About Pearson

Pearson is the world's learning company, with presence across 70 countries worldwide. Our unique insights and world-class expertise comes from a long history of working closely with renowned teachers, authors and thought leaders, as a result of which, we have emerged as the preferred choice for millions of teachers and learners across the world.

We believe learning opens up opportunities, creates fulfilling careers and hence better lives. We hence collaborate with the best of minds to deliver you class-leading products, spread across the Higher Education and K12 spectrum.

Superior learning experience and improved outcomes are at the heart of everything we do. This product is the result of one such effort.

Your feedback plays a critical role in the evolution of our products and you can contact us – reachus@pearson.com. *We look forward to it.*

Consumer Behaviour

The Indian Context (Concepts and Cases)

Second Edition

S. Ramesh Kumar
Professor of Marketing
IIMB Chair of Excellence
Indian Institute of Management Bangalore

Pearson

Editor—Acquisitions: Pradeep Kumar Bhattacharjee
Senior Editor—Production: G. Sharmilee

This book is intended for marketing students and practitioners interested in knowing the conceptual aspects of the fundamentals in marketing. Various brands have been cited as examples to explain these concepts. While the brands have been shown in a positive manner, academic interpretation of the

examples linked with the concepts is not intended to support or malign the handling of product and brand strategies. All references pertaining to public domain information have been provided wherever appropriate, and brand advertisements have been reproduced with due permission from the respective companies.

ISBN 978-93-325-8649-9

First Impression, 2017
Sixth Impression 2024
Seventh Impression 2025

Published by Pearson India Education Services Pvt. Ltd, CIN: U72200TN2005PTC057128
Head Office: 1st Floor, Berger Tower, Plot No. C-001A/2, Sector 16B, Noida – 201 301,Uttar Pradesh, India.
Registered Office: Featherlite, 'The Address' 5th Floor, Survey No 203/10B, 200 Ft MMRD Road,Zamin Pallavaram, Chennai -600044
Website: in.pearson.com; Email:companysecretary.india@pearson.com
Digitally printed in India by Trinity Academy for Corporate Training Ltd, New Delhi in the year of 2025.

Contents

Preface

Since the last edition of the book had been published, the environment has radically changed. The emergence of new phenomena like digitalization, cultural shifts and changes in consumer behaviour, I thought it was time for a new edition. After getting in-depth feedback from experts in the field, students who had gone through my courses, executives who had attended my programs, and my own observation and analysis of the changes in academic content, I have improved this edition with new examples and cases that are drawn from the Indian scenario. The online resources can be accessed via www.pearsoned.co.in/cb2rameshkumar

Please do write to me about your comments and suggestions at rkumar@iimb.ernet.in.

Acknowledgements

The second edition of the book stems from the feedback and wishes of several individuals and I am thankful to all of them. While it may not be possible to acknowledge all of them, I have made a sincere effort to reach out to some.

I would like to reflect on my grateful remembrances towards Dr B. Ilango, Former Vice-Chancellor of Bharathiar University for his unstinted support and motivation at a crucial point of time decades back in my career. Prof. K.R.S. Murthy, former Director of IIM Bangalore, who was instrumental in recognizing my potential and passion that have taken shape in whatever I have done in academics. I thank several of my students, especially Mr S. Swaminathan, Mr Madhurjya Bannerjee and Mr Sairam Krishnamurthy, who over the last three decades have rejuvenated me and encouraged me in my academic journey.

I thank IIM Bangalore for its support in terms of its infrastructure and academic ambience, without which I would not have the motivation to write books and cases. I would also like to mention my colleague, Prof. B. Shekar, who has over the years shown keen interest in my publications and provided suggestions on the presentation of the content.

I thank Mr Pradeep Kumar Bhattacharjee of Pearson Education and Ms Sanhita Sinha, editor of the book, for being highly involved and putting in their hard work to bring out this edition of the book.

I remember with limitless gratitude and would like to acknowledge the unparalleled efforts and limitless wishes of my parents, without whom every aspect of my life would have presented itself as an unsurmountable task. Finally, I would like to mention the positive support provided by my wife, Amrith, and daughter, Sahana for tolerating several episodes of idiosyncrasies that I may have exhibited while working on this book.

I also wish to thank Zomato, Paper Boat, Titan Edge, Globus and Soulflower for kindly sharing their respective company image with us. Their help and support have truly enhanced the value of this book.

S. Ramesh Kumar

Consumer Behaviour and Brands in The Indian Context: Consumer Behaviour Builds on The Basics of Marketing Principles

There have been radical changes in the environment in the Indian context—not just the initial challenges of an emerging market or diverse cultures within the country, but the onset of e-commerce and digital technologies. India, thus, faces unique challenges from the viewpoint of marketers. These challenges have been created by a medley of several and diverse factors like cultural practices, exposure to Westernization, the emergence of technology-savvy teenagers and young adults, a growing population of senior citizens, the culture of price-consciousness introduced by online retailers like Amazon, the demand for luxury brands, growing hospitality and healthcare, rural consumption of categories and the growth of modern retailing along with the traditional *kirana* stores. Consumers in several developed counties is the back office of branding, and in the Indian context, consumer behaviour is the backbone of branding. This is because obtaining nuanced insights in a complex environment requires the application of consumer behaviour. This book provides a quick reference to executives and students by simplifying the complex subject with concepts, examples and cases from the Indian context.

The following are examples drawn from the Indian context that reflects the need to understand consumer behaviour from the viewpoint of its application in the Indian context:

- If consumers in developed markets had been consuming cornflakes with cold milk for decades, why should a brand like Kellogg's advertise that cornflakes should be taken with hot milk, almost two decades after its entry into the Indian context?
- Hair creams had been marketed in the Indian context from the sixties. Why should after-shave brand of hair cream become so popular among youngsters? Why should a brand of mobile phone position itself on selfies?
- Why did Cadbury start marketing Bournville dark chocolates actively with ads decades after it was present in the context?
- Why should a brand like Surf (or for that matter most detergent brands) weave a "story" around its brand with a drama-like ad?
- How do *kirana* stores co-exist with modern retail outlets? What is the role of digitalization towards the development of attitude towards a store brand?
- Why should Indian brands spend so much on cricket or film celebrities?
- Why do consumers get influenced by sustained reference to brand associations (for instance, as in the case of Santoor soaps that had been using youthful skin as a proposition for the soap?
- While the brands in the perfume/deodorant industry was built with proposition on being attractive to the opposite sex, did a brand like Fogg attract consumers with its "x number of sprays" proposition when it was launched?

This book may not provide quick answers to these questions. But consumer behaviour as a body of knowledge will make the reader think about approaching such questions conceptually; this is perhaps a strong value addition to understand branding issues in the Indian context.

CHAPTER 1

Consumer Behaviour and Brands in the Digital Era

Relevance of Consumer Behaviour to the Indian Context: An Emerging Market

The classic four P's of marketing, namely product, price, promotion and place (distribution), still hold true in the digital era with respect to the conceptual thinking associated with marketing strategies. Consumer behaviour adds value to these strategies by providing the behavioural perspectives that get integrated with the marketing mix elements (4P's). It also takes into consideration an important aspect–the context in which branding strategies need to be formulated. Without the interface of consumer behaviour and context, the marketing strategy of any brand would exist in isolation. There are many aspects in an environment that are important from the perspective of consumer behaviour.

This chapter addresses four topical issues associated with both consumer behaviour and the context that we witness in India. These four issues will enable the reader to appreciate the viability of consumer behaviour in formulating brand strategies in a specific context (in this case, the Indian context).

The four issues are:

- The power of ethnicity and branding.
- The differences between Western and Indian cultures and their impact on branding.
- Consumer behaviour and the power of unconscious that refers to branding.
- Consumer behaviour and technology with its implications to brand and product management and the emerging aspects of online retailing and its association with psychological aspects of branding.

The Ethnic Route to Branding

India is a unique example of a convergence for displaying a tradition of cultural heritage and the influence of modernity and Western ideas. While lifestyles and consumer preferences seem to evolve towards Western tastes, some brands still have that adequate bandwidth to appeal to Indian consumers through various traditional ways. They can also use ethnic aspects to reflect changing cultural values. Good Knight mosquito coil, Robin Blue (from Reckitt Benckiser), the liquid that provides a blue tinge to white clothes; Himalaya, one of the chiefly recognized brands that offers over-the-counter tablets for personal care and healthcare based on Ayurvedic system of medicine; Chik shampoo has a fragrance with a whiff of jasmine; and Kurkure, the brand of snacks, are all examples that reflect how brands have successfully used ethnic cultural aspects. Hair gel or cream was never a popular category. The launch of 'Parachute After Shower' was instrumental in the diffusion of the category of hair cream that had never taken off for decades. Hair cream is not a part of the grooming routine among males in the country. The brand is positioned towards urban youth and had S. Sreesanth, a former Indian team cricketer, as its brand ambassador. The use of actors and sportspersons in brand advertising has always dominated the Indian scenarios as movies and sports are extremely popular and revered across the country. Coconut oil has been a part of the grooming routine in several parts of the country for decades. Basically, women apply it almost every day, believing in its benefits for hair care. 'Parachute', with its packaging innovation, provided the offering to the lower economic segment of the mass market. Its 'Advansed' variant's positioning makes very good use of established cultural beliefs. Over the years, the youth have shunned the traditional oily-look associated with hair care, preferring the non-greasy dry looks with urbane hair grooming styles.

"Parachute's Advansed" was targeted towards the beauty-conscious young women. There were also several variants of the brand, including a 'herbal hot oil'. Traditional folklore has always insisted the importance and application of coconut oil and specific herbs heated mildly for healthy hair. The brand also had a website that encourages consumers to check their 'hot oil factor'. From being a traditional product, the brand has adapted certain advancements to cater to the urban youth with an appropriate combination of contemporary model and product benefits.

The brands in the food department reflect the essential need for brands to be sensitive to Indian culture. Kellogg's probably did not expect the consumers to mix warm milk with cornflakes. (In fact, milk is usually consumed warm/hot in India.) After years of adaptation, the company now advertises that the cornflakes are to be had with hot milk. Nestle introduced the dark chocolates more than two decades ago and the offering was withdrawn soon enough and it was reintroduced as soon as the chocolate eating culture among adults bloomed up. Cadbury, one of the other major brands of chocolates, had only recently introduced advertising its dark chocolate combo, named as 'Bournville'. The brand was selectively distributed by the company for the last several decades without being advertised much. Earlier, Cadbury's advertising for its moulded chocolate bar alternative emphasises the enjoyment of Cadbury's on the first of every month as it is a 'pay-day'. Culturally, Indians have a strong sweet tooth and the first of every month is perceived as the day to celebrate with a sumptuous chocolate. Cadbury focuses on this strongly entrenched practice among the Indians.

The entry of the 'Quaker Oats' brand marks an interesting point in dealing with the cultural nuances. The brand's timing was in tune with the health and fitness culture that is trending among the urbanites. Oats were not a part of the food culture in this country, largely. The brand 'Quaker Oats' has positioned itself initially as a breakfast item with several health advantages. The brand's imagery ensured that the breakfast proposition was not strong enough to attack traditional eating habits. More importantly, it also emphasized the availability of ₹25 packs as consumers would want to compare the price of the brand with the existing alternatives (besides the cultural fit).

Family orientation is a brand description which is frequently used across various product categories, ranging from soaps to cars. Hindustan Unilever repositioned its soap Lifebuoy (a soap that has been in the Indian context for several decades) with a family imagery. Its Lux brand is associated with celebrities (which is a part of the fan-frenzied Indian culture). The company also has a brand Hamam (one of its oldest brands) advertised by focussing on majority of Indian families. Tanishq, a jewellery brand from the house of Tata, elevates the importance of nurturing family values with their elegant diamond advertisements. It introduced an advertisement that portrayed a young widow entering into remarriage, a progressive value in the Indian context. Culture in the Indian context has many unexplored strands that will benefit branding.

Touch of Reality

The Indian take on motherhood and brands[1]

The word and picture of 'Mother' is special in the Indian context and it is associated with several associations of joy, warmth, caring and sacrifice. The religious facet of Hinduism also portrays the Goddess as mother in several beliefs associated with religion. The country itself is often referred to as 'Bharat Mata'. There are several brands that have been projecting the idea of a mother in a number of ways. Vicks Vaporub has been a part of the Indian context for several decades and has always maintained a strong association with 'Mother' across a number of its ads over the years. In an attempt to connect with the modern mother and more as an emotional connect with the brand being secondary to the mother–child emotions, the brand had launched 'Vicks Touch of Care' campaign in 2017. The ad showed a transgender individual adopting and taking care of a child. It portrays the universal emotion of unconditional love that a mother has for her child, irrespective of their own struggles and tribulations. The brand's attempt to adapt to the changing environment reflects the importance of culture and emotions in consumer behaviour.

The 'Cultural Divide'

For any student who pursues marketing as their major stream, then the fundamental platform that triggers conceptual thinking are the differences between Western culture and the ethnic Indian culture, and how such differences can affect the branding associations and its related decisions. Apple, Chanel, Nike, Longines and Mercedes are few examples of Western brands that believe in minimalist design and communication. Paper Boat and Titan Edge are among the few Indian brands that have adopted minimalist packaging and communication. They are positioned at the higher end of the market in terms of their prices, and therefore, it is bound to target consumers who prefer costlier brands for a variety of reasons–minimalistic looks being one. Given the influence of Western cultures on the Indian context after liberalization, the consumers at the higher end of the price spectrum seem inclined towards brands that have a Western orientation, and hence, they become more acceptable.

At a fundamental level does culture play a part in making brands minimalist or otherwise? Culture at a basic level is shared meaning in context and has a number of dimensions associated with it. There can be eating habits, habits of hygiene, grooming culture, dressing culture and culture of addressing others, to name a few. One of the distinguishing features of culture is the 'high-cultural context' and 'low-cultural context' (the concept was introduced by Edward Hall).[2] This categorization has interesting implications on conspicuous consumption as well as on the mind-set of consumers who are a part of the marketing environment. Both factors have been known to influence branding. Low-cultural context is one where cultural cues add little meaning when communication/interaction takes place between the consumer and marketer. There is a little influence of emotions, gestures and implicit understanding of cultural cues and symbols. Germany is a low-cultural environment and so is Sweden. In a high-cultural context, inherent cultural cues that include symbols and emotions have an impact on communication. Water given to a stranger (hospitality), exaggerated expressions of emotions (Surf Excel's advertisement which depicted a boy getting playful in the mud and dirtying himself to bring a smile to the face of his teacher who has lost her dog, thus linking to the detergent brand's proposition is an example), story-telling that is inherent in Indian ads, and most Hindu women not wearing a white sari to a wedding are examples of 'high-context culture'.

Ethnic mainstream culture includes a mix of colours, diverse emotions that include 'story-telling', familial relationships and images that reflect symbolic meanings and an exaggerated expression of emotions. The standard communication of marketing and the packaging design is largely associated with the mainstream culture and is quite complex as compared to those in the low-cultural context settings. 'Top Spin' is a biscuit introduced by Parle and its ad depicts an airhostess getting confused about the destination of the aircraft because she is lost in its taste. It is humour that conveys the taste of the biscuit, which is particularly aimed at adults and can be understood by many. 'Maggi' noodles, which has over 70 per cent of the market share in the FMCG category, has introduced an advertisement that involves the interaction between a daughter and her mother. The daughter, who is about to set off as an independent adult, makes 'Maggi' noodles that leaves her mother exclaiming with joy that they taste exactly like hers, and the daughter says "that's because it's your recipe" (and this is a part of brand revitalizing in a competitive environment). Raga's recent advertisement that reflects the concept of gender equality and self-reliance of the protagonist is another example of a simple story-telling that creates a comparison with the self-concept of the consumer. The lady tells her former boyfriend in a chance meeting that she would rather have her job than have continued the relationship which expected her to be home-bound after marriage.

The mother–child relationship is universal in its bonding, but the Indian cultural context seems to have had a major impact on the ads of brands that have used such relationships for the past several decades. Horlicks, Vicks, Complan, Clinic Plus, Kellogg's, Dettol, Glucon D, Rasna, Tang, Parachute's sub-brands, Surf Excel, Raga and Bournvita are just some of the brands that have used these relationships in ads with the power of story-telling.

Exaggerated Emotions

An interesting example of exaggerated emotions was recently reflected in an ad by Johnson & Johnson's 'One Touch (Horizon) Sugar Monitoring Meter' intended to diagnose diabetics. The ad showed a happy family with a kid celebrating the happiness of using the meter to monitor the sugar level of the father. Onset of diabetes is a concern and the sugar meter provides valuable and timely inputs with convenience to overcome the disease. It may be interesting to study how such 'exaggerated emotions' are conveyed in other cultures by marketers promoting similar products.

The ethnic cultural context seems to continue with several product forms/preparations that have existed for decades, despite new forms of substitutes appearing. Detergent bars (non-existent in the West), use of turmeric for the skin (one is reminded of the success of 'Vicco' turmeric cream) and the advertising of herbal shampoo products in line with the Indian tradition of using herbs for the hair are some examples. Package designs are quite complex due to the priority of using loud colours (Parachute and Reynold pens are some of the exceptions and they may have benefited by the unique pack/product designs due to the contact they had created with the products from the unorganized sector which is yet another feature of the Indian marketing culture). India is too eclectic and vibrant to be contained only by the cultural fantasies of the West, at least at this point in time.

Making Sense of Irrationality (The Power of the Unconscious in Consumer Behaviour)

- Why are you continuing to buy the same brand of detergent for the last 20 years much after your children have outgrown their white uniforms?
- How did you get into the habit of eating Marie biscuits with tea?
- Do you 'anticipate' drinking a chilled bottle of Coke on a warm day?

Consumers want automatic (auto transmission) cars, automatic washing machines and automatic Bluetooth systems. It may be amazing to know that many of our behaviours are an outcome of automaticity, the degree to which our neuro-systems react to trigger without our conscious knowledge or control. Evolutionary neurobiology and cerebral processes are receiving as much importance as digital technologies and the marketers are attempting to find out how brands can become a part of such automatic actions of the consumers. This article makes use of several research studies that have been published by reputed researchers. Coke was one of the earliest brands which was a part of neuro-experiments. When the consumers were asked to select between two unbranded colas (one was Coke and the other was Pepsi), the majority selected Pepsi as they found it to be too sweet (subjective but still based on the same logic). When the brand names were revealed and they were asked to choose the majority selected Coke.[3] It was found that those parts of the brain associated with zones known for pleasure as well as decision-making skills had been activated when consumers were exposed to Coke. Dopamine triggers the pleasure zones when a likable cue (a brand name) is seen by the consumer. Sheer anticipation of the consumption produces a surge of pleasure and the brand is a part of such repeated experiences. The intangible effect of brand associations (impact of the brand name, its associations, logo and shape of the bottle) on the consumer's mind produces an effect that is significantly different from rational thinking.

The placebo effect has been demonstrated with respect to consumer behaviour.[4] Consumers who had consumed an energy drink based on a discount felt that the efficacy of the drink was much lower than those who had bought the drink on its full price. Consumer perception is based on how consumers interpret information based on their own experiences, past exposure and motivation. Interpretation influences brands. The quality-price association is almost universal when applied to consumer behaviour. Park Avenue, Giny & Jony, Monte Carlo, Del Monte and Vertu, do these brands have a country-of-origin relationship that implies a higher quality because of the perception of foreignness and the symbolic appeal of being associated with foreign names? Stella Artois, a commonplace beer in Belgium, is a premium beer in the US with its quality-centric approach aimed at its brand motto 'Perfection has a price'. Several years ago, Britannia introduced a carton soft drink 'Zip Sip' that was focussed on nutrition when the category was dominated by 'Frooti', a similar soft drink from Parle Agro India. Under such a context there are chances that the consumers would not have expected a milk-based drink in a carton. Sensory interpretation of brands may also be culture-specific. Dettol, the antiseptic lotion with its burning sensation and pungent odour, appeals to consumers just like the 'heat generating' pain balms appear to them. Krackjack biscuits created a new trend of providing both the taste of sweet and salt in a single pack before when 50-50 biscuits was launched based similar taste. Kurkure appealed quite interesting to many consumers due to its close similarities to the taste of many Indian snacks.

Kellogg's probably never advertises its cereals by pouring hot milk in it anywhere in the world as it does in India (after being present for almost two decades in India)! Dark chocolates were still not accepted by the mass media in a big way as Indians have a sweet tooth (it relates to the fact that Cadbury had developed in its recent campaigns). Consumers remember the past and connect well with it when brands send out messages that are in tune with the past. Britannia's cheese spread equated itself with the cow's milk and Tropicana soft drink associated itself with the oranges. But how do consumers respond to novelty? Novelty activates a part of the brain called *substantia nigra*. This area is closely associated with learning, memory and emotion. When novelty acts on a number of zones in the brain the release of dopamine influences the consumers' receptivity. This may not mean that everything that is novel will be accepted by consumers. While Crystal Pepsi (colourless cola) failed in the market, Red Bull, a unique energy drink thrived to be a global brand. Several soft drink and beer companies have tried launching many energy drinks but Red Bull remains as the leader. The contradictory aspects of the brain are the ones that make the job of the marketer exciting and challenging. Novelty is to be viewed in a cultural context. Dry shampoo may not pick up in the Indian context but may be sought after in some other culture. Novelty is just not limited to product inventions. Unpredictable rewards are three to four times more 'exciting' to the neurons, say scientists at the University of Cambridge. Would that explain the success of 'time-based' promotions from online portals that announce huge discounts that last for just a day?

The wonders that creative visuals and celebrity tie-ups do for a brand are almost unbelievable, given the objective that a consumer has to buy a brand that provides a benefit. The point is that the benefit may be emotional in nature and that is the reason why brands use what is known in marketing literature as the 'peripheral' route. The global relaunch of the historical brand Old Spice is an example (Refer to Plate 1.1). In a timespan of less than a minute, the commercial shows that the protagonist moves from one scene to another indulging in a host of activities such as going into the wilderness, carrying a cake, remodelling his kitchen and riding a motorcycle. Psychologists term this kind of action as 'pattern interrupts'.[5] By using several formats and variations to convey the same message, brands can prevent an advertising wear-out, a situation where consumers will not suffer from the fatigue of having to see the same advertisement repeatedly. This is not to say that just using 'pattern interrupts' can work for any brand or to say that the equity of Old Spice brand is not at work. The campaign had 1.4 billion impressions, 32.4 million downloads and had a 55 per cent increase in sales over three months after the campaign was launched. This

Plate 1.1 Digitalization had enabled the successful relaunch of the brand

shows that emotional appeals are as important as rational ones. 'Irrational' means getting away from arguments that are product-centric from the parameter of tangible outcomes. While the emotional drama of Old Spice is consciously noted and watched by consumers the brand's message, 'the man your man can smell like', gets into the mind without the brand being rationally evaluated by consumers.

Changing environment, lifestyles, fragmentation of markets and the digital impact on consumerism has created several opportunities for branding and product management. These opportunities may not be readily discernible (in terms of managerial perspectives).

Consumer Behaviour in a Digital Era

Traditional product management brought in consumer perspective to design and execute a product. While it is equally significant in the digital domain, it is important to understand that the consumer may not realize the best alternative to satisfy his needs given the diversity of needs and the infinite ways to digitally satisfy them. Fitness, for example, is an action that can have several contexts and segments. Apps for this domain not only just require consumer inputs; but they also require insights that are triggered by the marketing team and 'innovatively' implemented by the product management team. Innovation, here, means quickness and extrapolation of the trigger associated with the consumer. Customer inputs to a fitness app like Fitbit may only include things like 'I want to track the number of kilometres I ran'/'I want to know the number of calories I burnt (Refer to Plate 1.2).' But a mobile app that connects to the internet can get a lot more details from the context of usage like current weather conditions, knowing where the customer is (in a gymnasium or outdoors on a trek), points of interest (like a shop that sells nutritional drinks) around the location, interacting with other fitness products such as wrist bands, running shoes, and so on.

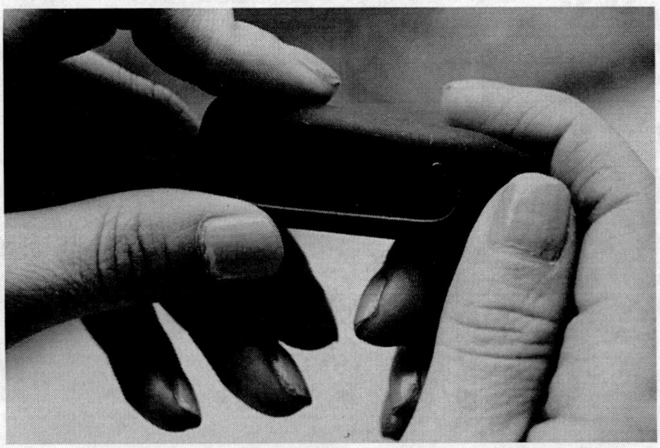

Plate 1.2 Fitness and self-image go together in this digital era

Depending on the availability of these external inputs, the app's behaviour and output should be enhanced. This will require the user experience, design, product management, engineering and marketing teams to come together and brainstorm its potential. In the near future, these approaches are likely to spread over to every product category. Kindle readers, iTunes and video streaming for entertainments (like Netflix) are few examples of the advancement of how digitalization is taking over the books and the conventional modes of entertainment. Taxi and travel services such as Uber and Ola Cabs are taking the very mundane taxi booking service to its next level through their mobile apps with location capabilities, dynamic demand-based pricing, secure credit card linkages and such.

Marketing and product teams work together to identify a product opportunity and the segments the product is meant for. Product managers then work with user experience designers and engineers to create a product that is valuable (product manager's responsibility), feasible (engineer's responsibility) and usable (designer's responsibility). For instance a brand may have to delve into psychographics (why of the behaviour) of consumers commuting and using their mobile to understand their preferences while commuting. It could be movie clips or even shopping interests.

The consumers' self-image and social image also have to be kept in mind for developing a product design. For example, a digital product could contain interface support in multiple languages. A consumer might prefer to use the interface in his native language when he is alone if he thinks his understanding of English is not good. When he is with his friends, he may feel self-conscious about using his native language and want to use English. A digital product should be able to understand the context and change languages appropriately or at least have an easy option for the user to quickly change the language of the interface.

With revenue models of several digital products built on advertisements, product managers need to control the number of advertisements that appear in the product. For example, a search engine with more advertisements (even relevant ones) than real search results will be perceived as inferior by consumers. Similarly, a social network with more advertisements than original posts shared by their friends will quickly jump to another network. Therefore, digital product managers employ various research methodologies to arrive at the right mix of advertisements so as not to put off consumers. A digital product can consider the motive to use (if it is used with a 'promotion' focus or with a 'prevention' focus) and change its interface appropriately. For example, a product that shows the status of utility consumption (say, 3G data usage of a mobile service) may be used by two sets of consumers, (a) Who are worried about their current usage and need reassurance that they are well within their allowed limits ('prevention focus') or (b) Who do not worry about their limits and like to know about more services to consume ('promotion focus'). In both these cases, the consumer will use the product to know the status of their current consumption but what to display to them is entirely different.

In the former case, there could simply be an indicator (in green/amber/red) with the balance highlighted. In the latter case, the indicator could be very small and more services can be shown to drive consumption. Consumer behaviour and product management together can open up new avenues in an era of convergence of technologies and real-time applications.

Touch of Reality

E-Commerce In India[6] and Consumer Mind Set

- 2016: $ 38 billion was the amount traded through Indian e-commerce portals
- 65% of online purchases are done through PCs
- 70% of online orders were cash-on-delivery products.
- 60% of impulsive purchases were found in the category of apparels
- First quarter of 2016 had 2 million plus transactions across 100 online retailers
- 65% growth was registered in e-commerce growth in one year.

Consumer Behaviour provides several perspectives to analyse the data. For instance, how is the attitude towards apparel category different from other categories? Jabong.com the online retailer, for instance, repositioned itself as a premium apparel seller as discounting, price-offs and low prices are against its strategy of providing fast fashion and latest collections.[7] 7.9 mn shoppers had bought goods from Jabong.[8]

New Categories and Digitalization

Online-based digitalization had opened up a new kind of service in the Indian context. Faircent had entered the peer-to-peer platform by which individuals and firms can borrow or provide loans to unknown individuals or firms when they are on the online platform.[9] This may evolve into a revolutionary concept because an emerging market like India has a significant segment of population that struggles for economic sustenance and also a segment that may require start-up funding for a variety of small ventures that may not be able to get funding from the regular funding agencies.

Digitalization and Indian Markets

The mobile category has created a revolution in the Indian Context. The ₹10 mobile recharge is the largest-selling pack in India. In rural markets, consumers prefer recharging their mobile as a top discretionary expenditure over several categories like biscuits, chocolates and soft drinks. The Indian market is likely to reach US $60 billion with respect to the e-commerce industry by 2020; 175 million consumers

consumers are likely to shop online by 2020 (in 2015, the number of e-shoppers were 50 million and e-commerce was worth US $ 10 bn).[10,11]

Online retailers are making an attempt to avoid discounts. Paytm had planned to open several virtual shops, enable consumers to buy durable goods ad also open up a channel for unbranded products and source products from their collaborators abroad to make them available to Indian consumers.[12]

The various aspects of consumer behaviour are likely to help brand managers in a variety of ways.

Importance of Digitalization and the importance of Emotions in the Digital Age

There is a proliferation of internet usage, mobile apps, online shoppers and social media interactions. The number of online shoppers increased by 95% between 2013 and 2015. It is estimated that online shoppers reach around 220 million by 2020 (36% of the total internet users).[13] The non-urban markets are also likely to contribute significantly to e-commerce. Given this scenario, several aspects of consumer behaviour that are applicable to traditional shopping will also become applicable to online shopping. For example, would the brand personality of online portal like Myntra matter to consumers?

*Note-figures from different sources may reflect some variation.

Digitalization–Can it ever Replace Emotions ?

Closeup, the brand of toothpaste introduced during the seventies, with the proposition of "toothpaste cum mouth wash" had all along positioned the brand towards youngsters with "closeup" propositions that symbolically signaled romance. Almost after five decades of launching several variants, including the Diamond attraction one, the brand announced the "First move party" on September 30, 2016 to draw the attention of youth. An ad for the event announced "Make your first move at the closeup first move party' (firstmoveparty.closeup.in).

Digitalization of a brand (especially the ones positioned on emotion) needs to combine technology with emotions.

Psychological Aspects of Online Retailing

The Indian marketing context has seen an explosive growth of online retailing in recent times. Other than the consumer durables and apparels, FMCG brands are also gearing up to enter into online retail. Britannia even launched 'Good Day Chunkies' exclusively online, at first. Myntra, Flipkart, eBay and Snapdeal are already some of the major brands with a significant following. Some brands of Motorola and Xiaomi mobile phones launched exclusively online were major hits. Online retail in India, according to media reports, will cross about $16 billion by 2018. One of the highlighted aspects of this growth is that it has been fuelled by unprecedented discounts across various categories and brands. The size of these discounts and their perennial nature (unlike the seasonal discounts that the Indian context is used to) has created a stature that will force branded products to not just revisit their strategies but also question the rationale for the existence of the brands that have endured for several decades. This situation throws up few interesting issues:

- Can brands sustain what they stand for? (Unless they belong to the luxury category, such as heritage brands like Ferrari, Mont Blanc or BMW in which case the brand associations are created by their legacy.)
- If an unknown brand of microwave ovens offers a good product, then it has the potential to replace an established brand through the digital word of mouth.
- While established brands may lose their brand associations, unknown brands may enter the considered set of consumers.
- Development of private label brands by the online portals themselves.
- Satisficing behaviour of the consumers (the term 'satisficing' was first used by political scientist and economist Herbert Simon, a Nobel Prize winner.)

Companies that offer a product line (a string of products at different price points) may have a price-fighter brand exclusively for online channels and strengthen the emotional or symbolic lineage of higher-priced brands. Apparels, mobile cameras and watches are few examples of the categories that may take this route. Furthermore, the functional aspects of brands at a higher price point may assume a direction that discounted brands may never be able to match. Sony's pocket camera and smart watch are examples that indicate this trend. Sony's smart watch has several features that other brands do not offer. Innovations like sensor-based apparel that can read the mood of the wearer and change colours accordingly may be launched.

Cross-selling among the brands of a company may become widespread with business analytics and data mining. Millions of consumers may be associated with the products of a company such as Unilever or Procter & Gamble. India's fast moving goods sector is also undergoing radical shifts in the online space with Amazon taking the lead. The brand offers 1.9 million products in this sector from 9000 sellers and also has the loyalty program Prime.[14] There may be clusters of families that use various products from the same company. The challenge for the brand managers is to utilize the data on consumption and develop micro-segments that can be effectively targeted with offerings and promotions. For instance, a consumer who cooks using organic ingredients may be different from one who likes to experiment with her cooking. Both consumers may use different sets of ingredients. The personal connection between the brand and consumer connection would be heightened (like Allen Solly's customization of colours to reflect one's individuality). Consumer relevance will be built into the brand and it would require a continuing relationship enabled by the company/brand. Nike+ in association with iTunes had several features to enable a user to monitor his performance and connect with others.

Consumers having access to digital media will be able to connect with their friends and contacts and obtain information on unknown products and their performances. This will be an opportunity for online portals to develop their own brands. An example is Myntra, it had attempted to launch private labels in apparel. Shoppers Stop will shortly be introducing its own brand, Haute Curry, online as well. A author was looking for a mobile phone for the elderly that would have bold letters on the keypad. Brands such as iBall, Philips and Samsung were the ones that showed up on Google search. iBall was good but pricey for the 'conversation only' requirement (basic need). The other two brands were unavailable in retail search. An unfamiliar brand called Swingdel, priced around ₹1,000, was ordered from Flipkart. The entire search and purchase of the unknown brand took about 10 minutes (online). The brand's rating and reviews online also influenced the choice. The brand's performance was much more than what was expected from an unknown brand at the given price point.

In an emerging market like India, there are millions of consumers who would fit this with their needs, understanding the whole concept that other better options exist in the market. Though there would be a few personality traits that motivate a consumer towards satisfying behaviour, there is likely to be a huge segment of consumers who would satisfice due to reasons of affordability. Little-known brands that are priced lower than branded offerings and the ones that do not have the luxury of launching an advertising blitzkrieg will have tremendous opportunity to break into the considered set of consumers through online retailing. ShopClues is a website that lists several manufacturers who may have the potential to develop their products into powerful brands, adding to the intense competition faced by the established brands. Online retailing companies that offer more discounts will pose emerging challenges to brand managers while benefiting consumers in the emerging market.

Behavioural Dimensions, Marketing Mix Elements and the Digital World*

Success of a brand depends on how well the consumer behaves (behavioural dimensions of consumers), digital initiatives and marketing mix elements that are combined in a competitive context. Motorola introduced its Moto-G exclusively through online channels. Dove soap strengthened the self-concept of consumers by introducing its 'Real Beauty' campaign online. Fastrack's brand of watches has a strong online presence. Urban Ladder is a furniture company that allows consumers to customise the product according to their expectations. Ford's Ecosport had posted online the experiences of its drivers. Consumers compare prices of brands of cameras in online channels. 'Share the load' challenge from Ariel brand had observed the current mind-set of consumers among who

---

* The content was first published as follows:

S. Ramesh Kumar (2014), 'Ethnic Route to Branding', *The Hindu Business Line*, 24 October.

S. Ramesh Kumar (2015), 'The Power of the Cultural Context', *The Hindu Business Line*, 3 April.

S. Ramesh Kumar (2015), 'Making Sense of Irrationality', *The Hindu Business Line*, 6 March.

Karthik Srinivasan and S. Ramesh Kumar (2014), "Beyond the Consumer's Perspective", *The Hindu Business Line*, 22 August.

S. Ramesh Kumar (2015), 'When Other brands Discount Online', *The Hindu Business Line*, 13 February.

think that doing the laundry was the work of the wife in a family and created a sensation in the social media by asking husbands to help in the laundry. Following this, another speculation that had happened recently is when Lakme announces its beauty contests through Twitter.

Changing Environment, Brands and Consumer Behaviour

Marketing has gained importance in India after the liberalization of markets during the 90's. In today's world of competitive products, the diversity of consumer preferences and the evolution of brands have taken a new turn, consumer behaviour has become extremely important for marketing decisions, be it marketing mix elements, segmentation changes or exploring new dimensions in consumer behaviour required in a changing environment. Several interesting trends can be expected in the new millennium. Leisure and luxury markets have boomed in the recent times. The shampoos and creams, which only the elite could afford a decade back, are marketed in sachets across the country today. Westernization has made an impact in the selection of product categories and brands. Denim clothes and the brands that exist in this category are an example of this impact. Even in such a category, an innovative marketer has come up with an ethnic brand (for example, 'Paper Boat' soft drink) by applying the principles of consumer behaviour. Psychographic and lifestyle changes have given rise to new eating habits (fast foods, eat-outs and food socials). A section of consumers may eat while driving. Interestingly, this trend is called grazing and has fast caught up in the developed world. In turn, this may give rise to products like refrigerated glove compartments and cup holders in cars and perhaps, yoghurts in tubes. Consumer behaviour provides the 'behavioural fit' to marketing mix elements that need to be changed from time to time by marketers. Repositioning of brands like Xylys watch or Lux soap are few examples of how brands need to revitalize themselves in a changing environment.

Consumer behaviour deals with the psychological process of decision making by consumers in a social context, which also exerts group pressures on them. A consumer buying a brand of two-wheeler, for example, is motivated by the need to own that specific model and the particular brand (based on functional and emotional benefits) and buys that brand from an outlet. This buying behaviour involves several psychological factors. These factors govern the individual thinking process (like motivation, personality, perception and attitude), steps involved in buying (decision-making process), interaction of the consumer with several groups like friends, family and colleagues (group-oriented concepts) and selection of the brand and outlet depending on the price, features and emotional appeal (marketing mix elements in a given environment). Consumer behaviour links these four aspects to enable a marketer to formulate the marketing strategies. The basic elements of consumer behaviour–what the consumer buys, how he/she buys, when and where he/she buys and how much he/she buys–is understood by the interaction of different factors associated with consumer behaviour as shown in Figure 1.1.

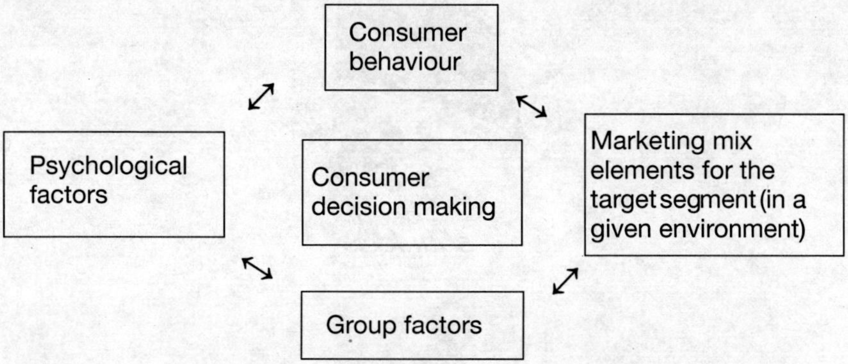

Figure 1.1 A Snapshot of Consumer Behaviour

The psychological processes are built into the individual's consumer system. The important aspect to be noted with regard to these psychological factors is that these factors are interlinked, resulting in behaviour. For example, though perceptions and attitudes are conceptually different in terms of their applications in a marketing context, attitudes also contain a perceptual component. The body of consumer behaviour views them distinctively to focus on specific applications. This is done to provide a conceptual clarity to the students of consumer behaviour. For example, in a product category like soap or tea, perception may be important, as positioning a brand indicates the differentiated advantage/proposition associated with the brand. In a product like the dishwasher, attitudinal models may be important, as the objective of a marketer will create an attitude towards the product as a stronger attitude towards a brand will translate into purchase. Personality concepts are important among the psychological factors because they pack a brand with emotional appeal to the appropriate target segment of consumers. In most categories, the consumers don't just look for functional benefits. They also seek symbolic gains. Symbolic benefits are those, which consumers perceive as beyond the functional qualities of a brand. These may be emotional in nature (Titan's gifting proposition has been around for decades), it may revolve around self-concepts (Louis Philippe), be associated with group appeals (Pepsi) or with human traits (adventurous and rugged as with Thums up) or even with status (Mont Blanc pens). The personality of the brand (which is formulated with the personality or reference group principles) may be reflected through brand imagery. Brand imagery is strongly associated with perception (image of Mercedes among interested consumers)

Learning is a concept that deals with the strength of associations and the impact of a stimulus on consumer response in a given situation. A stimulus is an information input to any of the sensory organs (an advertisement visual is an input to the eye and the accompanying jingle is an input to the ear). The strength of associations is used extensively in crafting the advertisement to create the desired feeling for the brand being advertised. Concepts of learning are also useful in exploring the brand loyalty—an area of interest to marketers, given the cost of acquiring new consumers. Brand associations are learnt (Tropicana with healthy juices or Head & Shoulders shampoos with strong and beautiful hair (Refer to Plate 1.3))

Plate 1.3 Functional and psychological benefits are important for brands that also symbolize personal grooming

Environment and Consumer Behaviour

Environment is not isolated from consumer behaviour. Perceptions and attitudes of consumers are shaped by the environment. The Indian Government initiated the Swachh Bharat Abhiyann campaign and resulted in the sale of hygiene brands like Dettol hand wash, Lizol, Harpic and Colin.[15]

'Kodaikanal Won't' was a You Tube campaign against Unilever on the mercury poisoning caused by the company's thermometer factory at Kodaikanal.[16] Such aspects need to be taken into consideration by brand managers in a digitized environment.

Consumer's decision making is about the sequence of steps involved in the decision-making process and distinguishes the products in terms of the level of involvement–low or high that needed to make a purchase decision. Consumer decision making (CDM) is helpful for the marketer to focus on a specific stage of the process. Even an established brand of mobile like Samsung will have to maintain a 'top-of-the-mind' recall through constant advertising (to maintain the visibility of the brand) and continue with its demonstration (which it has for a number of years) at a retail outlet. Demonstration at retail outlets (for instance, demonstration of a roti maker) is important because when a consumer enters the stage of 'evaluation of alternatives', he/she is faced with a barrage of options, including local brands.

The post-purchase phase of the decision-making process is essential for marketers to ensure that consumers are satisfied after the purchase. Another complex, but interesting aspect of this phase is how consumers reconcile to (or are satisfied with) the brand they have purchased when they are faced with similar or equally attractive propositions of competing brands. LG refrigerator offers to preserve the nutrients of the foods stored in it and Samsung may offer the option of converting the freezer into storage space in the refrigerator. Competing brands tend to impact the consumer's psyche a lot more in the post-purchase phase.

The concept of reference groups plays an important role in marketing communications. Celebrity advertising has been used widely in recent times. Testimonial advertisements and endorsements is another area of interest to marketers. Colgate, Coke, Pepsi, Lux, Boost, Kurkure and Raga are some of the brands that have used celebrity advertising. Word of mouth is another powerful group concept. There are a number of conceptual aspects that marketers need to consider before finalizing on celebrity advertisements. The clutter of advertisements in a category, the characteristics of the celebrity, the target segment and the objectives of using a celebrity are some of the important considerations while applying group concepts of celebrity advertisements.

Consumer behaviour involves the study of individual thinking processes like perception, attitude, learning aspects and personality. It also involves group concepts like group behaviour, reference groups and socialization within a cultural context. While several aspects of consumer behaviour and its linkages provide a framework for its study; the motivation, ability and opportunity (MAO) concerned with the consumer provides a fundamental and important foundation for strategies formulated by studying the consumer behaviour.

Motivation is the drive that activates a consumer to accomplish a goal.

A consumer who wants entertainment may see You Tube, go for movies or watch TV. It is important to note that the motivation will depend on personal relevance, self-concept or his/her involvement with a specific situation/product category. A consumer buying a soft drink may be motivated by a need to quench his/her thirst. But just wanting a drink may express low involvement in this situation vis-à-vis the same consumer buying a TV. Involvement levels are likely to be more significant when a consumer selects apparel according to his/her status. It should be noted that engaging in goal-related behaviour is different from achieving the goal itself. Motivation creates goal-related behaviours but there are other dimensions that help accomplish the goal. A consumer may want to be fit and may have the motivation and ability (intelligence, knowledge and money) to select and become a member of a fitness club. But the accomplishment of the goal will also depend on the opportunity he/she has. This may simply depend on the availability of time to execute or stick to the fitness club schedule.

MAO presents a number of important dimensions that cannot be ignored by the marketer. For example, even for a brand of soap (which figures in a low-involvement situation), opportunity with regard to factors like distraction and repetition of the advertising message may have to be considered when the promotional strategy is formulated. A premium brand of soap, which targets an upper-crust consumer, may prefer to advertise on radio (FM) if it finds out that this segment tunes into this channel while driving to work or back home. This strategy will provide an opportunity to the marketer to avoid the distraction caused to the consumer by other advertisements on TV (which may be many in number) and also cash in on the brand's unique strategy of advertising on FM. This will provide an opportunity to 'reach' the consumer more number of times (repetition also influences information processing) to carry the brand message. Besides, the consumer may also be 'time-compressed' (pressurized because of time) because of his/her busy schedule and may spend very little time watching TV. A direct marketing company may offer 24-hour ordering if it targets nuclear families in urban areas where both the husband and wife go out to work. MAO provides several interesting combinations that marketers can explore before they formulate the marketing mix strategies. Airtel, Vodafone and other brands have priced their offerings and also have a vast distribution of network to ensure that consumers will have an opportunity to recharge their mobile and also have the affordability (ability in this context) to execute their motivation to speak on the mobile.[17]

Consumer Behaviour, Marketing Mix Elements and Brand Success

There may be a need to analyse the consumer behaviour strategies in combination with the marketing mix elements of specific brands to obtain insights into the success or failure of a brand. This kind of analysis may involve more than one concept of consumer behaviour and cover a combination of concepts. These concepts, which explain a brand's success, may vary from one product category to another, given the nature and the intensity of competition in each product category. Marketers will benefit if they understand the linkages across concepts in a given product/market situation. This kind of analysis will result in the following advantages:

- **(a)** A marketer can formulate the brand strategy after considering a number of concepts associated with the competitive situation.
- **(b)** A pioneering brand will have followed a specific strategy for success and it will have to combine a few strategies to sustain the success achieved.
- **(c)** A follower brand will be interested in identifying the 'gaps' in the strategies made by the pioneering brand and a combination of concepts are likely to be helpful.
- **(d)** In a number of consumer product categories (both FMCG and durables), advertising or marketing communication (positioning strategies in particular) is given much importance in the formulation of a brand's strategy. While this may be critical, marketers will also have to be aware of the fact that other elements of the marketing mix are equally important. In a competitive environment, positioning will have to be strongly supported by the other elements of the marketing mix.

(e) A combination of concepts in analysing a brand's success or failure can also help in viewing the brand differentiation in terms of the total offerings of the company in the respective product category. For example, in the category of beverages, tea is an important product-line for Hindustan Lever Limited. While Red Label may use the functional attribute of vitamins to enhance the brand perception among consumers, Lipton's iced lemon tea may have to use certain strategies to create an attitude among the target segment. Taj Mahal is another brand targeted towards the lower end of the tea market, positioned on the aspiration of the masses. While brand personality may be important for all the brands in the product-line, the marketer needs to decide the extent to which they need to be differentiated on brand personality

The Indian context has a number of product categories that are dominated by (or where there is a significant share of) the unorganized sector. Biscuit is a category which has a high share in the unorganized market. A major part of consumption occurs at the lower end of the market (in terms of price points). The unorganized market consists of several local brands (catering to localized markets in terms of geographical regions) and a number of unbranded offerings from bakeries. Here was a distinct and definite need for a brand that could offer value at an appropriate price point (competing in the unorganized market). There was a need for a brand to convey the value proposition through an effective advertising campaign reassuring the consumers about the quality of the product. Britannia introduced Tiger biscuits for the lower-end market by making use of its huge network of retailing. They created a campaign that conveyed the value perception among the targeted consumers. The value was not just in terms of the price point; it was also in terms of how crisp and nutritive the offering was. Britannia's association also enhanced the brand perception among the target segment. There was a past stimulus (a stimulus is any input to any of the sensory organs): the Britannia brand, then a stimulus from the present. Tiger brand was introduced to signify the new offering and also an effective communication strategy was imposed, which reinforced the positioning of the brand–high value (as compared to rival offerings in the unorganized market) at a relatively lower price point. The retail network in the semi-urban and rural areas conveyed the aspects of affordability by associating itself with the brand (as against some offerings of the company, which are urban-centric). The overall brand perception was created through a combination of elements associated with the marketing mix.

Consumption of biscuits (probably even as a breakfast item) is a familiar practice in India. It is a part of the eating culture of the country. Britannia, by offering a product that was affordable for the masses, provided values and reinforced the cultural practice. The value would have created a favourable perception among the target segment, which would have compared the offering with the ones from the unorganized sector. This was made possible in a category in which the diffusion was high, but there was a 'gap' (in terms of value) at the lower end of the market. The characteristic of diffusion, namely relative advantage in terms of value was instrumental in making the Tiger brand a success.

The marketing mix elements form the foundation of any marketing strategy. This mix establishes the strategy of the brand in a systematic and structured manner. It helps the marketer to establish linkages with the focused target segment. In the pre-liberalization era in India, there was practically no competition and few brands dominated the market (in several product categories). Today, even brands that have been in the market for several decades make a planned attempt to construct a strategy by carefully identifying the scope for providing a competitive marketing mix. Amrutanjan has used a number of marketing mix elements to become competitive in the recent times, with several product variants for different market segments. Iodex is another brand that has modernized its marketing mix elements. Though Maruti has been in the Indian market only since early eighties, it has been forced to strategize variously so that it stays at the top of the automobiles market. So, it has launched new models and sub-brands and provided several services, which includes trading used cars and expanding its distribution. Marketing mix elements are important not only in their combination but also in the timing of such combinations. Kores was a well-known brand in the category of copiers; Rajdoot the two-wheeler brand had considerable amount of brand equity even during the eighties; HMT was the time-keeper to the nation before digital watches entered the country. Zodiac was probably the earliest readymade shirt brand available for men. While Eveready may offer alkaline (longer life) batteries, the marketing mix for this offering has to carefully take into consideration that majority of consumers in India still buy conventional batteries. Merlin came out with home-theatre systems in the mid-eighties when consumers were just getting used to two-in-ones (mass market) and televisions.

In a competitive situation, a firm has to priorities the marketing mix elements. This does not mean that concentrating only on a few elements and ignoring the others. Prioritizing emphasizes the need to recognize that some elements may be important than the others at a given point of time. When Samsung entered the Indian market, it offered the state-of-the-art product line. But the priority was to develop a brand with such associations (promotion) and also to develop a distribution channel. Heinz, the globally-known ketchup brand, entered India where Kissan and Maggi were already well-established brands. Though Heinz may have had a superior product in terms of its attributes, there was a need to create that brand awareness and link the attributes to the name of the brand.

Prioritization of the marketing mix elements starts from the clarity associated with the definition of the target segment. If a brand of cereal is set to be a niche brand (which is a small cross-section of consumers in India), it should have a marketing mix priority that creates awareness from the offering. Quaker Oats had done it in urban India. Fogg deodorant prioritized its number of uses as the proposition and Xiaomi prioritized its features and pricing when it introduced the mobile offering.

Titan, which holds a significant share of the organized quartz watch market, has been able to plan the marketing mix priority and also synchronize the linkages between different marketing mix elements. The unorganized sector in the quartz watch market is larger than the organized sector and the brand's progress has been due to the carefully orchestrated marketing mix. As discussed earlier, prioritization of marketing mix elements (a combination of them) should lead to the synchronization as demanded by the situation. The basic decision of Titan during the mid-eighties was to be only in the quartz watch market (which is a product decision). The initial campaigns of the brand created awareness by stating Titan to be as good as any foreign watch. Then, it made an emotional appeal by coming up with the popular Titan jingle. Simultaneously, the brand transformed the experience of buying a watch into a pleasurable one by offering the right ambience and comfort. Thus the brand has commemorated its watches by placing its products in exclusive Titan outlets. Several variants were created at different price points for various segments and perhaps, the initial problems in differentiation between various models were overcome by the effective application of sub-brands (World Time, Nebula, Raga, Zoop, Fastrack, etc.). The brand also developed an effective retail network with its presence in multi-brand outlets. All the efforts on the count of marketing mix have put Titan well within the 'top-of-the-mind' recalling while purchasing an exquisite watch.

Panasonic in televisions, Reebok in footwear, Ray Ban in sun glasses and Mercedes in cars are some foreign brands that entered India with a tremendous degree of equity and a well-planned marketing mix that could adapt effectively to the local context.

India is probably one of the very few markets in which the brands need to compete with the unorganized sector (biscuits, pens, detergents, footwear, dish-washing powders, traditional snacks, tea, edible oil and commodities, to name a few product categories). The most important aspect of marketing mix in most of these categories is the quality of the product and the price at which it is offered to the low-end consumers. An equally important element is promotion—a high-visibility campaign that creates awareness about the brand. Vim brand stands atop in the utensil cleaning category; Lakhani in footwear, Tiger in biscuits, Haldiram's and MTR in snacks and Nirma in detergents are some of the examples that have demonstrated the usefulness of the approach.

Marketing mix is equally important in international marketing as well. It even influences the manner in which a brand's associations are formed in the consumer psyche. Rolls Royce brand is a luxury car that has a fanfare among many consumers all around the world. Marketing mix elements and the consumer behaviour aspects are largely responsible for these kinds of associations. These elements have to be dynamic in a digital environment as well as within the capabilities of an organization.

While the behavioural aspects concerned with marketing are dealt with in this book, consumer behaviour is only one of the inputs for a successful marketing of the brand, the nature of the category, the kind of competition, the number of product categories the company is in, its infrastructure with regard to manufacturing and the capabilities of the competitors to swiftly address the changing consumer needs are some of the other vital aspects which serves as inputs to a brand's success. Parachute is an example of how consumer behaviour had supported its offerings strategy. Culturally, the coconut oil was used by consumers for several decades and Parachute had branded its offering powerfully with this practice. It's after-shower cream appealed to the psychographics of the modern youth; its Advansed sub-brand appealed to young and fashionable consumers (who had used this product before their bath as suggested by the associations of the brand); its offering with the Lite sub-brand had created a favourable attitude among youngsters who did not want the 'oily' look along with the benefits of hair oil.

Horlicks is another brand that had used the perception and attitudes to successfully relaunch itself targeting the likings of kids only decades after when this brand was overshadowed for its convalescence qualities(as a drink for the sick who were recovering).

END NOTES

1. Amit Bapna, (2017), 'Why is the image of a heteronormative family the hallmark of ideal advertising?', *The Economic Times,* April 12.
2. Edward T. Hall, Beyond Culture, Garden City, (NJ: Doubleday, 1976).
3. Douglas Van Praet, *Unconscious Branding: How Neuroscience Can Empower (And Inspire) Marketing,* (Macmillan, 2012), 19–20.
4. Baba Shiv, Ziv Carmon and Dan Ariely. (2005), Placebo Effects of Marketing Actions: Consumers May Get What They Pay For, *Journal of Marketing Research,* 383–393.
5. Douglas Van Praet, *Unconscious Branding: How Neuroscience Can Empower (And Inspire) Marketing,* (Macmillan, 2012), pp. 99–104.
6. 'Always on my mind', *The Economic Times,* May 23, 2016.
7. Richa Maheshwari (2016), 'Jabong sheds Brands with Low Margins', *The Economic Times,* May 23.
8. Shelley Singh (2016), 'India's ecommerce firms brace for a life without discounts', *The Economic Times,* July 12.
9. Nupur Anand (2016), "Faircent breaks into a new market, builds a brand," *Business Standard,* August 29.
10. Ratna Bhushan & Writankar Mukherjee (2016), 'Rural India cuts down on discretionary spends to save for internet and mobile talk-time packs', *The Economic Times,* July 12.
11. Shelley Singh (2016), 'India's ecommerce firms brace for a life without discounts', *The Economic Times,* July 12.
12. Ibid.
13. The Economic Times (Bureau) (2016), 'Ecommerce will Trigger Big Innovations in India: Study', *The Economic Times,* April 23.
14. Payal Ganguly (2017)," Amazon takes Prime Spot with Loyalty Programme," *The Economic Times,* May 9.
15. Ratna Bushan, (2015), 'On Mission Swachh Bharat Rekitt Homes in on Varanasi', *The Economic Times,* August 4.
16. Ravi Balakrishnan, (2015), "Ex Ad Executive Takes on Unilever", *The Economic Times,* August 4.
17. Wayne D. Hoyer and Deborah J, MacInnis, *Consumer Behavior,* Houghton Mifflin, 1999, 28.

EXERCISES

1. Collect the marketing mix elements of three brands in the shampoo category and their ads. How do you think the basics of consumer behaviour will help these brands selected?
2. Digital marketing: find three examples of brands from any category that have used digital marketing with principles of consumer behaviour?

CHAPTER 2

Consumer Decision Making and Branding Strategies

While a number of psychological variables are useful in understanding the consumers' mind-set, it is worthwhile to probe into some specific aspects of consumer decision making (CDM) in order to formulate the marketing strategies.

CDM enables marketers to visualize a broad framework of the stages and apply the psychological or/and group variables to a specific product/market/brand situation. The process of decision making can provide several trigger points at a conceptual level, especially when a brand wants to standout in a crowded product category or enter a 'new-concept' product category or elevate itself.

CONSUMER DECISION MAKING: IMPORTANT DIMENSIONS

- What kind of approach (strategy) should a brand have when it enters a crowded category with which the consumers are familiar (for example, products like soaps, shampoos, two-wheelers, etc.)?
- How should a brand promote a product that has a 'new-concept' and how are the stages in the CDM framework useful?
- What strategies, other than advertising, might be useful in the specific stages of CDM (consumer decision making)?
- How can the celebrities be used at different stages in the decision-making process?
- What are the different kinds of decision making that consumers indulge in?
- What are the specific differences in CDM between FMCG products and durables?
- Can the needs be differentiated based on what a brand offers?
- Do consumers have different kinds of 'sets' from which they select brands?
- What kind of strategies can a brand use when consumers search for any information?
- How do consumers use their evaluative criteria to take a decision across brands?
- What kinds of factors influence the selection of retail outlets when a consumer decides to buy a product?

These dimensions are strongly linked with one another and also play a significant role in CDM. They focus the attention of any marketer in consumer product categories towards how consumers perceive a category, a brand and their own needs.

Consumers and Brands: Not All Relationships are Created Equal

Branding in the present day's context uses several media channels and differentiation strategies. Every brand makes an attempt to relate to its target segment with the presumption that connecting with the customers would provide a sustainable relationship with them. There are two basic considerations with regard to such an approach. Firstly, a brand manager needs to understand brand relationships before investing in brands, especially in this digital era of quantifying customer lifetime value (CLV). Unless brand relationships are understood, the quantification of CLV itself may not be appropriate at the extreme end of building customer relationships. Secondly, brand relationships require a marketer to understand category relationships that consumers reflect in their interaction with the brands.

Do mothers have a sustained relationship with brands of milk additives like Horlicks, Bournvita or Complan? While brand image or associations play an important part in building customer relationships, how are most associations constrained by the related category? How is the relationship built by an anti-ageing cream like Pond's differ from that built by Lux in the soap category? Some of these complexities are addressed by the sociological model of Sternberg.

Sternberg's model consists of three aspects.[1] Originally the model was developed to explain the relationships between people but the model can be used in consumer behaviour as well, given the plethora of brand strategies attempted by brands across categories. The model has three dimensions that are simple to understand: intimacy, commitment and love. Intimacy is how well a brand and the user know themselves (applied to a consumer behaviour context); both the consumer and the brand are involved in this situation. Would a brand of pen like Reynolds like to have such a relationship and to what extent should the brand make an attempt to build the relationship based on intimacy? Mont Blanc, a premium brand of pen, that addresses the self concept of a consumer in the respective segment may like to develop a brand story that reflects an intimacy. This intimacy may be about how the brand's hand crafted techniques and special diamonds selected to make the limited edition a special one to possess. The buyer's sensitivity to his own self concept responds to the brand's story with the perception of how the brand understands him and the need for his social status. So, when the buyer buys several offerings of the brand, there is development of intimacy (perceived development of intimacy reinforced and rewarded every time a friend enquires about the offering) that offers a possibility of being committed to the brand. It is to be noted that the commitment in this case has been enhanced through intimacy. Commitment in isolation and without intimacy can also take place. A mother who has been a buyer of Complan (with its 'grow tall' proposition) may switch to Horlicks (that has a 'taller, sharper and stronger' proposition). This explains more of commitment to the category and to some extent to the brand and it happens without intimacy being a dominating factor. Unless, we reach an era of marketing where milk additives are customized, the brands in this category may find it difficult to use intimacy as a strategy to build brand relationships. Commitment in isolation is a decision to sustain the relationship and may not have true intimacy.

Love for a product may entail passion coupled with a high degree of liking, but may or may not have intimacy or commitment. Categories like biscuits, soft drinks and even mobile gaming may have strategies that focus on 'love' rather than intimacy or commitment. Mobile handsets, too, (the handsets that are a part of fleeting fashion) may focus on 'love'. A brand like Samsung may build a strong relationship with the use of Galaxy Note but may have a range of colorful and fun range of phones that are oriented towards 'love'. There may be brands like Britannia that banks on a variety has shifted to the health platform (Nutri choice and other offerings) that relies more on commitment rather than the taste proposition associated with "love". There are brands in the energy drink sector like Red Bull where 'energy-love-racy' associations of the brand go together. Red Bull's over a billion dollars in brand sale can be attributed to the impact of spreading excitement about the brand. This is a form of 'love' (passion) that has a remarkable sustaining power over its consumers. Though 'energy' is the proposition of the brand, the type of energy that a consumer expects from a soft-drink brand is different from what he/she will expect from a sports drink like Gatorade. In the case of the latter, consumers are more committed to the brand (commitment dimension).

The important point in Sternberg's model is that a brand's ultimate relationship (as derived from its implications on human relationships) has to have commitment, love and intimacy as part of its strategy. There are several implications to marketers who would like to explore the possibilities of this model. For example, Nike's 'love'-based strategy may be supplemented by its good quality offering (commitment aspect) that is, responsible for the consumer's relationship with the brand. The online platform of the brand can make use of the knowledge base it develops on consumers to supplement its strategy with the intimacy aspect of the brand (knowing about everything a customer would need his/her footwear needs). Such strategies are likely to augment a brand's strategy that had been primarily constructed on the 'love' platform. The brand's 'just do it' proposition, its appeal to the cajole consumer segments (and not just to serious sportsmen) along with fashion orientation over a period of time had created a strong platform and the 'passion or love' aspect of the band. Fastrack brand initially launched on the 'cool and urbane' platform continues to get strengthened with its social media campaigns. The brand's foray into sunglasses and bags (accessories) also strengthens the association as these offerings do have an association with 'passion'.

Consumer behaviour, with its inter-disciplinary orientation can generate several dimensions that can be applied to contemporary branding decisions.

The Basic Model of Consumer Decision Making

Figure 2.1 shows the several stages involved in consumer decision making. Before studying its detailed aspects, it is useful to understand the basic model of CDM quoted in several text books over a period of many decades and its implications for marketers. Whenever marketers introduce a new product category with a new concept, they have to do concept selling at the need stage. This is the stage where the actual and desired state of the consumer is examined. 'Ceasefire', the mini fire-extinguisher kick-started a wave of demand for the product among households (The brand does not retain its hold over the market for a variety of reasons but the objective here is to reflect on how the brand used an approach to market a new concept). It has marketed the concept using the primary advertising. Though the concept of fire-extinguisher, by itself, was not new to the market, the idea of introducing its mini version was a novel idea. It triggered off a perception of being a very different product than the huge, unwieldy ones encountered in office buildings or movie theatres. The primary advertising (with fear overtones) said different kinds of fires required different kinds of extinguishing gases and Ceasefire was the answer to the need. Concept-selling discusses the product benefits and how these can be solved by taking into consideration the existing problems of consumers or helps them reach a 'desired state'. While primary advertising concentrates more on product benefits to create a market need for the product, the secondary advertising discusses the brand. In case a pioneering brand brings in a new-concept product, the secondary advertising has to supplement the needs of primary advertising to ensure that the brand gets the competitive advantage of having promoted the concept. Titan may not be a pioneering brand in quartz watches. But it is currently one of the leading watch brands because of its brand-building efforts.

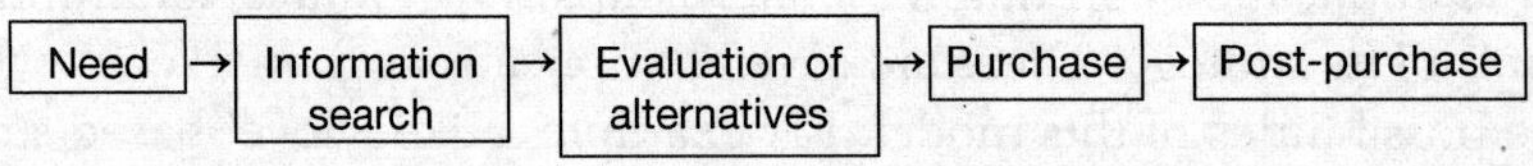

Figure 2.1 Stages in Consumer Decision Making

Heuristics and Consumer Decision Making

Heuristics are psychological shortcuts (literature mentions them as mental short cuts) or 'rules of the thumb' that consumers devise while taking buying decisions. There is a wide range of heuristics reported in the marketing literature. A consumer who prefers to have the lowly priced offerings may always shop at Reliance Mart as their prices are marked below the MRP (Maximum Retail Price) for most items. Consumers may decide to buy a brand of water purifier like Kent as some of its advertisement carries extensive information of its attributes. 'Special K' from Kellogg's may be chosen by a consumer who is looking for a cereal with low calorie. Consumers may eliminate several brands of cars that have a large number of features because they may require a simple car (as in the cereal case it is the choice that will come into play). Some may use the country of origin heuristics to select only the cars made in Germany.

Marketers who spend huge sums of money on promotional activities need to be sensitive to heuristics. This is to ensure that their promotional activities aimed at the segment that uses such heuristics are in line with the consumer segment's expectations. It is to be noted that not every category and every segment may reflect this characteristic of decision making.

Types of Consumer Decision Making

There can be different degrees of CDM depending on the unit cost of the product, involvement levels of consumers with regard to the categories, the efforts involved and the importance attached to the purchase. At the outset, there is a need to differentiate between purchase involvement and the product involvement. Purchase involvement is the interest in purchase process triggered by a need to consider a particular purchase. This kind of involvement is short term and may involve an individual or a family. Product involvement is enduring and the consumers may be involved with a brand (Colgate, for example) or with the product category of toothpastes. A high degree of involvement with a brand may form the basis of brand loyalty and a loyal consumer may prefer the brand without gathering much information on it or evaluation. Purchase involvement and product involvement may have several implications for marketers. For example, a situation can be highlighted to create purchase involvement while brand attributes may be focused on to create brand involvement. A new kind of offering from an insurance company can highlight the needs for the offering (purchase involvement) and also underscore the benefits of the brand (brand involvement). The types of decision making have been widely reported in the marketing literature and have been a part of it for the last several decades.

Habitual Consumer Decision Making

This kind of CDM involves no decision making at all. The consumer buys his/her preferred brand whenever a need arises and the evaluation of the brand may take place only when it fails to perform as expected. This kind of CDM happens only when there is very low involvement with the purchase (involvement levels and decision making have been treated separately). In such situations, even the alternative of not buying the product may not arise. A consumer who is running low on toothpaste may buy the same brand. There can be two types of decisions under habitual (also referred to as nominal decision making) decision making: brand loyalty and repeat purchase decisions. Repeat purchase decisions (without loyalty) are the ones that the consumer makes without staying committed to the brand. This may be out of sheer inertia or non-availability of other brands or alternatives. There is another situation in which the consumers may buy a brand without any commitment. A consumer may keep buying a brand of detergent until another brand challenges the logic of buying the former one.

Limited Consumer Decision Making

This CDM exists between habitual or nominal CDM and extended CDM. The difference between habitual and limited CDM is that the consumer may search for limited information before taking the decision. A consumer who is running out of tea may compare the brand prices or sales promotion offers. He/she may want to try a new brand, and hence, they may get information on the quality of the product or even consider the novelty of an offering. In limited CDM, there may be an internal and a limited external search (from memory). It normally occurs in low-involvement conditions. In both nominal and limited CDM, the post-purchase dissonance is highly improbable.

Extended Consumer Decision Making

This kind of CDM reflects a high level of purchase involvement. An extensive memory search or an external search, results in complex decision making with a number of alternatives/choices opened up for the consumer. However, there is only less chance of dissonance right after the purchase on the correctness of the decision. (This aspect of cognitive dissonance has been dealt separately.) Extended or complex CDM is likely to occur when the unit cost of the product is high and when there is a great deal of involvement as stated earlier. Products like cars, PC's, homes and televisions are such categories that are likely to go through this kind of decision making. There are also certain products/services that are likely to receive significant emotional inputs in the CDM process and they may be as important as the cognitive information associated with the evaluation of high-involvement products. For example, health resorts/holiday packages are being heavily advertised. Besides the financial aspects and information about specific locations, the decision making draws heavily on the importance of the consumer places on the experience which he/she is likely to have, moments of happiness he/she can gather or how important the memories are for the consumer and how well does the family, if involved, perceives the experience.

The Power of Emotional Decision Making

For several centuries, exchanging of gifts has been an universal culture.

In today's context, the positioning of emotions has become an important part of the consumer's decision making process. If the emotion is powerful enough then it can cut across several decision-making rules.

When iPhone 6S was launched, Croma, the retail chain, came out with an interesting advertisement that explained the emotion between a young husband and spouse. The wife gifts a splendid product to her husband(who is always fond of Apple products), especially because she is unable to spend her first wedding anniversary with him.

> The act of giving gifts is dotted with a prestige-based brand, emotional relationship and the self-brand connection (husband's fetish for Apple products). A reference group that symbolically identifies with the ad and the act of the protagonist is likely to relate more with the brand (the ad also had the actual names of the husband and wife).

The conventional CDM model deals with different stages, namely the need stage, information search stage, consideration of alternatives, purchase and post-purchase stage. While these aspects are very much valid even in today's context, it may be appropriate to take into account the several aspects of CDM that have become relevant to consumer segments in today's world. There are eight factors that are critical even to decide on the type of CDM. The conventional model mentions the routine decision making (routine decisions associated with daily purchases), limited decision making (consumers may shop for a variety of products in a category and look for limited information) and extended decision making (a consumer buying highly priced product like a car or house with huge degree of involvement).

In today's context of product proliferation, the brand completion and the limited resources available with most consumers, the following factors become very important:

Involvement level of consumers Contrary to the widely held perception, consumers may not only be involved in buying an expensive or luxury product but they also might be interested in buying a low priced product like toothpaste. Take a product like Colgate Sensitive—for instance, it may be used by several consumers who are suffering from sensitive teeth after they had carefully considered several toothpaste products. In contrast, youngsters with a relatively lower involvement may use Colgate Max, the gel variant. An anti-ageing cream advertisement may create a tremendous degree of involvement in a middle-aged woman who is highly concerned about her growing age as it reflects in her looks. TRESemme shampoos may create a high degree of involvement among its users who are particularly conscious about their hair appearance.

Need/Value A need state in the CDM process is triggered when there is a gap between one's real (actual) state and the desired state. The interesting point is that the individual should recognize this gap to advance into the next state (information state). Several two-wheeler owners may think that a four-wheeler is preferable; but only those who are deeply aware of the 'gap' will search for cars and may start searching for information about the car brands like Alto, Eon or Swift. Many consumers may believe that herbal products are desirable but only few will search for information about Himalaya's or Body Shop brands. The instalment schemes (payment tenure available for a period of time) offered by 'Tanishq' is an interesting example to reflect how the dormant need for jewellery among young women may be triggered by marketing. Social media interaction among a network of friends may also trigger the dormant interest across several product categories or even create interest in brands (for example, in the apparel category).

Value is the 'benefits–sacrifice' equation where benefits (tangible and intangible benefits) are offered by the marketer and the sacrifice is made by the consumer in terms of money, time and psychic costs of searching for a product. eBay may offer value to several thousand consumers; a premium shopping mall like UB Mall in Bangalore may also offer value to several thousand consumers who shop for their beloved products that are available on eBay. Value is an important aspect that provides a shape to the needs; it is also influenced by a consumer's involvement. A consumer who desires to buy a soap that has moisturizing qualities (due to its mildness and action) may be more involved in the attribute. Such a consumer is likely to perceive a better value in the Dove brand of soaps among several other brands in the provided choice.

Discretionary Income and Priority A consumer prioritizes his purchase depending upon his involvement and affordability. A daily wage worker may use a sachet of Ariel detergent or buy a sachet of Red Label tea depending on his income for the day or week. For many consumers, children's education may be top priority instead of buying several durable categories. A young man who has discretionary income may prioritize Bacardi as a part of his weekend expenses due to his involvement in hedonism (pleasure) associated with the consumption of the brand (discretionary income is one where the consumer may have extra money to spend on products and services after his basic needs for living are met). Several online buying channels like Amazon, Snapdeal, Flipkart and Myntra are in aim for the discretionary purchases of young consumers across various categories like electronic accessories, gadgets and apparels.

Personality The needs generated as well as the degree of involvement greatly depends on the inner characteristics of the individual. A consumer who has a high sense of belongingness is likely to buy several souvenirs that are associated with an IPL cricket match to experience the sense of belongingness with his group of friends. A self-motivated consumer is more likely to select a brand that is in tune with his self-concept (for example, the individuality associated with the customization of colours offered by the brand). A consumer may have a regulatory focus (an individual has a promotional or prevention goal where a prevention goal is more about being conservative, avoiding losses and taking less of risks and a promotional goal is about aspirations and opportunity to maximize the gains). A promotional goal-oriented consumer may choose a cosmetic brand that promises enhanced appearance that the consumer may believe to be important for his/her aspirations. (Fair & Lovely/Fair & Handsome cream, for example). While this does not imply that a prevention goal-oriented consumer will not choose the brand, it is a symbolic example to reflect the pattern of choices that may be associated with a consumer who may be under the dominant influence of promotional focus (goal).

Brand Communication Brand associations, brand imagery, brand personality and brand relationships are largely a result of brand communication. Gilmore (1919) was one of the earliest authors who had written about human beings associating human-like traits to inanimate objects (the study is termed as *anthropomorphism*).

The relationship between self-concepts and brand relationships provide the basic platform for brand associations to take shape. From fast moving goods to durables and services, brand associations have an impact on the brand choice. Mercedes, TVS, Hero Pleasure (two-wheeler for women), Taj Mahal (tea connoisseur's preference), Ariel detergent(choice of a discerning women), the macho appeal of Thums Up, the 'togetherness' of 'Close Up' toothpaste and the mother-daughter association of Clinic Plus are some of the diverse associations of brands that have impacted consumers in their respective categories. Over a period of two to three decades, the brand associations have played a major role in the decision-making practices of Indian consumers. What is important to be noted is that when a consumer chooses a brand offering in his/her 'choice set', both the functional and psychological aspects are important. The 'Fogg' detergent that had positioned itself as a 'no gas' deodorant had overtaken the leader in the category, despite being a late entrant. The brand traditionally associated itself with a symbolic category (that symbolized several psychological aspects among the youth) was able to create a functional association that had added to the psychological dimension.

Alternatives When it comes to consumer preferences, there may be several brands that offers alternative choices. Mountain Dew is not only a lemony drink but it is also associated with the spirit of adventure. Fair & Lovely is a fairness cream that promises fulfilment of aspirations (as against Fairever that has an herbal touch). Himalaya's face wash promises blemish-less complexion through its herbal action (as against Dove face wash which is associated with 'Real Beauty' and mildness). Horlicks is associated with 'growth signs' among kids (as against Bournvita which is able to absorb the vitamin D in milk).

Digitalization and Online Retail Channels Earned media (media that is associated with the good will of consumers) is an important aspect of social media like Facebook or YouTube. Social media is all set to overtake 'paid media' (conventional media used by marketers for several decades) as it involves friends or other acquaintances of the consumer. Online channels have opened up another dimension that will have important implications to the brands. Consumers can order lesser known brands from their favourite ecommerce portals like Flipkart or Amazon. If social media carries out favourable opinions or polls about such new brands being offered by the well-known portals, then highly visible brands are more likely to get affected. Walmart, one of the world's largest retail brands had explored the possibility of marketing its apparel brand (private label) 'George' in India, and if such a brand is marketed online, many consumers who are considering that the term 'value'—which is associated with price and quality—may consider such brands. Consumer ratings for products besides personal sources will emerge as an important word of mouth tool for many brands (Zomato app for restaurants is an example). Consumer's reviews and ratings can have a powerful impact on choice decisions of consumers. Maggi noodles is such an example of how negative word of mouth can affect a brand. The product was withdrawn from markets across India following reports that it contained harmful elements. The credibility and sales of the brand was affected tremendously. Usage of mobile is another major factor that can have an impact on brand choice. Unilever India's radio station (KKT) is meant only for mobile phones, especially in regions where there is scarce electricity. It is a contextual initiative that could attract consumers to the brands of the company. These radio stations stream entertainment content along with brand advertisements.

Consumer Decision Making and Celebrity Usage

Santro cars from the Maruti stable (the brand has been discontinued by the company but the objective in this context is to illustrate how a new brand had made use of a celebrity to establish itself in a new market) is an interesting case of celebrity usage in the context of CDM. As the brand was new to the Indian context, it just used a celebrity to get into the 'attention span' (which can be associated with the information search stage) of consumers. The brand ran a campaign which explained the problems associated with cars and how Santro was built to address these problems. The next was an advertising campaign comparing Santro with competitive brands like Matiz (from Daewoo). These strategies associated with the information search stage reduced the perceived risk among consumers (since the brand was new in India, perceived risks that had to be addressed) and it garnered huge sales. The excellent service provided by the company (in the perception of consumers) led to a positive post-purchase feeling. This would have resulted in the positive word of mouth (see Figure 2.2).

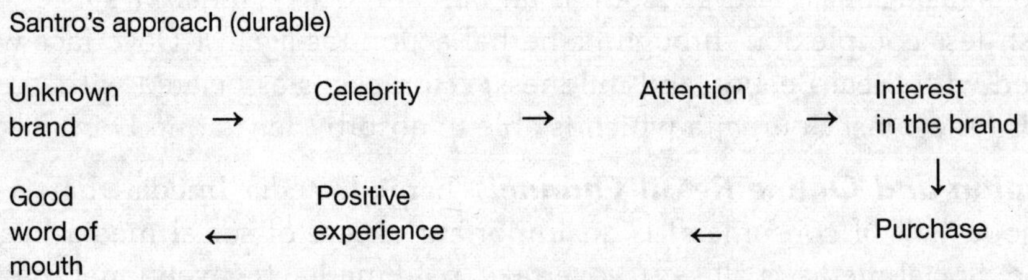

Figure 2.2 Celebrity Usage: Santro's Approach

Impulsive Purchase and Consumer Decision Making

Soft drinks, chocolates, branded blades, biscuits and ice-creams are products that fall under the impulsive-buy category. The needs that are reflected at the beginning of the CDM model are associated with an urge to buy the brand regardless of the consequences of purchase. (Impulsive buying is treated in a separate section.) This need can be triggered off by attractive display or brand packaging or POP material. Across markets, Gillette attempts to trigger off impulsive buying with an attractive display at the point of purchase (Refer to Plate 2.1). Consumers (a significant number of them) do tend to buy more blades than what may be currently required and keep them in stock, probably due to the impulse triggered by the brand. When such purchase takes place, the consumer may move directly from the need stage to the purchase stage. A large retail outlet like Reliance Fresh may be interested in researching the impulse profile of its consumers across many product categories to take decisions on display arrangements. The impulse profile of consumers may vary in terms of psychographics and demographics. Hence, it should be obtained for different

Plate 2.1 Gillette attempts to trigger off impulsive buying with an attractive display at the point of purchase

kinds of segments. Normally, the impulse products are low-cost items unless the target segment is at the upper end of the social strata and is willing to splurge on expensive items as a result of impulse.

Substitutability of Products

The need stage has assumed significance in today's competitive world when brands may compete in related product categories ('related' in terms of the needs of consumers). The competitive aspect of some categories may be indirect or direct. For example, ice-cream may compete with soft drinks, *mithai* or snacks and this can happen in an indirect manner. Though substitutable, it does not occur in the real sense of the word, the consumer prioritizes his/her need before making the purchase. There is a possibility that he/she may even postpone the purchase of other prioritized items. On the other hand, such a thing may not happen at all in the case of durables. Running a high-visibility campaign for both the product category and the brand can help a marketer 'place' these on top of the consumer's priority list (in FMCG categories). Kwality Wall's ice-cream adopted this approach and created interest in the category by having a number of price points in the category. In the case of durables, the brand can be prioritized by offering a value/benefit, which is of interest to the target segment. In entertainment products, TV is a highly prioritized product in both urban and rural markets.

Another interesting product category is that of the branded mineral water. A sizeable chunk of the market is in the unorganized sector, with Bisleri being the market leader in producing mineral water supply. Aquafina from Pepsi and Kinley from Coke targets the youth and have been launched based on its lifestyle-centric approach. Nestle and Britannia is some of the other companies attempting to build brands in this category. The reasons why soft drinks and mineral water are consumed is due to thirst, group activity and fun. In fact, soft drinks are more associated with fun than thirst. Each category is likely to substitute the other, depending on the positioning. For example, if the fun element is associated with the positioning of a brand of mineral water, it may be perceived as a substitute for soft drinks (aerated or others), not just during summer but throughout the year. Bisleri may have to increase its retail availability to match that of Pepsi and Coke if it aspires to be a substitute for colas/soft drinks. The need and purchase stages (during which the positioning strategies of brands are likely to work) are important for building brands.

Consumer decision making does not progress in a linear fashion. There are many aspects that can bring a brand directly in to the consideration or choice set. Choice architecture is about how a choice is being presented to the consumer and its influence on consumer decision making.[2]

A brand like Croma or LG that is desirous of having a sustained contact with the customer who has bought an appliance can either ask for an 'opt in' or 'opt out' choice among consumers when they need to approve of the brand's on-going contact with them for subsequent information on the brand's products or schemes that may be introduced. According to the default choice aspect of choice architecture, large percentage of consumers who need to 'opt out' by performing a task (for instance signing a form to opt out) are likely to choose the default option of being 'into' the brand's contacts than the 'opt in' consumers who have to perform a task to 'opt in' with respect to the brand's program associated with the on-going relationship with the consumers.

Brands and Consumer Decision Making

It would be of great interest for the marketers to examine how consumers decide to buy a brand. This has a number of implications on brand positioning like introducing trial offers or examining what kind of objectives the advertising campaign should address with regard to a given brand. Should the advertising enhance the brand awareness so that consumers consider it or should it mention and highlight the brand benefits so that consumers use the information in the final phase of decision making? It will also be useful for the marketers to find out about consumer-readiness with regard to purchasing the product category so that it can be appropriately used for communication strategies. For example, an answer to what kind of hair dye and how many consumers use a hair dye currently and how many are prepared to try it can provide useful information. Doing further research into the category and awareness levels of brands (old brands under the category like Godrej and new brands like L'Oreal) will also be useful. At the next level of product differentiation, it may be worthwhile to find out how many consumers are willing to try out a brand that can be used as well. As it is obvious, the awareness of the category, brand, benefits, perception of benefits and intention to buy the category/brand are critical when the specific stages of considering a brand are thrashed out for formulating a strategy.

The only difference in this era of digital and social media is that several brands that may not be a part of the awareness set may become a part of consideration set. For instance, an unknown brand (from the viewpoint of advertising blitzkrieg) of mobile can enter the consideration set of the consumer from an interaction with a friend on Facebook. And there is also a possibility of a failed brand getting revived after when it relaunches itself with a good word of mouth across social media.

The consumer of any product category progresses from total number of brands to choice set (impact of different stages may vary from FMCG products to durables). The total number of brands refers to the total number of brands in a category available in the market (for example, may be over 100 in the category of mineral water). Awareness set refers to the set of brands the consumer is aware of in a specific category. Ray-Ban launched a campaign to enhance the awareness levels of the target segment during its entry stage into the Indian market. Consideration set is a set of brands a consumer is likely to consider based on his/her criteria and choice set is the set of brands from which the consumer takes the final decision on buying a specific brand.

While product/market situations and the USP of a brand and the other details from primary research data are to be considered (as stated earlier) before the brand can finalize its strategies using the 'brand set' model, there is a growing research evidence to show that point-of-purchase (POP) material at retail outlets is useful in influencing the purchase decision of the consumer. This means that in certain categories (especially FMCG's), POP material can take a brand into the 'choice set' stage at the point of purchase (retail outlets). In certain categories of durables, the information on new features can place a new brand in the choice set of consumers. This is advantageous to the brands in durables that are high-involvement purchases where there can be a number of established brands strongly placed in the awareness or consideration set. For example, there were a number of well-known/established brands in the refrigerator and TV markets when LG entered into these product categories in India–Godrej, BPL, Videocon, Akai, Whirlpool, Kelvinator and Voltas to name a few. But LG's success can be attributed to its positioning based on its novel features in these categories, which placed the brand in the 'choice set' stage of CDM model.

LG's TV had the golden eye feature ('wrinkle-free', easy viewing) and its refrigerators came with the 'nutrition-preservation' feature when most competitive brands were positioning themselves on traditional propositions. It should be noted that the 'choice set' connected with LG in this situation is relevant to those consumers who were looking for novel features in their TV's or refrigerators. In the TV category, LG appealed more to the replacement (CTV) segments.

The following are the important aspects about this CDM model:

1. It provides directions for a new brand to make an impact on consumer's mind-set.
2. With appropriate strategies, it may be possible to eliminate stages or at least ensure a short period of transition across the stages in the 'brand set'.

3. There is a need to use specific strategies (communication as well as other aspects of the marketing mix elements) to take the consumer quickly to the 'choice set' stage. For example, Gillette ran a campaign in India for a shaving gel (a niche market) by associating this version with shaving brushes. (Shaving brushes are part of the shaving for a majority of consumers even though gel can be used without a brush). Besides, the brand also came out with special packages that could get the attention of consumers in the retail environment.

Information Search and Consumer Decision Making

Consumers tend to increase their effort on searching information in varying degrees. Some make an extra effort to probe and explore the information about product categories/brands while some others go through sources other than advertisements, such as the positive word of mouth. Information search may be internal or memory-based. It may be external, in which the consumer scans the environment to offer inputs to the CDM process. Information search takes effort, time and money. There are benefits of information search, which includes the selection of a brand that has a better value or higher quality or one that reassures the consumer against his/her perceived risks associated with the purchase.

Nature of Information Search

Whenever a consumer feels a need, one has to scan the memory to determine if a satisfactory solution can be found and if there are any alternatives to that solution. A consumer who is hungry can think of a fast-food restaurant, a brand of fast food or even prepare a meal by himself/herself. The consumer may also consider the type of food and associated costs. This is internal search. If he/she cannot hit a solution, he/she may undertake the external search. (The same consumer may also want information about the eateries when he/she is in a new city.) A number of decisions that consumers take with regard to low-involvement products are likely to be based on internal search. External decision making may include the following aspects:

- Opinions and attitudes of friends, relatives or opinion leaders.
- Information provided by promotional aspects associated with the brand like advertising, personal selling or brochures.
- Direct product trials (two-wheelers or cars).

There is another type of 'on-going' information search, which consumers undertake without a specific problem. For example, there may be consumers who are frenzied about motorcycles. They may or may not own the vehicle but may be interested in any information on motorcycles. These consumers are involved in an 'on-going search' with regard to this product category. This kind of information search occurs both because of the pleasure involved in seeking information and also because such information may be useful later.

This information search may be extremely useful to marketers. It may be worthwhile to identify a set of consumers who may not want to buy the product at a given point of time but are interested in the category due to their high level of involvement. A brand that is able to build a relationship with such consumers stands to gain attraction when the consumer is actually ready to buy the product category. There is a great possibility of consumers considering a brand with which they are not only familiar but have also had some interaction. TVS Scooty did just that through an online promotional method involving the target segment (youth) and collected the valuable information in a short period of time. Establishing contact and nurturing the established relationship through specific media and promotional methods appropriately to the 'on-going search' segment is extremely useful to the brand, especially when the category has competition.

Types of Information Sought

CDM requires the following types of information alternatives available, criteria for evaluating the alternatives and the performance of each alternative. A consumer is likely to search for information until he/she is satisfied that he/she has gathered these types of information. Different brands with different USP's form the basic information with regard to the alternatives available. Normally, in a number of consumer product categories, consumers perceive and interpret this kind of information through the positioning strategies of brands. For example, Lux can be positioned as an entry-level soap; Sunsilk for specialising into hair care; Clinic Plus, a therapeutic shampoo for the family and Clinic All-Clear for the youth. In fact, the perception of consumers about the probable outcome of using the brand (getting rid of dandruff or having bouncy, glamorous, attractive hair) is also an outcome of the positioning strategy of the brand. The positioning should be such that consumers identify themselves with it and perceive the benefits of the brand. A brand of toothpaste that was launched a few decades back had fast-spreading action as its USP and consumers were not able to identify themselves with the benefit. Clear-cut positioning of benefits (functional or emotional) helps the brand to influence the evaluative criteria that consumers (targeted segment) may formulate through external search. The toothpaste gel, with its cosmetic white teeth and lifestyle positioning, has appealed to the youth and created a new criterion in the category. Consumers also have what is called 'inert set' of brands or 'back-up' brands about which they may accept information. A consumer who has made up his/her mind to buy Colgate Total based on the 'multiple benefits' criteria may choose Himalaya if the former is not available. This happens because consumers may be tuned to information that is close to their evaluative criteria. This can also happen in durables but branding plays a vital role because of the high degree of perceived risk in high-involvement products.

The expectation on the performance of the brand depends on four aspects: market characteristics, brand characteristics, consumer characteristics and situational characteristics. Market characteristics include available alternatives, how well the product category has been accepted, (diffusion of innovation—this has an influence on reducing the perceived risk and/or making the product category a necessity, for example, gas stoves) and availability of information through advertising or sales personnel, independent sources or through personal sources. Brand characteristics depend on brand differentiation and the value perceived (the benefits perceived also dependent on this). Consumer characteristics depend on learning and experience, social status, age in the life cycle, perceived risk, familiarity with the product and the level of involvement with the product category. Situational characteristics include availability of time, whether the product is for personal use or a gift, physical and mental energy to gather information and affordability to buy the brand. The outcome in terms of performance is complex and based on several factors associated with the types of information sought. This, in turn, depends on a set of characteristics.

The influencing factors (types of characteristics) have significant implications for marketers. A microwave oven, for example, may not be perceived as a high-priority durable item in households where one of the spouses does not go out to work. An online grocery store is likely to attract the attention of a busy, young and aspiring couple pursuing an active career. The search for information on brands like BMW and Mercedes may be important for niche consumers who may be actively involved in deciding on the type of car to buy, not so much for its utility as for its status. The kind of information search by this niche will be quite different from those who may also learn about this information without intending to buy those brands.

Perceived risk, as a consumer characteristic, can provide several dimensions in which marketers approach and provide information to a target segment (especially in durables). For example, there may be a brand in electric cars, which wants to be launched in India. The information search involved with regard to the perceived risks of the consumer can open up several strategies associated with the marketing mix elements planned for the launch. This can be shown as follows:

Perceived risks about and information search for an electric car brand	
Risk factor	Implications for the brand
Social risk	Will the appeal of an electric car be comparable with that of a traditional one? (in terms of status)
Financial risk	If the brand is going to cost as much as a regular car at its entry level, will it provide value? Is buying the brand an experiment?
Performance risk	Will this new type of car perform as well as a traditional car with which the consumer is familiar?
Operational risk	Will consumers be comfortable with the driving and getting used to the operations of the electric car when they have all along driven the conventional car?

Financial operational and performance risks may be associated with the perceived benefits of the brand and can be addressed as value risk.

It may be worthwhile for the marketers to obtain primary information from the prospective consumers on the types of perceived risks associated with a product category or a brand introducing a new feature not associated with the category. For example, if a brand in air-conditioners (like LG) advertises a feature that provides 'clean air', there may be certain perceived risks associated with the feature like after-sales service because of the complexity of the product, the value provided by the feature or even certain apprehensions about the process through which the brand gives such a benefit.

Strategies of Applying Consumer Decision Making[3]

The strategies provided are not exclusive ones, though they are categorized into specific aspects/contexts. They provide an idea about how brand strategies can be formulated in a CDM framework.

Maintenance Strategy

This strategy is quite applicable to the regular FMCG products like soaps, toothpastes, tea, coffee, biscuits and soft drinks. The brand is in a situation where it is bought regularly (or habitually) and it has to ensure that the commitment levels of consumers are sustained. Sustaining this favourable or habitual behaviour may involve product development, launching variants, ensuring that advertising keeps the brand on top of the consumer's mind and avoiding stock-out situations in distribution channels. The last one is as important as the others because in a competitive situation, especially in low-involvement categories, consumers are likely to try another brand in case when their favoured brand is not available at retail outlets. POP is important to ensure that the consumer is further motivated to buy the brand. Colgate, Close-up, Surf Excel, Horlicks, Britannia, Lux and Red Label are some of the brands that can be associated with this strategy. Red Label launched its brand with natural ingredients, Britannia offers a number of variants and Pepsodent introduced a 'two-in-one' toothpaste (gel with the usual white toothpaste). The objective of such a strategy is to ensure that consumers do not leave the brand.

Disrupt Strategy

When a brand is not a part of the habitual buying pattern or not in the 'consideration set', then there is a need for the brand to disrupt the existing decision-making pattern. This is difficult because the consumer may not seek any external information (under nominal decision making). Free samples and coupons are such ways to break the habitual decision making of consumers oriented towards a competitive brand. This strategy can be very useful for brands that are new to the market and have to compete with a number of established brands in the categories. A significant and a relevant brand benefit can also be useful to break the habitual decision making. Fair & Lovely is strongly associated with manufacturing fairness creams. The brand is being used by a large consumer base. A new brand—Fairever (with the addition of saffron) was able to capture a sizeable 'trial share' when it was launched in the market.

There have been several brands like Ovaltine, Ragi malt and Drinking Chocolate that are in the last several years in the category of malted drinks. But Horlicks continues to dominate the market. Competitive brands in this category could have built up an effective disruptive strategy. Good retail brands offer excellent scope to disrupt FMCG purchases associated with the leading brands with which consumers have been familiar for decades. Penetration pricing with the visibility of advertising at times when the consumers 'down-trade' may be a very effective disruption strategy. Low prices, especially with no-frill services, have succeeded as disruptive strategies in the airline services sector all over the world–Southwest Airlines, being a globally known example. Penetration pricing backed up by good brand equity can also be an effective strategy in the fast foods category. A value based on a higher price point may also be a good strategy. Reynolds was introduced at a higher price point but consumers accepted the brand because of the superior benefits associated with it (the point here is not to discuss the overall strategy of the brand).

In a number of FMCG categories, the close competitors keep resorting to both maintenance and disrupt strategies, especially when there is a need to achieve market share. Bisleri introduced a number of stock keeping unit (SKU) with a view to increase its market share in the category of mineral water, in which the unorganized market accounts for almost half the market.

Capture Strategy

Limited CDM is an area in which the consumers look out for very little external search and they may purchase the brand again (unless it is not available). A brand which is currently being used by consumers should ensure that it captures a large share of the consumer's purchases (large because despite the limited nature of decision making, consumers may try other brands in categories like soaps and toothpastes). The evoked set has to have the brand on top of the consumer's mind. There may also be a need to introduce a number of SKUs to ensure that consumers do not leave the brand (Close-up, Fair & Lovely, Surf Excel and almost all the leading brands in the shampoo category are examples). This is important in the Indian context because the unit price of the product holds a significant value and the consumers may buy different brands for different occasions. The dominant brand should ensure it increases the consumer's share of purchases. In-store information (discussed later in the chapter) may be a useful strategy. This may be a prerequisite for leading brands. The in-store merchandising adopted by brands in supermarkets is likely to influence the purchase decisions when the consumers are present at the retail outlet. Brand loyalty assumes a lot of significance in the capture strategy. There may also be infrequently purchased items like antiseptic lotions and air-fresheners. A leading brand like Dettol or Lizol (in branded floor-cleaning category) should ensure that it develops the market, builds the brand and captures a large number of consumers as the market for the category evolves. For example, in a largely unorganized market for floor-cleaning products (household care), Domex and Lizol have built the brands and are attempting to expand the market. If a leading brand in a category, which is yet to evolve into a mass market, does not take the lead, then late entrants may make a dent into the market share of the pioneering brand when market evolves. In the dish-washer category, Vim held its own throne for several decades. But it was forced to come out with many variants and promotional campaigns in the recent times because of the growing presence of regional brands. Vim launched the major 'Vim Challenge' campaign to ensure that it sustained its pioneering lead. Capture strategy also emphasizes the need to introduce a downward stretch in a product-line, especially when a company is a market leader. Hindustan Unilever, a leader in the detergents market, was forced to introduce Wheel because of Nirma's onslaught at the lower end. Monitoring the environment and developing the product-line as the market evolves is an important strategy. Colgate launched its gel version after a competitive brand like Close-up was launched in the market to attract the youth segment.

Intercept Strategy

When the consumer is in the limited CDM mode and the brand does not exist in the evoked set, a marketer has to intercept to ensure that the brand gets into the (evoked) set. Sales promotion is one way of getting there and ensuring brand trial, but the brand should not get into the sales-promotion trap. Else, the brand is likely to get into the evoked set only when there is a sales promotion announced. New brands can use intercept strategy by getting consumer attention through strong positioning strategy, even in a limited CDM situation. Promise toothbrush highlighted itself on its angled design and Tropicana boasted itself for being a 'pure-juice' producer; these are such examples of intercept strategy. Another intercept strategy can be to reposition competition (though sometimes there is a risk of using positioning against established beliefs). Savlon, the antiseptic brand, repositioned its competitor Dettol by positioning itself as an odour-free brand without harnessing the tingly feeling when applied on cuts. Moov pain balm repositioned Iodex for its 'non–staining' effect when applied by a consumer.

Preference Strategy

As CDM involves extensive information collection, there are the situational possibilities that can make use of this strategy:

1. When the intention to buy the brand is high (as it is already in the evoked set of brands).
2. When the consumer has already bought the brand and wants to consider replacement of the product.

There is evidence to show that the intention to buy may not be a strong indicator of the final purchase, though a number of studies in India are conducted in this dimension. However, the intention to buy indicates brand awareness and even a preference for one. The gap between the intention to buy and the actual purchase can be traced to the point of purchase or retail outlet (especially for durables). The retailer's recommendation carries weight in the Indian context. A brand should ensure that the retailer commends a brand only if it fits into the 'need structure' of the consumer. This is in the interest of both the brand and the retailer. The retailers have to be trained in this aspect.

A durable national brand may have around 5,000 to 6,000 retail outlets in which it is offered and a majority of these are likely to be multi-brand outlets. It is essential for a brand to ensure that the retailer recommends an offering as per the needs of the consumer and the one that may be updated in terms of features. A consumer desiring a 'no-frills' TV will develop dissonance towards the brand and the retailer if he/she is pressurized into buying an expensive TV. The preference strategy should ensure that the brand is viewed positively even after it is bought. Another possibility of a change in the intention to buy may be due to the word of mouth (on a competitive brand) obtained from a personal source. A marketer may not be able to experience this directly but it is useful to have done a primary research on the decision-making process of consumers who have already bought a specific brand. Researching can be sourced from the past information on how the consumer knew about the brand he/she purchased, the various brands that were considered, the gap (if any) between the intention to buy and the final purchase and the various personal sources he/she used for information search. This research can enable a marketer to get inputs for preference strategies.

The preference strategy may also be associated with the existing brand that the consumer is using at a point of time. These are brands that exist in several categories. A brand, which a customer had bought (in any category) goes beyond the evoked set of brands and creates an 'experience' for the customer. This relationship phase based on the experience determines not only the evoked set of brands when the customer wants to replace the product but also when he/she desires to buy a different product category in which the brand competes actively. Right from the installation or giving information on product usage (by sales personnel or a brochure) to the stage of reminding the customer about the replacement of the product at an appropriate time, a brand (and hence, the company) can work out a number of dimensions associated with the preference strategy. This is a powerful strategy for customer retention. There are several brands (in durable categories) offering exchange promotion for the replacement market. There does not seem to be a single brand that offers privileges for a consumer who has bought the same brand in his previous purchase cycle. The frequent flyer program offered by airlines is a pure example of the preference strategy being used to retain consumers.

Acceptance Strategy

While the preference strategy tries to capitalize on the positive impact of the brand on the consumer, the acceptance strategy attempts to create an acceptance for a brand, which is not in the evoked set of brands when the consumer is about to begin the process of decision making. Moreover, this becomes difficult because of the strong and well-entrenched brands that are already in the evoked set of consumers. A strong brand name (with 'value' perception) can be a good acceptance strategy to get into the evoked set. Akai created a value-oriented exchange program when it entered the Indian TV market. Indian experience in durables shows that value is as important as or even more important than the brand name. LG and Samsung (Whirlpool's strategy was discussed earlier) are few examples of acceptance strategy which is successfully created by marketers through useful features. Santro's strategy (discussed earlier) is also an effective acceptance strategy. An acceptance strategy should ensure that consumers visit the retail outlet to know about the features and benefits of a brand. Automobiles and two-wheelers can advertise trial runs. Long-term advertising, with an emphasis on attracting attention (resulting in incidental learning among the prospective consumers) is another type of acceptance strategy. The objective of such a campaign is to get the brand into the evoked set of consumers.

The different kinds of strategies suggested across the CDM types are suggestive and a number of variations are possible with the marketing mix elements. This framework only attempts to provide a structured perspective on CDM.

Dimensions of Information Search

Information search can be explained in terms of degree, direction and sequence. The degree of search represents the total search. This is associated with the number of brands, stores, attributes and other information sources considered during the search process. Category killer like Vivek & Co (seller of various durable products like kitchen appliances, air conditioner, etc.). carry a number of brands and it becomes easy for consumers to compare the brands or attributes. Consumers may not visit many stores for the purpose of comparison.

The degree of search is significantly dependent on the decision-making process. Extended decision making will involve considerable information search. In the case of durables, if the consumer is satisfied with the purchase, then he/she may minimise the search time by considering the same brand during the replacement cycle. Consumers can be segmented based on the degree of information search (based on primary research) and grouped into a number of categories (suggestive) like low-search group, purchase-friend assisted group (assisted by a known person), high-search group or a moderate search group. A manufacturer of a durable like a TV or a refrigerator may find that consumers in the high-search group are more likely to buy the brand than others. The brand can come out with advertisements which may encourage the consumers to search for any available information. This is more applicable to the durable that offer new features to maintain a competitive edge. For example, Titan Edge was introduced as the slimmest watch in the world. (Refer to Plate 2.2). Consumer segments that engage in a considerable amount of external search may be easier to reach than those that rely on internal search. Consumers who rely on internal search may be approached through direct marketing.

Distribution decisions may be fine-tuned based on the type of retail outlets and specific geographic locations that consumers visit. A brand may find that a specific store in a geographical area enjoys a lot of consumer loyalty. The company may not appoint additional retailers in that area. In consumables like FMCGs or house ware, the in-store information or point-of-purchase material may play an influential role in CDM. There is a growing evidence to show that in some categories, buyers make their decisions using the in-store information. Electronic information kiosks may be useful in large stores if consumers need any information about specific brands, sales promotions or about the ingredients of brands. This may be applicable more in supermarkets that attract a large number of consumers. The search dimension is concerned with the order of search activities. Consumers may be involved in the brand search sequence (processing by brand), in which each brand is examined along various attributes or they may be interested in attribute search sequence (in which the brand information is collected on an attribute-by-attribute basis). For example, a consumer may process by price, warranty and features and in that order. A brand confident

Plate 2.2 Titan Edge was introduced as the slimmest watch in the world

of emphasizing its superiority over competitive brands can use comparative advertising. Marketers may also be interested in finding out the sequence in which the information sources are used by consumers. The consumers, for example, depend on TV for awareness, newspapers for specific details and word of mouth for a final endorsement by a source, which they consider credible. It may be worthwhile for the marketers to prioritize the dimensions of information search.

Affect/emotion and Consumer Decision Making[4]

Emotions (affect) can have a significant impact on consumers. Zumba dance (of Colombian origin) is being practiced by 14 million enthusiasts in 140 countries. The founders of the company associated with this unique dance were initially trying to spread the dance through the fitness route (logical manner to attract the people). It was able to create a cult following with the slogan 'Ditch the workout: join the party', thus signifying the fun element in it and the emotion associated with the brand. Closer home, merchandise are bought on festive occasions like Diwali or Vinayaka Chathurthi because of the excitement and emotion of masses besides the religious fervour associated with these festivities. Ginger.io is an app that monitors the moods by analysing the messages of a consumer, the frequency of messages and the locations. This concept can be used in a variety of ways: Kraft Foods monitors the moods of its followers on Twitter and decides to send coupons. Sentiment analysis is used with digital platforms to get an idea about emotional responses towards a brand and its attributes.[5]

Importance of In-store Research (FMCG Products)

- Do consumers compare prices when they buy commodities/essentials?
- What is the time spent by consumers in reading the in-store promotional material?
- How many consumers check if a price deal is available at the store in the product category they are about to purchase?
- Do consumers read the labels of the brands they select (especially, if they make a brand switch)?
- Do consumers spend time on brands placed at the entry point of the store?
- How many consumers buy products based on advertising/word of mouth when they make a brand switch? How many does change their decision based on the POP material?
- Do the children influence the consumers at the retail outlet?
- Do consumers change their decisions when cooperative sales promotion is involved? (One brand from a category given free with another in a different category, for example, a Dettol soap given free with Lizol?)

These questions are likely to be useful specifically for a large retail outlet dealing with FMCG products in an urban context (like the 'Food World').

Emergence of Shopping Styles

A few decades ago, such an article may not have been applicable to the Indian context. As markets grew and brands proliferated with a variety of propositions and positioning strategies, the shopping styles began emerging at least in the urban context. Consumers have also developed a lifestyle which has emerged from changing attitudes and mind sets, exposure to Western influences and a need for self-gratification. Beauty parlours in cities, eateries, time-share vacations, designer wear, watches and even soft drinks are a few instances that reflect these changes. The sellers' market is slowly moving towards becoming the buyers' market—though not in the same manner as in the developed world—but with a slew of variants among the products and its offerings. Soaps, shampoos, air-conditioners, televisions and washing machines, with their many features, are available aplenty. As the point of brands reaches 'commoditisation' in several categories (where differentiation may be getting narrowed down), the companies are endeavouring to highlight the value in their offerings. (Value, in simple terms, is the enhancement of the price-performance equation or 'more for the same price' approach) Value, by itself, has triggered off a shopping style even in the premium product categories. A few years back, a 29-inch TV was once placed in the premium category. The growth can be largely attributed to Akai, which brought in a value-based exchange scheme. The value has also reflected in 'price bundling'. Akai introduced a scheme that had the TV and refrigerator built into the same price in such a way that it resulted in a positive bargain for the consumer. Lizol, a brand of floor-cleaner had offered a value-based promotion of giving Harpic free with every bottle of Lizol. (Both products come from the same company.)

Quality–oriented Style

Consumers, here, look for quality in brands when shopping. They may choose expensive brands as they feel that the price is an indicator of quality. In the absence of well-known brands in a product category, these consumers are likely to take cues from the retail outlets ('Food World' or 'Nilgiris') hoping that these outlets will carry quality products. Small or regional brands, which cannot afford high-visibility campaigns, have an opportunity to get into the 'consideration set' of consumers by constantly supplying good quality products to these retail outlets. This they can do by conveying the brand name on the packaging. Vegetables, fruits, commodities and snacks are some of the product categories that offer scope for such strategies. It is also imperative for some brands to maintain quality (especially for FMCG brands like tea, coffee and soaps) to ensure that quality-oriented customers remain with them. These customers may also try out brands within a specific price range. A user of the Dove moisturizing bar may buy Mysore Sandal Gold, which is a soap in the same price range. In case of durables, the quality-conscious consumers may obtain references from friends on performance and after-sales service. They may also look for specific features that they are interested in. Automatic cut-off in gas stoves may be a feature that appeals to some consumers. It should be remembered that the quality, for this category, does not mean only the performance but also the convenience and comfort. These consumers are normally price-insensitive if 'quality' products enhance the degree of comfort and well-being. The 'feature' oriented 'quality' consumer may form a profitable niche for marketers. The LG brand that offers preservation of nutrients in its refrigerator and microwave is an example.

Brand–conscious Style

Consumers, in this category are brand-conscious because of the prestige associated with these brands. They may be drawn towards brands that have lifestyle appeals, in addition to promises on quality. A brand-conscious shopper will be found more enthusiastic in purchasing categories like two-wheelers, cars, televisions, textiles and watches where the brand is likely to reflect the social status of the buyer. Brands can also be built in impulsive product categories like soft drinks and chocolates through which the consumer would like to identify himself/herself in a social setting. Brands like Pepsi that carry group appeals may have an impact on this consumer type.

Another kind of brand appeal that may draw these consumers in is the extent to which they internalise it. Apart from projecting the social status through the ownership of certain brands, the consumers may also identify themselves internally with these brands. Brands make use of brand personality techniques, which are very useful.

The freshness associated with 'Liril' appealed to the housewives who wanted a break from their daily routine. Raymond's 'complete man' will appeal to consumers who consider themselves to be down to earth, if not ideal, guys.

Novelty–oriented Style

A small section of consumers may want to try and experiment with new products, new variants of existing product/brands and new brands. This shopping style may be found in almost any category where a number of brands compete with each other. The soap category may be fickle and one in which there are frequent brand launches. This style is also relevant to electronic products, a category with consumers who may like to try out the product/brand as soon as it is launched. Companies will benefit if they have a database of these innovators (depending on the product category) so that direct marketing may supplement other marketing mix strategies. This consumer-type may either be drawn towards the novelty of the product or derive internal gratification of being an opinion leader by trying out the new brand/product. An opinion leader in one category may not be so in another category. It may also be worthwhile for a marketer to research the market for novelty products (or products offering a number of features) to be sure of the availability of this niche. Decades ago, a novel product like record-player, transistor and tape-recorder combined has failed to take off in the market. Similarly, the picture-in-picture televisions have also failed in the competitive market.

Shopping as a Fun/Pleasure–oriented Activity

There may be shoppers who consider shopping as a fun-oriented pleasurable activity. Retail ambience, layout and in-store music may be factors that keep these consumers longer in retail outlets. While it may be possible to create brand awareness in such consumers in the case of durables, consumable product marketers can gain directly through this kind of shopping activity. Research shows that the right type of music (depending on the consumer type) makes consumers stay longer and spend more time in the outlet. There is another implication of this shopping style. Consumers should be encouraged to stay longer in the retail outlet without being pressurized into buying things. This increases the store traffic and results in better volumes. 'Kids Kemp' at Bangalore is a good example of how consumers are encouraged to stay on in the outlet. Fountainhead and Landmark book stores also encourage prospective shoppers to spend more time at their outlets.

Shoppers' Stop advertises and positions itself on the space and ambience created for a shopping experience. It came out with a television commercial saying shoppers can shop at a snail's pace.

Shopping as a recreational activity may be acceptable as a shopping style. Carried to the extreme, this shopping style may result in a compulsive behaviour called shopaholism. Shopaholics buy excessive products and brands to merely indulge themselves and serious cases may require medical attention. Incidentally, psychiatrists in the US have come up with a treatment for shopaholic behaviour. The major symptom in a shopaholic is that he/she feels guilty after when the initial thrill of shopping is over.

Value for Money Style

This style attempts to focus on the best bargain—not just the price but enhanced price and performance equation. A consumer with this orientation may gather information about several brands and retail outlets before finalizing the purchase of a brand. He/she may compare the prices, features and promotional offers and employ extensive decision making before clinching a deal. This consumer is different from the quality-oriented consumer in that he/she is concerned about the total offering (or total product experience) than just the quality. Bajaj has a value perception based on its initial cost, cost of maintenance, ease of reparability, resale value, service centre backup and ruggedness of the vehicle.

'Impulsive' Style

Unlike the shopaholic, this consumer buys without much analysis or information. The impulsiveness mentioned in this context is not the impulsiveness associated with most consumers when they buy things on impulse. The impulsive buyer is in a hurry to finish off his/her shopping (occasional hurry is not considered here) without much planning even while buying expensive and risk-oriented durables. This consumer does not seem to get involved in the learning process associated with the buying or decision-making process. Well-known brands can reassure this kind of consumer through a distinctive advertising campaign. For example, a hi-tech brand like Philips introducing a new version of a product can bring back its signature line it used a decade back "If it's Philips, you are sure".

Companies can also interact with retailers to ensure they do not take advantage of the impulsive nature of consumers in attempting to offer them products or features they may not need. An impulsive consumer may experience dissonance when he/she finds that the retailer has sold something that he/she does not require. This aspect of matching the offering with the needs is especially important to sustain and nurture a good brand image. Impulsive consumers can bad mouth a brand if dissatisfied.

Shopping Style under Information–overload

In crowded categories like electronics and entertainment equipment (generally durables) or cars, the number of claims and counter-claims made by brands can confuse a consumer. The confusion arises out of the fact that consumers don't understand the technological terms well. Besides, they may feel that they are losing out on certain features for the money they are paying (though they may not use all the features) if they decide on a specific brand. The retailing aspects are of vital importance in this situation, be it concept-selling for a new type of water purifier or detailing the features of a new model. These consumers are likely to stop in multi-brand outlets and hence, the retailer should make a planned effort to enable comparisons across brands (on technological claims, service, warranty, etc.) so that the consumer will have a clear idea about his/her buying decisions.

Loyalty Style of Shopping

The ultimate shopper, for any marketer, will be a committed loyalist who selects and reselects the brand out of conviction and involvement with the brand. The consumer may even stick to the brand across product categories brought over a period of time. Direct marketing, systematic creation of a database of loyal consumers and attractive schemes for these consumers are some strategies that will yield long-term gains for the marketer.

The shopping style would indicate different mind-set of diverse consumers. It should be noted that the consumers cannot be branded on these styles. These styles may vary across product categories even for the same consumer in different situations. Analysing the shopping styles will enable marketers to enhance the marketing mix strategies of their brands.

Consumer Decision Making and Brand Imagery

Though there may be many kinds of models on consumer decision making, brand imagery plays an important role among several consumer segments and across product categories. For instance, BMW, Audi and Mercedes may almost offer the same features; it is the congruence between the brand imagery and the perception of the interested consumer. (Some old examples have been used to convey the conceptual aspects)

Consumers are exposed to several kinds of advertisements during a day—some of them may have a conscious impact and some sub-conscious. (A consumer may start liking the brand or develop a certain association with it because of the constant exposure over a period of time even without realizing it.) In a span of one TV program, we are bombarded with numerous ads of consumer products.

There are durable category brands and there are services brands. Some of them use lifestyle appeals and some use celebrities. Given the clutter of marketing communication and the limited time in which consumers have to comprehend these, it is critical to have the right kind of imagery associated with the brand.

Imagery is the kind of associations a brand could get linked with over a period of time. It has an impact on how consumers perceive the brand and how they will react to it in the long run. For example, Horlicks had created a 'drink for the sick' effigy among many consumers a few decades ago. Will consumers have a clear thought process for Boost? What kind of image would a niche drink like drinking chocolate have in the minds of consumers? Brand imagery plays an important role in shaping the connotation in the consumer's mind-set. Several years ago there were only a few brands in most categories so it was easier to develop an image-status with a brand. Once an image was developed it stayed with consumers for a long time. Today's context is different as several brands attempting to create a similar image.

Old brands are in a complex situation—it will be difficult for them to suddenly develop trendy new imagery and the images which they have developed are either not very relevant today or competitive brands are developing more relevant images. For several years, Robin Blue was meant for bringing whiteness in fabric wash. The packaging and the bird on it symbolized the whiteness and was used as a household brand. Bajaj Scooters had a 'family vehicle' image. Now Honda, the leader in the scooter category, has developed a unique image. Iodex, a brand which was identified for sprains, is overshadowed by other brands which have developed several associations which may be relevant to the times.

It may be interesting to find out how many consumers currently think of the pioneering brands in any category and the reasons they probably do not think about them when the need arises. (Several pioneering brands have a low market share or are no longer there in the market. The inability of brand imagery to sustain it is one of the reasons for them being absent in the consumers' consideration set.)

Why is Brand Imagery Important?

It is important because it conveys the stance of the brand. Raymond's current TV advertisement shows that the corporate guy playing with pups. The evolution of this stereotype is conveyed by this positioning, which places an emphasis on the finer aspects of the lifestyle which executives would like to follow. It uses imagery which goes beyond the functional attributes (for which the brand has established a reputation).

Imagery is important because a brand has to adapt it to the changing environment. Vicco's facial cream for skin has all along been positioned amidst the occasion of a wedding. Fair & Lovely, a brand which was launched later, had taken a different kind of imagery and is adapting it to the changing scenario with the use of variants. HMT, which was positioned as a value-based Indian brand of watches was overshadowed by Titan which developed distinctive and memorable imagery (besides providing sophisticated technology).

Imagery is important because a company which has several brands for several segments could use it to ensure that strong associations are created with each of its brands. Creating the right kind of imagery prevents confusion arising in the minds of consumers. Fastrack and Sonata brands are both from Titan but have a clear image with regard to their target segment associations.

Imagery is useful for a brand to create a contemporary image. VIP, the luggage brand, for several years relied on the 'attribute' image but has taken a new approach to create a 'mood' around the brand with its 'Bye Bye' commercial. The commercial, apart from bringing emotion into the travel situation, also showcases the ease of handling which may be an attribute which consumers look for when they select their luggage brand.

Imagery is required to sustain a brand's association (managing the imagery is a different aspect in itself and is not addressed in this section). Imagery has to be sustained, especially when competitive products arise. Imagery may also be useful to create fresh associations with a brand (circumstances under which such strategies could be adopted is again a conceptual issue which requires an in-depth understanding of the market and consumer behaviour). For almost three decades, Liril was associated with fresh, green scenery with waterfalls in the background. It is now trying to create novelty through the 'orange' variant through its packaging and visuals. The new bike brand, Centra from TVS, attempts to create imagery associated with fuel efficiency.

When several brands in the category were using functional attributes, TVS Caliber motorbikes introduced a brand personality to convey the self-esteem associated with the brand by the use of a story with appropriate imagery. Fortitude, courage and perseverance were the personality traits which could be associated with the brand.

Imagery could also involve logos to enhance awareness levels among consumers about a brand's proposition like Air India's Maharaja symbolizes hospitality and has been instrumental in promoting the brand.

Imagery is very useful when a brand attempts a new and radically different strategy. Timex entered India with its low-end offerings, and in the last two years it has introduced a number of high-end watches creating the appropriate imagery in its advertisements. Without such a change, consumer perception about the brand cannot be altered. Eno's (digestive powdered drink which probably created the category in India several decades ago), Iodex pain balm and Cadbury's Drinking Chocolate, Ezee liquid detergent from Godrej and the Brylcreem brand of hair cream are probably some of the brands from the past which could have made better use of imagery to create a contemporary perception about themselves.

Decades-old brands such as Lifebuoy and Lux have managed themselves with several kinds of imagery during this period of time with variants. Imagery is useful when a brand introduces a variant after it has established itself on a specific benefit. Dettol soap, after establishing itself on the 'protection-from-bacteria' proposition, introduced a variant with moisturizer and employed a different kind of imagery.

Kinds of Imagery

There are various kinds of imagery that brands could use. Attribute imagery consists of amplifying the specific characteristic which is being used by the brand. After a long interval, Promise toothpaste has started using its clove oil attribute in its TV spots.

Imagery could be created through visuals or copy in the advertisement. PUF (Polyurethane Foam), a thermal insulation was highlighted by Godrej in its refrigerators to create 'attribute-based' imagery and to enhance the brand's perception. The current positioning of several brands in durable categories attempt to sport attributes type of imagery supported by visuals. The 'Sixth Sense' pitch of Whirlpool refrigerator and the Atom (denoting the compact size) air-conditioner from Hitachi are such examples.

This imagery helps a brand if it is able to convincingly stay ahead of its competition through its attributes which are well received by consumers. Sony with its strong thrust on technological innovation is an example. Its Trinitron and Wega TV's were advertised with this kind of approach and they were hugely popular.

An attribute conveying a strong benefit could also be used by a pioneering brand if the benefit is relevant to the consumer. Herbal ingredients as an attribute were blended with the stereotype of an elderly lady by Himalaya (formerly Ayurvedic concepts), which specialises in herbal 'over-the-counter' products. Certain kinds of attributes such as oxygen in a toothpaste or colourless cola may not convey clarity for consumers.

Colgate was perhaps the earliest of toothpastes to advertise the benefits of using the brand. Low-involvement categories such as lubricants can also use such benefits. BPCL's Speed brand showed the reliability of using the brand through an emotional reunion of alumni. Ericsson's mobile phone advertisement illustrated the compact size of the brand. Samsung conveyed its 'extra-space viewing' through one of its TV models using a theme. LG's Golden Eye, too, used a 'story' to convey its benefits.

For certain categories of products, benefits could be conveyed directly for better understanding. Fast-moving goods which do not have a glamour aspect (like a dishwashing bar) could make use of this approach. Vim followed this approach to reinforce its durability. Sunfill, the soft drink concentrate from Coca-Cola, conveyed the benefit of economy to appeal to the segment which may not be consuming soft drinks frequently.

Moov, which was not the pioneer with regard to pain balm, created an appealing benefit-based imagery leading to the brand's acceptance. It also effectively used the imagery to compete with Iodex on the 'staining' aspect of the offering. Britannia's success in the biscuit category could be attributed significantly to the use of imagery with a focus on health. Kanan Devan's tea brand (a Kerala-based brand) captures the freshness benefit in its packaging.

Symbolic imagery which revolves around fantasy, status, self-image and group fun is popular in certain categories such as soft drinks, cigarettes, apparel, liquor brands, cars and television.

Onida was probably the first TV brand to use the status appeal. It created the Onida devil which symbolized the jealousy of the neighbour. The visual was effectively complimented with the slogan "Owner's pride: Neighbour's envy." It should be noted that in a durable category the brand should offer technological features concerning the quality of the offering or the aesthetics to sustain such a symbolic imagery. It could be observed that this imagery did little for the brand when it came out with other electronic products.

Even well-known brands such as Mercedes and Rolex strengthened their symbolic imagery with attribute-based positioning at periodic intervals so that consumers would be able to perceive the brands as superior offerings. Coca-Cola and Pepsi are well known for their imagery associated with symbolism in the Indian context against the backdrop of celebrities.

As mentioned in the earlier part of the article, this approach is used by apparel brands for men and women equally (Allen Solly and Van Heusen respectively). Almost all cigarette brands at the higher end of the market were using this approach. They may continue to do so with the new categories they are venturing into in the form of brand extension (Wills Lifestyle apparel brand). Hero Honda's Passion Plus and Kinetic's Zing had 'cool' features to back up their use of symbolic imagery.

Imagery and its management is a crucial aspect as brands are perceived through associations and not reality. Brand imagery impacts the perception of consumers and provides a platform for strong associations in the psyche of consumers . Such favorable associations in turn adds to the equity of a brand.

End Notes

1. Sternberg, R.J. (1986), A Triangular Theory of Love, *Psychological Review, 93 (2)*, 119–35.
2. Richard H. Thaler and Cass R. Sunstein, *Nudge: Improving Decisions about Health, Wealth and Happiness* (New Haven: Yale University Press, 2008).
3. Hawkins, Best and Coney, eds, *Consumer Behavior: Building Marketing Strategy*, (McGraw Hill, 1998), pp. 537–541.
4. Michael Solomon *Consumer Behavior: Buying, Having and Being* (Pearson, 2015), pp. 63–66.
5. Ibid.

Exercises

1. Choose laptops and analyze the strategies of three leading brands of laptops after going through their ads and website. Comment on the usage of decision making strategies by each of these brands.
2. Analyze how consumer decision making strategies can be with reference to health and fitness associated with smart watches. Investigate the features and benefits of smart watches of leading brands? Select a specific segment.

CHAPTER 3

The Concept of Perception and Its Impact on Marketing Strategies

Sony, Raymond, Mercedes are some of the familiar brand names that spark off associations (brand images) based on past encounters that consumers may have had with these brands. These encounters may be purchase associations or the exposure consumers may have had through advertising. As in several aspects of life, it is the perception that matters in a marketing context in which brand names and company names trigger associations and images. Perception is unique to each individual and it is not just objective reality. Different individuals may have their own version of brand description or associations based on their perception. Rolex, an up-market global brand, may be viewed by some consumers as a brand that reinforces their personality by reflecting a prestige appeal. It may also be viewed by some as an expensive brand but a wasteful indulgence.

Perception and Value: A Prerequisite for Branding

With the diversity of lifestyles both culturally and lifestyle-wise, India presents the emerging and challenging opportunities for marketers with respect to pricing products and services. It is pricing from the marketer's point of view but it is the value perception from the consumers' perspective. The Indian context offers a wide variety of examples with regard to its value. Chik shampoo had introduced ₹ 1 pack during the 80's, Reynolds pen established itself during the eighties when the pen market was a huge unorganized market (an unorganized market has unbranded and substandard offerings as one of its characteristics), Maruti car was introduced to break the stranglehold of Fiat and Ambassador brands, Maggi noodles offered value (and continues to offer value as a breakfast option for students and several other groups of consumers), Titan watches offered value, Nirma detergent powder offered value, VIP's Alpha suitcases offered value, Peter England apparels offered value, the Ford EcoSport car offered value, a *kirana* store may offer value to consumers through monthly credit to consumers, McDonald offers value and so does Rolls Royce.From these examples it is clear that

1. Value is dependent on the respective target segment.[1]
2. Value need not necessarily mean that it is reflected only at the lower price end of the market.
3. A brand has to work dynamically to be perceived as providing value to the consumer.

Brand Management and Perceptual Factors

Upward stretch of a brand, especially associated with a brand that was basically launched for the lower end of the market, is always a challenging exercise. Micromax entered the Indian context in 2008. After establishing itself in the lower price ranges of the mobile category, it launched the smart phone Canvas 2 A110 in 2012 at a price point of ₹9600. The feature rich phone was a success in the market. Micromax launched Canvas HD A 116 in 2013 at ₹13990 and it also launched Canvas 4 and Canvas Turbo and had offerings at price points of ₹17999 and ₹19999. During the last quarter of 2013, Micromax's share of smart phones had fallen. While the case of Micromax shows how features and trendy advertisements can enable a lower-price brand to stretch itself upwards (upward stretch), a brand stretching itself upwards should take into consideration the perceptual factors like 'first impression' and brand stereotype while taking such important decisions. It may be worthwhile to think of a moderate strategy when such higher-end brand stretches are attempted to ensure that consumers do not form a perception that a brand that was well-known known for lower-end offerings had gone overboard with higher-end offerings. Also, it is to be noted that Micromax had used the sub-brand Canvas for such offerings.

*Inputs from Abhilasha Ojha (2014), "India Calling", *Business Standard*, April 28.

What is Value?

Value is the ratio of benefits to resources used to obtain those benefits. Benefits are delivered by the brand and the consumer undergoes the sacrifice.[2] Benefits can be in terms of functional benefits (Colgate Total), emotional benefits (the film *Neerja*) or it can be consumption that is sensory in nature which is termed as hedonism (Red Bull). A paint company like Berger Paints or Asian Paints may offer value to its consumers in terms of total painting solution from the selection of the colour desired by the consumer to the final completion of the painting job for the consumer's home. Value of a brand needs to be differentiated from its competitors; the brand may have to compete with itself and it has to appeal to a consumer who may decide not to buy it.[3] For example, when iPhone 6 was launched it must be differentiated from its competitor's offerings (for example Samsung). A consumer who owns Apple iPhone 5 may want to think why he should upgrade to Apple iPhone 6 and a consumer who may not own a smartphone or a consumer who wants to replace his smartphone should find compelling value in iPhone 6 (as otherwise he may not buy it). The sacrifice a consumer makes may be in the form of money, efforts, time or even the psychic costs associated with his decision making.

What are the Important Aspects of Value?

Value is context-dependent, it can have multiple dimensions and it may not be articulated by consumers and involves compromises from the end of the consumer.[4]

A car like Audi offers excellent engineering, status and comfort (multiple dimensions of value), Amazon and Starbucks were not born out of consumers articulation of their needs and a consumer frequently buying a sachet of tea (many brands of tea are available in the sachet packaging) for various reasons of affordability is compromising on quantity discounts and the ready availability of that product.[5]

Marketing mix elements, namely distribution, promotion, price and the product/brand offering, provide a synergy that is important to the consumer's perception of value. The design of Santro and its advertisement compared the brand on various aspects with its competitors to assert its value. Several variants from Britannia biscuits do not contain saturated fats (product offering) and the popular strategy of using psychological pricing like ending with odd numbers such as 99 (₹ 599 and ₹ 1099 was made popular by Bata in the foot wear industry decades back) is the signal perceived value. Vending machines for Coke, tea and coffee add distribution value. ITC's products like Sunfeast biscuits and Fiama Di Wills have made good use of the modern retail outlets. The exclusive showrooms of Titan add value to the perceived value of consumers through its service and ambience. Tanishq has added value through its karatometer that checks the purity of gold (a value that matters very much to consumers).

Perception and Value

Consumer behaviour plays an important role in shaping the value of an offering. Essentially, perception is a process by which consumers add value to what they see. This is an important aspect that triggers value to the brand. Videocon adds value to the respective segment by having three types of distribution channels: Retail Next, Retail Planet M and Digiworld.[6] Amazon and Flipkart had added tremendous value to the Xiaomi brand (introduced in India) and Motorola brand of phones during their launch by offering them at competitive prices. This had added to the inherent features of offer by these respective brands. In this case, both the brands and the online channels had added to the value perception of consumers. With online retailing channels offering significant discounts to consumers on a variety of product categories/brands, the brick and mortar shops need to think of innovative ways to provide consumer value to ensure that consumers keep visiting them frequently. Certain target segments require a high variety of product categories and variety of brands within a product category to ensure 'one-stop shopping'. Departmental stores like Hypercity offer such value to consumers. Big Bazaar offers discounted prices on a wide variety of product ranges with special sale offers on certain occasions annually. Several brands offer value through positioning their offerings at a higher price. In this context, the value added to the offerings is psychological. Louis Philippe, a premium apparel brand, De Beers diamond ring (trending as engagement rings), BMW cars advertised as the 'ultimate driving machine' and Dove soap with its 'moisturizing advantages' are such examples. The bottom line of using perception with respect to pricing is positioning the same offering at two different prices across two segments of consumers. 'Stella Artois' is an ordinary beer outlet in Belgium but it is advertised as a premium beer in the US with its slogan 'the choice of perfection!'[7]

Brand managers face a highly competitive challenge in today's context—all their activities need to appeal to their consumer through the value they create for the offerings.

A stimulus is an information input to any of the senses. One smells, hears, sees, touches and feels because of the stimuli sensed by the respective sensory organ. The immediate or spontaneous and direct or 'head-on' response of the individual to a stimulus is called sensation. The minimum level at which an individual experiences sensation is the absolute threshold for him/her.[8] Two persons travelling on a highway may notice a billboard advertisement from a different distance and may have different perspectives in their absolute threshold.

> Country (place) of origin is an important aspect of perception, Mysore sandalwood, South Indian filter coffee and *Lonavala Chikkis* are such examples. Yardley, the British brand of deodorant, advertises in India with a British-origin celebrity, thus reinforcing the geographical significance of the brand. Park Avenue, Kenstar and Monte Carlo are Indian brand names that suggest a foreign origin.

Applications of Sensation

Marketers constantly attempt to get through the 'sensory adaptation' of consumers. Consumers get used to the clutter of advertisements in the media and may fail to notice advertisements unless they stand out and attract attention. A creative advertisement will attract consumers' attention. Attention is a prerequisite for the perception to occur because it is the medium through which an attention that stimulus is generated for sensation. There are several strategies that marketers use to gain consumer attention. The '7up' soft drink used cartoon animation when a number of soft drink brands were using celebrities in their advertisements. Itch guard (a brand that offered solution for itches) used humour in its advertisement. Polo used an unusual theme for its advertisement (TV commercial). Impulsive products like confectionery rely on fun themes and Polo used a 'student–professor' fun theme. Bingo also used a fun theme showing humorous visuals when the brand is tested under 'normal' and 'extreme conditions'. Creativity which is relevant to the brand is required in an advertisement to ensure that consumers' pay attention towards the brand. A direct marketing company selling up-market durables may send a CD along with the product information to select prospects instead of spending indiscriminately on advertising. The consumer is likely to load the CD on the computer and go through the brand information rather than read through a half-page newspaper advertisement. The idea of using such strategies should be taken into consideration.

Another interesting application of sensation is the ability of individuals to differentiate between two stimuli. This can be best illustrated through an example. A company manufacturing chocolates may add to the quantity contained in each unit of chocolate without increasing the price. If the present weight of the chocolate is 20 grams, then there is a need to ascertain from consumers what additional quantity would be perceived as more (the options may be 22, 24 or 25 grams). The marketer in this situation (particularly in a competitive situation) has to consider the following facts:

1. The quantity at which consumers will consider that the brand is offering more chocolate—the point at which consumers will perceive the difference between the earlier version of the brand and the newest version.
2. They need to ensure that more chocolate is not offered beyond the differential threshold as this will cause a dent into the profitability per unit and also a cut into repeated purchases.

Marketing research information obtained with 'Just Noticeable Difference' (JND) as the focus will enable the marketer to add just that quantity required to create the awareness in which that extra quantity has been added in the new version of the chocolate. Cadbury's chocolate introduced its newest version during the eighties as 'Dairy Milk' to highlight the significant changes made in the product. This enabled the brand to create a perception about the enhanced newer version of the chocolate to the consumer. Positive changes in the brand may have to be highlighted to make use of the JND concept.

- A number of shampoo brands offered 10 ml sachets at ₹1 when the sachets were introduced in India. Over a period, the price points have been increased by a number of brands while decreasing the quantity in the sachets to 8 ml or less. It may be difficult for the consumer to notice the difference from the packaging unless one specifically looks for the quantity label on the package.
- When coffee prices increased during the mid-'90s, marketers may have wanted to bring down the quality (taste) of coffee by using the right mix of chicory to the point where consumers do not perceive the change.

The Concept of Perception

In simple terms, perception is the meaning an individual adds or subtracts to the information he/she receives through the sensory organs. The incoming stimuli interact with the stored information (memory) to give rise to perception. Figure 3.1 illustrates the mechanism of perception.

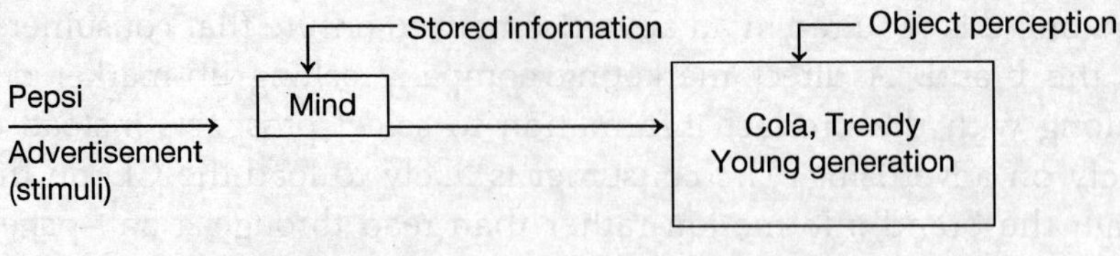

Figure 3.1 Mechanism of Perception

A Pepsi commercial telecasted during a cricket match may be a stimulus. The stimulus interacts with the information already stored in the mind of a consumer. This information may be associated with cola advertising, specific brands in the aerated soft drink category or its implications that have been added to the brands in the cola category. (These aspects are covered in the Chapter 4 on Learning Principles). The individual is able to spontaneously associate Pepsi with Cola, or a trendy, young generation. A distinctive brand meaning is triggered in the minds of consumers. This can be extended to create a brand personality (dealt later in the Chapter 5 on Motivation). Any competitive brand has to develop unique associations that originate from perception. The concept of positioning has its foundations in perception.

Perception and Brand Exclusivity

Maruti had been offering premium car models for many years. In a changing environment, consumers expect a differentiated experience in the on-going premium car models and the retail experience is a significant part of the whole experience. In 2015, Maruti introduced the 'Nexa' version, an exclusive dealership network for premium cars. S-Cross was an offering introduced through Nexa.

Dynamics of Perception

Perception consists of several elements and involves selection, organization and interpretation of stimuli. All these elements offer useful points to marketers regarding the formulation of communication strategies.

Selection of stimulus, as stated earlier, depends on attention that can be brought into communication through contrast. Jenson & Nicholson, the paint brand, used full-page magazine advertisements with only a few lines of copy to stand out from the rest. Levi's used black and white advertisements in a magazine published with full of colour advertisements to highlight the contrast. Contrast helps a brand to obtain the involuntary attention of consumers.

'Premiumness' and Alphanumeric Brands

A stimulus is interpreted by the consumers to make sense to them. Alphanumeric brand names seem to denote premium perception among the consumers of durables.[9] Car models such as i10 and i20, XUV 500, SX4, TUV300 in cars and Nikon D700 and Cannon 400D in cameras are such examples.

Branded Entertainment in the Indian Context

Product placement or branded entertainment that involves placing a brand as a part of the movie scene was effectively used in the movie *Happy New Year*. The movie that had Shah Rukh Khan as the hero had earned ₹30 crores from more than 20 brands that were placed in the movie.[10] The list of brands that were placed in the movie included Nokia, Renault Duster, Microsoft, Baskin and Robbins, Hitachi and Videocon. Earlier Kick, Ra.one and Krrish 3 were some of the movies that had used this concept. While a brand using product placement gets mere exposure through it, using product placement frequently and inappropriately may erode the equity of the brand, apart from creating fatigue in the minds of consumers.

Lack of Contrast and Perception

Lack of contrast can also be used to attract attention. Advertorials (advertisements on the lines of editorial, write-ups), can be placed close to magazine articles in such a way that consumers get into such advertisements immediately after reading the article. Dabur's Honey carried such advertorials. Bru coffee, when it was launched, identified itself as a drink that is close to the South Indian filter coffee through its advertisements. A branded curd (curd is used as a household item in several households) should taste as close as possible to which was made at home. Kurkure resembles and tastes like an ethnic snack.

Selection of a stimulus is also based on a consumer's motivation regarding a specific product category. A consumer interested in buying a television (selective attention) is likely to be attuned to advertisements of television brands. Selection is also based on an individual's expectations. Some brands use unexpected visuals/audio effects in advertisements to drag attention. But such elements should be taken into consideration, the match they have with the category and the benefits a brand offers. For example, a brand like Apple that offers innovative and high-quality features with regard to its products may start the advertisement saying, 'Apple is expensive', followed by a copy which substantiates the claim (hypothetical example). This is likely to attract attention of the consumers who are used to be freebies and low-prices will suddenly encounter a contrary and unexpected element in the advertisement. Bacardi, the liquor brand, pulled attention through its unexpected visual and jingle when such advertisements were allowed on television (the example is used for illustrative purposes to convey the concept through liquor advertisements on TV channels. They are no longer telecasted in India).

The organization of stimuli involves figure and ground, grouping, and closure. All these concepts offer insights into how an advertisement may have an impact on consumer perception. The figure in any advertisement is well defined, concrete and upfront. The ground is hazy and continuous. In an advertisement, the figure should always be the brand name and the 'Unique Selling Proposition' (USP) of the brand. The jingle, humour or creativity should also be the basic ground for the promoting the product and should not affect the figure negatively. Ericsson's advertisement for its cellular phones is a good example to illustrate the point. The brand used humour in its 'Black coffee, please' commercial and it became a famous advertisement. A study by the author conducted among the prospects revealed that though the advertisement was recalled well by the respondents, they associated the advertisement with another brand which, incidentally, had launched a press campaign. The press campaign was in operation while the Ericsson brand was being advertised on TV. Such an observation reveals that it is not only important to attract attention through advertisements but also it is more important to ensure that they have the appropriate figure and ground elements.

Grouping enables marketers to create associations by combining the stimuli in such a way that brand associations are developed when consumers associate the sets of stimuli. Force 10 brand of shoes from Liberty used this technique to project it as a lifestyle brand. The brand was grouped with burgers, jeans, cola and shades. Titan's Fastrack watch was (initially) associated with a can of soft-drink to imply a trendy, young and Westernized lifestyle. Charms, one of the earliest Indian cigarette brands associated with the "youth's attitude", grouped the brand with denims to appeal to the urban youth. Grouping is extensively used to shape the perception of brands. LimeRoad, an online fashion portal is trending with latest women's fashion garments.

The concept of closure is associated with an incomplete stimulus. Individuals express the need for closure by organizing their perception to form a complete picture. If they are exposed to an incomplete stimulus, they will make an effort to complete it. A circle with a small portion of its periphery missing will be perceived as a circle. When an individual is exposed to an incomplete stimulus, there is a build-up of tension, which motivates him/her to complete the picture. Closure leads to a very interesting application in marketing. A brand may broadcast the audio track of a TV commercial on radio (especially, since FM channels are catching up) to create an incomplete perception of the TV commercial. This is to induce the consumer to complete the perception by recalling the visual associated with the jingle. For instance, imagine Titan's jingle tune being played on a FM station that brings to you the images of Titan.

Yet another associated application is the development of unique brand elements that have a long-term impact on the brand association. This association based on the property of the brand (achieved usually by repeated advertising and sustained association) serves as a differentiator, thus enabling the brand to maintain a unique image in the category. Titan's usage of Mozart composition for its ad jingle and 'Give me red' associated with Eveready batteries are unique brand elements. These are extremely effective in a low-involvement category like batteries. The 'red' (power association) combined with the 'youth' image appealed to the younger generation, particularly at a time when Walkman, cameras and cellular phones were catching up in the urban markets. These examples may be old but are useful to illustrate the concept powerfully. Kellogg's, in certain markets, uses hoardings that do not spell the brand name completely and forces the viewer to mentally experience closure. Each time this happens, it has a cumulative impact on the consumer.

Perceptual interpretation, unique to the individual as adding meaning to what has been sensed, is based on the individual's experience. Marketers have to be careful when they choose brand names for their product categories. Dove soap positioned itself as moisturizer in a soap that competes with similar products, thus clearly establishing its competitive frame of reference. Product design may also influence the interpretation of the stimulus (picture of the product). Hero Honda Street (two-wheeler) had several city-friendly features. But the design probably reminded the consumers of the M-80 mopeds that were popular in several urban areas during the '80s. Further, there was a price difference between the two offerings. Street was introduced at the upper end of the then two-wheeler market, while M-80 was associated with the lower segment. Perhaps the design of Street could have been different from that of M-80. Categorization is also an extended concept associated with the interpretation of stimuli. Consumers tend to associate a stimulus with a group of stimuli they are familiar with. For example, when microwave ovens were introduced consumers may have associated them with kitchen appliances before the product concept became familiar to them. Marketers should be careful in product design, advertising and branding to avoid unfavourable categorisation in the mind of the consumer. 7up re-launched itself as an 'Uncola' drink in the US and opened up a new category in the mind-set of consumers. Branding jewellery as Mystic Gold and advertising it with a celebrity endorsement may make consumers think of it as an expensive brand even if the price is not explicitly stated. Advertising a beer brand as LITE may give the impression that it is 'light in calories' even when it is not explicitly stated. Positioning strategies should be taken into consideration along with the interpretation of the copy and the visual of advertisements.

Brand Positioning and Perception

As stated earlier, positioning has its foundation in concepts of perception. A positioning (or a perceptual map) provides an idea about how consumers perceive brands specific to relevant dimensions. In Figure 3.2, two dimensions are chosen. They are traditional to trendy and economy to premium. It is possible to map the existing brands and this enables a new brand to enter the consumer's mind. Perceptual maps enable the marketer to provide the competitive angle to the brand. It should be noted that considerable primary information is required to obtain the two dimensions in a map. When there are more dimensions preferred by consumers in a product category, the marketers need to use sophisticated marketing research techniques to simplify the dimensions chosen for the positioning exercise.

Positioning that starts as an attempt by the brand to understand the likings of the target segment should be nurtured in the long run to build a sustainable association. Pepsi's association with the younger generation, Titan's depiction of lifestyles for its consumers and Volvo's association with safety are such examples. When a brand develops an additional association, it has to ensure that the additional association supplements or complements the original association without contradicting it. Raymond's association with the 'complete man' lifestyle proposition strengthens its earlier positioning as the 'guide to a well-dressed male' (which was the positioning of the brand during yesteryears).

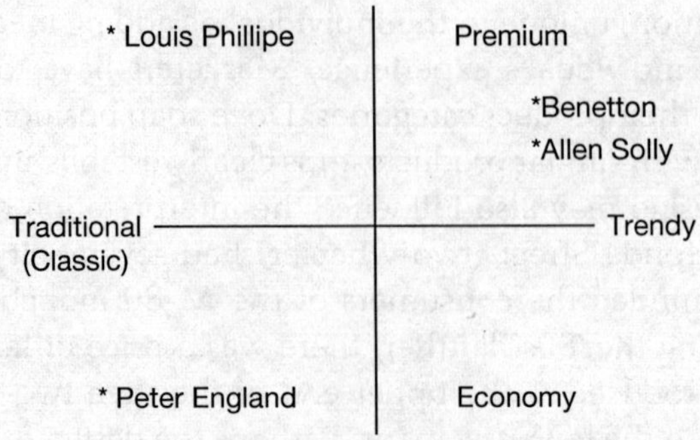

Figure 3.2 Positioning and Perception (author's perception of brands based on marketing communication of brands may not reflect the respective company's strategies)

Perception and Prices

Prices have been used by marketers as an input signal to the perception of quality among consumers. It is not uncommon for consumers to equate high prices with high quality, particularly if backed up by appropriate associations like a premium brand name or an up-market retail outlet. In several product categories like televisions, confectionery and fast foods, consumers compare the brand's prices with those of the one they have in mind. These are internal reference prices. A number of brands of colour televisions used to mark the price tag below ₹10,000 as consumers may have this as their internal reference price. A popular blade among the masses did not increase its price for a long time as this may have affected the perception of consumers. Soft drink manufacturers like Coke, Pepsi and confectionery brands like Cadbury's and Nestle are concerned with price points, especially at the entry level minimum prices. The re-emergence of 200 ml bottles in soft drinks (some years back in the Indian context) and the ₹5 price point in chocolates or the 50 paise point in confectionery and candies are examples of value perception in the respective categories.

External reference prices are those that consumers compare across outlets for the same brand. A price discount offered by different retail outlets in the category of consumer durables is a good example. A consumer wanting to buy a model of LG TV may compare the external prices for the same brand and its model across all retail outlets. Similarly, for men's readymade wear, leading brands like Louis Philippe, Arrow or Park Avenue may have factory outlets that offer a discounted price for selected products. These outlets may appeal to a segment, which may likely to have the brand after comparing prices across retail outlets. This segment may also be prepared to select from a smaller variety (designs) if they get the brand of their choice at economy outlets. These consumers compare external prices, probably after compromising on the variety.

Transaction utility is another factor that has an impact on price perception. This relates to the satisfaction of a consumer that derives from making a deal within a particular price range. This is closely related to the internal reference prices. Transaction utility may be applicable to a cross-section of consumers who may predominantly have their satisfaction tied to the transaction limit they have in mind. There may be a cross-section of consumers who may not mind crossing over its internal reference price and may not want to come across as stringent 'price hunters'. But a brand would do well to research its customer segment to find out the degree of association with transaction utility. Brands that have successfully used penetration pricing like Nirma, T-Series and Tiger have used the transaction utility to satisfy consumers.

Acquisition utility is the extent to which a consumer feels that the brand purchased has matched his/her value perception. Though prices are important, a consumer who is drawn towards acquisition utility may be prepared to pay more for a brand if he/she is convinced that the price adds to the value of the acquisition in terms of features or convenience. The implication is that a brand that carries a premium over other competing brands should communicate the value it offers to consumers, after choosing a segment that will be interested in acquisition utility as against transaction utility. In this context, value does not necessarily mean functional utility; it may be symbolism or emotional or group-oriented appeal. Red Bull in soft drinks and Fastrack watches are examples of how advertising/marketing communication can play a role in acquisition utility. Perception also gets associated with discounts offered by marketers. Tensile price claims can be used to promote a product or a retail store. 'Save up to 50 per cent' is an example. Objective price claims provide a single discount level (save 30 per cent). Marketers find it useful to conduct primary research among the appropriate target segment before choosing the discount method.

Can Brand Images be changed?

In a competitive context, there may be a need for a brand to change its image depending on the product/market situation. There may be a few brands that have successfully transformed their images. Cadbury's Dairy Milk chocolate (moulded version) was positioned towards children during the eighties. As the chocolate market expanded over the years and as adults were also interested in the product category (due to in the changing lifestyle), Cadbury's transformed the brand image of the moulded variant in such a way that it was repositioned for adults. The target segment shifted from children to adults. The warmth proposition of the previous positioning (a gift for the children as a reflection of parental warmth) gave way to spontaneous and enjoyable 'celebration' associated with everyday life (cricket field dance commercial was a popular TV commercial for the brand). Another instance is Gems, also from Cadbury's. It was positioned for children in the past but now it has been targeted towards adults as well.

Perceived Risks

There are many kinds of risks perceived by consumers. They are functional (a huge investment in a durable may pose a performance risk), physical (preparing food in a microwave using radiation), financial (if buying a water purifier will justify its cost), social (will the designer jewellery attract attention in a public or private gathering), psychological (will the consumer feel happy about the in-flight services of an airlines) and time risk (will the consumer waste time evoking a warranty). Different categories carry different risks depending on the consumer's familiarity with the product, his/her economic status and perception with regard to brand association. Marketers have to examine these risks, especially when they launch new products. For example, an electric car, which is a new concept, may have to address several perceived risks during its launch. Retail outlets can provide the support necessary to address some of the perceived risks through demonstration or creating 'customized' product awareness based on the queries of the prospective consumer concerning perceived risks. Such a strategy is likely to be very effective in the diffusion of products in an emerging market like India where penetration across categories is quite low. Word of mouth, too, is an important source of addressing perceived risks (for example, a brand of shaving system for women). With the emergence of digital media like Google and YouTube, word of mouth is critical for a brand's success. This is because unlike advertisements created by marketers, some of the digital media carry user-generated content and consumers may attribute more credibility to it (or as much credibility) than what they perceive from advertisements.

Figure 3.3 shows the various aspects of perceived risks associated with an electric car.

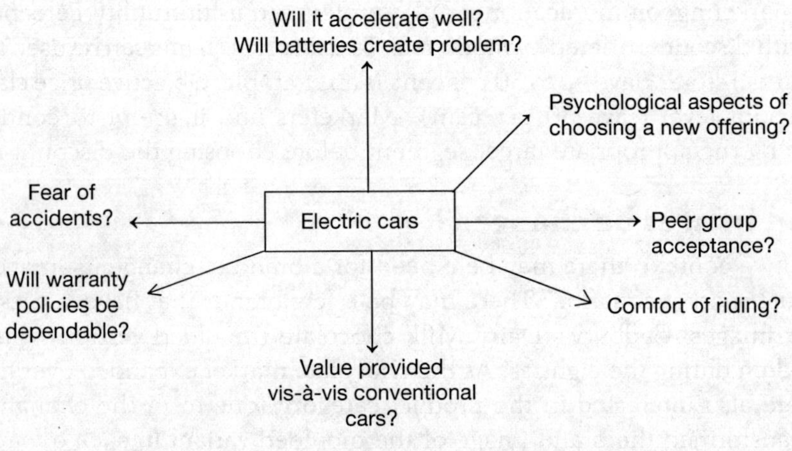

Figure 3.3 Perceived Risks and Electric Cars

Managing Category/Brand Image (Indian Context)

- During the mid-'80s, Cadbury's made an effort to change the image associated with its chocolate drink by bringing in a new brand 'Choco Cheer' which is positioned for the youth. The change was focused more towards the youth and the product category was positioned using a new brand as Cadbury's has had a long association with its classic 'Drinking Chocolate'. Such an approach may be useful in the present-day context to connect with the urban youth population (Coffee might be an age old-drink but has a renewed youth market in cities with Café Coffee Day and Barista on the lines of Starbucks in the US).

- Videocon introduced its sub-brands like Challenger and Bazooka to reach out to the higher end of the colour TV (CTV) market.
- Brands like Mercedes, Nissan, Renault or Peugeot are plying as taxis in several parts of the world, but they do not have the 'taxi' association (unlike the classic Indian Ambassador) because of their brand-building efforts.
- Nesfit, a glucose powder from Nestle, failed possibly because of its white packaging when consumers related and confused glucose with green packaging (although even it had used some favourite sports celebrities like Sachin Tendulkar).
- Johnson & Johnson named its prickly heat powder 'Shower to Shower' to reflect the new version without the traditional 'baby' version of the product.
- Rooh Afza, an herbal fruit drink was marketed in India for several decades; it attempted to change the image by bringing in a youth-centred visual imagery in one of its ad campaigns.
- Madura Coats introduced Louis Philippe as a premium readymade (shirting) brand. The company also has Allen Solly, Van Heusen and Peter England in the category. Careful advertising and retailing ensures differentiation across the brands in terms of consumer perception. Pond's used the concept of "Pond's Institute" a few years ago to convey an updated image of itself when it introduced the up-market cosmetic products like anti-ageing creams.
- Titan focuses on retail outlets to enhance the consumers' perception of the brand. Titan's Sonata (at the lower price end) and Xylys (at the higher price end) do not have Titan's conspicuous associations attached to them.
- Sony used Trinitron, a sub-brand to project its state-of-the-art offering in CTV's.
- Park Avenue is a formal readymade wear brand from Raymond. The company introduced Parx when it entered the informal readymade wear segment.
- Cadbury's Dairy Milk chocolate was targeted for children in the mid-'80s and for adults in the '90s. It introduced a variant called Cadbury's Gold positioned towards adults but used its permissiveness in its advertising. Cadbury's Gold was quickly pulled out of the market. Would it be that the permissive association of the variant Gold contradicted the associations of the original CDM (both were moulded chocolates)?
- Onida TV advertised itself as a premium brand during the eighties with its famous tagline of "Neighbour's envy, owner's pride" with the devil symbolizing "jealousy'. Such a firm positioning—especially as a pioneering brand in the market (when the market was just developing) provides a strong foundation for a brand to come out with excellent products in future.

- Burnol was an ointment for burn injuries. The target segment was housewives who were using traditional techniques while cooking. When stoves (gas versions and others) started picking up, the brand attempted to position itself as an ointment for burns and also for cuts and wounds. Despite the best efforts of the brand to manage the image, a number of consumers may still associate the brand with burns. The brand attempted to position itself with 'Plus' and '3-in-one' prefix but the 'burn' proposition is a strong one that may continue in the consumer's mind-set.

Brand Perception and Country of Origin

Perception of brands is also affected by the country of their origin. The following brands have invariably carried their 'country of origin' associations:

- UK (Class and Heritage) – Rolls Royce car
- France (Style and Class, Fashion) – Wines, apparel and perfumes
- Germany (Quality and Reliability) – BMW car
- Switzerland (Precision) – Watches and knives
- Japan (Miniaturisation, Values and Features) – Consumer electronics and cars

The country of origin enables marketers to develop stereotypes (words and pictures that consumers carry in their mind). South Indian coffee, French fashion or glamour-related brands can take the consumer to the countries of their origin. Bru, the instant coffee brand, has used this by positioning itself as a coffee with the taste of filter coffee. Sometimes, a brand may not use the country of origin. Perfetti, the Italian chewing gum manufacturer, has an American (sounding) brand name called Brooklyn. Chewing gum is more associated with the American culture and the brand name would be useful to position it for the youth who follow or are likely to follow the American way of life.

Levi's, Coke, Pepsi and McDonald brands have American-ness to them. This has been most instrumental to their success. The US triggers off associations of hi-tech, entertainment, enjoyment and diligence. In fact, the association (perception) is so strong among consumers that they give more importance to brand names of US origin like Mattel, IBM, Nike, Walt Disney and Walmart though a number of products marketed under these brand names have the label 'Made in Thailand/Malaysia' or 'Vietnam/China'. A country's name can also change in consumer perception. About three decades back, Japan was associated with economy goods. Today, there are several Japanese brands like Lexus, Honda and Sony being bought by hundreds of people in the US. Taiwan and Korea have also been successful in changing the perception of consumers about their country of origin. LG, Samsung and Hyundai are successful brands across the world in several countries. Vodka brand names are strongly associated with Russia and Sweden. In the recent times, a brand called Finlandia has made a mark in some of the markets with its association of Finland's geographical qualities with that of clear vodka (a very creative positioning stance, given the strong country of origin's association with the drink).

The Concept of Brand Repositioning

In today's world of cluttered communication, positioning in a market provides a mental angle with regard to competition. This mental angle is the competitive differentiation that marketers attempt to provide for their offerings. This aspect is associated with consumer perception of specific product/market, in the backdrop of which a marketer makes an offering. Positioning is what a marketer does to the mind of a prospective consumer. Positioning is associating a specific image with a brand name. It is the act of designing the company's offering and image so that they occupy a meaningful and distinct competitive position in the target consumers' minds. While positioning is a well-accepted concept in marketing communications, the concept of repositioning does not seem to have been adequately explored by marketers. Positioning does undergo changes. In a dynamic marketing environment, repositioning a brand is as important as formulating the original positioning strategy for it. The concept of strategic brand concept (SBC) probes the three stages (introduction, elaboration and fortification), through which a brand passes.[11] While SBC delves into brand strategies that are appropriate to the different stages of a brand's lifecycle, it does not probe several possibilities of brand repositioning. Ries and Trout, pioneers of brand positioning, provided some examples of repositioning (Aspro vs. Tylenol comparison is one of them). Jack Trout with Steve Rivkin gave examples of how a brand (Carnival) of ice cream could be repositioned with a renewed perception of itself among consumers (a range of ice cream cakes was launched and the brand was positioned as one associated with ice cream bakery). Calvin Klein modified its range of cosmetics (with SPF) and repositioned the range through departmental stores associated with lower prices. Ries and Trout have suggested the usage of marketing mix elements in repositioning of brands. Repositioning is not an isolated marketing exercise. It has to be considered with product-line management, sub-brands and new kinds of imagery in a changing environment and a specific brand has to be repositioned in an appropriate manner.

Segmentation—Repositioning Linkages

Segmentation is the process of dividing a cluttered market (in terms of a mix of consumers) into homogeneous markets in such a way that a company can target specific consumer segments with its positioning strategies. Segmentation variables are used to divide the market. In a dynamic competitive context, marketers should consider the constant changes in their target segments and reposition the brand accordingly. The following aspects provide linkages between segmentation-related changes and brand repositioning directions:

(a) How should brands be repositioned when a segment of consumers buying brands offering value shift to unbranded offerings? This happens in unorganized markets in categories like edible oil, pens and moulded luggage. An unorganized market is one which has a number of unbranded offerings promoted only through low prices in local markets. They are generally not branded and fall short of quality expectations. These offerings are sold within a vicinity of about 20–30 km from the place of manufacture and some of them may also be illegal offerings (duplicates).

(b) How should a brand that wants to appeal to a different segment be repositioned? (Gems)

(c) How should a brand that wants to supplement its existing brand personality position for an additional segment be repositioned? (Fair & Lovely Face Wash)

(d) How should a brand, successful with a functional proposition, be repositioned to another segment that may require a symbolic orientation apart from the functional qualities? (Mouthwash brands)

(e) How should a premium brand be repositioned that wants to enlarge its niche segment after it has created brand awareness? (Close-up Diamond attraction variant)

(f) How should a brand be repositioned when it wants to reach out to consumers at the upper end of the market? (It has to be ensured that the brand does not get into an 'image trap' as it is moving from a cheaper market to an up-market position). (Micromax)

(g) How should a brand be repositioned when it wants to shed its image (due to competitive reasons) after maintaining a proposition for a period of time in the market? (Lactocalamine)

Brand Associations and Sustainable Core Proposition

A brand is a competitive offering (product, service or concept) with unique functional and/or emotional associations. Hence, the associations connected with a brand may reflect rational and emotional benefits. Brand personality is one of the tools to achieve them. The associations need to be enduring because they give the brand sustainable differentiation in the long run. Strategies associated with brand or product-line management should be taken into account for the long-term impact of brand associations. The brand variants should ensure that their associations do not contradict the original associations of the brand.

Brand associations should consider the facts of sustainable core proposition (SCP). An SCP is a brand proposition (functional, psychological or both) that needs to be nurtured and developed during positioning and maintained during repositioning. It gets reflected in associations relevant to the brand. The concept is vital because it can trigger off anchored perception. Anchored perception is the cumulative impact of consistent brand associations developed over a period of time. This essentially requires the core proposition of the brand to be maintained, regardless of the variants launched or how the brand is extended or repositioned.

In simple terms, brand repositioning can be associated with a change in the perception associated with a brand and its new associations gained, nurtured or strengthened for such repositioning. There may be a few instances when the brand completely changes its associations in order to appeal to a new target segment but these instances are unusual. Cadbury's (moulded version) repositioning towards adults after strongly focusing on children and Pond's association with high-end products after being a lower-end talcum powder for many years are such examples.

Sustainable Core Proposition Strategies and Brand-related Dimensions in Repositioning

There are seven kinds of repositioning strategies based on the segmentation repositioning linkages and the basic idea of SCP and brand-related dimensions.

Value-oriented Repositioning

This strategy is useful in two situations; in one situation, when a brand offering value is competing against the unorganized sector (explained in the examples given below) and in the second situation, when a brand has strongly established a value proposition. The examples given below are old ones but ones that offer insights for a conceptual direction.

Reynolds is a brand of ball-pen that was launched in India during the '80s. It was nearly double the price of the other competitive offerings in the market. These offerings, which were in the unorganized sector (without registered brand names and marketed in a small territory), were of poor quality. Reynolds used the skimming price (higher price point) strategy and became a successful brand. Besides, Reynolds also had a sturdy product casing, apart from a good, uniform flow of ink that ensured easy writing. Though consumers paid more for Reynolds, they perceived it as a reliable brand. Reynolds created this positioning and association through a good product and higher price. Its advertisements created awareness but the associations came from a 'price-quality' perception in the ball-pen market. Repositioning Reynolds should involve a better-quality product and higher price (even if variants are launched), especially when a number of brands have entered the market with similar offerings.

Akai was practically institutionalised in the second-hand TV market in India. At a time when consumers perceived 'price-number of features' combination as an indication of value, Akai created value perception by announcing exchange schemes. There were schemes by which consumers could exchange their existing television for a new one and pay around 50 per cent of the price for a new television. In a market where brands were attempting to position themselves as 'no frill-low price' or 'feature-ridden' or through comparative advertisements that emphasized a few extra features, Akai entered the mind of prospects through sales promotion schemes. It could position itself as a brand that offers value through good sales promotion schemes. Repositioning, for Akai, will work through sales promotional schemes that are enhanced through proper value addition. The creativity in repositioning exercise for Akai will lie in the ability of the brand/organization to launch innovative and competitive sales promotion schemes. If a brand relies on certain unique characteristics of the market (large number of second-hand buyers in this context), then it may be effective to use a similar approach while repositioning it. Of course, there are other options like creating a high-quality product and its symbolic aspects. But the unique association of a brand is carried over with an innovative approach that is associated with the original positioning strategy.

Segment-oriented Repositioning

This strategy is useful when a brand wants to change the segment to which it is currently catering.

Sunny was a two-wheeler scooterette (a hybrid between a moped and scooter), which was initially targeted for teenagers. The brand was endorsed by a well-known sports celebrity. The initial positioning was through a novel product (scooterette) and the glamour of the celebrity both of which may have appealed to the target segment. The company probably realised that the product (60 cc) was not much of a success in the market. This was reflected when the brand was repositioned as 'Sunny Zip' and it was upgraded to 75 cc. The target segment for the repositioned product was women, mostly housewives and college-going girls. The repositioning involved upgrading the product, change of segment and a sub-brand (Sunny Zip). The advertisements did not incorporate a celebrity. They showed typical users of the product. Brand imagery was used to strengthen the brand association. This is an example of brand repositioning for a new target segment after the product is modified.

Another interesting example is the Fair & Lovely fairness cream. After decades of positioning on the fairness platform for young people, the brand started targeting middle-aged married women. The TV commercial amplifies the usage of the brand by a married woman (user imagery) and not so much of the brand benefit (which has been hammered in for years). This approach also shows how a benefit can be extended to different segments at different times, especially when the original target segment may be exposed to new brands. This approach may require development of a strong brand before such a repositioning is done. Fairness, as a benefit, was being extended to married women at a time when personal grooming has become important for consumers in the Indian context. The brand did not continue the repositioning (as evident from the commercials not being re-telecasted) presumably because of strategic reasons. In consumables, the Cadbury chocolate (moulded variant in the rectangular slab) was positioned for children in the '80s. In the '90s, the same variant was directed towards adults using a change in the brand imagery. The objective of the brand was to expand the market and bring in adults into its segment. Cadbury introduced a variant of the moulded version under the sub-brand Cadbury's Gold. This sub-brand was positioned on a permissive and mischievous personality platform with appropriate visuals (in the TV commercial). The TV commercial showed a lady clad in permissive apparel in a gymnasium embracing men. This association contradicted the 'fun-loving adult' association of the earlier moulded variant that was not considered as permissive in the Indian context (during the time when the brand was launched and the context has changed since then). Cadbury's Gold did not sustain itself in the retail shelves. Was it because of the contradictory brand associations? Does the conceptual angle that needs to be addressed while discussing repositioning strategies? This example reflects the impact of positioning a new variant using the overall brand associations, which is also associated with the earlier variants.

Celebrity–oriented Brand Enhancement Repositioning

This strategy is useful when a brand uses imagery (or a celebrity) to strengthen its association and makes an attempt to enter a new segment based on the strength of the same imagery.

BPL, a brand in consumer electronics originally operated in business-to-business marketing (X-rays and telecom) before moving into televisions. This brand of TV was initially positioned itself as the one manufactured with high-end technology. This is a typical example of a brand attempting to use technology as an intangible feature. Consumers may have exhibited a strong preference towards the brand because of its technology association without even knowing its intricacies. During the mid-'90s, the brand repositioned itself using a celebrity model. The celebrity had a charismatic appeal (for the masses as well as the elite) and would have been a good fit for the brand, which was targeting the rural Indian population. The company is also marketing refrigerators, microwaves, radios, CD's and kitchen appliances. The repositioning using a celebrity did not elaborate the details on the product attributes or benefits. It used ethnocentrism, a personality-related concept that reflects a strong tendency on the part of an individual to buy products that are made in his/her own country. The celebrity in the TV commercial spoke about the conviction that consumers should have on the Indian-made products. This was an effective strategy considering that there are a number of multinational companies in the consumer electronic categories in India. The repositioning exercise added a favourable Indian association to the brand that had a positive image. The repositioning may have also helped the brand to make an impact on rural consumers for whom the celebrity held a tremendous charisma.

Symbolism-oriented Repositioning

This strategy is useful when a brand with a strongly entrenched functional image wants to expand its market using a symbolic positioning without losing its earlier association.

Raymond is a well-known up-market brand in textiles. The brand initially positioned itself as a 'guide to a well-dressed male'. The brand is priced higher than a number of other fabric brands and it has a network of exclusive outlets throughout the country. The brand repositioned itself a decade ago as the fabric for 'the complete man'. The repositioning attempted to emphasize that the offering was meant for an up-market consumer who also has his/her share of family experiences in life. Repositioning of the brand involved lifestyle aspects after the functional proposition of the brand was well-accepted by consumers. The lifestyle repositioning of the brand has created a strong differentiation for the brand.

Up-market Technology-oriented Repositioning

This kind of strategy is useful when lower-priced brand attempts an upward stretch, apart from continuing to serve its current consumer segments.

Pond's is a household name in India. The brand repositioned itself as a contemporary skin-care brand using the technology and research association. The brand used the concept of "Pond's Institute" which was associated with state-of-the-art products. Pond's currently has skin-care products at the upper end of the market. The repositioning of the brand created a perception that helped it to 'move' to the higher end of the market without a new brand or sub-brand from the perception of consumers. It is also worthwhile to note that the brand could stretch itself upwards without getting into the 'image trap'.

Niche-oriented Repositioning

This strategy is useful when a niche brand (premium one) is interested in expanding its consumer base after it has created brand awareness.

Dove is one of the premium soaps at the upper end of the soap market and the brand has a small overall market share. Initially, the brand attempted to reposition itself as a moisturizer bar. Dove's TV commercial compared other soap products and conveyed that the brand is superior to other brand of soaps (establishing the point of difference after conveying the point of parity to enable the consumers to know that the brand competes with soaps). The positioning focused on the advantages of using a moisturizer bar. Dove's positioning in a niche market involved the repositioning of the soap category. The brand continued to reposition the soap category with a new TV commercial on the same theme. Similarly, ITC's Fiama Di Wills used 'gentle naturals and effective science' to position its range of shampoo and soaps at the higher end of the price structure in their respective markets.

The Perception–Intention Framework

A brand can use the SCP along with a framework, which offers other alternatives (along with the brand-related dimensions) that do not involve SCP. The two dimensions that can be used for a 'perception–intention' framework are: (i) intention to buy and (ii) anchored perception. Anchored perception is associated with the brand's association and with the cumulative perception of consumers (this is a figurative concept and the marketers need to use some measures associated with a brand on many counts that enhance the value of the brand depending on the context of the brand) and the intention to buy is associated with several aspects of the marketing mix elements along with the brand's associations.

The intention to buy can be the final stage in decision-making when the consumer has adequate knowledge of the product category, competing brands and has evaluated their benefits and associations. There may be a gap between the intention to buy and the final purchase. This gap can result from several factors like the availability of cheaper brands, display of point-of-purchase posters of a competing brand, a sudden recommendation (from personal sources of information) for a competitive brand or the consumer's perception of the proposition of a competing brand. A marketer has to decide the appropriateness of using anchored perception based on the competing brand associations in the environment, the period of the brand's visibility campaigns (involving the associations of the brand) and the measure of its share after it was launched. The degree of recall and recognition needed to categorise the anchored perception as low or high also depends on a specific market situation. Anchored perception needs to be high or low based on the information available on the various aspects of a brand.

Sustainable Core Proposition-oriented Approach

In Figure 3.4, the top right quadrant can be associated with a brand that scores high on both counts, the intention to buy and anchored perception. This indicates that the existing brand associations put it on top of the recall hierarchy. This increases its chances of being purchased. Pepsi and Coke in the Indian context are examples of soft drinks, which consists of several brands in the aerated fruit drink and fruit juice (fruit drinks contain some percentage of fruit juice) that belong to this category. The cola brands continue their respective proposition to build brand equity. The principle of SCP can be followed if there is a need for the brand to fine-tune its positioning associations. Successful brands in this quadrant need to sustain their strategies to continue their leadership in a given market. It may be worthwhile to find out if brands with dominant market shares in a specific category fall under this classification.

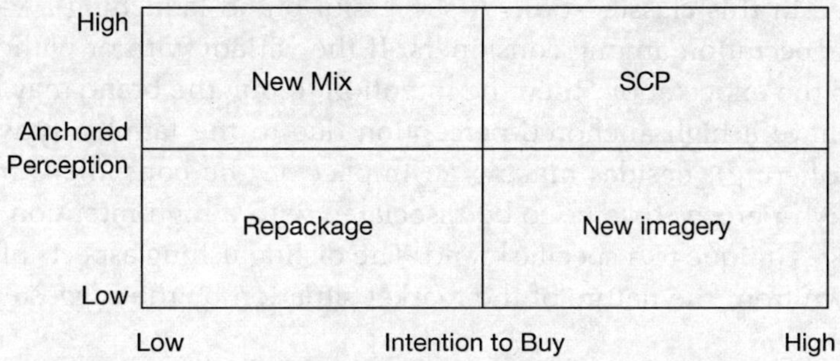

Figure 3.4 The Perception–Intention Framework.

New Imagery

When the intention to buy is high and the anchored perception is low, the brand may have an attribute/benefit association that appeals to the consumer but the anchored perception has not been strengthened as reflected by the low recall. A brand in this quadrant can also have a significant market share but weakened anchored perception over a period of time, can lower the intention to buy it.

Brands that have been very successful in the past but have experienced considerable decline in recent times may have to create new imagery to appeal to its consumers. Consumers may be aware of the brand and may even have a mild intention to buy the brand. But lack of contemporary associations may have motivated these consumers to buy some other brand. Sometimes, the offering needs to be updated and followed up through appropriate imagery. A brand of popular pain balm has recently introduced a number of new and updated offerings. This was backed up by the marketing communication.

Repackage

This strategy can be applied to brands that are associated with a low intention to buy and a low anchored perception. This is a situation when the brand fails after initial positioning. There needs to be a new offering and sometimes there needs to be a new brand name as well. Repackage is also applicable to those brands that have been successful in the yesteryear but have declined gradually over a period of time. This can happen because of low-anchored perception and the offering lost its relevance because of environmental changes affecting the intention to buy.

New Mix

A 'new mix' alternative can be considered for brands associated with a high anchored perception and a low intention to buy. In terms of brand visibility, positioning associations can have a positive impact on the target segment but they may not trigger off a significant intention to buy. Non-availability of the brand through a strong distribution channel may be a reason for the low intention to purchase. There are brands in the Indian context that advertise effectively before a distribution infrastructure is developed. Consumer expectations from a brand when a variant is launched may also be the reason for a brand to get categorised in this classification. A successful brand launching a variant triggers a certain kind of expectation among consumers. If the variant with or without a sub-brand fails to live up to the expectation, then the intention to buy the brand may be low (though consumers will have a high anchored perception due to the familiarity with the brand). A good brand (offering), besides making an impact on the consumer's mind-set should also provide a high-perceived value to be associated with a high intention to buy.

Repositioning is unique to a specific brand. The distinguishing aspects of a repositioning strategy are drawn from the nature of the market situation by the suggested framework.

Perception and Marketing Mix Elements

A brand, Milkfood, launched yogurt (sweetened curds in different flavours) and its proposition was that it offered tastier curds than the homemade ones. (Curd is used as a staple food item in most parts of the country). It also launched ice creams in different flavours. Both the categories were sold through the same retail outlets in most areas. The pricing of the yogurt was higher compared to that of the home-made curds. Given this background, consumers may have mistaken yogurt (taken as an alternative to ice cream in the US for health reasons) to be a special kind of ice cream that does not taste like ice cream. There may have also been some confusion because of the flavours. The proposition of taste at a higher price may have also discouraged trials and repeat purchases.

When a brand introduces a product that has close substitutes:

1. It has to have a distinctive brand name that ensures that there is no confusion. It should not be common to the other products of the company.
2. Point-of-purchase posters on the new product must be put up at the retail outlets to ensure that consumers associate it with a new category.
3. When very close substitutes are available, skimming the market with a high price may create transaction/acquisition-based satisfaction and this influences the perception about the purchase of the new offering (even in FMCG products).
4. Communication about the brand (new offering) has to revolve around an aspect that is not oriented towards changing the strongly entrenched beliefs (especially with regard to foods as they are a part of consumer's culture).

Touch of Reality

India's Macho Motorbike

Bullet motorcycle (from Royal Enfield Motors) is a 50-year old brand. It has been traditionally associated with the macho image. While several brands are vying with one another on the aspects of contemporary styling and technologies, Bullet[12] has the opportunity to become India's macho motorbike. The passionate 'die-hard' followers could create the right kind of buzz among the youth to create a cult brand image in a niche market. In the year 2007–08, the brand sold around 38,000 units. Bullet's example reflects how perception plays a role in shaping the image of a brand in a competitive market in which a brand image is very vital. Uniquely, this brand has a right gear shift (when all other bike brands in the world have moved to left gear shift). The company has launched a new model with a different brand name, 'Thunderbird' to target up-graders from small bikes. 'Bullet Machisma 500' targets young bikers. The brand does not advertise as aggressively as other brands in the current market. Being a niche brand with a macho image, the strategy encourages word of mouth (buzz). The brand has done away with discounts, thereby not linking price sensitivity with the brand. This strategy, along with the brand's past image, adds on to the perception that consumers would buy the brand more out of passion than because of a price deal. The Royal Enfield brand stores attempts to provide an experience to the prospective buyers.

Inddiethumpers Club is a community formed by the owners of the brand and the company has a separate website to encourage online interaction among the owners of the brand to enhance affinity among the owners (another form to spread word of mouth).

The website is related to stories, problems and solutions about the brand. In a world that is getting ahead with functionality and benefits, heritage brands with more of symbolism than benefits can be created to hold consumers' attention, if the principles of perception are appropriately applied.

End Notes

1. https://www.youtube.com/watch?v=xP9zqcUn6jQ, accessed on 9 January, 2015.
2. Leon G, Schiffman, Leslie L. Kanuk and S. Ramesh Kumar (in collaboration with J. Wisenblit), *Consumer Behavior*, (New Delhi: Pearson Education, 2010), 11.
3. https://www.youtube.com/watch?v=xP9zqcUn6jQ, accessed on January 9, 2015.
4. http://www.cio.com/article/2441854/it-organization/the-seven-fundamentals-of-value--according-to-mohanbir-sawhney-.html,accessed on 9 January, 2015.

5. Peter Skarzynski and Rowan Gibson (2008), *Innovation: A Blueprint for Transforming the Way Your Company Innovates to the Core*, (HBS Press), pp. 69–70.
6. Writankar Mukherjee (2015), 'Videocon Merges Backend Operations of Retail Arms', *The Economic Times*, 5 January.
7. Doughlas Van Praet (2012), 'Unconscious Branding: How Neuroscience can Empower (and inspire) Marketing', Palgrave Macmillan, 36.
8. Leon Schiffman, Leslie L. Kanuk and S. Ramesh Kumar (in collaboration with J. Wisenblit), *Consumer Behavior*, (New Delhi: Pearson Education, 2010), 161.
9. Lijee Philip (2015), 'Safety in Numbers', *The Economic Times*, 26 August.
10. Ravi Teja Sharma and Pritha Mitra Dasgupta (2014), "SRK does a Rocket Singh with Latest Flick", November 1.
11. C. Whan Park, Bernard J. Jaworski and Deborah J. Maclnnis (1986), 'Strategic Brand Concept-Image Management', *Journal of Marketing*.
12. All about ads, NDTV Profit channel (interview with Prahlad Kakar), 18 October, 2009 (10 p.m.).

Exercises

1. Investigate the influence of Perception on the category of mobiles. Use the ads of various brands after selecting a specific price range.
2. Analyze the influence of perception on the category of ready-made apparel. Use the ads of leading brands to investigate how the basics of perception are used?

CHAPTER 4

Learning Principles and Their Usefulness to Branding Associations

In a cluttered environment, marketing communication depends on focused creativity that involves differentiating between brand associations. Focused creativity (a) has to be meaningful to the target segment; (b) has to have a competitive orientation so that the communication gets differentiated and (c) has to make an impact on the consumer mind-set to the extent of at least reminding the consumer about the functional or emotional proposition of a brand. An established brand has the advantage of having 'entered' the mind-set of the consumer. Colgate is associated with the prevention of tooth decay and Lux is positioned to take pride in rendering beautiful skin. The three aspects of the message (related to creativity) formulated by a brand has to take into account how information is processed in the mind of the consumer. Incidentally, knowing the process may also enable a marketer to identify a brand proposition.

Developing and Nurturing Brand Associations

Branding is a psychological process. A significant aspect of learning principles is concerned with how consumers learn brand associations. Consumers provide meanings to the offerings made by marketers. Brands evolve their communication strategies that shape brand meanings and consumers perceive these meanings based on their own experience with the brands they use; consumers also form perceptions about the brands pre and post-brand usage. Brands get differentiated from commodities that are sold on price differences. The simple difference reflects the fact that a good brand should not just rely on price reduction eternally, specifically in a dynamic environment. The psychological aspects of branding are illustrated by a popular experiment conducted among consumers.[1] When consumers were asked to choose between unbranded offerings of Pepsi and Coke, they chose Pepsi based on its taste; when the brands were identified and they were asked to choose, so they chose Coke. All along their brain activity had been mapped by magnetic resonance techniques that revealed that when they heard Coke, the portions in the brain associated with pleasure and decision making had flashed. This confirms the psychological linkages between brands and consumer's mind beyond functional utility.

A brand is a unique offering from a company that offers a set of values*. The uniqueness of the brand has to emphasize the following:

1. Brand differentiation (that is associated with brand positioning).
2. Brand relevancy (that is also associated with brand positioning).
3. Brand equity (how a brand adds value to a category and how a consumer realises this value).
4. Brand reinforcement (how the brand positioning can be periodically reinforced to make the brand relevant in a changing environment without its associations being lost).

Horlicks, Dettol, Santoor, Parachute and Raga (in their respective categories) are such examples of how these brands had successfully managed themselves over a period of time.

Brand associations have to be managed over a period of time after selecting the brand strategy associated with a product line. Unilever India has several brands in its product line-up like tea and soaps. It has Liril, Lifebuoy, Hamam, Lux and Dove in soaps and Taj, Red Label, Three Roses, Taaza and Yellow Label in tea (to name a few brands). There may also be sub-brands in the product-line. Gillette has Sensor Excel, Mach 3, Fusion, Vector Plus and Guard. Guard, the sub-brand is a 'non-frill' version which is at the lower-price end category that tends to attract consumers into the category of twin-edged blades from the conventional category of blades that majority of Indians use for shaving purposes. As it is evident, the various sub-brands that target different groups of consumers need to be managed differently from the viewpoint of branding.

There are three kinds of brands, namely functional brands, self-expressive brands and hedonic brands (sensual consumption of offerings).[2] While this distribution may not offer absolute exclusivity among brands, it provides a useful and conceptual direction to manage brands. Colgate Total offers '12-hour' protection from several aspects of teeth problems and is a problem-solving brand which is strongly associated with the functional brands. Himalaya Complete Care toothpaste is another such example. Fastrack watches symbolizes urban, hip and a progressive attitude towards the opposite gender among youth and it is full of symbolism. Tanishq stands for modernity, traditional values and freedom of choice. Café Coffee Day is something more than a cup of coffee. It is about coffee consumption in a social setting. Consumption experience makes it a hedonic brand. Red Bull energy drink is another example of a hedonic brand. There may be certain brand strategies that a brand may adopt to move from one category to another. Volvo vehicles was strongly associated with safety (functional association) had introduced a sports model that have earned the likings of the modern-day youth and driving experience. Each brand needs to decide its strategy considering both its context and objectives.

---

* For further reading, please refer to any basic textbook on marketing

Brand relevance is about a brand making an attempt to change with the environment. Horlicks had launched Women's Horlicks to cater to the growing trend of women in urban areas who require appropriate nutrients that are in line with their aspirations. Sunsilk's 'Gang of Girls' (www.gangofgirls.com) was an online platform that engaged girls on a host of topics beyond haircare that were of interest to them. Saffola edible oil's 'heart foundation' initiative is not only in line with its proposition; it addresses the fitness trends among consumers. Complan's Multigrain variant for adults and Vicks Multi-pain pain balm for adults are such examples of well-entrenched brands stretching their equity to be in tune with the changing environment. Digitalization of brands also provides an opportunity for brands to engage today's consumers. Ceat Tyres had launched an app that could be used by consumers to drive safely.

Brand equity is the value a brand adds to a product category. Satisfaction of needs, trust and commitment, identification with the brand and the utilitarian value of the brand are some of the important dimensions of brand equity.[3] Strong brands that have been a part of the lives of consumers are likely to rank high on these dimensions of brand equity. Dettol that has a presence in antiseptic lotion, soaps, hand-wash, utensil washing gel and wipes is a strongly entrenched brand. Johnson & Johnson's baby products that include soaps, creams and oil are widely trusted by mothers due to the nature of perceived risk associated with the category. Identification with a brand may be because of status, a sense of belongingness among the users, trustworthiness or any other aspect that may involve emotions. Dove brand has extended itself into soaps, hair oil, shampoo, face wash and body lotion in India. The brand's mildness and its imagery of 'Real Beauty' is likely to have added to its equity. Brand equity is also equally important for brands at its lower end of the price spectrum. Parle-G in biscuits, Chik shampoo and Rin detergent are such examples of well-established brands. There are brands that have recently used their equity to revitalize themselves after an extended length of time. Vaseline from Unilever India had launched a few variants that had 'healing' as its advantage. Fair & Handsome, the pioneering brand of fairness cream for men, had built up a proposition about the suitability of the offering to men. The diversity of examples reflects the usefulness of the various dimensions of brand equity.

Brand-consumer relationship is an area of interest to both academics and practitioners. There are many types of relationships that a brand can have with consumers.[4] A consumer using Raga watches for many years may have a committed relationship; one who likes using Nescafe coffee may have a daily-dependent relationship and someone who is always buying at a leading retailing store like 'Reliance Mart' may like the prices but feel that he cannot change the shop as he perceives that alternative shops do not provide the same value. In this case the relationship is 'Master–Slave'. Stenberg introduced three other dimensions with regard to brand–consumer relationships namely passion, intimacy and commitment.[5] A housewife can be committed to Horlicks because she believes it is good for her child while a teenager may be passionate about Red Bull. Branding in combination with consumer behaviour may open up several unexplored avenues for marketers.

The Concept of Conditioning

The principles of learning provide interesting insights into the understanding of information processing. There are a number of theories associated with these principles. This part of the chapter deals with theories of learning and attempts to highlight those areas, which have a direct implication on the creative aspects involving brand messages.

Classical Conditioning

Classical conditioning deals with the process of associating messages/feelings/situations with a brand on the assumption that the feelings/messages/situations get strongly identified with the brand. Such a process is aimed at creating the brand's associations in the mind-set of consumers. For example, cricket, films and pranks, besides many other aspects, denote youth associations. Hence, having identified the younger generation as its target segment, Pepsi has used visuals of these three aspects in their brand messages. The basic point in such a context is that there are specific situations, which trigger off pleasant sensations and feelings and these situations are being associated with a brand. When a brand aggressively creates visibility using these visuals for a period of time, consumers may internalize the brand as a part of the feelings and experiences associated with these situations. Pepsi is associated with film stars or cricket celebrities or the fun that young people indulge in. A marketer of photographic films may associate the brand with the feelings of warmth. Titan's association with gifts and the warmth is interesting from the perspective of its brand identity. The situation chosen has to be one that elicits a known response from the consumer, preferably a favourable and emotional one. Classical conditioning develops brand associations that reside in the memory of consumers creating a favourable opinion towards the respective brand.

Branding and Licensing in the Indian Context

Classical conditioning is closely associated with licensing brands. The Indian context is full of examples of how licensing is used by brands to appeal to consumers. Parle had embossed Tom & Jerry on their Milk Shakti cream biscuits (these are liked by children but resisted by mothers as cream biscuits are perceived as being bad for health). Hero cycles introduced Mickey Mouse brand for children. Over ₹1000 crores is being spent on Disney offerings in India that include stationery, fashion, home products, health and food items. Chhota Bheem, a character that was launched in India, has 3000 SKUs covering many categories like shoes, school merchandise and apparel. The movie *Dhoom 3 had* Ceat (tires) and Barbie dolls. Also, Myntra, the online brand, had entered into licensing arrangement with Disney.

Inputs from, Amit Bapna (2014), 'License to Sell', *The Economic Times*, September 3.

Branding Challenges and Classical Conditioning

Classical conditioning is all about managing associations. How should brand associations be developed and sustained? Changing environment poses unique challenges to marketers who are dependent on associations.

Chotukool refrigerators from Godrej were introduced in 2008 in the price range of ₹ 3500 to 3800 in the rural markets. Later, based on consumer insights, the company, its design was altered to focus on different segments (to be used as a lifestyle product in cars, for instance).[6] The challenge in such a context is to explore the complexities of positioning the same offering to different segments. Such a strategy is dependent on differentiation of brand associations across segments.

Brand Associations to Relationships

Associations with brands trigger certain thoughts that are stored in the schema which is a collection of knowledge about a domain that is associated with the consumer. Strong brand associations lead to a brand–consumer relationship. Susan Fournier has published several research papers on this topic. One of the relationships mentioned in her papers is that a consumer may view a brand as a friend. MTR foods, a Bangalore-based brand known for its traditional snacks, had planned to position its ready-to-eat product range as a woman's helping hand on all occasions and not as a substitute.[7]

While there may be arguments about the reality of how a consumer can associate with a brand as a friend, the nature of such associations may not be within the conscious mind-set of the consumer. He/she may find that mentioning the respective category will subconsciously direct them towards the brand.

The following have to be taken into account before a brand decides to use a specific feeling/situation:

1. Researching the market is a prerequisite, as a suitable emotion is required to be paired with the brand. The emotion or a specific situation, (which may be called based on the relevant stimulus) is likely to be the core aspect of the brand imagery and has to be selected with great care. When an international brand of jeans entered the Indian market, the brand chose a celebrity who may not have appealed to the target segment of the brand.
2. The imagery selected to be paired with the brand, should have some relevancy to the product category. Selecting a heart-warming emotion for a brand of photographic film is very meaningful as warmth is closely related to bring back the nostalgia or memories. This becomes the brand's benefit for the consumer.
3. It is essential for a brand to plan a specific emotional proposition (it can even be functional) to ensure that the brand offers a sustainable differentiation in the long run.

4. A marketer should be extremely careful in selecting an association (it can even be a jingle) especially, when stimuli (picture/visual or song) selected is over-exposed to consumers. The over-exposed stimulus can be a film song or even a celebrity who has endorsed many brands. A brand of chocolate may associate itself with a popular film tune but the popularity of the tune can take away the novelty associated with the brand–tune pairing.
5. Negative emotions may also be used. An insurance company can use a degree of fear appeal. Using strong fear appeals may be counter-productive. A brand of edible oil had initially used appeals associated with heart attacks and then it had changed the appeal. In the recent times, several insurance brands have focused on positive aspects of life like an enjoyable retirement or a fine future for children to ensure that fear appeals do not create a negative feeling towards the brand.

The initial success of Onida based on its 'devil' ad symbolizing neighbour's jealousy used a negative emotion in an interesting manner. Onida was one of the earliest brands in the Indian context in the eighties and probably the first to be advertised on a premium plank. The off-beat execution may have generated interest and taken it into the consideration set of consumers along with a few brands that existed at that time.

Fear/negative appeals can be used in a creative and meaningful manner from the viewpoint of a consumer's mind-set.

Memory, Learning and Brands

Memory is an integral part of learning. Associations and networks are formed in memory. A consumer may have a schema about a specific domain and this is the knowledge structure about the respective domain. There can be a schema for a brand, a person, an event or a place.

Self- schemata indicate the associations about self that is contained in one's schema. Consumer preferences and brand associations/personality take shape only from the schema of the consumer. Consumers who have an incomplete self of themselves seek to complete themselves with appropriate brands (symbolic self-completion theory).[8] Memory holds the key to several decisions made by the consumer. Memory may also be activated by the type of goal.[9] For instance, a consumer may think of Red Bull drink when the goal is to spend time with friends, but think of many other beverages when he is hungry. Memory is stored in engrams (electrochemical etchings) that get activated due to stimuli that the consumer experiences (a friend's recommendation about a restaurant when a consumer's memory is also mood dependent).[10] A consumer who learns about a brand like iPhone and feels good about its attributes is likely to recall the attributes of the brand when he is in a good mood. (The consumer needs to attribute his mood elevation to the brand's attributes during his initial exposure).

"Memories are fragile but powerful products of what we recall from the past, believe about the present and imagine the future" – Daniel Schacter.[11]

From nostalgia to aspirations, memory and brands are intertwined.

Taste is the Reward

SOSYO, a Gujarat-based cola-like drink launched during the 1930's, had a 29 per cent market share of aerated drinks in Gujarat. Currently, it competes with leading brands like Coke and Pepsi.[12]

Taste can be a strong reward in such categories and can build a base of loyal consumers.

INSTRUMENTAL CONDITIONING

Instrumental conditioning is a concept which deals with the desirable reward a consumer gets when he gives a favourable response. A brand of shampoo may prove to be a good choice for dandruff and a brand of readymade wear may be both comfortable and appealing to the peer group of the consumer. Service provided at retail outlets (quick check-out during peak hours in a retail outlet like Food world) can also reinforce consumer behaviour in terms of repeat buying or patronizing a retail outlet. This conditioning can also be applied creatively on the Internet. The basic assumption of applying these principles on the Internet is that reinforcement of this behaviour can also result from the experience (and not only from a good product) provided to consumers.

Amazon makes recommendations to consumers based on the purchases of other buyers who had reflected similar preferences. In such an example, the consumers have a motivation to return to the website and this may also creatively reinforce the brand in the consumer mind-set. While instrumental conditioning helps FMCG consumers with regard to repeat purchases, marketers of durables may also benefit by ensuring that consumers keep coming back to them, so that they can be targeted during the replacement cycle or for marketing other products of the company. BPL may have millions of consumers using at least one product of the company. The importance of ensuring a sustained contact with the consumer need not be over-emphasized.

New Brand , Instrumental Conditioning and Associations of Value

Vistara, the airline that was launched in India, was analyzed for its performance in its first 100 days and the following conceptual aspects could be identified with the points raised in the analysis with regard to brand positioning, value and brand associations.[13]

- A new entrant in service (intangibles) needs to all the more careful to ensure value perception with reference prices taken into account. Premium economy offered by Vistara is a good concept but because it is associated with economy schema, thus price schema would also be closer to economy. Schema is the sum total of all associations and schemas are formed in the associative networks. For instance, when a consumer thinks of air travel, several schemas associated with different brands may be triggered in the associative network concerned with air travel. There may be schemas associated with business and economy classes of airline brands.
- Experiential aspects (sensory on this case) are important in creating instrumental conditioning that leads to the consumer preferring the stimuli that had been rewarding.
- Selecting the right segment
- Leisure travelers on vacation routes are likely to prefer economy as compared to corporates who may prefer premium economy.
- Contrasting signals
- Reducing prices by sixty percent in economy segment takes away the value association of a new offering and affects it's positioning. In any case there seems to be no clear positioning of Vistara despite its association with Tata.
- Brand relationship dimensions can be strengthened as associations if specific dimensions are identified.

Gamification and Instrumental Conditioning[14]

Gamification makes routine actions into interactive experiences by adding gaming elements. It has some degree of uncertainty, short and long-term goals, feedback, competition that is not hostile and a digital platform.

Fitocracy is an app that has gaming principles for physical fitness and awards badges to the user after completing a milestone. Vitality is a game in which players can exchange points for groceries and air tickets.

Closer home, apps like Zomato (Refer Plate 4.1) has introduced its own gamification features. Online grocery apps in India too may start such initiatives. Digital initiatives that have rewards built in them make use of the basic principles of instrumental conditioning.

Customer Relationship Management and Instrumental Conditioning

A company can plan a contact program with consumers after the sale is over. Instrumental conditioning, in such a situation, triggers off (customer relationship management) CRM. CRM has several complex dimensions. In this chapter, a reference is made to the concept in association with instrumental conditioning because of the basic fact that mutually rewarding relationships last for a long time. There are four phases identified with regard to customer-interface in durables.

Plate 4.1 Zomato has introduced its own gaming features

Traditionally, after-sales service has been the only phase associated with customer-interface. This offers very little scope for a marketer to have a sustained interaction with the customer. For example, after the installation of the durable, it may be a month or even years before the customer thinks of the company. The post-sale phases help in planning, monitoring consumers and formulating specific communication strategies in distinctive stages extending the 'response-reward' mechanism associated with instrumental conditioning.

The satisfaction phase immediately follows the purchase phase. The customer wants to fully explore the product using its features, finding out its benefits and experiencing how he/she has benefited from the purchase. Though the 'reward' is the benefit itself, it may be worthwhile for a marketer to reinforce the customer's decision of selecting the brand. This reinforcement may start with a personalized 'thank you' letter and be followed up by company personnel by explaining the brochure accompanying the brand and/or taking a personal interest in familiarizing him/her with the product. There is also a need to provide an exclusive telephone/web access to consumers who may have bought the brand in the last two or three months. This exclusivity, apart from addressing the queries of new consumers, also helps to enhance the satisfaction levels and promotes a good word of mouth (WOM). Today, WOM may be a more powerful weapon than advertising, especially for durables, as consumers look for sources of information other than advertising. This phase should reinforce the feeling of consumers that they have made the right choice. This is a basic step for any kind of on-going relationship program. Reinforcement can also be brought in through innovative warranties. A futuristic offering from a brand that was bought by the consumer earlier will enhance the reinforcement model if it offers a longer warranty.

Sustained Value and Rewards Associated with a Brand

Instrumental conditioning is based on rewards experienced by consumers. The 75-years-old Parle G brand is a very good example of how consistent value of the offering can result in brand success. 4551 Parle G biscuits are being consumed every second, 400 million biscuits are being produced every day and 100 crore packs across sizes are sold every month through 5 million outlets.[15]

Online Gaming and Rewards: Transactional Advertising

Transactional advertising involves rewarding an online game player when he responds to ads while playing the online game.[16] The player may get virtual points or currency that can be used in the game or he may be able to crack a code associated with a game. With millions of active gamers across mobile devices, transactional advertising seems to be futuristic.

Using this concept, Farmville, a popular online game in association with Lady Gaga, an American singer created GagaVille.[17]

Closer home, an online service provider like Zomato can use the concept and provide rewards that can be used in restaurants.

The Impact of Customized Communication: A Form of Reward

As a market expands, different needs emerge from different kinds of customers. Companies usually take care of this aspect by offering many variants from the parent product. A skincare company may have a plain cream, moisturizing cream and an herbal variant. This enables consumers to try out from the range and select a product suitable for their skin type. Creating awareness on skin types, the problems associated with skin and the impact of seasonal variations on the skin may be some important aspects that need to be communicated even before consumers consider buying the variants.

Communication in this situation is time-oriented, sequenced and may even become customized after a stage when an individual consumer starts looking for specific advice on skincare. Special efforts are required by a company to formulate communication. This includes not just information on skin types but also the right kind of appeal for the products offered by the company. Besides, the communication should also consider the time factor effectively for introducing the brand during the different phases of communication with the consumer.

The communication involved in the relationship-building exercise is different from one that happens through mass media. A brand of cosmetics targeting young teens in urban markets can create a website and carefully involve consumers who are highly beauty-conscious with a variety of information on skin care. This advice can also be customized to individual tastes. Reward (instrumental conditioning) need not be only associated with freebies or money, timely advice on several perceived risks associated with a category may also be perceived as a reward by consumers. Such consumers are likely to become loyal to the brand.

Loyalty Programs

A company interested in loyalty programs should consider transaction and non-transaction methods of building loyalty. This may depend on the specific product or service category.

For example, customers are likely to choose an airline that offers the most attractive frequent-flier program. There are product categories where consumers may like to get as much information as possible on the usage and other aspects of the product. This is applicable in the Indian context where an increasing number of consumers are attempting to be aware of buying and using several products they have not been exposed to.

Health supplements, branded nappies, branded baby food, mouthwash and fast food are some examples that require intense information that is backed up by credibility. Consumers may be concerned about the frequency of use/intake or the nutritional ingredients used. This offers tremendous scope for marketers to provide information to prospective consumers, which in turn, achieves their confidence and builds goodwill.

Consumers may begin to perceive that the knowledge base provided by a company reflects its concern towards its consumers. Loyalty programs that are based on non-transaction methods provide the basic foundation for transaction-oriented reward schemes. They emphasize that the brand/company is not just a price warrior but one that is aware of the kind of customer orientation required in the category.

Pricing and Loyalty

A limitation of heavy sales promotion is that consumers are inducted into a 'price war' mind-set. This may prove counter-productive for loyalty-building as consumers tend to pick up the cheapest brand in the market or the one that is offered under similar sales promotion (price-off or a free gift with purchase). Soaps, toothpastes and noodles are some examples.

While sales promotion, by itself, may be an effective tool, a brand will have to carefully plan the objectives of sales promotion, considering the aspects of loyalty objectives. This may not be done by most brands.

A large company marketing a brand of noodles (with a considerable amount of brand-building efforts) can use relationship pricing through cross-selling of other fast food products made by the company. This is different from sales promotion. A combination of units purchased across product categories over a period of time and the resultant savings—besides contests—provide a useful relationship program. This need not be a short-term benefit because the consumer would be motivated to buy offerings of the brand by factors other than those provided by price. The underlying assumption in such programs is that the products are good. Loyalty programs must be planned using the information on the various segments of the product/product-line and the corresponding demographics and psychographics. In the Indian context, a major chunk of sales happens at small retail outlets. This is unlike the departmental stores of the West where a number of data-capturing tools are used to obtain valuable information on consumption patterns.

Hence, companies have to make efforts to collect the required data before attempting to formulate programs. It may be possible to collect such data in the case of durables, if a company has a proper system to follow up and track customers after the sale is over. Marketers can explore unlimited possibilities if they synergize databases and loyalty patterns to develop relationships.

Consumer Behaviour and Information Processing

There is another school of thought on learning, the information processing theory on learning or the cognitive theory on learning, which is based on mental activity. The basic assumption of this theory is that consumers are likely to search for relevant information and get involved in complex problem-solving situations with regard to their needs. Consumers may process information on attributes, brands, product categories or a combination of these aspects. Individuals also have a different orientation towards imagery—the ability to form mental images. A marketer can research the target segment before formulating advertisements focused on consumers in the target segment. The research can deal with (a) tests of imagery vividness, which are concerned with the ability of consumers to evoke clear images; (b) tests of processing style, which are concerned with the preference of consumers towards visual or verbal messages; or (c) tests of daydreaming, which are concerned with the fantasy context. The utility of such research can be explained by the fact that specific guidelines to the advertising executives can be formulated. They would deal with questions like 'Should the advertisement for a brand of soft drink contain attractive visuals based on a high degree of fantasy element or should it have a tuneful jingle or both?' The impact of media on the target segment would also have to be researched. The information processing theory is based on mental processes rather than on the strength of associations, which forms the basis of behavioural theories.

Important Aspects of Information Processing Theory

There are certain critical aspects of the information processing theory and each of these have an impact on the behaviour of consumers and also on the formulation of marketing strategies (Refer Figure 4.1)

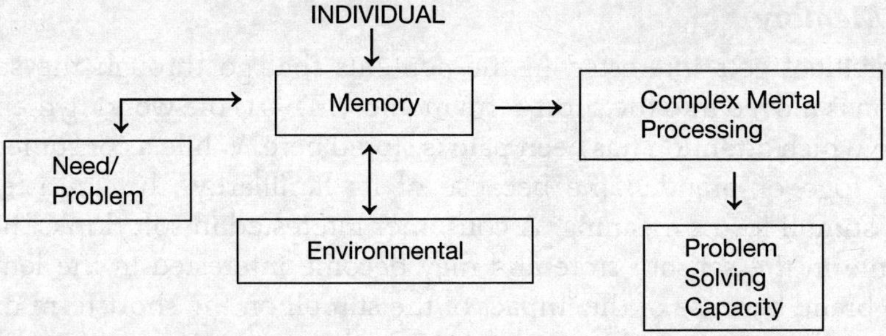

Figure 4.1 Basic Aspects of Information Processing Theory

Sensory Store

Stimuli (sensory information, which acts as inputs to our senses) from the environment enters the sensory store in the memory. Senses together do not transmit complete messages to the brain. Each sense receives only one part of the information (sound, colour, touch, etc.). Perception takes place in the brain and the individual perceives the complete image. The image in the sensory store lasts for a few seconds and is lost instantly if not processed. Hence, the individual's current interests and motivational pattern may filter out a plethora of information not required by him/her. While it may be possible to gain entry into the sensory store with catchy and creative advertisements/visuals, it may be difficult to make a lasting impression on it, given the clutter of communication in today's context. These aspects have a number of implications for marketers. The right media have to be selected to ensure that the target segment gets interested in the communication after being impressed by the visual. However, even a creative advertisement for a foreign vacation when advertised on a wrong TV channel will not hold any viewers to capture its significance. While the viewers may appreciate the creative aspects of the visual, a large chunk of viewers of the TV channel may not even fall in the demographic and psychographic profile of the target segment. A niche channel like Discovery or Travelxp may be a better choice as the interest levels triggered off by the advertisement in the sensory store will ensure that the context of communication moves on to the next stage of the memory.

Companies with seasonal products like soft drinks or textiles, (which may be bought more during festive seasons) can have special communication strategies that may be of interest to the target segment which is something like a sale/contest. This will be different from the regular campaigns of brands in terms of the brand personality aspects. A TV channel may use humour during such a campaign. This can have an additional impact on the sensory store in terms of its 'attention-grabbing' power. In-store displays like the ones at POP and even the location of brands (especially, new brands in a category) are other aspects that are connected with the sensory store.

Short–term Memory

When an individual gets interested in the contents that go through the sensory store, the information is moved into the short-term memory. This is the working memory and the information to which attention has been paid is stored here. While a consumer may readily recognize the logo or brand name because of its familiarity, the short-term memory examines the stimuli for its meaning. A consumer interested in soft drinks may recognize the brand name in the sensory store and may become interested in the lemon or grape variant of the brand because of the impact of the stimuli on the short-term memory.

Short-term memory can hold only limited (and distinct) pieces of information. The process of evaluation of information with regard to its relevance to the individual is very brief and takes place within 30 seconds. If the information is not evaluated within this time, then it is forgotten.

The implication of short-term memory for marketing communication is interesting and useful. In order to transfer the information from short-term to long-term memory, the short-term store undergoes a process called rehearsal, which is a silent, mental repetition of information. This memory contributes significantly to the 'top-of-the-mind' recall of brands. This characteristic is extremely useful for FMCG brands that have a strong brand image. Close-up in toothpastes, Red Roses in tea and Surf Excel in detergents are strong brands as they are generally advertised throughout the year. When brands (or logos) are advertised continuously, the 'top-of-the-mind awareness' is enhanced and there is a probability of the information getting transferred to the long-term memory. Hence, the very thought of a product category can trigger a few brands in the minds of the consumer. These are likely to be the strong brands as the ones mentioned above. Some may be pioneering brands like Pepsi and Coke, which are spontaneously associated with the cola category of soft drinks. Building brands is also useful in evoking the 'experience imagery' associated with a specific brand, a process by which information from long-term memory appears in the short-term memory. For example, the very mention of Cadbury can evoke the shape, taste and colour associated with the chocolate.

Novelty and Memory

Do novel stimuli or associations trigger or recall better? According to the Von Restorff Effect, any unique stimulus in a set of stimuli seen by the individual will be recalled better. Applying novelty to this effect enhances the effect on recall.[18] A brand of mixer-blender called Blendtec depicted an advertisement where iPhones/iPads were being blended to pieces in its 'Will it blend' campaign. In India, Bingo, Polo and Fevi Stik have used novelty in a variety of ways. However, given the diversity associated with several psychological effects and the context that surround such ads (competitive clutter as well as the context in which the individual views such ads), effectiveness of such ads on consumers may vary. It may be a good idea to use novelty associated with the benefits of a brand like Itch Guard (medicine to treat itches) had created a humorous ad that conveyed the benefits of the brand.

Long–term Memory

This memory has the capability of retaining information for a long period of time. The information that enters this memory keeps getting organized and reorganized as new information enters the memory. Information gets updated with appropriate linkages when new and relevant bits (with regard to a specific domain of product categories or brands in the marketing context) of information get into the memory. The process of activation links new data to the old information stored in the memory.

Another distinguishing feature of this memory is 'schema' or a total package of associations brought into an individual's mind when he/she feels a stimulus. The stimulus can be an advertisement or simply a need felt by the individual.

Marketers can use long-term memory and schema in a number of ways. The following points will enable them to appreciate the value of long-term memory in analysing or shaping the behaviour of consumers:

- Consumers can have a schema for product categories, brands or even retail stores. Different consumers may have a different schema for different product categories. A type of schema for soft drinks is shown in Figure 4.2.

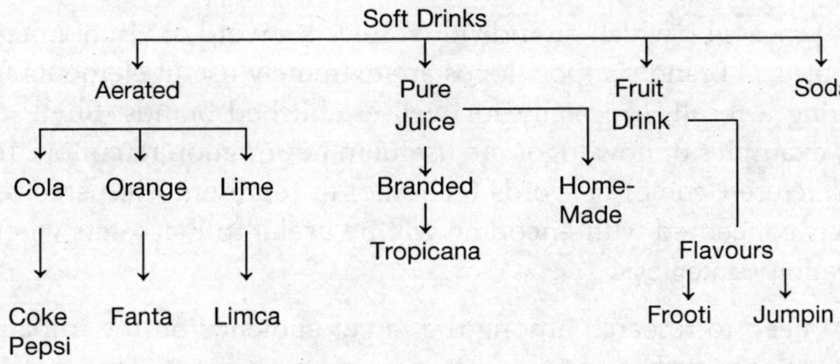

Figure 4.2 Schema for Soft Drinks

- As brands begin to pack a new product category, the effectiveness of the USP of the new product decides how the brand will impact the existing schema in the mind of the consumer. If a new brand of cola is to be launched, marketers should consider how it can enter the existing schema for soft drinks. Red Bull created the 'energy' association with regard to soft-drinks in the schema of consumers.
- When a 'new concept' of product category is being created (electric cars or a tablet-based soft drink), the pioneering brand has an opportunity to become an inherent part of the relevant schema. Hence, such a brand should strive hard to build itself. Though Titan was not a pioneering brand in the digital category of watches, it is a very strong brand in terms of associations.
- Marketers can explore gaps in the minds of consumers to formulate an appealing USP. For example, Promise toothpaste used clove oil as its USP when it launched the brand. This made a tremendous impact on consumers. (The example is used to illustrate the concept rather than to analyse the brand.) Maggi used the convenience

plank to get into the minds of consumers. Care should be taken to ensure that the USP so formulated appeals to the target segment. Being unique is one thing and making the consumer buy the brand is another. Hence getting into the schema should be done with the overall objective of influencing the purchase decision of consumers. The USP of a brand has to be unique, relevant, acceptable to consumers and identifiable with the target segment.

- A well-known scooter brand of the yesteryear was positioned on the comfort plank. The visual of the advertisement showed the brand being used for countryside rides. While the positioning was effective in conveying the 'ultimate experiential comfort' (and probably making an impact on the existing schema for scooters), it is doubtful if prospective consumers would have identified themselves with the idea of using a scooter for a countryside ride, especially when the visual did not have an adventurous, young person. The example might be old but reflects the importance of formulating a USP from the viewpoint of the schema.

Encoding and Information Retention

Encoding is the process by which an individual selects a word or visual image to represent the perceived object.[19] Brand symbols/logos are extremely useful elements from the viewpoint of triggering a recall, especially for well-established brands. Shell, Mercedes and Dettol are such examples of how logos are useful in information retention. Individuals can assign a visual/picture (iconic) or words (echonic) to represent the perceived object. The following aspects concerned with encoding will be useful to marketers when they formulate communication strategies:

1. There is a need to research among the target audience on the impact of the visual with regard to the verbal components in an advertisement. This can differ from one product category to another (a brand of FMCG can call for a different approach, from a brand of TV).
2. There is research evidence to show that TV viewers can commit a large portion of their thought and involvement to specific parts of the program(s) they view. Hence, apart from introducing TV commercials at prime time (when viewership is large) for an appropriate brand, marketers can also research the TV program or serial and pre-test it among a cross-section of the target audience. This will enable them to get some idea about the degree of involvement that viewers have in a program. This, in turn, will help them place the TV commercial 'adjacent' to the 'high-involvement' parts of the program.
3. When consumers are exposed to a lot of information (as in the highly-crowded FMCG product categories), they are likely to experience 'information overload'.

Research is inconclusive on how much information consumers can handle when brands disseminate it. Marketers can determine the point where information overload occurs with regard to a product category in a specific medium. For example, marketers can find out the impact of brand advertising the toilet soaps on TV. This helps them decide on alternative or supplementary strategies with regard to encoding. If the consumers find it difficult to encode information about a new brand of herbal soap on TV, marketers may choose the point-of-purchase material as having a better impact. This can be useful, especially for new brands entering a category which already has strong brands.

Retention and Long–term Memory

Long-term memory has two ways of storing information. It can store information episodically (according to the sequence in which events take place) or semantically (according to relevant concepts). An individual may remember the various brands of he/she may have used during different stages in his/her life (based on episodic component) or remember how specific brands are useful for specific purposes (or end benefits) depending on their features (based on semantic memory). Episodic memory is also known as 'autobiographical memory' as it records one's experiences in the world. Research evidence shows that a pioneering brand in any category will have an impact on consumers with its novel and unique features. A pioneering brand may also have an edge over the other entrants in terms of its impact on consumer mind-set because of episodic memory. This may not always happen in practice, as there are a number of other factors which must be considered while evaluating a brand's success. The follower brands may be successful because of enhanced marketing mix elements. (Maruti, Titan and Dell were not pioneering brands). The inference is that a pioneering brand in a category can sustain its success if it can fine-tune its marketing mix elements over a period of time. Reynolds is one such example.

Semantic memory gets organized when there is activation or when new information gets clubbed with stored information to result in meaningful chunks of information. Brand comparisons take place because of semantic memory. Another implication of semantic memory is that the consumer is also able to fulfil his/her needs (since organization of information happens according to meaningful concepts). A consumer may prefer a car brand because of certain specific features that matches his/her needs. This is meaningful to the consumer, and hence, the brand gets into his/her memory.

Retrieval of Information

Retrieval is the process by which individuals are able to recover information from long-term storage. Research suggests that consumers remember the benefits rather than the attributes of a brand (there can be exceptions like PUF used in refrigerators). Godrej made use of this attribute to make a significant impact on the mind-set of potential consumers. There are two causes that interfere with the retrieval process. Recently-learned material or retroactive learning can interfere with the retrieval of previously learned material and material learned earlier or proactive learning can interfere with the retrieval of newly-learned material. The implication is that marketers should provide effective 'retrieval cues'. These cues can enhance well the effectiveness of advertising campaigns, especially over a period of time.

Consumers may like advertisements but the respective brand has to be recalled when they make a product choice, especially at retail outlets. This is very essential for FMCG products where there is a proliferation of brands. Soaps, tetra-packed drinks and food are such categories where cues may be very effective.

Life, a brand of cereal in the US, used a method which provided a strong retrieval cue; a photograph from a certain TV commercial of the brand was used on its package. Point-of-purchase material, which is associated with TV advertising, can also be provided at the retail outlet.

A relevant contrast provided in a TV commercial can also be an effective way to trigger off recall among consumers. Itch Guard, a brand for skin-infection ointments used good contrast by inducing humour in it. It showed a man in plush surroundings feeling itchy and wriggling due to an infection, toppling things around and interrupting the proceedings. The context of the advertising theme is a tradition of 'meeting-the-bride/groom' ceremony.

Priming[20] is another technique that can provide strong retrieval. It is a process of triggering the schema in the mind-set of the consumer by using one of its aspects. For example, a brand using comparative advertising can trigger off several brands and their attributes or benefits. Santro introduced a comparative advertisement to get itself into the consideration set of consumers (the example may be old but it is appropriate to illustrate the concept). A brand should use priming only if it is sure of gaining a competitive edge over other brands. Prior research is a prerequisite for using priming. Another method of using priming is to highlight a problem that can trigger off associated problems. The brand can then convey how to solve or avoid the problem (Surf Excel's stain removal campaign involving two children who playfully fight with one another is an ideal example). Even services can make use of this technique. A brand in the category of insurance can show a powerful visual, which may trigger off several aspects related to the benefits of a policy.

Other Aspects of Retrieval

Prototypicality is a concept that may result in high recall of an advertisement.[21] Consumers tend to remember a brand if it is positioned as an ideal product in the respective product category. Prototypicality can be applied by brands that offer to have an edge over competing brands in the category and also to have pioneered a product in a category or sub-category. For example, Maruti was the typical 'small' car when it was launched with several aspects that are associated with a small car that had the characteristics of initial cost, fuel economy, compact looks, etc. The entry of Santro, Indica and Matiz made Maruti a 'mini' car. Dove, the brand of moisturizer bar, which pioneered this product is another example of prototypicality with regard to moisturizer bars. Brands entering the market with liquid detergents (a few brands have been in the market for a long time) and shower gels (a few brands have attempted to make a mark in the market) have the opportunity of creating prototypical brands in the Indian context.

Salient attributes in a product category are recalled better. Hence, marketers need to research on them for a given target segment of consumers. These depend on the goal consumers have while choosing a product/service. Globally, McDonald is associated with the characteristics of fast food, good value, convenience and hygiene.

Recall of experiences is an effective way to enhance the recall of a brand. Constant research is required for an insight into the motivational aspects of consumers. In certain markets, consumers may have the desire for new products that look like old products. This can contribute to the style and looks of new products in the pipeline, and these in turn can have a positive impact on the recall of the brand. A brand of health drink can position itself as a drink of 'simple and happy times', making it a family drink.

Congruence is another concept that contributes to a high degree of retrieval. Congruent associations establish strong linkages and lead to effective retrieval.[22] The words 'refreshing', 'emerging' and 'recharging', when used for a soft drink for sportsmen, may be effective because of the congruence in the words.

Redundancy is a variation of congruence and a process that enhances memory.[23] This occurs if information that has to be learned has visual and copy elements that fit together. Hence, the recall of a brand name, advertising message and pictures can be enhanced if they have similar or common elements. The similarity in verbal and visual message is encoded both verbally and visually. This results in two retrieval paths. A brand namelike Frooti can have a visual of fruits and the copy can talk about the fruits used in the drink.

Mood or a temporary emotional state has an impact on retrieval of information. A positive mood enhances recall of positive information and vice versa.

Split–Brain Theory[24]

The split-brain theory emphasizes that the right and left hemispheres of the brain processes different kinds of information. The left is concerned with activities like reading, speaking and other verbal aspects while the right takes care of non-verbal and pictorial information. TV viewing is concerned with the right side, and hence, learning is passive. Due to the visual element, the information processing occurs in a low-involvement environment as against the information processing which occurs in print, a high-involvement media.

The split-brain theory has a number of implications on consumer behaviour. It says there are high and low-involvement consumers; high and low-involvement purchases and that there are a number of purchasing factors responsible for the involvement levels. A television and facial cream may both reflect high-involvement buying as both the purchases involve financial and social risks respectively. The medium of TV becomes important for conveying symbols, brand logos or short visual messages repeatedly. Visual cues enhance brand recall. Marketers should research the involvement profile of consumers to get an idea about the target segment's interest in the product and its benefits, consumers' perception of its associated risks and the symbolic nature of the respective product category/brand.

Learning theories and concepts offer a number of creative avenues for marketers and advertisers.

Old Brands and New Communication—Applying Learning Theories

The application of learning theories along with appropriate marketing research to find out the relevance of visuals/copy can be useful to old brands with which consumers are familiar. Some of the old brands may trigger strong brand recognition, but consumers may not have used them and hence forgotten about them (though, at some point in time they may have been familiar with them) or they may have perceived a weak link between the brand (stimulus) and the benefit of the brand (reward). Forgetting a brand is known as decay and a weakened link between the stimulus and reward is known as extinction. This can happen to a number of well-established brands over a period of time, when a number of new brands enter the category. For example, in the category of antacids, currently there are several offerings of tablets and liquid forms available in the market. Eno is a well-known brand in the context and the brand has been in the market for several decades. In an effort to reposition itself, Eno came out with an interesting campaign that repositioned the tablet and liquid variants in the category of antacids.

The TV commercial showed Eno in comparison with a tablet and a liquid (both unbranded ones) and explained how the offering is more effective than the other two variants. The sensory store may be receptive to the old brand that is familiar to consumers and consumers may recollect the advertisement (if repeated frequently) when they have a need for it from the short-term or working memory. When the consumer is exposed to such communication over a period of time, the brand name may enter the long-term memory (the process by which consumers are familiar with several brands like Lifebuoy, Titan, Cadbury or Dettol). The relief (benefit) experienced by consumers in using the offering will further strengthen the brand's association with the need and benefits of the offering.

Strengths of Brand Associations

The following are some examples of how brands have built up their associations. It should be noted that as a result of classical conditioning (in the form of associations); brands create a focused perception in consumers. To that extent, classical conditioning is linked to perception (though for conceptual purposes of comprehension, these two are treated as distinctive).

- Margo brand of soap's associations with neem (which is considered good for the skin) over several years (later was endorsed by a celebrity).
- Café Coffee Day's associations with relaxation and socializing.
- Rolex and Omega watches with the prestige of the consumer owning them.
- Nike's associations with a youthful attitude (Refer to Plate 4.2).
- Saffola's association with healthy cooking oil.
- iPhone's associations with technological trends and fashion.
- Lux soap's associations with celebrities for several decades (Refer Plate 4.3).

Plate 4.2 Strengths of Brand Association

Plate 4.3 Strengths of Brand Association

End Notes

1. Douglas Van Praet, *'Unconscious Branding: How Neuroscience Can Empower (and inspire) Marketing*', (Palgrave Macmillan, 2012), pp. 15–30.
2. Alice M. Tybout and Gregory S. Carpenter (2006), *'Creating and Managing Brands' in Kellog's on Marketing,* (Wiley India, 2006), pp. 74–101.
3. Banwari Mittal, Morris B. Holbrook, Sharon Beatty, Priya Raghubir and Arch G. Woodside, *'Consumer Behavior: How Humans Think, Feel, and Act in the Marketplace*, (2007), pp. 527–552.
4. Felicia Miller, Susan Fournier and Chris Allen, *Exploring Relationship Analogues in the Brand Space*, ed. Susan Fournier, Michael Breazeale and Marc Fetscherin, *Consumer-Brand Relationships*, (Routledge), pp. 30–56.
5. Robert J. Sternberg (1986), 'A Triangular Theory of Love', *Psychological Review 93*, pp. 58–83.
6. Kala Vijayaraghavan (2015), 'Boyce to Men', *The Economic Times*, 7 October.
7. Amit Bapna (2015), 'Can Homegrown Snacks Make Hay While the Market for Instant Noodles Flounders?', *The Economic Times*, 9 September.
8. Psyclopedia, http://www.psych-it.com.au/Psychlopedia/article.asp?id=292, accessed on 20 August, 2015.
9. Gerald Zaltman (2003), How Consumers Think: Essential Insights into the mind of the market, (HBS Press), pp. 165–86.
10. Ibid.
11. Ibid.
12. Shramana Ganguly (2015), 'Rolling Out the Social Network', *The Economic Times,* 19 August.
13. http://economictimes.indiatimes.com/industry/transportation/airlines-/-aviation/how-tata-sia-joint-venture-vistara-fared-in-first-100-days-of-operation/articleshow/47076179.cms, accessed on April 28,2015.
14. Michael Solomon, *'Consumer Behavior: Buying, Having, and Being*', (Pearson, 2015), pp. 216–218.
15. Delshad Irani (2015), "Common Man's Biscuit", *The Economic Times,* 12 August.
16. Michael Solomon, *'Consumer Behavior: Buying, Having, and Being*', (Pearson, 2015), pp. 523.
17. Ibid.
18. http://changingminds.org/explanations/memory/von_restorff.htm, accessed on 30 September, 2015.

19. Hoyer and MacInnis, *Consumer Behavior* (First Indian ed), (Houghton Mifflin, 1999), pp. 162–186.
20. Hoyer and MacInnis, *Consumer Behavior* (First Indian ed), (Houghton Mifflin, 1999), pp. 162–186.
21. Ibid.
22. Ibid.
23. Ibid.
24. Leon Schiffman and Leslie L. Kanuk (2000), '*Consumer Behavior*', (Pearson, 2000), 183.

EXERCISES

1. Analyze the influence of learning on soft drinks with the ads of leading brands. Comment on how perception aids the respective brand's positioning strategies.
2. Analyze the influence of learning on electronic wallets. How do you think classical and instrumental learning play a role in developing the brands in the category?

CHAPTER 5

The Role of Motivation and Personality Dimensions in Brand Associations

Smith and Mackie (2007) defined it by saying 'The self-concept is what we think about the self; self-esteem is the positive or negative evaluations of the self, as in how we feel about it.'[1]

Some brands make an attempt to connect with the self-concept of consumers. Rin detergent launched a campaign wherein a young girl with her mother makes a 'bold statement' about herself in spite of the negative comments that the hotel manager makes about the girl based on his perception of her 'shabby' clothes

In a subsequent campaign 'Rin' created an impressive portrayal of a young girl in a rural area where an industrialist keeps wondering about qualified personnel in the area (the brand's role in the confidence reflected by the protagonist comes through clearly in both the ads). The Rin Career Academy advertises (along with one of the ads) that it can assist young women to gain skills that will propel them towards professional success.

The self-brand connect made possible by the concept of self-esteem is likely to create a strong and favourable associations of the brand in the consumer's mind.

Motivation and personality are powerful concepts as they are closely linked to the self-concept of consumers.

Needs, motivation and personality are related concepts and it is appropriate to consider them together. Need is a state of deprivation that produces discomfort (widely quoted in literature). Motivation is the drive which impels a person to achieve his/her goals. Personality is a set of inner characteristics that enables a person to decide how he/she should consistently respond to the environment. Motivation and personality are linked—a person with a high degree of confidence may be assertive. There are a number of theories on personality. The Freudian theory assumes that the behaviour of individuals is based on unconscious needs and drives. Accordingly, human personality consists of three parts—'id', ego and super ego. 'Id' is the component that consists of impulses and primitive instincts that urge an individual to seek immediate gratification. The thoughts associated with 'id' are primitive in nature and are associated with baser instincts. A number of product categories, which may not have well-defined functional attributes and are oriented towards sensual pleasure, formulate communication which may appeal to 'id'. Perfume, cigarette, liquor and condom are some categories, which are oriented towards the usage of appeals with baser instincts. Axe and Set Wet brands seem to have adopted the 'id' route. The categories mentioned have an association with 'id' in several parts of the world where these are advertised. Liquor brands may resort to surrogate advertising (involves advertising the brand by creating another category) and use 'id'-oriented appeals to the extent permitted by a society. McDowell soda is an example.

There are two kinds of needs, primary and secondary. The primary ones are physiological needs like thirst, hunger and sex. The secondary needs are acquired, such as a sense of belongingness, status and self-esteem. Consumers may not consciously know their secondary needs and it is in this situation that the symbolism associated with brands may appeal to consumers. Louis Philippe and Park Avenue in apparel, Mercedes in automobiles and Fastrack in watches are some examples that reflect a consumer's symbolism in terms of association with prestige. Consumers, by associating themselves with these symbolic brands, are able to gratify their psychological needs. Liril soap was launched in the 70's. The Liril advertisement captured exactly the experience of indulging in a bath. The water-fall, the greenery around and the model indulging in fresh water was in synergy with the lime soap offering freshness and a refreshing experience, the green packaging of the brand and the image of lime on the advertisement (TV commercial). The example reflects how psychographics and brand proposition can be creatively combined for the brand success. Liril was very successful for several years after such a brand positioning (the focus is on the concept rather than on the performance of the brand). In 2015, after almost forty years, Liril brought back the same theme that reflected 'freshness is back'.

Self–control and Brands

In today's world, the fitness-conscious consumers are split between gratifying themselves with eating, or drinking hedonic or pleasure-based offerings and protecting their health. Coke in the US had introduced smaller packs that cost more than the regular packs in terms of price per/litre.[2] Locally, MTR, a brand well-known for making traditional snacks has, ₹10 packs across a variety of food offerings.

Multiplicity of Needs

Normally consumers have more than one need and analysing the multiplicity of those needs (with their importance) provides insights for marketers. A buyer of 'no-frills' Maruti Alto may be interested in the brand because of its low price, fuel economy and comfort, but the low price may be the pre-potent need, which will take the brand into the 'consideration set' of consumers.

Types of Goals

Goals can be positive or negative. Behaviour is directed towards a positive direction (approach) or away from a negative direction (avoid). This concept is useful when the unique selling proposition (USP) is researched. For example, do consumers want white teeth or prevention of decay from their toothpaste? The choice of the product's (in this case the toothpaste's) USP is a decision that a marketer needs to take and the concept of goals is likely to be useful in this situation. Axe's (deodorant) advertisement (TV commercial) shows the image of a pig and the communication is oriented towards the behaviour of an individual avoiding the negative direction (of smelling bad).

Extrinsic and Intrinsic Needs

Needs, from the viewpoint of application to a practical context, can be classified as extrinsic and intrinsic. Extrinsic needs are those that motivate an individual to achieve the end result. Buying a status symbol (designer watches or furniture) to impress others is associated with extrinsic needs. If an individual buys a car for his/her won comfort and enjoyment, it is associated with intrinsic needs. It is worthwhile to find out the linkages between intrinsic and extrinsic needs before a communication package is formulated for a brand. Table 5.1 explains the concept of examining the linkages between the two needs.

Table 5.1 Intrinsic and Extrinsic Needs for a Brand of Television

	Intrinsic	Extrinsic
Aesthetic appeal	Gratification on the offering (TV) and affordability	Status symbol and premium-ness
Sound quality	Sensual pleasure innovator	Appear as a state of the art output device
Brand equity (associated)	Reassurance (perceived risk)	Symbolic association
Special features	Variety-seeking tendencies about self	To encourage the word of mouth

The list of needs provided in the example is suggestive and illustrate the concept. In-depth research is required to find out the degree and importance of these needs. This is useful to select a brand's associations with the chosen USP.

SELF–CONCEPTS AND THEIR IMPLICATIONS

In almost any category of consumer products, symbolism makes use of the concept of 'self'. Self-concept is the image an individual holds of himself/herself that includes various associations about self. There are a variety of self-concepts, which are useful in marketing communication. They are:

1. *Actual self-concept*: It is the way the individual perceives himself/herself. A group of consumers may perceive themselves as rebellious non-conformists who seek individuality and freedom in their lifestyles. 'Charms' cigarette was perhaps, one of the earliest brands in India to create a brand personality using the power of self-concept. 'The Spirit of Freedom' and 'Charms is the Way You Are' were some of the style statements in the advertisement featuring young models. In order to enhance the claims of freedom the brand had endorsed its package in a unique pack featuring a denim look. This was around the time when denim was getting accepted in India for its functional and symbolic appeals. The lifestyle type of advertising and the symbolism of denim association was normally related to the West with casualness and freedom and this made the brand an inherent part of the youth culture during its time. The brand used the actual self-concept and/or the others concept of a person.
2. *Ideal self-concept*: It is concerned with how an individual would like to ideally perceive himself/herself. The individual perceives the ideal image of the self, based on aspirational needs and this depends on the individual's financial and educational status, upbringing, exposure and personality traits. An upcoming businessman who is driven by aspirations may buy the Tag Heuer brand of watch that may be associated with globetrotters, certain exclusivity and even an up-market sport. There may be a variant of this self-concept in the form of 'others ideal self-concept' (how others should ideally perceive an individual). The individual may use the status symbol to impress others (others ideal self-concept) but may resist from doing so if it is a situation in which he/she feels others do not matter (personal discretionary time, leisure, etc., with regard to professional work). Marketers can use such psychographic information with lifestyles (how individuals spend their time) to come out with appropriate appeals for products and services (vacation and weekend cars are such examples of categories where the kind of orientation is likely to be useful). Consumers who are relatively low on their self-esteem are likely to depend more on prestige brands to boost their confidence. A consumer who has affordability and has a low self-esteem is likely to buy a car like Mercedes to perceive that his self-esteem among others has risen. The demand for high-end mobile phones like iPhone may be partly driven by this aspect.

Inner–Directedness and Other–Directedness

There may be broadly two kinds of consumers, inner-directed and other directed. Inner-directed consumers lookup to 'themselves' for following a specific lifestyle, formation of attitudes towards product categories and brands and in general, for purchase decisions. Other-directed consumers are influenced by their peers, neighbours and aspirational groups with whom they interact on a regular basis. Sprite, the soft drink that positioned itself as a 'non-pseudo' drink, is targeted at inner-directed consumers. Other-directed brands are those that strongly emphasize the group and symbolize others self-concept orientation. i10 from Santro that connects with the young target segment, the old advertisement of Onida

("Neighbour's envy : owner's pride") and the status factor associated with the various mobile phone brands, as reflected in the advertisements, are such examples. Socially conspicuous categories like cars, two wheelers, mobiles and apparels are likely to use other directed appeals. But if the target segment is otherwise inner directed appeals and are also useful (Allen Solly's unique proposition that emphasizes individuality, and hence, the inner directedness).

Psychographics and Choice of Cars

The Sub-4m Sedan (mini sedan) is a compact car that had appealed to the value conscious Indian consumer with its utility with respect to space and the feeling of owning a prestigious sedan. Dzire, Amaze and Zest are the brands in this segment and the offering that is unique to India had also attracted Volkswagen and General Motors.[3] The psychographic profile of the mini-sedan buyer is different from that of the hatchback buyer (most car brands in the mini-sedan segment also offer hatchbacks). The former is conservative, family oriented and traditional while the latter wishes to experiment and dabble around with choices.[4] This reflects the importance of psychographics associated with the personality of the buyer in an emerging market, even when brands develop offerings that are unique to India.

Personality Traits and their Applications

Traits are enduring and distinguishing. They are helpful to marketers in a variety of ways.

Consumer Innovativeness

This aspect of personality may be useful for both FMCG products and durables. It enables the marketers to identify and target consumers who are receptive to new-product categories. A number of new-product categories are getting introduced and these benefits from identifying the innovators. Mobile phones, electronic toys, plasma TV's, Worldspace music systems, special types of watches like 'Ecodrive' from Citizen and electric cars are some categories which may benefit from the identification of innovator profile. Innovators also form a good base of consumers who spread the word about the category or brand by talking about it. There is a need to ensure that innovators are not only satisfied with the product but also with the service that is packaged with the product. It may be worthwhile for marketers to find out if these consumers perceive the benefits offered by the new product categories. For example, products like three-in-ones (transistor, tape-recorder and record player) introduced in the late 60's and early 70's did not catch up even though a few innovators bought this product. With small differentiation in the cola market, a brand may come out with a cola fortified with vitamins and one of the success factors will depend on the 'buzz' generated by innovators. The smart watch category with several well-known brands is likely to initially appeal to such consumers who consider themselves as innovators.

Ethnocentrism

Ethnocentrism is the tendency of a consumer to prefer products 'made in my country' instead of using a foreign product. 'Ruf and Tuf', jeans is a good case of a brand attempting ethnocentrism. Consumers have been used to a number of foreign jean brands. Arvind Mills, which launched 'Ruf and Tuf', found that the aspirational levels of consumer groups in semi-urban areas were high but they could afford to buy only cheap clones/duplicates of well-known brands. There was a need for a good quality brand at affordable prices. 'Ruf and Tuf' was launched with a celebrity endorsing it and the brand followed this up with a campaign that emphasized its ethnicity. The campaign was effective in ending the perception that only foreign brands had quality in the category of jeans. The brand was priced with penetration pricing, tailors were trained and roped in to tailor the jeans (as against readymade jeans) and the product itself was presented in a unique manner (the fabric plus other accessories were given as a set). This is an old example but effectively illustrates the usage of the concept even in a category that is strongly associated with an American origin.

Optimum Stimulation Level

The intensity of physical or mental or sensory activity an individual experiences is referred to as the stimulation level. Due to the differences in personality and lifestyles, individuals vary in the stimulation levels they experience. Individuals with a high level of stimulation are likely to find ways to reduce stimulation levels and individuals with a low level of stimulation are likely to attempt to increase their levels of stimulation. The marketing implication is explained through the example of vacation packages that range from high adventure to the ones offering tranquillity and peace.

Another application of stimulation levels can be associated with the management of product-lines in FMCG categories like biscuits, chocolates, toothpastes and even cigarettes. One of the objectives of launching variants of brands (in the form of flavours and tastes) is to ensure that consumers do not change their brand. It may be worthwhile for a brand to find out through research if loyal consumers need variety to gratify their stimulation levels. Revenue from variants is carefully managed for product-line profits and the stimulation levels of consumers are worthwhile to be considered. The concept can be further explored with a trial of variants in consumables to check if it answers the question 'Do consumers who are highly stimulated try out more of its variants in a specific product category?'

Dogmatism

This refers to a trait that is responsible for the individual's resistance to information which is not in tune with his/her beliefs. Consumers who are not very dogmatic are likely to be more open to marketing communication than those who are dogmatic. Exploring the cognitive attitudes in the target segment is useful to marketers, especially before they formulate broad communication. For instance, among the target segment for water purifiers there may be some who strongly believe the process of purification is likely to be hazardous to health. This kind of belief has to be carefully dealt with, using a combination of promotional methods like advertisements, personal selling and perhaps, demonstration with sophisticated methods and research data. Permission marketing, which involves creating an involvement of the consumer (by obtaining his consent towards receiving information about the company's offering) is likely to be effective in providing a foundation for communication and reducing the dogmatism. From among the target segment for the water filters, it may be useful to gather data on how many are interested in obtaining the information on the brand, which also includes the kind of information addressing wrong beliefs. If the brand is able to communicate effectively to the selected cross-section of consumers, there are chances that the word of mouth will take over and the positive effects of such word of mouth will be associated with the brand. This approach is likely to be more effective than a high-visibility campaign that directly attacks the dogmatic beliefs of consumers. Advertisements may become counter-productive if they generate counter-arguments in the mind-set of dogmatic consumers. Consumers may feel that the brand is attempting to force itself through an advertising blitzkrieg.

Figure 5.1 reflects the different stages involved in addressing dogmatism among prospective consumers. Apart from research results, other kinds of 'credibility' models like doctors and scientists who are noted for their eminence can be used, to address the dogmatic consumer.

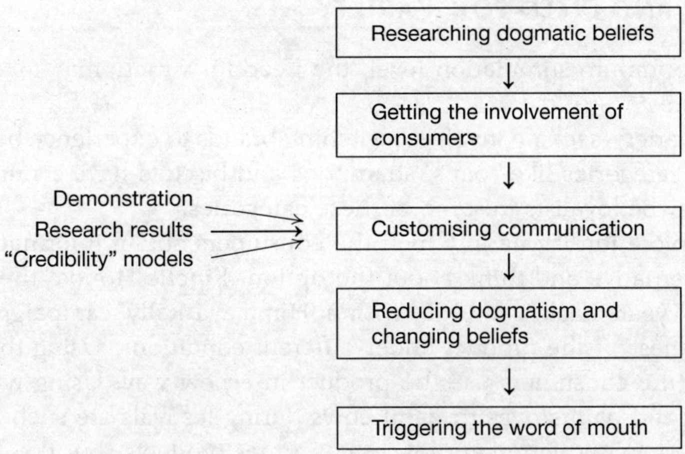

Figure 5.1 Dealing with Dogmatism

Importance of Cognition

This refers to the consumer's orientation towards the marketing communication associated with brands/categories. Consumers who have a high need for cognition are likely to respond favourably to marketing communication that is high on product-related information. These consumers may not be as responsive to peripheral cues of marketing communication like a jingle or model in a TV advertisement. Researching consumers' need for cognition will be useful for marketers as the insights gained will help formulate communication strategies. This aspect of the consumer's personality will be useful for consumer durables. Given the type and variety of target segments in a number of categories of durables, a marketer may have to decide on specific strategies for each segment. For example, in the category of washing machines, the semi-automatic one is likely to attract a target segment that is not interested in the upper-end 'fuzzy logic' of washing machines. Research information can give insights on the need for cognition across these segments. If the company finds that a particular segment is not interested in certain product-related information, a different kind of appeal can be used in advertisements. This can be backed up by customer-friendly information provided at retail outlets. Advertising campaigns in both television and automobile categories have compared different brands. A brand may also propagate a major end-benefit (without much product-related information) as it will attract prospective consumers who may not have a high degree of cognition.

Saffola's Heart Foundation initiative coupled with their proposition of 'healthy heart' which is a good example of cognitive aspect. Kent water purifier had carried several ads that provide a great deal of information about the brand and its features.

Personality and Need for Variety

With regard to optimum stimulation level, the need for variety may take different forms among consumers.

Exploratory variety-seeking involves switching brands to experience better alternatives. FMCG product categories like soaps, shampoos and biscuits have a number of variants, though there may be loyalists in some of these categories.

Vicarious exploration is one in which the consumers obtain information about a new and different alternative and think about the option. Kinetic Honda, the gearless scooter launched several years back, came out with a 'Himalaya Rally' campaign, which emphasized the ruggedness of the product under different conditions. Using the innovativeness is one in which the consumers use the product in a new way. Using washing machines for making lassi and paints/dyes to paint cows during festivals are such examples. Using the innovativeness is not very common in consumer products (but the Indian context is unique, as indicated by the examples).

Interpersonal Influence

This deals with the responsiveness of consumers when they are subjected to other interpersonal influences. There are three types of interpersonal influences used by marketers.

1. Information influence is the tendency of a consumer to accept information from others about reality. This aspect may be useful to decide on the 'word-of-mouth'

strategies. In the category of durables, demonstration at retail outlets may spread the product benefits among the target segment through consumers attending such demonstrations. A consumer enquiring about washing machine brands on his Facebook groups is an example.

2. Value-expressive function is the tendency of consumers to enhance their standing with others by attempting to be similar to those with whom they compare themselves. Reference group appeals in several categories as examples. This involves expression of a specific value. Fastrack watches and Rolex watches symbolize certain values associated with the respective target segment.
3. Utilitarian influence is the tendency of consumers to conform to the wishes of others in order to obtain rewards (or avoid punishment). This aspect may be indirectly reflected by the behaviour of some consumers. The peer pressure to buy a brand of car within a price range is an example of such behaviour.

Self–Image and Possessions

There is a strong link between the consumer and his/her possessions, the product categories and brands he/she buys. It is a part of the consumer's 'self-defining' process and the consumer is likely to select a brand which is in congruence with his/her personality. Consumers are likely to acquire products which enhance their self-image. These possessions may be bought for functional or symbolic purposes (status) or both. There are 'self-altering' products, which consumers seek whenever it is appropriate. A young executive who is about to begin his career in the corporate world may choose Van Heusen if he believes that the brand is likely to enhance his self-image (Refer to Plate 5.1). A middle-level manager promoted to a senior position may acquire a specific brand of mobile phone if he believes that it draws 'respect', apart from serving functional purposes. Cosmetics, apparel, watches, cars and jewellery are such categories in which the consumers seek to modify or alter their self-image. Consumers may alter their self-image out of physical vanity (inflated view of one's physical appearance) or achievement vanity (excessive concern about one's achievements). As materialism increases, consumers get increasingly concerned with enhancing their self-image.

Fixated buying behaviour is concerned with the addiction of consumers to buy products to display them and they share the tendency with consumers who have similar interests. Unlike shopaholics who are addicted to shopping indiscriminately, the fixated behaviour is normally associated with specific categories of products like watches, electronics, gramophone records, cigarette lighters and automobiles. There are advertisements in several newspapers inviting sellers to sell old watches and this aspect is a reflection of the fixated behaviour of consumers who may be watch collectors. Fixated consumers have a deep interest in particular product categories and are willing to indulge in extensive search (efforts and money) by 'going after' the products.

Brand Personality—Lessons from Indian Brands of the Previous Decades

In the category of soaps, Hamam, Cinthol and Liril have been in the market for a number of years. Hamam has limited variants. Liril tried a few but Cinthol has had the maximum number of variants. Liril has a very strong brand personality developed over almost three decades. 'Refreshing', 'enjoyable', 'indulgent' and 'fragrant' are the characteristics of Liril. Hamam has been a family soap and it was positioned (at some point in time) as an 'honest and clean' soap without harmful chemicals. Lux, for many decades has been using celebrities and is associated with skin-friendliness and glamour. Aramusk was a macho soap launched for men during the 80's. The brand had immense potential to strengthen its personality, being the pioneer in creating a macho soap. Developing a personality in this category is extremely important for a long-term association with the brand. Lifebuoy with its 'germ-killing' personality is an example.

In the category of scooters, LML Vespa created a personality around itself when the scooters category was dominated by Bajaj. LML projected its personality as 'suave, sophisticated and standing apart from the crowd'. Yamaha was strongly identified with 'youthfulness and adventure' during the late 80's. In the recent times, the brand attempted an association with a celebrity popular among the youth. Hero Honda redefined the market with its path-breaking 100 cc economy bike and went on to create Hero Honda Splendor and Passion. The latter was advertised as a classy, lifestyle product. Rajdoot was another bike brand with a very strong 'personality orientation'. It was perceived as a 'rugged and tough' bike and was even endorsed by a film celebrity who had a similar image. The brand was popular in the rural markets and even in today's context such a brand can be revived through the creative use of imagery linking the contemporary aspects with the personality associations of the past.

Caliber, the four-stroke bike from Bajaj, developed its personality differentiator from other 'macho' associations that were popular with motorcycle brands. The imagery and the storyline of the TV commercial reinforced the idea of self-esteem through perseverance, fortitude and spirited approach under adverse circumstances. While it is true that the functional aspects of a durable brand in any category need to be competitive, the emotional associations through brand personality add to the appeal of the brand (as in the case of LML Vespa or Caliber). Zodiac, the readymade brand of apparel, was probably the earliest of brands to create a personality in this segment with its iconic model symbolizing formal, elegant and professional look. Allen Solly, with its semi-formal (or semi-casual) approach of Friday dressing may have appealed to 'non-conforming and casual' executives in software companies and advertising agencies. Raymond, after hammering down its USP of being a 'guide to a well-dressed male' during the 80's, created 'the complete man' during the 90's. In the women's wear, there were two brands—Vimal and Garden—which successfully attempted a different brand personality orientation during the 80's. Vimal was portrayed as 'lively, other-directed and full of verve' and the Garden was oriented towards 'proud, aloof and distinctively classy' self-image. Siyaram (suitings) attempted the ethnic route to create a personality association—'young, modern and highly educated with a strong orientation towards the country'. A certain degree of ethnocentrism was also involved in the approach. Double Bull and Charagh Din, the readymade brands marketed in Mumbai held significant appeal for a niche up-market segment. Consumers may have perceived the brands to be 'elegant and exclusive'. Though both the brands advertised in a few up-market media vehicles, the limited availability of the brands also added to the 'exclusive' image. As a number of personality dimensions have been explored and used in the fabric/readymade category, it would be a challenge for new brands entering the category to cultivate a distinctive personality.

Brand Life cycle and Brand Personality

The concept of brand life cycle provides a framework for marketers to manage the meaning of the brand and hence, its personality. The framework also provides scope for marketers to get into product categories that are within the 'image domain' of the brand's meaning and personality. The following are the advantages of the brand life cycle:[5]

1. The firm can plan the brand's personality.
2. During the follow-up stage, the brand imagery and variants of the brand can be managed in such a way that it is well within the image/personality selected by the brand.
3. The meaning selected by the brand can be nurtured in a predictable and enduring manner, enabling consumers to consistently identify themselves with the brand.

There are three stages in the brand lifecycle introduction, elaboration and fortification. The brand selects either a functional need (consumption related) which is external to the consumer or a symbolic one (internally-generated) which is oriented towards self-concepts, group identification, status orientation or a hedonic (sensory) meaning (pleasure-oriented). These needs may be reflected in the consumption or gratification involved in the variety experienced by the consumer in the form of product variants.

Figure 5.2 outlines the three stages involved in the brand life cycle. In the introduction stage, the brand gets associated with a specific meaning. For example, if Colgate has selected the functional benefit of decay prevention in toothpastes, it should introduce variants that reinforce the functional (problem-solving) orientation of the brand. In the Indian urban context, if it is assumed that the category of toothpastes has entered the elaboration stage, then Colgate is currently following the functional approach after establishing itself on the functional platform for a number of years. It has Colgate Herbal, Colgate Total, Colgate Gel and Colgate Sensitive Care. All the variants, including the gel version (if associated with whitening action), reinforce Colgate as a brand which is oriented towards solving dental problems and reinforcing the benefits associated with oral care (Refer to Plate 5.2). Though the brand is built on a functional platform, it is possible to develop a personality for the brand using appropriate imagery. As per the brand life cycle, Colgate may perhaps enter the mouthwash category in the fortification stage and use the personality cultivated over a period of time.

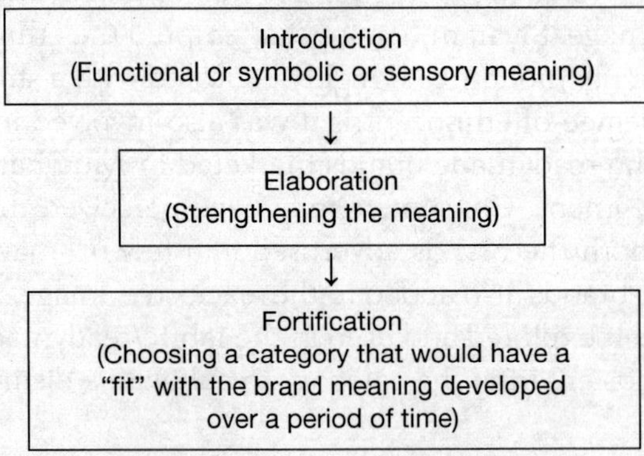

Figure 5.2 Brand Life Cycle

Among watches, Fastrack from Titan selected the symbolic meaning for its brand. 'Young', 'vibrant' and 'casual' may be the characteristics that are associated with the brand. If it is assumed that the brand is in the introductory stage of its life cycle, then the brand has the potential to intensify its personality by offering upper-end 'aspirational' watches to nurture the symbolic appeal when it enters the elaboration stage of the cycle. The category, for example (given the personality of the brand), may be a readymade apparel. Fastrack is already into the category of goggles and soft luggage. If a brand of perfume has taken a hedonic or pleasure-seeking meaning during the introductory phase of the brand life cycle, it can offer a set of variants (different fragrances) and emphasize its hedonism to

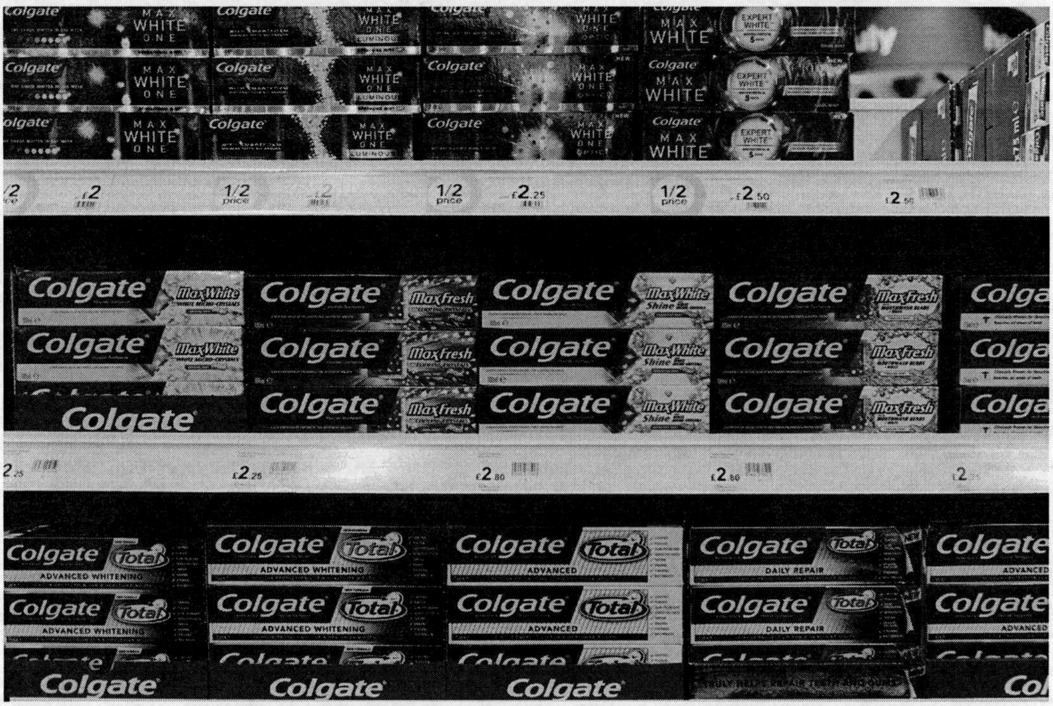

Plate 5.2 Colgate and its variants

strengthen its original meaning. The brand can choose to make use of the hedonic meaning and extend the brand name to the category of soap gels emphasizing the 'hedonic properties' of the brand.

Box 5.1 The Impact of Personality[6]

A researcher asked a set of consumers to watch the commercials of three beer brands. One brand was targeted towards the drinker who perceived himself as a failure; the second was targeted towards a social drinker and the third towards the reparative drinker—a middle-aged man who perceived himself as someone who would have achieved more in life but only because he has sacrificed a lot. The 250 consumers chosen for the study had watched and tasted the beer brands. After being given sufficient time to see each commercial and taste each brand, the respondents were asked to state their preferred brand and complete a questionnaire which measured their 'drinker personality'. The result showed that for most consumers, the preferred brand matched with their own 'drinker personality'. In fact, the impact of the brand personality was so much that many consumers thought that at least one beer brand was not fit enough to drink. The fact was that the kind of beer in all the brands was the same.

Touch of Reality

Brand Personality and Self-concepts

There are several personality traits that can be measured. Achievement, endurance, affiliation and aggression are some examples of personality traits. According to Banwari Mittal, Moris, Sharon Priya and Arch, self-concept is the 'sum total of all the thoughts and ideas the person who conjures up when he/she thinks of himself/herself.' The linkages between self-concept and brand personality can be understood from the definition. A brand of motorcycle like Rajdoot may position itself as a 'rugged, exciting and aggressive' bike while a brand closer to the urban youth segment may position itself as a 'youthful, romantic and contemporary' bike. Several combinations of positioning statements are possible if primary research investigation on the psychographics of the target segment is considered. The psychographics are associated with activities, interests and opinions. The target segment's psychographics may be reflected in a variety of ways. They may also perceive the brands they buy in accordance with the positioning of the respective brands. A buyer of Fastrack watches may perceive the brand to reflect certain psychographic characteristics. While exploring self-concepts, marketers should use scales that indicate bi-polar dimensions. Rugged to delicate, rational to emotional, conformist to non-conformist and conservative to liberal are some examples.

End Notes

1. E. R. Smith and D.M. Mackie, *Social Psychology*, (Hove: Psychology Press, 2007).
2. "Coke's Big Bet on Smaller Packages Paying off in US (2015)," *The Economic Times*, August 5.
3. Lijee Philip and Ketan Thankker (2015), "Street cars names (not just) Dzire," *The Economic Times*, September 2.
4. Ibid.
5. C. Whan Park, Bernard J. Jaworski, and Deborah H. MacInnis, "Strategic Brand Concept-Image Management," *Journal of Marketing, 50* (1986): 135–145.
6. Hawkins, R. Best, and K. Coney, *Consumer Behavior*, (McGraw Hill, 1989).

Exercises

1. Choose the online jewellery category with three brands. Visit the website and apply how the target segment matches with the personality profile of the respective brand's target segment (that you think is applicable).
2. Use Personality traits and values to analyze the category fairness creams for men and women. After considering the major brands in this category. What is the difference you observe between men and women in terms of personality projection in the ads?

CHAPTER 6

Attitudes and Their Impact on Branding Strategies

- Is there a concept that can be used to gauge and evaluate the overall receptivity of consumers towards a product category or a specific brand (old or new)?
- How should a brand that wants to create a favourable impression on the mind-set of consumers approach its marketing mix elements? How can a brand pioneering a product category ensure that consumers develop a positive attitude towards the brand?
- Would the brands following a pioneering brand in a new category be in a more advantageous position from the marketing perspective?
- How is cultural value tied to the consumer mind-set?

Involvement and Digitalization

Involvement is the degree of personal relevance or interest that an individual associates with any object or brand or stimuli. This is an old concept that is central to the formation of attitude. Myntra, an online fashion portal that can be accessed also through mobile apps has a focus on personalization that creates better involvement (Refer to Plate 6.1). This makes the consumers spend more time when they are online.[1] Myntra's online fashion portal, for some time was only available on its mobile app. Though the company may have reintroduced its desktop version, the move of the company reflects a trend towards personalization on the go. Further the e-tailer (with Flipkart) also introduced the Big Billion Day during the festive season targeting 50 million consumers in about 70 types of categories.[2] The company had also sent half a million post cards to consumers in smaller towns. These initiatives are likely to impact attitude creation towards the brand.

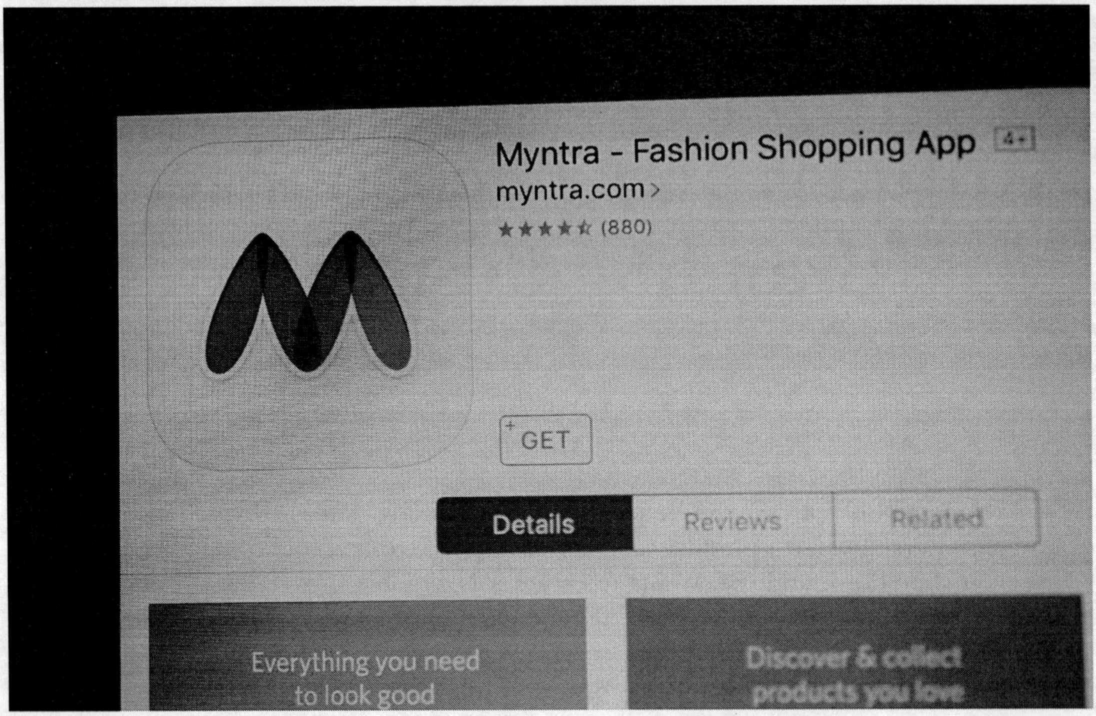

Plate 6.1 Involvement and Digitalization: Myntra

The concept of attitude will enable marketers to get several interesting and useful insights about consumers because the concept deals with both the internal aspects of the consumer mind-set and the intention to buy products and brands.

Attitudes serve as quick 'reference points' to consumer behaviour. In the case of a new-concept product, consumers develop an attitude towards the product category. When they accept the product category, they develop an attitude towards specific brands, which can be measured by appropriate marketing research techniques. There is a strong link between beliefs, attitudes and values of consumers.

Linkages in Attitude Formation

Attitude can be defined as a mental predisposition[6]—favorable or unfavourable, positive or negative towards a person, concept, product, brand, service or an idea. Beliefs are mental statements that may be concerned with any facet of life, religion, nation, product or brand. Values are an individual's convictions about his/her mode of living in a specific cultural setting. Values point out to the individual on how he/she should set and accomplish his/her own goals in life. Buying products and services is one of the major activities of

Attitudes and Revitalization of Successful Brands

Revitalization of brands is associated with adapting to the changing environment and involves a change in the perceptual field of consumers (keeping the earlier strengths of the brand intact in terms of its associations). Such strategies enable the well-known brands to sustain the positive attitudes they have been able to create through its success. Communication and associations with events or persons play an important role in brand revitalization. Allen Solly had initiated associations involving the youth and sports to signal that it is a youthful brand. It had acquired license to market a line of apparel inspired by Wimbledon.[3] Louis Phillipe had connected with Tedx golf and a TV series on Vijay Amritraj, the tennis star. All these associations symbolize success and hence reinforce the brand's associations with positive outcomes.[4]

Dabur Amla had conducted beauty contests at the village level to focus on women to convey the benefits of the brand.[5] Such revitalization strategies continue to provide a strong cognitive as well affective association to brands that have already created powerful propositions.

an individual's life and hence his/her beliefs, attitudes and values are important from the marketer's viewpoint. Values shape attitudes and beliefs and it differs from beliefs[7] and is explained in the below diagram as follows.

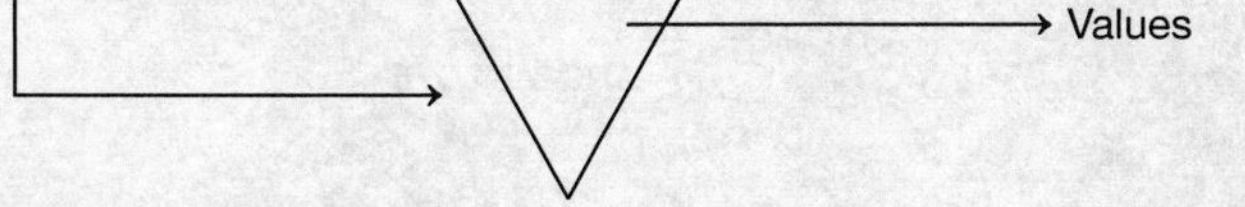

Figure 6.1 Linkages between Values, Attitudes and Beliefs

(a) They are few in number.
(b) They are enduring and difficult to influence.
(c) They orient the individual towards behaviour which is acceptable in his/her culture.
(d) They are not tied to specific situations.
(e) They are accepted by members of a society.[8]

The linkages are shown in Figure 6.1.

Marketing Implications

A belief is what an individual thinks about the several aspects of his/her life. In the marketing context, an individual may believe (for instance) that Godrej is marketing a number of product categories. An attitude has several components, which are an outcome of interrelated beliefs. The attitude of the individual towards Godrej will consist of (i) additional beliefs which are attributes and positive aspects of the company's products and its service, (ii) his/her behavioural response towards Godrej and (iii) specific feelings towards Godrej. (Feelings have an emotional component and can get developed because of a variety of reasons) In this situation, a value that may influence the individual's attitude towards Godrej may be a strong preference towards environment-friendly, green products. If he/she believes the company is environment-friendly with regard to its products and has a strong preference for such products, it is likely to have a positive impact on his/her attitude towards the brand. All beliefs need not necessarily become attitudes, –inter-related beliefs build attitudes. An individual will have a large number of beliefs, fewer attitudes and even fewer values. Soulflower is a cosmetic brand that is creating an attitude towards vegan-based offerings in India (Refer Plate 6.2).

Marketers normally attempt to reinforce existing favourable attitudes or create some when a new product category is introduced. Changing an unfavourable attitude is a difficult

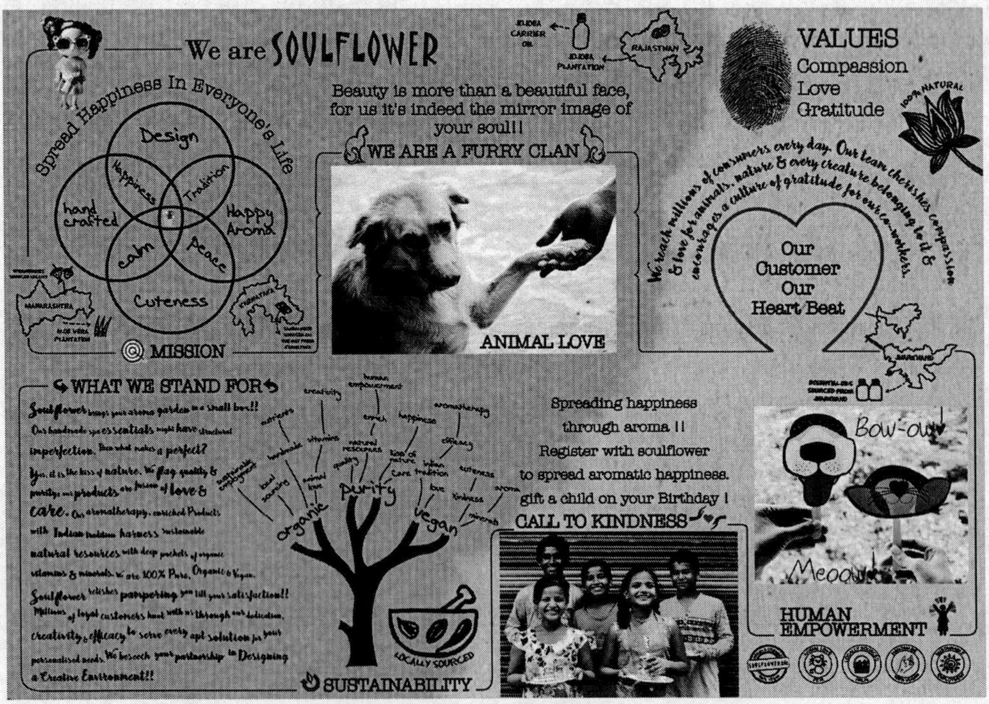

Plate 6.2 Soulflower is a cosmetic brand that is creating an attitude towards vegan-based offerings in India

task. Hence, marketers must be careful in the initial stages of brand communication to ensure that unfavourable attitudes are not created. They must also consider the 'value' aspect in a specific environment for example, in certain product categories like cigarettes for women, pubs for the youth and products that are not tested on animals. There are two aspects with regard to the association of values in a marketing context.

1. Marketers may have to wait and offer their products in a way that they don't have a negative impact on the values of consumers in a given context.
2. Marketers can monitor the centrality of a specific value in brands among the target segment. Centrality is the relationship between attitude and a value.[9] Stronger the relationship between the attitude and value, the more difficult it is for the marketer to break it. Consumers may differ in their centrality and so it is important for marketers to probe these aspects. If an apparel manufacturer is attempting to introduce a Western dress (which needs to be considered in the backdrop of values in a specific marketing context), there should be adequate consumers with low centrality. This will ensure that consumers will, at least, make a trial purchase. If the brand of apparel is launched for a segment with a high degree of centrality, the attitude towards the brand (even if it is new) will be unfavourable because consumers associate their values strongly with their clothing attitudes.

Even in a permissive/progressive city like Bangalore the number of women who smoke is insignificant as compared to men smokers. Cultural factors—especially taboo associated with women smoking cigarettes—inhibit them from smoking. Such categories that are culturally sensitive can be labelled as *neo-mindset* products. Marketers need to carefully research the values of consumers before launching such culturally sensitive products in the marketplace.

Multi–components in Attitudes

There are three components in attitudes, namely cognitive, affective and conative components. Cognitive aspects are linked to the beliefs and knowledge about a brand's features/benefits. A consumer can have a number of beliefs about a brand like Tropicana (the juice brand in the soft drink market). He/she can think of it as a global brand; that the brand uses the best fruit ingredients available in the market and the fruit contents in the brand are healthy as compared to the aerated soft drinks. Parents may believe that the brand of juice is useful to provide nutrition to children, who otherwise are poor eaters. A marketer needs to research the beliefs before planning a communication campaign. Affective aspects deal with how good or bad the consumer feels about a brand. This good or bad feeling has an emotional part associated with the brand. This is one of the reasons why brands use celebrities for brand endorsement. Some brands prefer to highlight the celebrity or the entertainment content rather than the features/benefits of the brand. Such brands employ the peripheral route to create attitudes (as against the central route that uses features/benefits of the brand). The emotional aspect of the attitude (affective) is important as it projects the 'overall' attitude of the consumer towards it.

A charismatic celebrity—especially in fast moving consumer product categories like soaps and chocolates—can have a strong impact on the affective component of the consumer's attitude. Such an inducement backed up by a good product creates brand loyalty. Conative aspect is the part of the attitude that motivates the buyer to buy the brand (action phase of attitude). In durable categories, the retail store ambience and attention provided to consumers play a vital role in transferring the positive aspects of cognitive and affective components into final purchase at the point of consumption. Brands that have already made a positive impact through cognitive and affective components on consumers are generally very successful when they run sales promotional campaigns. Several outlets in modern retailing have offers from established brands. The brands need to be careful about such promotions because the constant advertising of brands for sales promotion may have a negative impact on the mind-set of consumers.

Creating Likeability through the Digital Route

Paper Boat, Urban Ladder and Lifestyle are some of the brands that use Instagram to connect with the young consumer segment. Paper Boat initiated a campaign based on a social cause (Refer to Plate 6.3) and Lifestyle had a campaign called "InstaStyle" around its summer collection.[10]

Creating likeability is a part of the affect aspect of attitude. Instagram with its visual imagery is one of the digital routes to connect emotionally with brands.

Plate 6.3 Paper Boat initiated a campaign based on a social cause

How are Attitudes Formed

Learning and associated theories contribute significantly to the formation of attitudes. Positive reinforcement (satisfaction from a brand trial) and repetitive usage of the brand can lead to a favourable attitude formation. The assumption underlying family branding (using the same brand for a host of products) is that consumers generalise their learning with regard to a brand and extend it favourably to many other products for example Apple or Raga watches. The management of brand meaning over the brand life-cycle is of major interest to marketers. Celebrity endorsements (Lux, Head & Shoulders and Pleasure are such examples) are attempts to extend the positive attitude of consumers towards the respective brand. Both classical and instrumental conditioning contributes to attitude formation.

Cognitive learning which is oriented towards problem-solving can result in positive attitudes. Marketers should find out the receptivity of the target segment before they position the brands oriented towards problem-solving. Consumers are likely to assess the information about a brand during the process of forming an attitude towards it. They may not always process brand-related information, except in the case of high involvement purchases. It is also possible that consumers cannot take on too much information about a brand, particularly when there is already a clutter of information. Research provides useful information on how well the consumers are prepared to receive information. There is no point including a whole lot of features of a brand (especially in technical jargon) in the advertisement of a brand as they may not add points to consumer satisfaction. Marketers, therefore, have to carefully formulate their communication even if the benefits are strongly positioned.

Role of Beliefs in Attitude Formation

Beliefs are descriptive mental statements that a consumer may carry with regard to any domain-product, brand or even individuals. They play an important role in the formation of attitudes, and marketers have to be sensitive to the existing beliefs of consumers. This assumes significance, especially when the new-concept products are introduced. Beliefs form cognitions associated with attitudes. Stronger the beliefs about the brand, stronger is the likelihood of the consumer forming an attitude about a brand (marketers may have to correct the beliefs; for instance, Cadbury chocolates had to correct certain negative beliefs when the product was involved in a controversy involving worms. Hence, a celebrity was used to revitalize the brand's purpose).

When Zero B (water filter) was introduced, the initial communication attacked the existing beliefs about boiling water for drinking purposes. The campaign was later changed to 'Safe, Safer, Safest' emphasizing the use of Zero B as the safest of all other options.[11] When Kellogg's came to India and launched its cornflakes, consumers took it with hot milk (as drinking hot milk is a part of the eating/drinking culture of consumers in India). A brand that launches a new type of food needs to consider the beliefs of consumers towards their (traditional) breakfast habits. The habit of eating is part of a given culture and it is one of the most difficult habits to change. Given the cultural diversity of

India, consumers in different parts of the country would have different kinds of beliefs towards breakfast. Tang, the orange juice was initially positioned as a breakfast juice in India. Having the juice as a part of breakfast is not a cultural habit among Indians. Kellogg's, in recent times, has been positioning its products intended for children (as seen from the visuals of the advertisement). Chocos from the same brand, too, was positioned as a nutritious food for children and one of the advertisements highlighted the ₹ 10 package (enhancing the 'intention to buy' aspect of the attitudinal component).

Maggi is probably an unusual example in the food category that was a success in the 80's. The brand used the convenience plank made famous by the 'two-minute noodle' advertising copy. Such a positioning would have appealed to a number of urban, nuclear families. Such a brand also has the possibility of developing a snack for teenagers with the distinctive possibility of these consumers being familiar with the brand in their formative years. (Maggi as a brand may have had problems with regard to safety issues before being banned but the example is provided to highlight the conceptual aspect.)

Role of Beliefs in a Specific Context in the Environment

Beliefs associated with a brand are important inputs for the formation of attitudes. In 2015, Maggi noodles were taken off the shelves due to problems with regard to its safety. Yippee noodles from ITC made use of the opportunity to create an ad campaign that vouched for the scientific and hygienic processing of the brand. This is an interesting strategy to strengthen the attitude towards a brand when a well-entrenched competitive brand is facing problems due to credibility and trust-related issues.

Types of Influence on Attitude Formation

Marketers attempt trials for a brand with the idea of creating a favourable attitude towards it. Braun, a brand of shaving systems for women, attempted this approach in durables. Creams from the personal care category specify a time period for the consumer to note observable results. This kind of direct experience would have a substantial impact on attitude formation among consumers.

The opinion of family and friends can have an influence, particularly on the purchase of durables. Such opinions may lead to formation of attitudes towards specific brands. A consumer who wants to buy a TV, car or washing machine is likely to seek such information before deciding on a particular brand decision. The opinion he/she receives will have an impact on attitude formation. The presence of Internet has added another dimension to the word of mouth. There are several sites which badmouth brands and consumers vent their frustration through these websites when the brand they buy does not conform to their expectations. On the up side, a brand can have ardent followers who form communities, which forge and strengthen relationships among its users.

The mass media can also shape the attitude of consumers towards product categories and brands. Ideas, opinions and advertisements have an influence on them.

Direct marketing, which is capable of customizing messages to niche consumers, can create favourable attitudes among them such as an approach to addresses their specific needs. Certain product categories may be more amenable to direct marketing than others. Books, music and services (banking and travel) are categories where the interactive nature of direct marketing can enhance consumer attitudes. They can create a high degree of involvement towards the offerings. These categories offer tremendous scope to satisfy consumers during the pre-sale phase of selling which in turn enhanced attitudes.

Research has established that individuals who have a high need for cognition (who enjoy information processing) are likely to form a positive attitude towards advertisements with full of product information. But marketers must use this method with caution. Advertisements for televisions or cars are brimming with product-related information. A brand following this approach should ensure that the copy of the advertisement conveys the information in such a way that consumers are able to comprehend it.

New concept brands, for instance, the electric car like Reva would find that this approach can be used effectively with direct marketing. The brand can identify a small niche of consumers who are interested in trying out new-concept products and apply the approach choosing the appropriate channels of communication.

Attitude towards Product Categories/Brands

Though a number of articles deal with attitudes towards brands, marketers are not interested only in brands. They are also interested in product categories, especially when new product categories come into a market. Brands can diffuse in a specific market only when awareness about a new product category is created and a favourable attitude is built up towards these categories. Figure 6.2 indicates the manner in which attitudes develop towards brands or product categories.

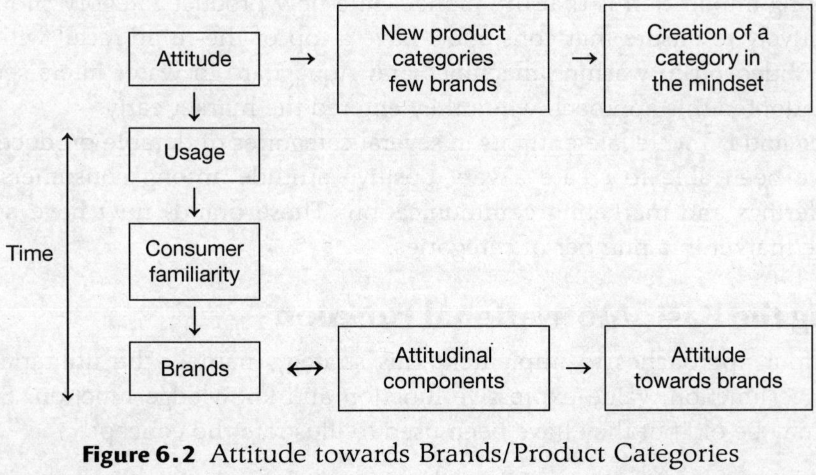

Figure 6.2 Attitude towards Brands/Product Categories

Brands and the Combined Effect of Cognition and Affect

Fair & Lovely has been a part of the personal grooming market for the last several decades and continues to be a dominant brand. Fairness as a benefit is cognitive in nature. The aspirational and self-esteem aspects are reflected in many of its commercials. This is the affect part as it is associated with the 'feel factor'. In recent years the brand mentions its international superiority over other creams that cost more than double its price. Another advertisement mentions that the brand is on par with skin treatments provided by various salons at quite a high price (cognitive).

The ads of the brand reflect the impact of the joint effects of cognition and the affect on sustaining a brand without losing its focus on its basic proposition of fairness to enhance one's self-esteem.

When a new product category is introduced, the market does not usually have too many brands. Washing machines, vacuum cleaners and water filters are a few examples in the Indian context. Consumers form an attitude towards the category, as in the Zero B water purifier as discussed earlier. A small section may start trying out the product. The new category gets diffused through 'word of mouth' of the users and also through communication strategies of the few brands in the market. It takes some time for a category to be 'created' in the minds of a larger number of consumers. Once many consumers start using the product, consumer familiarity with regard to the product category is established. Digital watches, for instance, came in the late 70s when not many consumers were familiar with automatic watches. But now digital watches have been well accepted and consumers are familiar with the product category. A number of brands enter a new category over a period of time. This results in a number of positioning strategies and brand associations/images. There are several attitudinal components that play a part in creating an attitude towards a brand. Eventually, consumers develop attitudes towards various brands. This, in turn, affects their decision making with regard to brand preferences. The marketing implication is that the pioneer in a new product category should build its brand effectively to ensure that consumers have a top-of-the-mind recall with respect to the brand. Videocon in washing machines and Aquaguard in water filters seem to have effectively adopted this approach when they entered the market early.

Samsung and LG were late entrants in several categories of durable products. But these brands have been able to create a very positive attitude among consumers with their product offerings and marketing communication. These brands now have a substantial share of the market in a number of categories.

Changing the Basic Motivational Function

There are four approaches to implement this strategy, namely the utilitarian function, ego-defensive function, value-expressive function and knowledge function. Some of the examples may be old but they have been used to illustrate the concept.

(a) Utilitarian function is a method that attempts to change the attitude towards a brand or bring in a new belief if it is a new one, by highlighting the utility aspect for consumers. Apart from the conventional route of using advertising to convey the relevant information, a few brands also use the direct marketing approach to highlight their functional aspect. When a brand attempts to bring in a new belief among consumers (in this case, the utility aspect), it has to have an attribute or benefit, which gives it a marketing edge over other brands. Nokia has models that have several features and benefits in mobile phones (the Nokia model 1100 had a torch and a radio and had appealed to consumers at the lower economic strata). Dettol floor cleaner positioned itself as an offering for healthy homes and for preventing illness. High-priced brands need to make the consumers aware of the application of the product, wherever applicable. For example, a brand of utensil cleaner may have introduced the liquid variant and also have the proposition of lower usage as compared to other cheaper variants. This needs to be communicated to the consumer. As a category gets competitive, differentiation is not achieved just by functional utility. It is achieved by the 'value' perception of consumers. Durables can also get benefitted from this approach (refrigerators, washing machines and water-heaters, to name a few) if a brand clearly demonstrates the effectiveness of not only the 'primary' benefit but also the secondary one. For example, all brands in washing machines make tall claims of high technology and its impact on washing fabrics. Utility, in the Indian context is the saving of power and water (secondary benefits) apart from the cleaning action, which is the primary benefit. If a brand can demonstrate its effectiveness on the primary and secondary benefits, it can create a new belief among consumers.

(b) **Ego-defensive function** is oriented towards protecting the self-image (self-esteem) of consumers. This approach is useful in personal and cosmetic products that guard consumers against embarrassment in a social situation. It is important for a brand attempting this approach to use appropriate imagery in the execution of an advertisement. During the 80's, Colgate and Lifebuoy's variant used this approach. Clorets, in the confectionery category, also positioned itself as a chewable gum that can consumed 'after anything'.

The 'Cool' Connect

The affective part of attitudes is a critical aspect for many categories of products. Online fashion portals have the affect or emotional component as a prerequisite for diffusion of clothes. LimeRoad is an e-commerce fashion portal that is exclusively targeted towards women. It is a good example of how a fashion brand had created a strong affect associated with the brand. The website targets about 25 million women in specific socio-economic classification and about 17 per cent of them were interested . The website has a scrapbook where consumers show case designs and about 3 million looks are created by the consumers in a month. The website has 10000 sellers on its platform. Online fashion retail is expected to account for 35 per cent of the total online retail by 2020.[12] This particular affect in a category like fashion is intrinsic to any fashion brand and in the case of 'LimeRoad', there is also a reference group effect where consumers may form preferences and attitudes based on their interaction with others.

(c) **Value-expressive function** is similar to the ego-oriented approach but deals more with the values and attitudes of consumers (target segment) rather than protecting their image/self-esteem. The visuals of an advertisement play an important role in reflecting the lifestyle associations. Charms cigarettes, launched during the early 80's, created an attitude based on 'freedom and rebellion' which served as a style statement. It was, perhaps, one of the earliest brands to create an attitude among youth. The brand was offered in a pack with a denim finish. This was when denim was becoming popular as a fabric symbolizing Westernization, rebellion and freedom. The advertisement copy said 'Charms is the way you are' and was one of the most memorable advertisements of that decade. Though the example may have been repeated elsewhere in the book, it enables the students to visualize the application of the respective concept. Lenovo, targeting the younger generation, used a celebrity to indicate its symbolic associations. The major limitation of this approach is that there are several brands in a category that use such celebrity appeals. This can fail to provide a differentiator for a new brand because a pioneer in the category would have already got associated with such appeals. An appropriate approach to overcome this limitation would be to follow the ego-defensive function (depending on the appropriateness of the situation) and follow it up with the value-expressive approach. Raymond was always advertised as a 'guide to the well-dressed male' in the 80's. (This can also be classified under the 'fundamental values'. But clothing has a social appeal and so, the end benefit for the consumer may be 'fabric confidence'. Hence, the ego-defensive function may also be appropriate.) During the 90's, it was positioned as a brand for the 'complete man', emphasizing his several roles and experiences with his family. The limitations of this approach is that it reinforces the fact that a brand needs to update its core offering associated with functional utility and that no brand can eternally bank on the symbolic appeals (a few categories like perfumes may be of use to the symbolic appeal for a longer period of time).

(d) **Knowledge function** serves as a cognitive need, the need to know. Marketers can explain the advantages of certain brands to make these brands competitive. In a competitive context, brands get associated with several features and benefits. This approach of attitude creation is useful in durable categories like TV, refrigerators and washing machines. Communication should ensure that consumers are able to effectively comprehend product-related information and benefits. The use of technical terms, even to convey the brand proposition, should be avoided if consumers find it difficult to understand the information at the retail outlets. Several TV brands advertise technical features. This requires the personnel at retail outlets to have not only a sound knowledge of the product but also the ability to match the needs of consumers with the product features.

The knowledge function is very important for new-concept durables. The vacuumiser was a new-concept product that could be used to preserve food. The difference between preserving food in the refrigerator and this appliance was that the latter did not cause odour and prevented food from going rancid. The product was launched with a basic pump and a number of containers. Consumers could choose the number of containers they required. The knowledge function would have been very effective in such a case. Consumers needed to be educated on their needs and how the containers would match their needs. Though awareness was created about the product using direct marketing, the retail network that marketed the product was oriented more towards selling the containers than educating consumers. The knowledge function can also be useful to position a brand in a multi-brand category like toothpastes. There is a great deal of marketing communication, and thus a strong need for a new brand to develop a convincing differentiator to slip into the 'consideration set' of consumers. A strong emphasis on benefits may be helpful in developing a favourable attitude towards a brand. Colgate Total was positioned on several benefits based on specific ingredients, as a toothpaste that gives 'prolonged freshness'.

Quaker Oats had created awareness about its offering with a knowledge base on fitness and health.

Association with Events

Attitudes can be created by relating a brand with certain events or social groups. Fosters, the well-known Australian brand, sponsored the Grand Prix with the idea of associating itself with the sports enthusiasts. Millions of viewers watch this event and reaching even a section of the audience interested in the brand will create a positive attitude towards it. Coke and Pepsi are other brands that sponsor events in which the brand connects with the target segment. This approach pays if sponsoring is even a part of the overall brand-building strategy. Of course, the event itself should be of interest to at least a section of the people. It is imperative that the brand association, along with the event, should strengthen the personality of the respective brand. Sponsoring a beauty contest or a sports event without considering the overall brand associations may have a negative impact on the brand.

Dealing with Conflicting Attitudes

Certain product categories may have given rise to conflicting attitudes over a period of time in the minds of consumers and these must be addressed to change attitudes.

Microwave cooking is convenient but consumers may think that the food made in the appliance is not tasty. Marketers should probe and identify such conflicting attitudes that cause the effect of a favourable belief to be nullified by another unfavourable belief. As long as conflicting attitudes are not addressed in marketing communication, brand-building efforts may not yield results. There have been beverages and fast foods with soya-based offerings that were not significantly successful in India. Though consumers may be convinced about the health aspect of soya, they may simply not like its taste. The affected component can be addressed using a celebrity who appeals to the target segment. This may have an impact on the die-hard fans of the celebrity. Marketers should also attempt to enhance word of mouth to remove these conflicting attitudes. A major share of the plastic containers market is in the unorganized sector. Tupperware, a brand of plastic containers, has a premium pricing and it positioned on lasting durability. Consumers may be convinced that the brand is durable but also expensive. Word of mouth on the value offered by the brand in terms of the durability associated with it versus the 'not-so-durable' offerings from the unorganized sector may convince the consumers of the 'value' of Tupperware. Nutrichoice biscuits had come out with a good campaign that illustrates the approach towards conflicting attitudes. Health biscuits may trigger the belief that 'they are healthy but would they be tasty?' Nutrichoice's campaign conveyed that the brand would be better than bread though not as tasty as fast food.

Changing the Relative Evaluation of Attributes

As a product category develops over a period of time (from ice-creams to up-market cars), more and more brands come up, with each of them offering a set of features/attributes and benefits. Consequently, there are several segments based on product features and benefits. In the refrigerator market there are consumers who prefer the 'no-frill' 165 litres model. There is a cross section of consumers that prefers the frost-free model. There are consumers who want a brand that offers them flexibility with regard to storage space and there are others who want quick-chilling features. LG, the brand that has made its mark in some durable product categories, positioned itself on the plank of preservation of nutrition. This positioning is in tune with the basic benefit that consumers expect from a refrigerator preservation of food and beverages. In the present-day context, consumers are familiar with refrigerators as a category and also aware that all brands offer cold storage. The core proposition of 'cold storage' is no longer a differentiating factor among refrigerator brands. If the consumer's evaluation of a brand can be upgraded with a useful feature/benefit, there is likely to be a shift in his/her intention to buy the brand. This approach also repositions what the consumer looks for in the respective product category. It is implied that there is a target segment which may be interested in such updated and relevant features, and hence, the approach need not necessarily cover the entire market during the same time period. The objective of a premium brand will generally be to capture a niche in the market. Hero Honda (motorcycles) changed the evaluation of consumers on various product attributes (looks, riding comfort, maintenance, etc.) with an overwhelming claim on just one attribute and which is economy (even though it could have presented other benefits). The positioning, when it was launched, was 'Fill it. Shut it. Forget it.'

Changing Brand Beliefs

A brand has to reinvent itself when competition sets in. There may be a need to change the beliefs of consumers towards the brand by using new attributes/benefits. Introduction of 'new' and 'improved' versions or relaunches are some types of situations where this approach is applicable. It is important for consumers to perceive the 'newness' of the brand and as far as possible, the benefit needs to be tangible if the brand is promising with its enhanced functionality/benefits. In the category of malted/milk additive drinks, a number of brands have made such claims and it will be worthwhile to find out how these claims are perceived by consumers. A belief towards a brand can change only when consumers perceive the benefit. In the recent times, Britannia has been able to change the belief towards the brand by using a number of variants and sub-brands in this category and consumers can perceive the changes through taste. Kellogg's, by introducing its biscuits, Chocos at lower-level price points, has attempted to change the belief that the brand is expensive. While attempting to change the brand beliefs, a brand should consider certain beliefs and habits of the people in the environment. Culture is a part of the environment and eating and drinking is a part of any culture. Great Shake was a tetra-packed soya drink from Godrej. While the initial campaign during the 80's positioned the brand as a quick, 'filling' drink, the later campaigns emphasized the goodness and nutritional aspects of soya and how the drink was popular in a few Asian countries. There are two aspects a brand may want to consider in this situation, a) what is the established culture with regard to eating in a given market? b) would a new offering of food appeal to the consumers in a specific cultural setting?

Another aspect which is important in changing beliefs about an existing brand is the importance given by the consumer to a specific attribute or benefit in the evaluation of a brand. During the early 90's, Ambassador (the dominant brand in the category of cars for several decades) came out with a campaign in an attempt to reposition itself. The campaign repositioned the brand as a one which is more suitable for the rugged and crowded Indian road. While any consumer will certainly agree with the factoid on Indian roads, the question was whether this benefit will be an important factor in the decision-making cycle of consumers, particularly when all brands are perceived to be adequately suited for Indian roads. With the changing brand beliefs, it must be ensured that the attribute/benefit chosen for the new belief must be relevant to the consumer.

Adequate research needs to be carried out to find out if consumers perceive the change in the position of the brand to be too radical. An extreme change advocated by a brand (compared to the past positioning strategy) is likely to be rejected and such a perception from the consumer's viewpoint is based on the assimilation-contrast theory. Marketers should be 'moderate' in their attempts to change brand beliefs. A brand of hair cream like 'Brylcreem' (a brand that has been already in the market for years) may not want to suggest that the brand is totally non-sticky because consumers expect a certain level of greasiness/stickiness in a hair cream. This is true particularly of this category that has not grown much or been attempted with too many positioning strategies. Parachute, the brand of coconut oil, avoided assimilation-contrast by bringing in a sub-brand; parachute light, in the coconut oil category. Parachute Light suggested that the offering is lighter in terms of greasiness and easier to use when compared to the conventional coconut oil. Another way to avoid a negative effect in a situation of this kind is to visibly demonstrate the feature or benefit the underlying change. When Kinetic Honda (the gearless scooter) was introduced in the 80's, it was competing against well-known brands that were rugged and oriented towards Indian-road conditions. The sleek look of the brand may have created a doubt in the minds of the consumers (who had all along been using conventional scooters) about the ruggedness and durability of the new offering. The band sponsored a 'Himalayan Rally' in which the riders of that brand participated. The event was effectively captured in a TV commercial. Parachute brand introduced 'After Shower' sub-brand in the hair cream category rather than attack the strongly entrenched belief about the greasiness associated with the hair cream category. Smartness, style and dressing for the occasion are certainly in tune with the 'grooming ritual' of youth in the present-day context.

Using a New Attribute Brand

Brand beliefs can also be changed by bringing in a new attribute that is ignored by competition or by adding an attribute based on the technical aspect. Godrej (refrigerators) emphasized the 'puf' usage during the 80's and highlighted this as its positioning plank. Though a number of refrigerator brands used PUF (Polyurethane Foam), these brands had ignored this aspect in their positioning strategies. 'Oral-B' tooth brushes introduced the brand with a mechanism that enables a consumer to know when he/she should change the toothbrush. This attribute is a result of technological innovation. Research on choosing attributes ignored by competitive brands can provide important insights. There is a need to consider the perception of consumers on what they consider as a favourable attribute/benefit. Bisleri, in the soda category during the 80's, positioned itself as the 'Quiet soda' (with less amount of carbonation). It was a new offering that could be categorized under changing the importance associated with the attribute (the positioning that carbonation is not an important attribute in this case). Red Label added vitamins and antioxidants as an additional attribute. For adding an attribute, it may be worthwhile to find out if consumers are interested in that attribute. A few years ago, refrigerators were launched with multiple doors. Research by a manufacturer showed that consumers did not perceive this as an additional attribute. Technology can redefine the market and the concerned brand can get a high visibility when an attribute conveys a strong benefit. Hero Honda, with its four-stroke engine (and hence, better mileage) redefined the category of motorcycles. Ever since, every manufacturer has introduced the four-stroke version. A brand should pre-empt competition while adding attributes because a number of brands are likely to follow the pioneering brand over a period of time. A few brands had remote controllers when colour televisions were introduced, but today, it is virtually impossible to find a CTV without one. This holds good for a number of categories like cars, watches, washing machines and two-wheelers. Another aspect of adding a new attribute is the cost involved in introducing the attribute. Even in FMCG categories, adding a new attribute may involve cost.

Overall Attitude towards the Brand

Another approach towards the changing attitude with regard to a brand is to have a global statement in the copy of the advertisement. 'Your guarantee of good impression' from Kores; 'If it is Philips, you are sure' from Philips and 'The Ultimate Luxury' from Esteem are some examples of this approach. Generally, such global statements are associated only with brands that have made an impact on the mind-set of consumers (the discussion in this context is not about a brand's success). In these examples, the brands were well known and had made an impact on their target segment at some point of time. For this approach to be effective, consumers should feel that the global statements carry adequate authenticity and credibility.

Focusing on Competitive Brands

Repositioning competition is another way to change the attitude of consumers towards a brand. One of the earliest brands to attempt this was Tylenol. It was introduced at a time when Aspro was the largest selling brand in the US. Tylenol, in its advertisement copy highlighted the negative aspects of consuming Aspro and said it (Tylenol) did not have features that caused the negative effect. The campaign is supposed to have had a phenomenal impact on consumers. In the Indian context, Kinetic Honda repositioned the scooters (as a category) as stylish vehicles. The market for gearless scooters (like Kinetic Honda) is growing and the market for traditional scooters is on the decline. There are two prerequisites to be followed before a brand attempts this approach and are as follows.

1. If the claims of superiority product are made, then the brand should be perceived as having a strong edge over the competitive brand on the claims made. Ind Suzuki, in the 80's, came out with an advertisement comparing the brand with Hero Honda on a variety of features. HCL did comparative advertising with Modi Xerox in the category of photocopiers. Consumers should perceive a brand to be superior and that is likely to happen only when the brand attempting the comparison has good attributes.
2. When consumers have a strong belief structure in certain product categories, the brands will have to be careful about repositioning competition. Savlon forced its competition, Dettol, to reposition itself using the Tylenol route and highlighted the burning and stinging sensation caused by Dettol. If many consumers had believed that the burning sensation triggered off the positive action associated with antiseptic lotion, the approach would not have been effective. Moov, a brand of pain balms associated with sprains and aches, repositioned its competitor Iodex saying that it (Moov) did not leave stains on the user's clothes. In this context, the consumers may have perceived the benefit to be very tangible.

The Elaboration Likelihood Model (ELM)

This model suggests that there can be two routes to persuade consumers. One is the central route or the 'product relevant' route and the other is the peripheral or the 'non-product' route. The central route has a focus on product attributes or core functional benefits and the peripheral route is oriented towards 'non-product' aspects like the celebrity and/or the background used in the advertisement, excellent packaging or free samples. The central route primarily seems readily applicable to consumer durables as they are likely to commit the cognitive resources of consumers (generally being high-involvement products). But even in certain product categories of consumables, there is scope for the application of the Elaboration Likelihood Model (ELM), well-established in the literature on consumer behaviour. For example, a brand like Colgate Total (which promises a number of benefits) may appeal to consumers who may like information on the chemicals used and their benefits. Mouthwash brands like Listerine can explain the rationale of the benefits they provide. The prerequisite of this approach is that the target segment, apart from being interested in the product benefits, should also be data-oriented. There may also be a few instances when a brand has used both central and peripheral cues to make an impression on the target segment. Samsung (TV category) came out with a model that had extra viewing space and the advertisement used humour, apart from highlighting the brand benefit. Whirlpool effectively used the 'ice, ice baby' campaign, which had certain peripheral cues like a catchy jingle and background setting. Whirlpool used this approach when it had created adequate brand awareness in India and took care that the peripheral cues did not overshadow the brand's benefit of making ice in a short time. If a brand chooses to use both types of cues, it has to ensure that the peripheral cues do not overshadow the central cues, especially for durable products. Santro effectively combined the two in a series of advertisements the initial one featuring a celebrity to capture the attention of consumers. This created brand awareness among the target segment. The campaign was followed by competitive advertising where Santro was compared with a number of brands on several features (central cue). Fanta (soft drink is an impulsive buy) has been using humour (peripheral cue) in the recent times.

Figure 6.3 shows the application of the ELM model with regard to attitude creation/ change. MAO represents motivation, ability (to comprehend several aspects of the given information) and opportunity (time pressure or a wrong media selection strategy).*

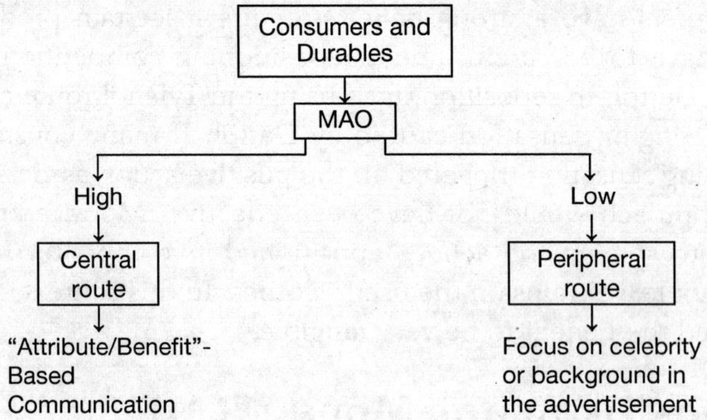

Figure 6.3 The Elaboration Likelihood Model

Convergence of Central and Peripheral Routes

What is a peripheral route and what is the central route is dependent on the context and the offering. A brand like Head & Shoulders, the shampoo brand in its TV advertisement mentions anti-dandruff as the brand's proposition (central), uses a celebrity (who advocates the benefit) and also provides a romantic aspect to the shoulders (symbolizes leaning on the shoulder as a romantic gesture) and associates the benefit with the romantic link. The ad—though uses celebrities (generally regarded as peripheral by the model)—is largely associated with the central route. Such a linkage is likely to be more effective than just a celebrity association without linkages to the proposition of the brand, especially if the benefit is tangible in nature.

* The MAO Model has been adapted from:

1. Hoyer and MacInnis, Consumer behavior, *Houghton and Mifflin*, (Indian edition,1999), 30.
2. Leon G. Schiffman, Joseph Wisenblit, and S. Ramesh Kumar, *Consumer Behavior*, (New Delhi: Pearson Education, 2015), 191.

IDEAL POINT MODEL[13]

Practicing marketing managers will find the Ideal Point Model effective in measuring attitudes. This model captures consumers' perception on the 'ideal' brand (with ideal features) and compares their perception on existing brands. The following are the components of the Ideal Point Model:

A_b	Attitude towards the brand
W_i	Importance of the attribute *i*
L_i	The 'ideal' performance on attribute *i*
X	Beliefs about a brand's actual performance on attribute '*i*'.
n	The number of salient features.

If the model is applied to a brand of TV, say *A*, the following attributes can be identified.

1. Picture quality
2. Audio quality
3. Usefulness of special features
4. Handling ease
5. Aesthetic appeal
6. Compactness

Consumers can mark the ideal brand and rate *A* on the attributes on a scale of 7 ((1) given to reflect the low perception and (7) to reflect the high perception on the respective attribute). The application can, for example, result in the following analysis.

Attribute	Importance (W_i)	Idea (L_i)	Brand *A* (X_i)
Picture quality	7	4	3
Audio quality	4	3	2
Special features	3	2	2(usefulness)
Handling ease	3	1	4
Aesthetic appeal	2	4	1
Compactness	1	3	1

The formula for attribute A_b towards the brand can be applied as

$$A_b = \sum_{i=1}^{n} W_i (L_i - X_i)$$

For Brand *A*, the resulting value is 28.

Implications of the Model:

1. A brand can find out how close it is to the 'ideal' brand. A value of '0' is ideal because at this point the brand is the 'ideal' brand.
2. Higher the value of a brand, farther away it is from the 'ideal' perception of the brand. (Minus sign does not alter the value as the objective of the model as it is to measure the distance of a brand from the "ideal" brand—W_i (L_i — X_i) is to be considered.
3. A brand can improve its attributes and move closer to the 'ideal' brand. In the example, except for the usefulness of special features, Brand *A* is farther away from the ideal brand on all aspects and requires improvement on these aspects.
4. A brand can shift the importance associated with an attribute. Brand *A*, for example, can alter the importance on aesthetic appeal (on which it is below the ideal brand) by an advertising campaign that stresses the attributes on which it is ranked high.

The approach needs to be preceded by research on the perception of consumers on this new attribute/benefit. For example, if a shampoo brand wants to shift the importance of attributes by introducing a new benefit 'spreading action to make the roots stronger', the perception of the consumer needs to be captured before the brand uses the attribute.

Touch of Reality

Attitudes Matter in an Emerging Market

There are strong Indian brands (from the viewpoint of market shares) like Amul (butter), Eureka Forbes (water purifiers), Nokia (mobiles), Maggi (noodles), Fair & Lovely (fairness creams), Cadbury (chocolates), Johnson & Johnson (baby-care products), Titan (watches), Dettol (antiseptic solution) and Maruti (cars).

While some of the brands may have faced competitive pressures from other brands in the category, some of the brands may have a large share in a thinly penetrated market. Attitudes are important, both from the viewpoint of category development and brand associations/beliefs. For example, in the categories of water purifiers or antiseptic lotion, brands may have to create appropriate beliefs to expand the market. In the case of a brand like Nokia, distribution channels have played a major role in shaping the beliefs of consumers towards the brand (display of the brand's range, price points being explained at the point of purchase and customized selling at the point of purchase). Mobiles phones are available at about one lakh outlets and Nokia is prominently displayed at most outlets. All these aspects get translated into a liking for the brand and this aspect is the 'affective component' or the overall evaluation of the brand. There may be a cross section of consumers that buys the SKU due to the influence of conative component (intention to buy) because of the price level affordability.

Case cum exercise based on an experience with reviving a category—answer the question at the end of the case

A Case Study from the Indian context — Attitudinal Linkages to New Product Category Creation: Attitudes and "Aftershower"*

MALE GROOMING—THE AFTERSHOWER JOURNEY

Background

The turn of the millennium was a harbinger of hope for a generation awakening. The Internet revolution had sparked a movement that had completely redefined the way people saw life and its tenets. It tore down barriers, both social and geographical and ushered in the era of globalization—an era where people, both young and old, started getting exposed to happenings in 'their' world and started to make 'choices'. Their lifestyle was no more a set of mores laid down by the society but a reflection of choice; a choice driven by individuality, of personal attitudes and a reflection of the changing world view.

India, as a country, was uniquely placed in this era of change. Post-liberalization, the country had for the first time shaken off its legacy of mediocrity and was looking to compete in the world market. It had emerged as an IT powerhouse like Infosys, Wipro and a host of other firms that had turned the spotlight on the nation; suddenly 'Made in India' was a good tag to have.

There was an enormous amount of positivism in the country, starting from the political parties to the media; everyone was talking about the future in a positive frame. Indian youth were making news all over the world, be it in IT space or in other business.

What this did for the country was that it brought about a change in the mind-set. Suddenly the masses were not content with what they had, but were actively seeking resources that were driven by individual choice.

MALE GROOMING—CATEGORY OVERVIEW

The male grooming category in India, at that point in time was dominated by shaving products like blades, shaving creams, and deodorants were the key segments that constituted male grooming. Vanity, for men, revolved around shaving.

The male grooming category was small and valued around 200 crores, the major players being Col-Pal, Gillette, Godrej, Old Spice and Park Avenue. The category had started registering growth with the entry of Gillette and Park Avenue in the market and because of category building communication by the two large players. It was a low

---

* The caselet was written by Mr Arnab Das, Brand Manager, Marico Ltd. in the conceptual format provided by S. Ramesh Kumar, Professor of Marketing, IIM Bangalore, who also prepared the solution note.

The author would like to thank Mr Sameer Satpathy, Head Marketing, Mr Arnab Das, Brand Manager and Ms Deepa Rajaram, Human Relations Manager, Marico Limited for their time, effort and support in preparing the caselet and advertisements featured in this book

investment, low interest category in which the key players were starting to create excitement through the launch of new products.

The hair creams segment was estimated to be around ₹ 22 crore (Nielsen off takes valued the category to be even lower at around ₹ 11 cr) the key players being Sara Lee India (Brylcreem) and Hindustan Lever (Clinic Active).

The category was on a hopeless decline. From a 400+ tons per annum (TPA) market in 2000, it had dropped to 200 TPA and slowly it had become unattractive. But the numbers actually had a deeper story to tell. The decline was driven by the absence of competition. HLL had withdrawn Clinic Active from the market leading to a category decline. To compound matters further, the only player left in the category is an MNC brand, which was not investing in marketing.

And all this was happening when the household penetration of the category was going up. Somewhere, there was a crying need being expressed by the consumers for an oil substitute for daily grooming whereas a product in a format that provided the benefits of oil but helped them stay away from the messiness.

Target Segment (TG) Profile: Cream Users

Cream users

- **Demographics**
  - Male; Socio-economic classification (SEC) A [upper and upper-middle class]
  - Age band 25 to 34
- **Psychographics**
  - Successful in career, working for a good organization
  - Image conscious
  - Confident
  - Fashionable
  - Self-driven in making choices

The consumer's basic need was to have a product that kept hair in place and made him look good.

Needs from Male Grooming

The Indian populace, by the turn of the century, had undergone a complete change in demographics. 54 per cent of the population was below 25 years of age. The arrival on the scene of a completely young consuming class had a telling impact on the marketing of everyday products; new trends had started to emerge.

The consumers had suddenly become young. The future was bright and there was a marked change in attitude. Gone were the days when the youth found conformance to be a virtue, conformance to rules laid down by an older generation with values based on machismo; today, it was all about "it's my life" and it was ok to indulge.

- There was a growing obsession amongst the consumers with the enhancement of hair. Hair was no longer an accessory that needed to be in place, but had become a conduit to look good, to look modern and to completely transform one's appearance.
- Hair care had suddenly become relevant to all sections of consumers.
- Hair had to look good for the 'package' to be valued as worthy.

Yet, the needs from hair care were limited. The key desires are listed below:

- Basic styling, epitomized by the monthly haircut was monthly. Hair styling, as a concept, had not evolved till then.
- Daily grooming needs encompassed the following features.
  - Basic setting of hair
  - Non-sticky/pleasant smelling product
  - Product not harmful to hair
  - Oil and water dominated, as a universal post-bath habit.
- Occasional fashion
  - Gelled hair
  - Very small number of people used hair colour.

Aftershower

Opportunities

In creating a new space

All the current players were playing in the style—cosmetic segment. The entire platform of natural style provided with an enormous opportunity to tap into. See Figure 6.4.

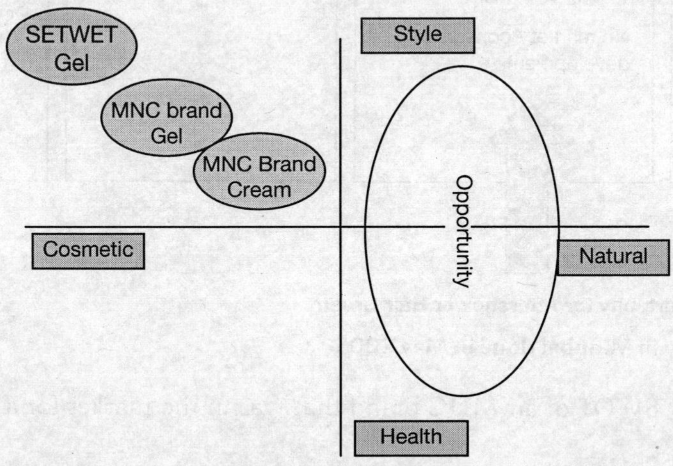

Figure 6.4 The opportunity for a new offering

Weak Competition

An MNC brand had been around for a long time. It was the first and the oldest brand in the category and had a large range, but it was perceived to be old fashioned "dad's brand", 'fuddy-duddy', etc. The brand had been seen around for too long and the consumers did not perceive any change to have happened. The core of the brand was built around 'experienced hair style' rather than being aspirational and hence, it was being lapsed out by consumers. Figure 6.5 presents a SWOT analysis of the MNC brand.

The consumers had become indifferent to the brand and the category at large, as relevance for the product in the changing scenario was not being built up.

Challenges

To get the marketing mix right.

- The new product had to be better than the dominant MNC brand.
  - The MNC brand was the global leader in male grooming.
  - A well-known Indian brand did not sustain itself in the market.
- It had to be distinctive.
  - Success would be impossible without a USP.

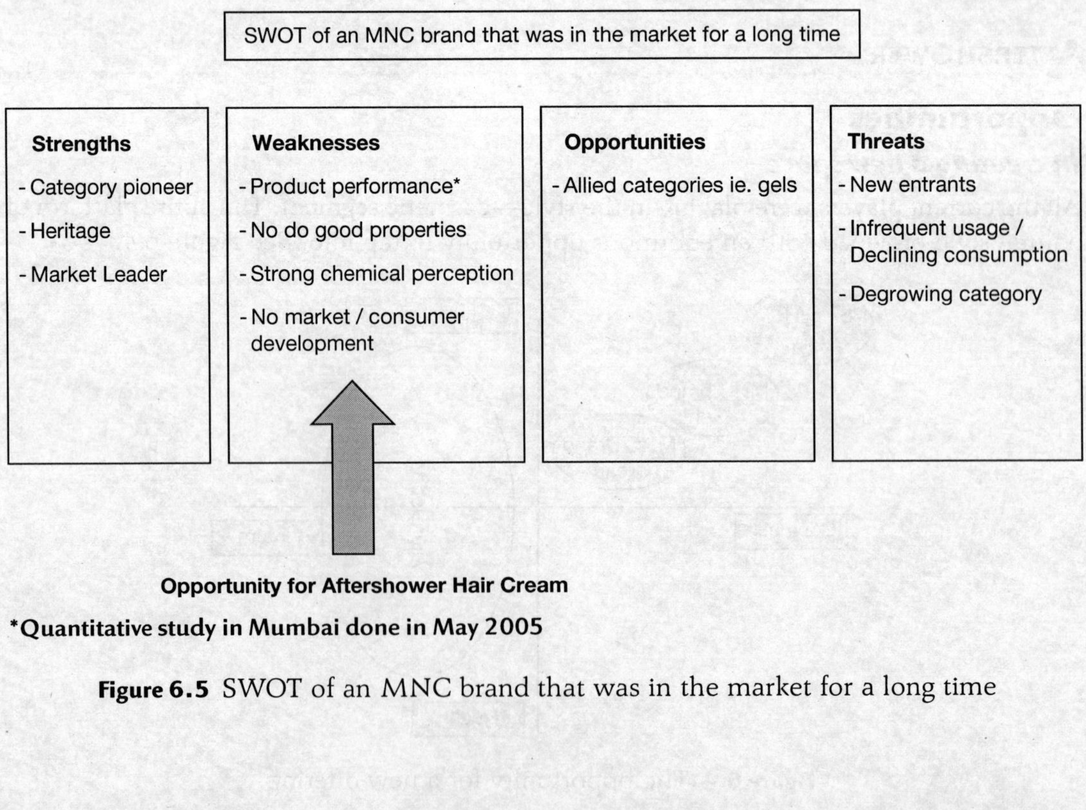

***Quantitative study in Mumbai done in May 2005**

Figure 6.5 SWOT of an MNC brand that was in the market for a long time

Product

The following were the differentiators in the product:

- Natural as it contained coconut milk proteins.
- With aqua moisturizers it helped aid the fresh feeling throughout the day.
- With refreshing zingy fragrance
- Completely non-sticky

The formulation was clearly superior to the MNC brand.

Packaging

The packaging was clearly superior to the MNC brand (Refer Figure 6.6)

Figure 6.6 The appeal of packaging

Proposition

The proposition was based on the following elements:

- Natural daily grooming
- Style and substance
- From Parachute Advanced

  This led to the communication tagline 'Style on . . . every day'.

  The proposition was clearly as a daily-use product that was not only non-sticky but also helpful in styling the hair and also helpful in nourishing it.

  The proposition scored highly with the consumers as they liked the element of style + nourishment.

  The proposition was very clearly distinct.

Physical Distribution

Distribution also emerged as a very clear differentiator

- Marico distribution clout was leveraged.
- The MNC brand, which had a distribution model that banked heavily on wholesale reach was outplaced.

Clearly, the retail muscle provided the ability for Parachute to outperform the MNC brand.

Targeting

Demographically the target group was defined as

- Male; Socio-economic classification (SEC) AB;
- Age 15 to 34

What this definition of TG did not define was

(a) Who would the cream user be?
(b) Who would not be the cream user?
(c) Amongst the cream users, who would still continue to use hair oils?

An extensive research has led to the clear understanding of the male consumer and his product preference based on his position in the 'do good look good' continuum (Refer Figure 6.7).

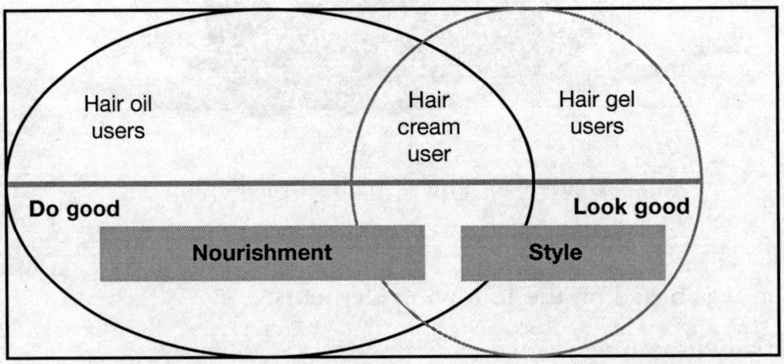

Figure 6.7 The 'do good look good' continuum

Consumers who had very strong health/nourishment needs would prefer to use oils as a preferred product, whereas those with only styling needs would use a gel. That left a substantial overlap of nourishment and style needs which is actually the core TG for creams.

The broad-based demographic group was further sharpened using psychographics.

Male consumers in the age band of 15 to 34, SECTION ABC, who may be just out of college in their first job and with an internal (driven by need for hair health benefit) orientation, who are users of hair oil, would be the ideal convert into creams. The consumer would be residing in town classes with a population of 10 plus lakhs, he would be ready to groom but may not be ready to show. The Gel user would have a strong external (hair appearance and sensorial's) orientation, so he would showcase his sense of style to the world and celebrate his individuality. There were certain other lifestyle traits that went into identifying the 'After Shower' user:

- He would either be in his first job or would be at the crossroads, out of college and into his first job.
- He would be ambitious; he would aspire for success in his career.
- He would have an active out-of-home lifestyle.
- He would love gizmos and girls
- He loves to watch TV, movies
- He loves sports, especially cricket
- He is confident but is unsure of how well he is matched with his peer group.
- He wants to look clean and presentable.

The consumer who had his grooming needs satiated by hair oils would not venture into the 'creams' space. But consumers who were not comfortable with the sensorials for oil would definitely be trying the offering.

Strategy

The tasks were simple:

- Category creation
- Share gain from competition

The strategic pivots for building the brand were given in Figure 6.8:

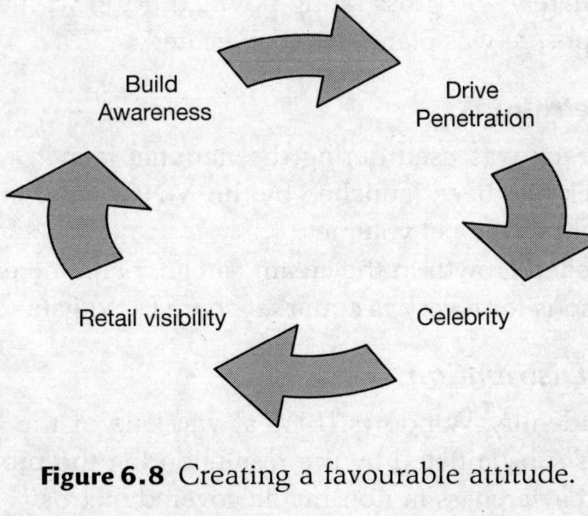

Figure 6.8 Creating a favourable attitude.

Celebrity

Communicating the proposition to the audience was the next challenge. There were barriers that needed to overcome to make the proposition salient:

- The category, to the youth, was being equated as unexciting.
- The style had to be made exciting so that people get connected to it.
- The communication had to cut through across India.
- Break media clutter, clearly, the brand needed an ambassador who could do it.
- Give a different dimension to styling.
- Appeal to youth all across the country.
- Lend the brand a youthful and sporty image.

Based on the above factors, Yuvraj Singh was chosen as the brand ambassador. He was a rising star and was performing well in the international arena (captured success), he was perceived to be stylish and played cricket which is frenzied as a separate religion across the country. The TV commercial established the key proposition of non-stickiness, unique style and its everyday usage.

Build Awareness

TV was used as the main medium to build brand awareness. The focus was to be on south India because

- It accounted for more than 38 per cent of the category volumes.
- It accounted for 23 per cent of TG and hence it was the only way to reach the TG in a cost-effective manner.
- It had media isolatable states; with higher return on investment (ROI) for the spent revenue.

Two bursts of approximately 750 gross rating points (GRP's) with a reach of 45 per cent TG at five times the exposure was planned and executed.

Drive Trials and Penetration

A new 14 gram ₹ 10 pack was used during the national launch to drive trials and also penetration. A ₹ 10 pack had been launched by the MNC brand in the gels segment and it contributed 22 per cent to the gel volumes.

The ₹ 10 pack propelled growth in the cream category and increased penetration. This was one of the key reasons for a very fast market share (MS) gain.

Retail Visibility and Distribution

Retail visibility/Brand Identity Windows [BIW's] was one of the key factors that drove awareness and this was substantiated by the results during the prototype. It was also an optimal way of creating awareness in non-media covered metros.

Results

In the Post launch phase, 'After shower' had become a benchmark for success in Marico.

By December 2005, 'After shower' had achieved a volume of 22 tons and a share of 33.3 per cent in the cream segment.

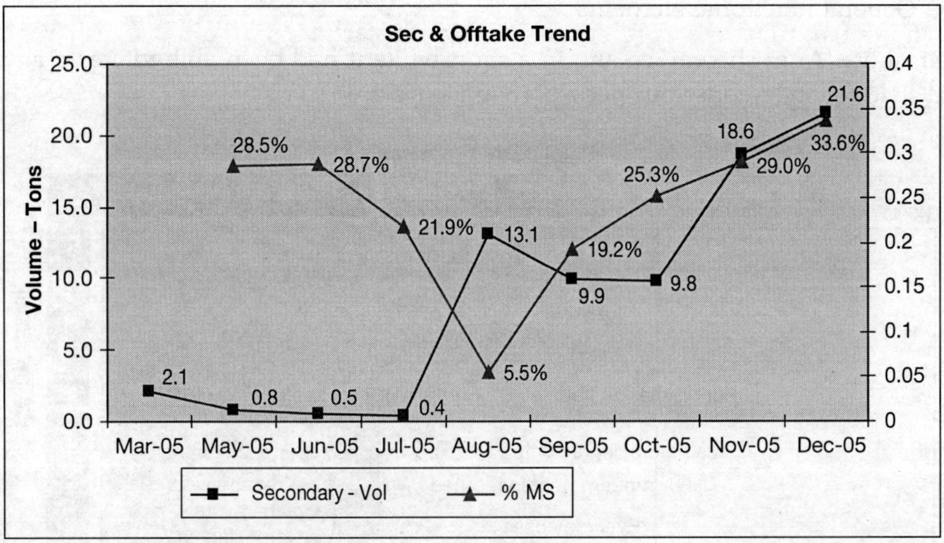

Pivots that Worked

The key pivots that have worked on the brand are

- A winning proposition addressing the consumer's needs gaps.
- ₹ 10 pack—driving trials into the category and also ensuring penetration.

This created good visibility for the brand in retail and helped create awareness of the brand. Good visibility enabled Marico to launch a new brand in a category that was dominated by the MNC brand.

Post Evaluations of Advertisement

- Awareness created 77 per cent of the TG.
    - o Source of awareness was via TV; also a lot of word of mouth was working on the brand.
    - o Overall success in creating curiosity about the brand.
- Consumers found it to be a new category product which is to be unique.
- Expectation from the product was also set high.
    - Providing shine and health were the key expectations.
- The likeability of the advertisement was very positive.
- The advertisement established credibility of the claims.
- Established relevance for the product.

- Yuvraj was a key element who was recalled and all the situations were registered with the consumers; he was a strong hook but did not hamper the brand communication. The situations registered were:
  - o Yuvraj applying cream
  - o Yuvraj and the girl
  - o General functional elements

The Parachute 'After shower' cream, in a short while it had been able to create an image around style for style-conscious people. (See Figure 6.9)

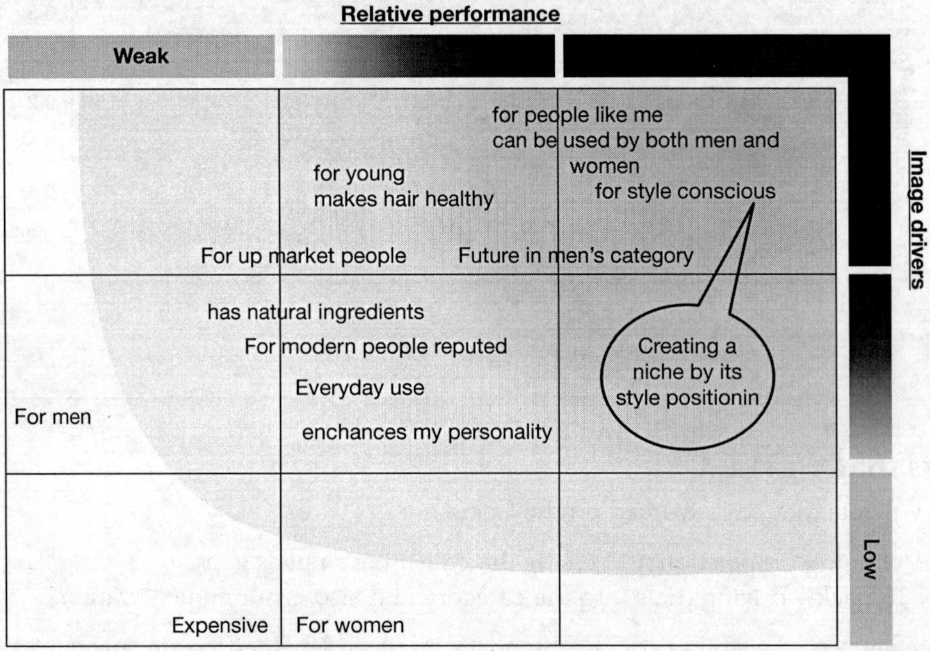

Figure 6.9 Image versus Performance

ANNEXURES

Product definitions

	Hair Cream	Hair Gel
Form	Opaque	Transparen
Product	Hair cream is oil and water based	Hair gel has no oil
	Hair cream gives nourishment because it contains oil	It does not give any nourishment

	Hair Cream	Hair Gel
Stickiness	There are less polymers;	There are a lot of polymers; hence, the cream is non-sticky and the gel is relatively stickier.

Retail POP's

Retail POP's were used extensively to create visibility for the brands. The different elements were

- Posters
- Banners
- Danglers
- Retailer detailers were used to differentiate the brand offering with regard to the competition.
- Product detailers detailed the product attributes and were a handy aid to the frontline sales force.
- BIW (Brand identity windows). They created a separate zone for 'After shower' products in the outlet.
- Floor dispensers, it is used for product displays in modern trade.

Question

How would you apply an appropriate theory of attitudes to analyse the conceptual learning from the case?

(There are no right or wrong answers to this question. You have to organize your thoughts on cognitive aspects and from affective aspects of the case information. Also think of applying and comparing the routes available through the ELM model. Explore the possibility of associating the TORA model explained in the reading suggested)

Suggested Reading

- Leon G. Schiffman, Joseph Wisenblit and S. Ramesh Kumar, *Consumer behavior,* 11th edition, Pearson education, 2015.

End Notes

1. 'Q&A with Ananth Narayanan' (2015), *The Economic Times*, 8 October.
2. Pankaj M. (2015), "You 'very got mail," *The Economic Times*, October 9.
3. Sangeeta Tanwar (2015), 'Experimenting with Communication Strategies to Beat the Clutter' (online edition), *Business Standard*, 5 October.
4. Ibid.
5. Ibid.
6. Leon Schiffman and Leslie L. Kanuk, *Consumer Behavior* (7 ed), (Pearson Education), pp. 186 & 323.
7. Ibid.
8. Schiffman Leon, Leslie L. Kanuk and S. Ramesh Kumar (in collaboration with J. Wisenblit), Kumar, *Consumer Behavior*, (New Delhi: Pearson Education, 2010), 342.
9. C. M. Judd and J. A. Krosnick (1982), 'Attitude Centrality, Organization and Measurement', *Journal of Personality and Social Psychology*, pp. 436–447.
10. Jessu John (2015),A Storm called Instagram, *The Hindu Business Line,* August 21.
11. Subrato Sengupta, *Brand Positioning*, (Tata McGraw Hill, 1990).
12. Ankita Rai (2015), 'Campaign Logic: LimeRoad sashays down the runway', *Business Standard*, 5 October.
13. Leon G. Schiffman, Joseph Wisenblit, and S. Ramesh Kumar, Consumer Behavior, (New Delhi: Pearson Education, 2015), 192.

Exercises

1. Analyze the impact of attitudes on one segment of two wheelers. Choose the economy or the premium segment of motorcycles. Develop beliefs associated with each brand and apply the affect part after collecting ads of brands?
2. Analyze the impact of attitudes on water purifiers and launch a new brand. Choose the leading brands to develop beliefs and comment on celebrity usage by a leading rand over a period of time.

CHAPTER 7

Diffusion of Innovation: The Acceptance of New Products and Brands

In today's competitive context, marketers are not only concerned with launching brands but also with how consumers accept them in the market place. Diffusion of innovation is associated with:

1. How consumers accept new products and brands (specifically the target segment of consumers in a given social context)
2. How they accept a set of marketing mix elements formulated for a brand over a period of time? Though traditionally, diffusion of innovation has been concerned only with new products, the concept can be applied to existing products and brands, given the intense competition in almost any product/service category.

Self–Concept and Diffusion of Fashion, and Personal Grooming Brands

Global research has shown that the physical profiles of recipients who attempt online crowd funding (democratic source of raising funds for a venture) play a role with respect to the funding obtained.[1] It seems that thin, fair-skinned and attractive persons were highly preferred by the donors. Given the implications of such research studies, fashion and personal grooming portals that operate online are likely to earn more attraction, given the reach of digital platforms.

Physical looks that is a part of one's self-concept is important to marketers, especially in this digital age. Flipkart and Amazon may bring in several aspects of virtual reality to promote fashion products.

DEFINING 'NEW' PRODUCTS*

New products can be divided into products that are a result of:

1. Continuous innovation
2. Dynamically continuous innovation
3. Discontinuous innovation based on the degree of innovation

The division of the term 'new' among products launched in the market is based on two aspects:

(a) The changes required in consumer behaviour to use the innovation
(b) Degree of innovation

Aeroplanes, computers and telephones were discontinuous innovations at the period of time when they were invented, as both the degree of innovation as well as the degree of changes required in consumer behaviour in adapting to these innovations was high. When buying a digital camera or considering Internet shopping, the change in behaviour on the part of the consumers is moderate as is the degree of innovation. Hence, these will fall under dynamically continuous innovations (since moderate changes of behaviour are involved with regard to the two basic factors applied to diffusion of innovation). When the remote switch of a TV is considered, consumers have to make only a small change with regard to their behaviour (or practice) to use the remote along with their TV. Hence, it is a continuous innovation.

The dimensions used for the classification of the 'newness' of a product should take a specific target segment's perception of 'newness' into account.

Diffusion of innovation in the Indian context has an interesting trail of history. Category development, timing of the brand's introduction and cultural aspects are some of the important aspects that affect the diffusion of brands. The following examples will provide an idea about the diffusion of brands:

Diffusion of Brands in the Indian context

Brand/Category	Comments on diffusion of category/brand
Ezee, Genteel Liquid Detergents	Available in the market for several decades. How should the brands in the category get into the ritual of consumer's washing of clothes?
Cadbury Drinking Chocolate	Available in the market for decades. Does cultural aspects of taste a barrier for diffusion of the category?
Detergent bars (Surf Excel, Rin)	Continue to be a popular choice by Indian consumers perhaps due to habits.
After-shower hair cream (Brylcreem)	Did after shower brand diffuse fast as it became a part of the dressing ritual among youngsters?

(Continued)

* Leon G. Schiffman, Leslie L. Kanuk and S. Ramesh Kumar (in collaboration with Wisenblit J), *Consumer Behavior*, (New Delhi: Pearson Education, 2010), 398

(*Continued*)

Brand/Category	Comments on diffusion of category/brand
Tea bags (Taj Mahal)	The brand created awareness about the tea bags during the mid- '80s. Have tea bags diffused adequately among consumers? Is taste and the ritual of making tea (cultural aspects) a barrier?
Hima Peas (packaged green peas)	The brand was introduced during the '60s. Was it ahead of its time ? Even today would packaged vegetables (frozen) be acceptable to consumers?
Videocon's Karaoke music	Targeted youngsters a few decades back. Was it ahead of its time? Would such a concept succeed in the era of digital music?
Café culture	Socializing over coffee was pioneered by Indian Coffee House-ICH (Indian Coffee Board) in a few cities and towns during the '60s. Consumers of the bygone era would have nostalgic memories of ICH. A contemporary version of ICH is perhaps the cafes we find today (Café Coffee Day and Barista, for example)

Diffusion and Existing Products

Diffusion can be applied to existing products. For example, marketers can consider (i) categories, (if not brands), with which consumers are familiar; (ii) brands with which consumers are familiar even if the categories are new to them (because of the high degree of advertising). New brands in familiar categories have to address diffusion problems differently from old brands in new or unfamiliar categories. Relatively new brands (late entrants) in consumer durables like Kenstar, LG, Samsung and Whirlpool have to follow a different kind of strategy in order to compete with strongly entrenched brands. LG, for instance, has been able to achieve significant diffusion by its focus on new features/benefits in familiar product categories. LG's proposition in refrigerators was 'preservation of nutrition'; in microwave ovens 'health'; in washing machines 'fabric care'; in air-conditioners 'healthy air' and in TV's, it was 'relaxed viewing' (Golden Eye). LG was able to capture a significant market share at the premium end of the respective product categories. Whirlpool was also able to diffuse itself in refrigerators by offering 'Indianised' features based on research. In the automobile sector Santro diffused itself in the Indian market by offering new features/design. Even in consumables, brands new to the market have to adopt strategies with a strong differentiation. A brand called Pass Pass offered dry fruits as a chewing option in direct competition with other chewing products. Red Label, though a well-known brand, introduced a 'nature care' variant when faced with competition. This was a case of an old brand in a familiar category reacting to competition. Britannia introduced a number of variants to diffuse itself in the market. It introduced Tiger biscuits, a new brand for the lower end of the market. Reynolds offered pens with superior features and gained acceptability.

There are categories like hair dyes, contact lenses and antiseptic lotions in which consumers may be familiar with brand names (Godrej in hair dyes, Bausch & Lomb in contact lenses, Dettol in antiseptics). But these categories require concept-selling for consumers to understand the benefits and usage of the products. Microwave ovens, a category that has been around for some years, has a number of well-known brands. The brands in such categories should formulate concept-selling in such a way that these product categories (and hence, specific brands) get prioritized in the minds of consumers. Marketers should remember that diffusion of a product does not just depend only on competition between brands. It may also depend on competition between product categories. After being in the market for several years, washing machines sell in much lesser numbers than the diffusion of personal computers. For instance, a middle class household may prioritize a PC for educational purposes over a fully automatic washing machine. Demographics and psychographics play an important role in generic competition across product categories.

Ice-creams can compete with chocolates, snacks and aerated soft drinks. L'Oreal has done extensive concept-selling for its hair colours and has, perhaps for the first time in India, positioned itself on the fashion statement plank. This comes at a time when hair colouring is becoming a rage all over the world (Refer to Plate 7.1). Companies in the

Plate 7.1 In India, L'oreal has positioned itself on the fashion statement plank

contact lens market are using a variety of strategies to diffuse the product. Positioning contact lenses as a fashion accessory is one of them (Bausch & Lomb). In a country like India, lowering costs and thereby, enhancing the total value of the offering (contact lens and its subsequent care) should enable brands to diffuse faster in the market.

A brand must maintain its pioneering lead, especially after it has gained acceptance in the market. Steel almirahs (cabinets) from Godrej have had a high degree of credibility for the last several years but they were priced far higher than competition in the unorganized sector. Doing a downward product-line stretch would have helped in faster diffusion of the brand in the category. Park Avenue, in the men's readymade clothes, has maintained its strong position for the last several years by launching variants. Launching variants, incidentally, has to be considered with regard to the cost involved. Cadbury, with its variants, is an example. Amrutanjan and Iodex have been well-known brands in the category of pain balms. These could have repositioned themselves with variants in the recent times.

In certain categories, sustained and contemporary communication can lend mileage to a pioneering brand. Bru, in instant coffee, is an example. After establishing itself strongly on the 'taste' attribute, the brand has been 'updating' its communication. Close-up also pioneered the other toothpaste gels and sustained itself for several years before the market developed into a substantial one for gel toothpastes. It effectively used communication strategies over a period of time. Top brands (which can be considered as pioneers)—Coke, Kodak, McDonald and Sony have sustained themselves along with the growth of the product category.

Category Creation and Brands

Toilet cleaners, despite being in the market for a long time, is a low-penetration category. Rural markets grew rapidly after the Government announced its Swachh Bharat project.[2] In one year there was an increase of 18 lakh households that were using cleaners. One crore commodes had been installed in rural markets. Domex Toilet Academy made toilets accessible and affordable. Harpic brand had roped in Amitabh Bahchan and companies had introduced smaller packs of 200 ml. Clean Mate was promoted by Big Bazaar.

While compatibility with earlier practices of consumers may have been broken, the concerted efforts of companies have brought in relative advantages of hygiene, availability of trial packs and observability aspects that are important for the diffusion of the category.

Characteristics of Diffusion of Innovation*

The following are the distinctive characteristics of diffusion of innovation:

1. **Competitive (relative) advantage**: A new product, regardless of the category of innovation, should offer a distinct advantage. Mobile telephones have the advantage of being used when on the move. Walkman offered the same advantage to music buffs. E-mails over snail-mails; mixers over traditional methods of crushing; iPods and plasma TV's over the conventional sets—all have definitive benefits. When marketers consider competitive advantage in relative terms, they have to consider (a) the target segment for the product and (b) the 'value', as perceived by the consumer. For example, a first-time buyer (a typical upgrader from the scooter) of the latest electric car in India will perceive its relative advantage differently from the one who wants a second car for his/her household at a price nearly equal to that of, say, a Maruti Alto. This perception will be different for the two segments in spite of the advantages of the electric car that offers compact size, environment-friendly features and easy manoeuvrability. If shaving gels have to catch up in the Indian context, they have to be priced competitively with creams. Value in price, features and psychological satisfaction are such features that a new offering must give and convey the value perception in the mind-set of the consumer. Maruti (when it was introduced during the '80s) in cars, Reynolds pen and Bajaj Chetak are brands that captured the 'value perception' of consumers. Reynolds makes an interesting case of value being conveyed at a higher price point. In a market full of unorganized 'brands', which compromised on quality, Reynolds followed skimming (higher-price than the existing rivals when it was introduced), but it still created the 'value' association. Ariel was the first brand to launch compact detergents in India. If the brand had created the value perception (cost per wash) in a realistic manner, it may have been a more powerful pioneering brand in this sub-category of detergents.

Value Through Technology

Value in an emerging market has to take into account the rural markets or towns (Refer to Plate 7.2). Dell had planned to have stores in several small towns. It had opened one in Hapur, a town in Uttar Pradesh that is surrounded by educational institutes and has a population of about three lakhs.[3] Dell had gained the insight that PC's are used for school home work through its survey. Diffusion a market requires several aspects of consumer behaviour and marketing mix elements.

---

* Leon G. Schiffman, Leslie L. Kanuk and S. Ramesh Kumar (in collaboration with Wisenblit J), *Consumer Behavior*, (New Delhi: Pearson Education, 2010), pp. 399–401

Plate 7.2 Dell had planned to open stores in small cities as well

2. **Compatibility**: Marketers have to examine the extent to which a product can be compatible with the existing habits, practices and cultural values of consumers (target segment). Gillette introduced shaving systems for women. Though positioned for urban women, it may take some time before the target segment takes some time to perceive the product as part of their personal care. Reference groups and word-of-mouth concepts are applicable to the diffusion of such a product. A brand should not normally communicate anything against the established practices and beliefs. If the example of the electric car is extended to practices or habits of a people, a consumer used to a conventional car (even if he/she is interested in it as a second car) has to familiarise himself/herself with a new set of usage practices like acceleration, charging batteries, driving within the city limits, changing speeds, etc. Some brands of electric toothbrushes are found in a few shops in urban Indian markets. Electric shavers (launched by Philips and Braun in India) may also have to tide over such barriers before getting diffused in a significant manner. Washing machines in urban areas of India had diffused due to the complexities of engaging traditional domestic workers and also due to the fact that in many households both the husband and wife are working and need a washing machine to save time. Gllette's introduction of shaving gel—to be used with a brush for shaving (unlike the Western markets where gel is used in a brushless shave)—is a fine example of compatibility-based offering in a market where majority of shavers use the brush.

3. **Complexity**: Complexity of products can put off consumers, however technologically advanced they may be. Except for two-in-one music (audio-cum-tape recorders) systems, there does not seem to be any convergence product that has taken off in any part of the world (including Internet TV's). However, in recent times mobile phones with additonal features such as MP3 and camera appear to have gained acceptance. With such significant advances in mobile, the telephony brands would be concentrating on 3G technologies. The success of convergence through mobiles (voice and data applications) would largely depend on the availability of infrastructure and also the extent to which such products remain within the affordability of consumers. India is probably one of the markets where there has been an exponential diffusion of mobiles, largely due to the declining prices. Millions of users are at the lower end of the market and the tariffs of mobiles in India are probably the cheapest in the world! Nokia had an interesting advertisement (TV commercial) for its Maps and Navigation mobile phone variants. Its 'turn left, turn right' campaign demonstrates the power of navigation and shows how a consumer is able to reach her destination in an auto rickshaw using the device without depending on anyone (GPS is available in most of the smartphones). Technological complexity may discourage target consumers from buying such products. Watch-TV is another example of an innovation that never took off in spite of the 'made-in-Japan' tag. Fear of technological obsolescence may be another reason for consumers not buying a product. Consumers may wait longer to invest in PC's, given that their prices have come crashing in the last 10 years. The downward lower-end offerings from leading brands like HP and Lenova added credibility to the perception of consumers that they will be able to obtain more 'value' from the buyer if they can wait longer. Complexity is not just restricted to durable hi-tech products. Products like contact lenses and hair dyes, may also diffuse slowly either due to complicated usage or fear of usage. Easy-to-use proposition and credibility through product demonstration may enable marketers to grapple with the perceived risks in such products.
4. **Trialability**: The extent to which a product can be tried out also affects diffusion. This may be extremely important, especially for consumer durable products like washing machines and microwave ovens, which are not conspicuous products (like two-wheelers, watches, cars or fashion apparel). Some of the brands of durables claim reduced usage of water or lower consumption of power. Unless backed up by the ability to be demonstrated at the point of purchase, the credibility of such claims would remain questionable. A leading store dealing with household appliances in the US has a retail showroom that permits consumers to use the offerings and satisfy themselves on several benefits and applications. Such an approach will be useful in the Indian context.
5. **Observability**: The degree to which products and brands can be observed by consumers influences diffusion of categories and brands. Mobile phones and fashion apparel are such good examples.

FMCG products, too, gain from observability of advertisements, others using the offerings and observability of offerings online (digital media). Several brands on online portals do not advertise widely but are bought by consumers.

Does Diffusion of Innovation Follow a Pattern (Adopter Categories)?

Traditionally, diffusion of innovation is supposed to follow a pattern with distinctive stages like innovators, early adopters, early majority, late majority and laggards. While the categorization of different groups of consumers at various points of time may be of relevance to marketers, the pattern of consumers adopting a product may vary from one category to another and the traditional curve may not hold good. Analysing specifically, the psychographics of innovators (among the target segment) may enable a marketer to target consumers who are likely to try the product. For example, the innovator segment for Levi's jeans may be the modern youth in urban cities, who are highly fashion conscious. The basic logic of targeting innovators is to enable the diffusion of the product among the target segment either by word of mouth or the influence of 'role models' (in fashion products). Targeting innovators may require a specific thrust on a few marketing mix elements. For example, in the case of jeans, the focus has to be on prime-area fashion outlets frequently visited by innovators. Organizing fashion-related contests at selected colleges may also help the fashion brand to get promoted. Campaigns in fashion magazines may help. In the case of consumer durables also, innovators may be critical for the brand to diffuse.

Box 7.1
Importance of Product Compatibility with Tends

Parachute Jasmine Hair Oil	Cultural Compatibility
Fast food brands	Compatibility with the trend of eating out
'Ramp-ready looks in a jiffy': proposition from brands like Fair & Lovely, Glam up, Close-up Diamond Attraction	Compatibility with the need to get presentable for a social occasion quickly.
Quaker Oats	Compatibility with the trend of fitness
Beauty salons	Enhancement of 'self' as a culturally accepted practice in cities and towns.

Brands with social appeal (Scooty) and utility products (Tupperware), too, require a positive word of mouth from innovators. In the case of utility-based products, geo-demographic segmentation (a housing locality with a specific lifestyle) may be useful. Demonstration at such places with a focus on selling the products may generate word of mouth, which in turn, will enable diffusion among the 'followers'. Tupperware uses a unique sales promotion plan where the demonstration of the product takes place at the residence of a host with prospective consumers in the neighbourhood attending the event. An innovator in one product category may not be an innovator in another category.

When the product/brand gets diffused over a period of time to the other categories of consumers like early adopters, there may also be a need to introduce variants as consumers become familiar with the product and may start developing preferences for variants (as in Close-up toothpaste, Titan watches and ice-creams). The categorization of a brand in the diffusion phase is possible with detailed research on target segments, potential for the product, competition, etc. Not all consumers (even in the target segment) may adopt the product even in the 'laggard' phase.

Another useful classification for diffusion of innovation for a new product (sub-category) like the electric cooker is given in Figure 7.1.

Consumer types		*Strategy*
Consumers who are unaware	→	Concept selling about what an electric cooker is
Symbolic rejectors know the product but decide it is not for them	→	Trigger word of mouth through personal sources of information
Symbolic adopters like the product and get to try it	→	Demonstration at retail outlets after getting them to come to the outlets
Trial adopters who have tried the product but not purchased it	→	Create a priority by outlining benefits (advertisements in specific media vehicles)
Trial rejectors who have tried the product but found it lacking	→	Researching the reasons– product development, if required, should be carried out

Figure 7.1 Diffusion of Innovation—Adopter Categories

Phase 2 Interest ↔ Persuasion

Strategy

A database on interested prospective consumers should be collected. This can be done through a contest among the target segment using appropriate media vehicles. One-to-one marketing should be done after the database is obtained.

Phase 1 and Phase 2 should lead to positive evaluation.

Box 7.2
Innovator Profile for Electric Cookers

Target segment: Married women in urban cities (nuclear families with both husband and wife working). Demographics have to be researched.

- Willingness to have an additional cooker (electric). It is preferable to choose housewives who are used to gas cookers and psychologically conditioned to the concept of the cooker.
- Working women who have to attend to multiple tasks before leaving for office.
- Married women who perceive little risk in the product.
- Married women who are likely to talk about the new products they buy.
- Married women who are oriented towards the 'novelty appeal' of their kitchen appliances.
- Married women who watch specific programs on the TV or read a specific magazine (appropriate media vehicle can be used to give them useful information on the product/brand).

Consumers who are interested in observing the trial may not visit retail outlets (point of purchase) just to express their interest in electric shavers. Most of the consumers would not make exclusive visits for this product. Hence, demonstrations should be done at 'high-service' outlets where prospective consumers visit for their regular shopping. These outlets should be dedicated to demonstration and spreading the benefits and usage of the product.

Phase 3 Decision ↔ Implementation
Strategy

As consumers for this product category are not likely to be price-sensitive, a discount may not be required to generate trials. Decision to buy could be reinforced by allowing life-time free service (at least during the initial launch period).

Phase 4 Confirmation
Strategy

This is, probably, the most critical aspect of the diffusion process. The satisfaction levels associated with trials, positive word of mouth and subsequent usage depends on this stage. All costs incurred by the brand at this stage should be treated as an investment in brand-building. The following strategies can be used in this stage.

1. In order to arrest dissonance (which may be just psychological), a full refund should be provided to a consumer who expresses dissatisfaction for a specified period.

2. An interactive division (accessible to the consumer at the cost of the company, especially when most users are likely to own a mobile phone) to help a consumer with product usage should be made available. The consumer may lose interest in the product if he is not able to get online suggestions when he requires them.
3. Apart from interactive assistance, the company should take the initiative to have face-to-face contact with the consumer. Based on feedback, it should strive to improve the product and ensure that consumers who have bought the original version can exchange it for the new one with free of cost. This builds confidence among consumers who are associated with the brand and hence, they are likely to enhance the word of mouth.
4. Finally, given the probable profile of innovators, there is scope for community-oriented brand-building. For instance, the brand's club can pursue a lifestyle interest that is common to the consumers belonging to the club. It may be worthwhile to find out from consumers what kind of lifestyle pastime will interest them and plan a promotional campaign based on the feedback.

Companies need to be careful about online media like YouTube or websites where the offering is being discussed. A good offering with strong functional and service benefits is certain to have a good word of mouth.

Dimensions of Brand Diffusion

At a time when new products are proliferating, a marketer will want to know how the target segment accepts the products over a period of time. It is important that consumers perceive the 'newness' in a new product as a consequence of marketing it.

Dimensions of 'Newness' in a Product

It may be worthwhile to analyse the kinds of 'newness' associated with products and apply psychological factors to convey it. Product attributes can create a feeling of uniqueness, especially in a highly-competitive category, be it toothpaste, TV or washing machine. Though marketers always feel that benefits are more important than features, consumers may also be drawn towards features. A brand should ensure that the novelty of the feature gets translated into functional benefits and emphasize the latter in its communication.

Awareness of a novel feature → Qudra Point Focus (QPF)/ "Golden Eye"

↓ ↓

Follow up after awareness — How does it improve the performance

↓ ↓

Reinforcement of the message at retail outlets (for durables) — Demonstration linking QPF/Golden Eye with TV viewing

Figure 7.2 Dimensions of Newness in a Brand

Box 7.3
Convergence and Concepts of Diffusion

With advances in technology, convergence products enable brands to be introduced in the market all over the world. Internet telephony, for example, is evolving in some parts of the world, but it is perhaps too early to predict if it will diffuse in a big way.

Huge investments are required to lay such networks. Some Japanese companies have introduced advertising between messages to strengthen the feasibility of operations. While diffusion may take time, studies in Europe and the USA on mobile advertising indicate that users who are initially drawn to such convergence products can be retained through careful customization of services and online information.

Nintendo, a Japanese brand of computer-based videogames, was one of the fastest brands to be diffused in the US. Computer games were innovated by a firm called Atari (US) during the '70s. Nintendo used academic concepts to achieve diffusion in a market where even retailers were wary of changing the product because of the products offering that had disastrous marketing history associated with Atari. Nintendo had competitive knowledge (high-resolution graphics) and a variety of games. It could observe the diffusion graph because it controlled the demand for its games.

Nintendo went on to become a rage in the country. The brand was also introduced as Famicom to avoid its association with computers, though it was computer based. Famicom, apart from sounding less complex, would have also generated curiosity among consumers. Trials were encouraged with kids being asked to try out the product. It was easy to operate and was promoted during Christmas at a time when people shop for novel presents, especially for their children. Nintendo also priced the brand to convey a value perception. It priced the hardware less, but priced the software higher. Such an approach of the brand was the 'razor and blade' strategy.

In the case of consumables, there is a need to introduce variants (after careful research) or features (an outcome of technology). Internal costs and profitability aspects are required to be studied before a brand plans the variants, especially in a crowded market. Little Hearts from Britannia, Polo from Nestle, the initial launch of Ariel's compact detergent, fairness creams from Fair & Lovely and the variants in soaps are interesting examples of how new brands gain acceptance by using either technology or product variants.

The 'newness' in durables can be a novel feature itself and the accompanying benefit may appeal to a section of consumers. In the case of consumables, the novelty can be

1. Unique taste/shape because of technology: Kurkure snacks (cultural taste made with a specific technology)

2. Innovative strategies with a 'value', Guard, the lower priced twin-edged blade from Gillete is an example.
3. Creating a concept that is acceptable to consumers based on the cultural beliefs.

Fair skin has always been perceived to be superior and beautiful in the Indian context. Fair & Lovely is a dominant brand in the fairness cream market. The brand has also triggered the growth of this market in the last few years. Though a number of brands have entered the market in the recent times and perhaps, even broken the monopoly of the pioneering brand, Fair & Lovely continues to be the dominant brand in the category associated with fairness creams. When a brand successfully introduces a concept acceptable to the consumer, the brand-building efforts enable the brand to be perceived favourably. Such efforts create a brand image with the relevant associations vital for a brand and attempts to diffuse a new concept. If this aspect of consumer behaviour is not employed, then the brand will end up in just conveying the concept while the 'follower' brands capitalize on the 'category awareness' (created by the pioneering brand). Taj Mahal tea is available in tea bags that has not only created awareness in a new product category (of tea bags) but also created brand associations.

Value in Durables

As in the case of Nirma in detergents, a brand of durables can also create 'newness' with a value proposition. eBay which institutionalised the second-hand market for various categories through online channel is a good example for creating value in durables for expanding the market and diffusing the brand. It is vital that such brands retain this 'value' in the long run so that the brand can sustain diffusion when competitive brands follow. This is a common problem associated with incremental 'newness' introduced by brands in a crowded market. In recent times, a brand has to commit itself to a proposition—especially if it is 'value' for the lower-end market to ensure that the brand continues to get diffused.

Symbolism as Newness in Durables

Symbolism also can be used in durables (as in the case of cosmetics, apparel, etc.). Onida used symbolism to its advantage in a TV market, which was just developing, during the mid-'80s. "Neighbour's envy, owner's pride", pushed the price to the background and created a higher-end segment that was able to associate with this appeal at a time when television was still a symbolic product to be displayed in the drawing hall of the house. But as in value, a brand can sustain itself on the platform of symbolism by launching innovative products which will appeal to the innovators. This it can do by combining symbolism with innovative features that enhances the psychological feeling of the owner of a particular brand. This is different from the novelty appeal as discussed earlier, which appeals to the curiosity of the consumer. In-depth research is required to find out the feasibility of such products for innovators. The earlier version of picture telephones by AT & T and TV-watches by some Japanese brands failed because the role of innovators was not duly considered. Innovators are extremely important in the cycle of innovation because of the word of mouth involved in the diffusion of products, especially in durables. Service provided during the launch of the new product is as vital as the latter's novelty. The service also influences the word of mouth, which has an impact on prospective consumers.

The Power of Trial

While marketers offer test-drives of automobiles to give consumers a feel of the brand, trials can be used powerfully even for the diffusion of a commonplace product like a dish-washing bar. This is a market that has 'no-cost' alternatives such as ash and sand. Vim Bar, in its improved version, adopted an effective sales promotion scheme along with a unique 'challenge-based' promotion to enhance brand trials. Rin Supreme, marketed by the same company and with a high level of penetration, roped in Vim Bar in a sales promotional scheme. The brand also sampled the product among the target segment with an assurance of providing a year's supply of the product if the consumer was not satisfied with the sample. The offer was filmed and the advertising campaign created on this basis enhanced the visibility of the brand apart from improving the word of mouth. In the case of durables like washing machines, a brand can combine demonstration with trial to increase the credibility of its proposition (such as saving electricity, removal of dirt though a specific and unique action, etc.). It is surprising that in a highly competitive market with widespread exchange offers and freebies, demonstration/trials at the point of purchase is not adopted as a brand strategy.

Functional Utility

While value is the determinant of the worthiness of a product for a specific price point, the functional utility has to be analysed in terms of convenience, ease of use or the manner in which the product benefits the consumer. Though value is important, an intensive analysis of functional utility can help a brand capture the perception of consumers in its 'newness'. Consumers readily pay a premium on shampoo sachets even at the lower end of the market because of the convenience and lower unit cost. This, in spite of the fact that some sachets cost more than the regular size shampoo bottles in terms of per ml cost. Weighing the functional utility against the novelty appeal may be important in certain categories. Four-stroke, by itself, is a favourable feature in two-wheelers. But consumers may compare the feature with its utility. Honda Activa's design, features and comfort may have appealed to several segments of consumers and is the leading scooter brand (in 2015).The brand has a leading market share in the scooter market that got kick-started after the market in this segment (Bajaj was a leading brand in the category for several years) had almost declined.

A combination of factors has to be considered while formulating strategies for the diffusion of products/brands. Detergents, shampoos or food are such categories in which consumers in the lower strata buy low-unit cost packs to exert their expenditure control. They attempt to consume less by buying low unit cost packs and this kind of buying may result in an overall saving in the household budget. Marketing communication should emphasize the product application costs (wherever applicable) to ensure faster diffusion of the brand.

Why Do Brands Fail?

In an era of brand loyalty and brand experience, it is important that marketers analyse why brands fail. There may be several reasons, both internal and external to the organization, for the cause of failure.

Category Development

Normally, brands evolve as categories and develop over a period of time. Soaps, biscuits, shampoos, pens, washing machines and audio products are a few examples. If a category does not evolve, chances are that consumers don't perceive it favourably. Or, they do not understand the nature of the product and so do not take it into their 'consideration set'. A lot of research is required on marketing mix elements to ensure that the category registers with the target segment. The onus of doing the research is on one of the pioneering brands that kick-starts the category. While this meant creating awareness some decades ago, it is a complicated exercise in the current context. Red Label, Horlicks, Surf, Dettol, Colgate, Cadbury and Scissors may be some of the classic brands that had been responsible for the growth in their respective categories. Incidentally, all these brands have also run successful advertising campaigns over the past several years. While some of them may have faced intensive competition in the recent years, they have also been a part of product history in the Indian market.

Brylcreem is a brand that may have contributed to the growth of the hair cream market. Clinic, the well-known shampoo brand, also moved into hair creams but later dropped such variants. Brylcreem was the pioneering brand in this category. There are certain interesting questions regarding the product category:

- What was the target segment for the brand when it was launched: executives, men who travelled on work or the younger segment who followed a particular lifestyle?
- What were the brand benefits, convenience in carrying the pack (as against a hair oil bottle) or better grooming?
- Did pricing restrict the growth of the brand (vis-à-vis hair oil) and, if so, did the brand attempt niche marketing strategies?
- What was the perception of consumers on counts of the frequency of usage, hair styling and 'stickiness'?

Development of the category, especially by the early brands in it, determines not only the success of such brands but also how subsequent the brands perform in this category. This is not to say that the late entrant brands will not succeed in developing that category. In fact, there are several brands that have successfully done so. A pioneering brand can become synonymous with its category and hence, be the first in the mind of the consumer. Later, it can make appropriate changes in the marketing mix to ensure it leads with a sustainable advantage. Close-up in gel toothpastes is a good example to show that a brand can succeed after pioneering the sub-category, even though it may take time to succeed. Ariel had introduced the sub-category of compact detergents. Parachute After Shower, a hair cream from Parachute, has made rapid strides in recent times in the category of hair cream with about 70 per cent market share over the last ten years.[4]) Communication had focused on the style aspects of personal grooming and also included a celebrity.

Timing of the Brand

Timing of a brand is important. There are two options for a brand to diffuse itself. It can either introduce a new concept and wait for the market to develop and accept it or introduce a new concept when the timing is right. The former approach demands more money, time and organizational resources. The latter can be successful if there is adequate and on-going research on consumer behaviour. Time-share in the vacationing market has evolved in India and is still a niche segment. A brand attempted this in the mid- '80s. The timing for pure fruit juices in today's context is probably right, even though it is still a niche market. For nearly two decades, there was only one brand of pure apple juice. Hima Peas, a brand of frozen green peas, was introduced during the '60s when lifestyles were far more laidback than they are today and people were not under pressure to buy frozen vegetables. Hero Honda's initial proposition of economy was timed well with consumers willing to purchase two-wheelers for personal transport and the improved purchasing power of the target segment. Brands in commodity items like salt and flour have been introduced when there was a need for convenience and good quality. There may even be situations in which timing plays a role with regard to changing lifestyles.

Contact lenses have been in the country for the last 30 years. Many consumers gave up the product after trying it. The branded offerings that have been in the market for the last few years have attempted to market the product through a mix of strategies. Changing lifestyles, coupled with aspects of convenience and personal grooming, may have changed consumer perception of contact lenses. Brands should adopt a well-structured strategy beginning with the identification of appropriate segments. Baby powders are another product category wherein a number of brands failed to make progress in a niche market (like Pond's and Glaxo). A related market of baby soaps has seen a few brands in the recent times. Given the awareness of consumers, affordability and the attitude of parents towards child care, it may be appropriate to build brands in such categories though the market for such products may only be niche. Brands like Itch-Guard and Krack have timed their launch very well. Offering for the elderly is a market that needs to be explored in India. Cadbury has introduced Cadbury Lite especially for people diagnosed with diabetics.

Cultural Dimensions

Culture is unique to a market and can offset several attempts of marketers. The clear lemon drink in the carbonated beverages or soft drink market (Campa Lime or Sprint in the '80s or the bitter lime popular in the West) may not do too well in the country because they are not a part of its culture and eating and drinking are strong cultural habits. While a number of consumer products may get diffused because of changing lifestyles, food products that are not a part of a culture will meet with resistance. Bread has low penetration levels in several parts of the country even though it has been around for a long time. The reasoning also holds good for shaving systems for women (Braun). Herbal soaps and shampoos, which have built brands on cultural practices, associated themselves with the usage of such ingredients Godrej's Storewell advertisements of steel cabinets used traditional marriage occasions as its theme. Brands that are associated with strongly-entrenched cultural practices/beliefs, have to be careful before using a Western appeal. The core benefit of Fair & Lovely, the leading fairness brand, draws from cultural beliefs. The brand has also launched a herbal variant. Mother–daughter associations have been a part of Indian advertising. Clinic Plus had all along used this association and created an aspirational association around the brand when the environment is all about women's aspirations.

Nestle introduced its dark chocolate version in India, and the variant was taken off in the market for a very long time before being reintroduced after decades. Bournville, the bitter chocolate brand from Cadbury, has been in the Indian market for a long time but caters to a small niche. Cadbury has been instrumental in expanding the market for chocolates among adults. New concept products can target youth. The advantage of targeting the young is that they are more open to new tastes than the older consumers. The youth may also be more amenable to changing habits. It is worthwhile for marketing academia and practitioners to give as much importance to failed brands as to the successful ones.

Branding the Unknown—Strategies for 'Small' Brands

Fairever in creams, Nirma in detergents, Narasu's coffee and MTR (Bangalore-based company) and other smaller regional brands in fast foods have stood out in a marketing area that deals with high-visibility advertising and expensive promotional 'push'. While major brands like Titan, Britannia and Colgate have used marketing concepts to build brands in a highly competitive scenario, marketing principles are equally applicable to brands that are manufactured in the small-scale sector. This is particularly true in the Indian context, which offers tremendous potential for value-based offerings, given the proliferation of unorganized markets in several categories like batteries, watches, biscuits, UPS, computers, moulded luggage, cassettes, detergents, sewing machines, ice-creams, jewellery, footwear and readymade apparel.

The Basics

An unknown product manufactured in the small-scale industry has to compete with several established offerings, especially brands that have been in the market for several decades. The unknown offering has to build itself up as a brand with limited resources in terms of advertising, distribution network and financial outflow. Consumers are becoming extremely discerning, apart from the fact that they have far more choices today. Several decades back, even established brands used to 'float' their offerings in the market because competition was not very intense.

A small-scale offering must research the market and select the appropriate target segment. While there is nothing new about doing this, it is true that the rule is practised more in its breach than observance. This is the foundation strategy for a small-scale unit as mistakes may be irreversible. Hindustan Lever can afford to introduce a variant of Close-up and remove it from the market, but such experimentation on product launches will not be feasible for a small-scale company. There are a few aspects that need consideration before a small-scale firm segments the market. Segmentation, here, refers to geographical, psychographic and demographic characteristics of the target consumers.

Caution 1: Non–branded offerings in the market–Scope for new offerings

A typical example is herbal soaps. While mega brands battle it out in an advertising-dominated category, Medimix has carved a niche for itself in the South Indian markets. In fact, there are several such brands in some other markets, like Krishna Tulasi. Mega brands may follow pioneers (herbal variant of Fair & Lovely followed Fairever). This cannot be avoided. But the leading product can build itself as a brand by being on top of the mind of the consumers. Product categories which can be researched on similar lines are baby foods, toys and traditional snacks and eatables.

Caution 2: Value matters

Consumers look for value, which is nothing but enhanced utility at a given price point. Enhanced utility can range from functional features of a toothbrush to an 'experience' in a hospital or clinic. Value orientation is so strong that small-scale industries can compete with mega brands like the way Nirma did in the detergents market. While Vim is a major brand in the category of scouring powders, Sabeena was a brand in South India and Shineit was popular in Western markets. Value has to be delivered at a lower price point, especially in a market where small-scale offerings will compete with mega brands. The latter have consistently followed this strategy. There were several small-scale offerings among ball pens but none of the brands had a value propositioned like Reynolds. There are several offerings in biscuits but none offered the value of Tiger. Heavy advertising may have had an incremental impact on the acceptance of these brands. But the core product at a specific price point attracted consumers to try out and remain with these brands. In fact, Reynolds delivered value at a higher price point. It is an accepted fact all over the world that 'word of mouth' is the most effective advocate of a brand and any offering from the small-scale sector has to be taken into consideration. There are several regional brands of clocks which sell by word of mouth. Gold Winner is a regional brand of edible oil that advertised through regional channels.

Caution 3: Do not overlook premium niche markets

Contrary to the popular perception, small-scale offerings can develop a premium niche market even in established product categories if such niches are identified properly. As mentioned earlier, small scale offerings should avoid mega brands. But if they have to, for some reason, compete with the latter, they must identify premium niches. While there are several packaged tea brands, a few brands of flavoured tea have appeared in the market through modern retailing. While these variants are available in limited outlets, a brand can be built at a high price in a geographical area where there is a demand for such offerings. While Titan and Ajanta may be well-known brands, an enterprising marketer has built a small niche for a clock cased in sandalwood, which is priced at a premium price. Furniture is another category that offers potential for a premium niche.

Caution 4: Cluttered retailing is to be avoided

A small-scale offering has to be very selective about the manner in which it chooses its retail network. This has to be done along with the 'value' proposition. But the suggested retailing approach cannot be a substitute for a bad offering. Mega brands with their established 'push and pull' strategies have little space for unknown brands to compete with them. Hence, a prudent strategy for an unknown brand to establish itself is to find shelf space at upcoming departmental outlets in upper-middle class localities. A number of unknown offerings in foods, candies, shampoos and floor cleaners are already implementing this approach. This will be particularly effective because of the thrust of departmental stores on cultivating 'store brands'. Once a brand gets established at such retail outlets, it can slowly develop a retail network in a specific geographical market. Starting with the usual 'grocery- store' approach will be difficult for unknown brands. Besides competition, there may also be doubts about quality perception.

Caution 5: Planning a promotional strategy

A careful planning is a must for using promotional methods, as expensive advertising is ruled out. Advertising on cable television may be cost effective but a brand has to make sure that the message reaches the target segment. FM radio stations have reactivated the interest of marketers with regard to radio as a media. Stations like 'Radio City' may be very useful to advertise lifestyle products like jeans or goggles, even if they are offered by an unknown brand. Given the profile of listeners, at least a section of them are likely to consider new offerings after becoming aware of them through such media vehicles. Point-of-purchase posters can be useful at specific retail outlets, especially for eatables and commodities. Regardless of the promotional mix used, an unknown brand should clearly convey its USP over the established ones at a given price point because comparing price points is part of the Indian consumer's behaviour. Event marketing,—normally thought to be the preserve of mega brands—is a very effective tool if the target segment is chosen with care. Organizing an event in a women's fashion institute/beauty parlour will create more awareness than advertisements in a shopping guide. The event has to be novel as well as meaningful to the product category and the brand.

While certain strategies have been suggested, these by themselves cannot guarantee success. They need to be customized to a specific product/market situation. While elaborate marketing research may be beyond the reach of the small-scale sector, it must attempt to build a knowledge base of consumer behaviour in whatever way it can. It is this base that can provide vital inputs to customize strategies.

Barrier Breakers: An Application of the Concept of Diffusion of Innovation

Insta Care, a well-known multinational in the field of eye-care and opthalmics, entered the Indian market in 1992. The company had invested around ₹ 75 crore in Pune to set up a factory, which would produce eight lakh units of contact lenses per annum. Given the huge market in Indian eye-care, the company's intention was to pioneer and create a market for contact lenses. Contact lenses are not new to India. People used them even in the late'60s. But no major player had made a concerted effect to market the product in a professional manner. There were six small manufacturers who manufactured the product and sold it to a few ophthalmologists and ophthalmic opticians. Insta Care made its estimates about the potential of the product in the following manner:

About 40 per cent of the Indian population required some kind of vision correction. Even if 1 per cent of these patients opted for contact lenses, the potential would be somewhere around 10 million units. Given the replacement cycle and product variants that could be introduced slowly, the company felt it could become the unassailable leader in the product category. Given the fact that Insta Care was a leading player in some of the developed countries and was backed by research, there seemed to be little risk in attempting to enter the Indian market.

Mittal, Marketing Manager, Insta Care was recapitulating the strategies of the company on a monthly visit to the corporate headquarters of the company at New Delhi. He joined the company in December 1995 and was based in Bombay. He knew the company had committed certain fundamental marketing mistakes in the last three years. With a new concept product like contact lenses, ('new' because consumer acceptance over the last two decades has been low), an in-depth analysis of consumer behaviour would have been invaluable. The company had banked more on the statistical route to get its estimates rather than getting to the underpinnings of consumer mind-set. The company's initial market study was sketchy. It concentrated on potential estimation and found that about four lakh lenses could be sold in 1992. The report also projected the figure over the next seven years and placed it at around one million by 2000 CE. On the behavioural angle, the study just probed into the perception of consumers from the viewpoint of convenience. But this study was unprofessional and superficial, according to Mittal.

Strategy of Insta Care

The company launched an advertising campaign, which concentrated on the aesthetic appeal of contact lenses. The TV commercial showed a group of young adults making fun of a friend because she wore spectacles. The model in the advertisement uses contact lenses and becomes the cynosure of all eyes as it were. The TV commercial ran successfully for almost a year. During this time the company organized what it called 'easy-vision camps' in schools, colleges and offices. The company demonstrated how to use contact lenses with doctors answering queries of the audience. The company also provided free trials of lenses during the camp. The camp was restricted to select institutions/organizations in urban cities. A year after the launch, the company also went on a huge sales promotion campaign that offered free gifts like cooling glasses and clocks against the purchase of lenses over a particular billing amount. The distribution strategy was surprisingly unusual. The company set up a network of optical dealers in around 200 cities and towns. Except for metros where a qualified practitioner was attached to each outlet in the evenings, the other outlets had 'eye care-takers', employed by the respective optical dealer. Optical dealers in metros had to take the company's approval for hiring practitioners, but the latter did not insist on this condition for other towns. The reason was that optical dealers were unable to find practitioners who met the job specifications of the company. A consolidated sum was paid to the practitioner in a metro, apart from fees on a per-patient basis. In other towns, the 'eye care-takers' were paid on a per-patient basis. The company reimbursed 60 per cent of the payment. The services were available at all the outlets only in the evenings.

Contact lenses can be of three kinds: the semi-soft or rigid gas permeable (RGP) lenses, which allow free movement of oxygen between the lens and the cornea, soft lenses which have a higher percentage of water content and frequent replacement, and disposable lenses. Soft lenses have an advantage over RGP lenses as they do not draw too much of dust. Insta Care introduced soft lenses (called Insta Care) for the first time in India when most consumers were using RGP. Soft lenses differentiated themselves from RGP lenses, which were sold by small players in specific regions with the help of practitioners. There were some dealers also in some of these regions but their influence on consumers was insignificant. Insta Care marketed its lenses in the range of ₹ 1200 to 1600 a pair. Added to this was the cost of cleaning and maintenance solutions amounting to about ₹ 100 per month. These lenses can last for about a year. The company's turnover in 1995 was around ₹ 25 crore.

Competition

Clear Vision, yet another multinational in the eye-care market, entered India in 1994. The company believed that the product was too 'technical' for consumers to pick up off the shelf. The company's market survey indicated that a majority of the urban people with vision problems visited an ophthalmologist. The concept of optometrists, who specialised in vision correction, had not caught on in India. The long-term objective of this company was to expand the market through optometrists. As this objective would have taken time to accomplish, the company made distribution network as its priority. It felt that the technicalities of the product needed to be customized to specific consumer needs. So, it launched the product in 10 cities. It approached well-known practitioners and opticians in these cities to form a network through which its brand credibility could be enhanced.

The company entered the market with regular soft lenses but a year later, it introduced disposable lenses. The idea behind the new offering was that disposable lenses dominate the global market. Apart from this, there was the differentiation aspect of disposable lenses that provided certain advantages over the regular ones. They were more hygienic, facilitated better vision and were easy to maintain. This could have been a move to pre-empt Insta Care, which also had its disposable lenses in the other markets of the world. Their price ranged between ₹ 3000 to 3500 for a pair. The company branded this offering as 'Crystal' with a six-monthly replacement package. Consumer feedback encouraged the company to launch its best-selling brand abroad called 'Freedom', which was a monthly disposable lens. Unlike its competitor, Clear Vision had a low-profile media campaign, which highlighted the convenience of disposable lenses. The company used practitioners to push its soft lenses and disposables. It believed that 'pull' strategies will not work well at that stage of market evolution without the usual heavy advertising and high visibility drives, which the company felt would be wasteful. It identified opticians in Bombay and Bangalore, who catered to upmarket consumers. And then, it introduced a cosmetic product-line for them. These cosmetic lenses came in six colours and targeted the upmarket party-goer who would use these lenses for their snob appeal. These were priced between ₹ 4000 to 5000 a pair. It was called 'Showtime'.

A Research Study

Mittal was convinced that the future strategies of Insta Care will emerge from more serious market probing. He selected the following issues, which needed to be addressed by the research study:

- What is the current user base of contact lenses?
- What is the consumer perception of contact lenses?
- Do consumers perceive cosmetic benefits or functional benefits from using contacts?
- What is the word-of-mouth on contact lenses, in general, from users?
- What is the feedback from the users of Insta Care?
- How exactly does a consumer decide on buying contact lenses?
- Perception of consumer disposables.

Mittal felt these issues, apart from demographic data, would provide a strong base for his future decisions.

Six months later, Mittal was going through the marketing research report submitted by an agency that covered 13 cities. Their study used a sample of 5000 consumers (past and potential users in the income bracket of ₹ 15,000 plus per month). The pilot study showed that the lower economic segment was not interested in the product.

The highlights of the study were:

(a) Eight lakh people use contact lens currently (obtained by the agency from several sources).

(b) Around 70 per cent of the users gave up contacts and switched back to spectacles. Of these, 50 per cent were users of RGP (hard or semi-soft lenses).

(c) The perception of most non-users was that contact lenses:
— are made of glass and harmful for the eyes
— are difficult to use
— can break easily
— are far more expensive than spectacles, which last for years
— are difficult to maintain.

(d) A majority of the users perceived the functional benefit of convenience associated with the product. About 30 per cent of the non-users associated 'looks' with contact lenses. Among users, pre-dominantly those who used RGP ones, there was dissatisfaction regarding the clarity of vision.

(e) Users bad-mouthed contact lenses on performance, price and weekly maintenance. Most of them used the RGP lenses.

(f) Most consumers who had tried Insta Care were satisfied with the product but felt that the product was far too expensive a replacement for spectacles. About 20 per cent users complained of a bad fit.

(g) The pattern of consumer usage that emerged from the research study is shown in Figure 7.3.

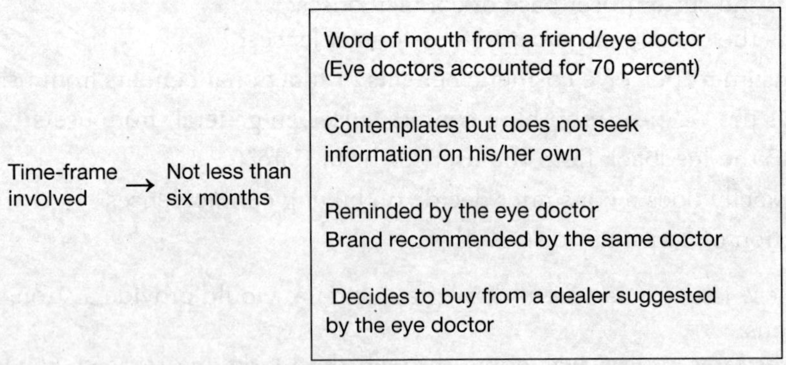

Figure 7.3 Consumer Decision Making Sequence

(h) A majority of the non-users and users perceived that disposable lenses are offering additional benefits, there was no maintenance involved. But most of them also considered the price as a demotivating fact. Respondents said they would wait for prices to come down before deciding on buying disposables.

Mittal was reminded of the innovation–decision model, which he was forced to go through as a part of his consumer behaviour program during his student days (Table 7.1).

Table 7.1 Innovation–Decision Model

Stage	Relevance to the case
Knowledge	Lack of understanding of the product itself
Persuasion	Negative attitude because of bad word of mouth of RPG users
	Need to create awareness not only on contact lenses but also on soft lenses
Decision	Consumer not convinced about the price of contact lenses. What kind of value can be introduced?
Implementation	Customization of lenses can play a vital role
Confirmation	Strategies to retain existing lens users

Promotional Issues for the Diffusion of the Product

(a) What is the functional benefit of both the product category and the brand?
(b) How can contact lenses fit in with the users of spectacles? (Barriers on usage aspects)
(c) Complex nature of customization – Implications on consumer behaviour? Encouraging the consumer to go to the expert doctor/optician.
(d) How can potential consumers try out the product?
(e) How can the 'visibility' of satisfied lens users (of the brand) be created?

Touch of Reality

Price Matters, but It is not the Only Factor

Dove soap bars, Raga watches, Allen Solly branded apparel, Sensodyne toothpastes and Bru Gold coffee are some examples drawn from the Indian context to reflect that if segmentation is right and offering provides value for the respective segment, pricing by itself need not be a differentiator. These brands provide value at a higher price point.

Opportunity with Respect to Low Penetration of Brands

Different brands attempt different strategies to get diffused in the respective categories. Lipton Iced Tea introduced the powder variant. Dettol advertises on a variety of applications that include keeping germs away from the steering wheel of the car. Maggi introduced sachets with a cap. Fair & Handsome introduced a ₹ 5 pack to increase trialability. Movie celebrities have been used to diffuse fad-life products. Dev Anand's hat (Jewel Thief) of the '60s, Rajesh Khanna's stereotype of a handsome man with a motorcycle (Andaz) during the '70s and apparel worn by celebrities in recent times are examples. Gillette's Vector Plus advertises its twin-edged blades as a durable offering at an affordable price (when the shaving blade market is dominated by conventional blades). Cadbury and Nestle introduced liquid chocolates at a low price point. Tex, a brand of toilet cleaner, positioned itself as a better alternative to acid with a low-priced packaging. Shampoo brands from P & G and Unilever are available in sachet packs. Parachute pioneered low-priced packs in hair oil. Given the large Indian population, even a miniscule additional penetration of the market will bring in a large volume of users for a brand.

Technologies, Company Strategies, Consumer Appeal and Diffusion

It is interesting to note that a company's strategy and its policy on several aspects concerning the offering have implications on diffusion of the product in the respective market. Decades ago, Sony's Betamax format of video recording failed, as it did not have any functionality to record football matches or movies in terms of duration without a change of operation. Matsushita came out with its VHS format, opened up the format to VHS equipment manufacturers and succeeded not only with its brand but also in expanding the market for video recorders.[5] IPods with its iTune ecosystem, iPad and iPhones with their features and symbolic appeals are examples of brands that have created history through rapid diffusion among consumers.

End Notes

1. "Thin and Cute? You'll get funds", *The Times of India*, August 10, 2015.
2. Sagar Malviya (2015), 'Toilet Cleaners Win the Day', *The Economic Times*, 2015.
3. Delshad Irani (2015), 'Dell Goes Rural with a Vengeance', *The Economic Times*, 14 October.
4. http://bigbasket.com/pb/parachute/?next=%2Fpb%2Fparachute%2F, accessed on 14 October, 2015.
5. http://drug-dev.com/Main/Back-Issues/Beta-or-VHS-When-Good-Is-Good-Enough-276.aspx?-When-Good-Is-Good-Enough!-276.aspx, accessed on January 11, 2017.

Exercises

1. Choose tea bag category. Comment on the diffusion of the category using the principles of diffusion?
2. Café Coffee Day (CCD) has an instant coffee bag named Filta Fresh. How would you diffuse this brand? Visit CCD to get details about this product or visit their website (product available as on May 17, 2017).

CHAPTER 8

The Concept of Reference Groups and Their Implications on Branding

Self–Brand–Celebrity Connect

Celebrity endorsement is a significant aspect of the Indian marketing context. Self-concepts consist of the actual image of self as well as the aspirational aspect of self. Reference group concepts are associated with the celebrity–consumer connect.

In an effort to have a fine focus on self-brand associations, the brand owners tend to select only the celebrities who can connect well with the target segment. Phillips had different celebrities for endorsing different products for instance, it used actor Arjun Kapoor for advertising its 'Beard Trimmer' for body grooming, Alia Bhatt for its beauty appliances and actor Varun Dhawan for advertising its unique 'Aquatouch' shaving appliance.[1]

The Power of Celebrity–brand Combination in Consumer Behaviour

Celebrities are important elements of reference group concepts. They have been a part of the Indian culture for several decades and they inspire consumers (in the respective segment) in various ways using their expertise, credibility, and charisma.

How can celebrities add value to brand positioning aspects and brand associations when concepts of reference groups are applied?

There are several ways by which celebrities can add value to positioning strategies. The Indian context perhaps offers the most diverse examples in the world, both in terms of product categories that employ celebrities and the nature of the celebrities employed by them. Sachin Tendulkar, Amitabh Bachchan, and Shah Rukh Khan are celebrities who have represented diverse categories over the years and it would be interesting to research if there are such examples in the world.

The following are examples from the Indian context (the examples present historical and contemporary ones):

Palmolive shaving cream	: Kapil Dev and Sunil Gavaskar's endorsement of its effectiveness (charisma of the celebrity endorses the brand; this is common even in the present day context).
Brylcreem	: Farokh Engineer, the dashing opening batsman and wicketkeeper of the seventies, endorsed the brand to give it a racy, sporty touch.
Lux	: Positioned as a luxury soap, topical celebrities are chosen time to time (Glamour, charisma, and endorsement add value).
Boost	: Sachin Tendulkar (a sportsman's knowledgeable endorsement of a brand on its supply of energy).
Raga	: Katrina Kaif's endorsement for a watch that was created for the ethnic woman to showcase her beauty and sensuality.
Reid and Taylor	: Amitabh Bachchan replacing James Bond for the higher-end brand from S. Kumar (apparel brand).
Gold Café	: Pataudi endorsed this classy, granular coffee brand.
Asian Paints	: Saif Ali Khan endorsed its brand and associated with fun and surprise.
Junior Parker	: Amitabh endorsed its class when Parker introduced a lower priced version.
XYLYZ	: The luxury watch brand from Titan launched a campaign that had a sports celebrity, fashion celebrity and a technologist endorsing it (to create a new image of a luxury watch.
Guess	: Priyanka Chopra was selected by this American denim brand because she resembled Sophia Lauren.
Fiama Di Wills	: Deepika Padukone endorsed the brand's 'science with nature' proposition.
Thumps Up	: Salman Khan's image provided the 'tough, rugged and adventurous' impression to the brand.
Pleasure	: A two wheeler launched exclusively for women had Priyanka Chopra breaking cultural beliefs ('That stupid Village girl' TV ad) to provide an image of 'modern, independent, and self-assured' user imagery.
30 Plus	: A tablet that was focused on energy had actor Jitendra (nineties) known for his 'energy-based' roles endorsing it.

Knorr Soup	:	Kajol endorsed the brand suggesting the fun involved serving it for kids. The ad shows the actress as a caring mother having fun with her kids.
Snickers	:	The brand of chocolate from Mars company had Rekha and positioned it as a Snack with the tag- line 'Hungry? Grab a Snickers.'
Cadbury	:	Amitabh was used to enhance the trustworthiness of (chocolate) the brand after there was a furore with worms being found in the chocolate offering of the brand.
Chinny Pickles	:	Used a regional celebrity in Tamilnadu to advocate for the regional delicacy.
Anacin	:	Used a regional celebrity to advocate the relieving (analgesic) action of the offering (observational learning is indicated in this example as viewers would observe the relief experienced by the model and by the tablet when required).
Van Heusen	:	The readymade apparel brand had Deepika Padukone to provide a modern and sophisticated fashion association among its target segment.
Nesfit	:	Had Sachin, Leander Paes, and Prakash Padukone to endorse the (Nestle) effectiveness of the offering.
Yamaha bikes	:	John Abraham to provide an youthful and modern association as the brand had not advertised as frequently as it competitors before.
Cinthol	:	Featured cricketer Imran Khan during the eighties when the he was at the peak of his career (per- haps to bring in a topical association).
Sun Feast	:	Featured Shah Rukh Khan in a playful sequence with children to cash in on the car's popularity with kids when the brand was launched.
Santro	:	Starring Shah Rukh Khan to endorse its brand and gain visibility in a market where the brand was completely new and competing brands were strongly positioned. The star was also used for its subsequent ilo launch.
Taj (tea)	:	The noted tabla player, Zakir Hussain, was used in the initial years to reflect the fine preference of the classical artist. Later Saif Ali Khan was introduced to make the brand connect with the target segment.

Note: The associations used in the explanation are based on the author's perception/analysis/interpretation of the ads and information. It was meant to provide academic understanding of the concepts involved; they may not reflect the perception of consumers.

> **Types Reference Groups and Online Initiatives**
>
> The age-old concept of reference groups seem to be getting revived with the diffusion of online buying and online sharing of consumer opinions. Myntra is planning to build a community of consumers through its fashion network by which consumers can exchange opinions about fashion and also use the platform for virtual wardrobes with pictures and image searches.[2] Online fashion is likely to create an ecosystem full of reference groups that would be able to multiply the number of online communities.

The examples reflect the usefulness of appeals that makes use of one aspect of reference group appeals. A reference group is a set of people with whom individuals compare themselves to shape their attitudes, values, knowledge and behaviour (including buying behaviour). When a celebrity is associated with a brand, the consumer who identifies with the celebrity feels that he/she is the symbolic member of the group that is represented by the celebrity (the consumer neither has a face-to-face interaction or relationship with the group). Brands use these concepts in a number of situations and using the celebrities is a vital application. A brand derives value from celebrity associations, if celebrity usage happens in a conceptual manner. Marketers should know the aspirational groups with which target consumers may want to associate themselves. These aspirational groups have to be represented in a manner that will appeal to target consumers.

Kinds of Reference Groups

There can be three kinds of reference groups. The aspirational group is one which the consumer admires and likes to emulate but of which he/she is not a member. The consumer does not have a face-to-face contact with this group. Hence, this is a secondary group.

Associative reference groups are those to which the consumer belongs. These may be his/her friends, family, college peers, sports club co-members and professional groups, etc. The consumer has a face-to-face contact with the group. Hence, this is a primary group. Besides the aspirational groups, associative groups are also useful to marketers in positioning strategies. For example, Allen Solly, with its semi-formal apparel, would have appealed to specific professional groups like software and advertising professionals who work in an informal culture. The very successful 'Lalitaji' campaign from Surf during the '80s would have appealed to a number of middle-class homemakers because they would have identified themselves with Lalitaji. While there may have been an overtone of aspiration in the 'hard-bargaining' character of Lalitaji, it typified the behaviour of a middle-class housewife. Dissociative groups are those that the consumer may like to avoid. Brands will avoid using Western models in the Middle East markets as consumers will disassociate themselves from such symbolic groups.

Reference groups can also be defined on the basis of degree of contact (primary or secondary) and degree of formality. An athletic club may have a number of formal rules, which its members have to follow. But an informal friends group does not have any formal rules. Homophily is another criterion that may be important, especially for products in the categories of apparel, perfumes, cigarettes and watches, etc. Homophily refers to the degree of similarity among group members. Consumers with similar interests are likely to meet frequently and exchange information on a variety of aspects associated with buying behaviour. In this case, word of mouth becomes a very strong influence. Density refers to the extent to which group members know each other. Even household neighbourhoods may differ in terms of density associated with groups. Families that follow a Western lifestyle as against an ethnic lifestyle are likely to reflect a lower degree of density. The degree of identification, though not associated with groups, may be important because this deals with how much a consumer identifies with a specific group. A consumer may be part of a software group but may like to dress more formally. Individual identification with the group has an impact on conformity or the extent to which an individual behaves accordingly to the wishes of the group.

Another characteristic of a group may be the strength of bonding or ties. Strong ties may indicate a close, intimate relationship and weaker ties may reflect a distant, limited inter-personal contact. Sometimes, weak ties may also result in 'embedded markets' because they can influence how a consumer reacts to them. For example, a consumer may prefer to buy an Amway cosmetic or a Tupperware container from an agent who is his/her neighbour rather than from an unknown agent, though the 'relationship tie' may be weak between the consumer and the neighbour.

Reference Groups and Digital Media

Yatra.com the online travel company had its 'Relive Happiness' campaign across its website and also on its Twitter and Facebook pages. The idea was to get responses from families that had availed their vacation services and they were invited to share their memories with photographs. The company went ahead with the campaign with just 150 entries. While viral campaigns generally are all about numbers, such a campaign may not have got numbers in terms of views but would be effective in connecting serious prospective consumers (high-involvement consumers) who are involved in family-based vacations.[3]

Reference Groups as a Powerful Source of Influence

Consumers try to use sources that are not dominated by marketers, like 'word of mouth' (WOM) from friends and families, WOM from clubs, internet forums and neighbourhoods. In fact, online social networking sites like Facebook, Twitter or Snapchat have added another dimension to WOM (apart from the contribution of review websites like mouthshut.com). Such reference groups are extremely important to marketers for receiving feedback about the product and for monitoring the discussion among its members. If there is any kind of negative opinion for the brand, the marketers need to probe further and take appropriate action using the cyber opinion leaders who may have a positive word of mouth about the offering/brand. While such channels are not entirely dominated by marketers, it is essential for the marketers to research and find the opinion leaders who would interface with other prospective consumers online. Profiling online consumers with regard to psychographics, interests and possessions will enable marketers to identify specific target segments for which messages can be tailored with the help of opinion leaders. For example, there may be a target segment interested in state-of-the-art features of a mobile, or another segment interested in the 'coolness' of the latest launch of an iPhone. Beyond the marketer or 'non-marketer-dominated' communication, the challenge for marketers today is to synergize communication emerging from the online and offline interfaces of reference groups. For example, a celebrity can endorse a brand in an advertisement and generate a positive WOM that can be continued online among a group.

It may be worthwhile for marketers to identify opinion leaders and market mavens through marketing research. Opinion leaders can also be used in advertising. Celebrities, models and representatives from various social groups can be used in advertising as opinion leaders. However, there may be subtle differences in the usage of such opinion leaders depending on the objective of the communication. 'Lalitaji' of Surf is an opinion leader (depicting a 'common man' appeal). Bournvita, Horlicks and Complan also use the mother-child model as an opinion leader in their advertisements. Kapil Dev and Tendulkar played the role of an 'expert' when they advertised for Boost (that had a style-statement, 'secret of my energy'). An 'expert' is an opinion leader who can endorse a brand based on his/her knowledge and in a specific field. As a sportsman, Kapil Dev has to have the knowledge and training to spot out a drink which gives energy. A celebrity can endorse a brand simply by reflecting his/her satisfaction with it (more by usage rather than expertise). Surf Excel detergent used the 'Slice of life' appeal in its reference group-based advertisements. It showed how a consumer can solve the problem (stain removal in this case) and the target segment is likely to associate itself with its model/housewife. This is the 'common man' appeal where the consumer identifies herself with the model 'who is like him/her'.

Normative Influence

This is a social pressure, which is designed to encourage conformity. Part of the normative influence is acquired by the consumer during socialization and interaction with the family, friends or colleagues. The consumer develops certain behaviour about the types of product categories and brands to be bought based on the interaction with the group. Normative influence affects the brand choice congruence in tune with the choice of the group. Consumers are very likely to buy what others in their group possess (generally, in certain product categories like clothes, mobiles and cars).

The virtual connect to reference groups

Colors, the TV channel had an interesting initiative to increase the online activity of reference groups (consumers interested in the channel). It had roped in celebrities and fans from all over the world and could ask them questions and get answers in the virtual booth.[4] Online channels can trigger several interactions among reference groups and create an engagement that goes beyond the transactional relationship between the brand and the consumer.

Product characteristics affect the normative influence depending on whether the product is consumed in private or in public. Water heaters and antiseptic lotions may be private products and cars and two-wheelers are public products. Products can also be classified as necessities and luxuries. Consumer characteristics also affect normative influence. Certain consumers are susceptible to interpersonal influences and may have a need to enhance their self-image by acquiring products or brands that they think will be 'approved' by the reference group, of which they are a part. They may exhibit conformity to enhance their self-image. Normative influence may be felt by the consumer in an indirect manner, he/she may feel that the group may not 'accept him/her' and hence may choose the category or the brand. A highly 'inner-directed person' is unlikely to yield to normative pressure.

Hoyer and MacInnis states that there can be predictions about when reference groups will influence decisions with the framework shown in Figure 8.1.[5] The framework reflects the degree of reference group influence on brand choice depending on the nature of the product:

	Product: Private	Product: Public	
Necessity	Mattress	Watches shoes	Low product preference
Luxury	CD player	Jewellery	High
	Low	High	

Figure 8.1 Brand Preference

Informational Influence

Informational influence is the extent to which sources offer information to help consumers make decisions. This influence is important because reference groups provide information to reduce consumers' information search. Informational influence can be triggered by specific advertisements that create awareness on products/brands/features. Informational influence may affect purchase decisions when offerings are complex and the perceived risk is high. This is also likely to work when perceived brand differentiation is high among durable products. Consumers, who are oriented towards informational influence, will seek product-relevant information. As for the characteristics, informational influence is likely to be greater if the source of information is regarded as an expert. (For example, an ace racing champion communicating the benefits of a car's features will carry credibility with consumers planning to buy a car.) Informational influence may also benefit the FMCG products. An event associated with coffee sponsored by a company like Hindustan Lever or Nescafe can trigger off product-related exchange of information on coffee. Such events can provide the content for informational exchange to take place. The 'common-man' appeal may have informational and normative influence on the target segment because of source similarity, since the latter perceives the source to be similar to itself. Facebook and other digital platforms have opened up a new era with respect to informational influence. For instance, ShopClues, an e-commerce portal deals with several unknown offerings and consumers may buy them based on informational influence that is associated with search on the digital platform.

Word of Mouth and Reference Groups

Word of mouth (WOM) refers to information about products or services communicated verbally. WOM can be persuasive because of the credibility associated with it (in the 'marketer-dominated' media) and also the face-to-face association involved in the communication process. The credibility is higher because the consumer usually chooses his/her sources for WOM. Research shows that WOM can be seven times more effective than the print media, twice as effective as the broadcast media and four times more effective than sales personnel. WOM can have a dramatic impact (positive or negative) on the perception of consumers. WOM referrals can be very effective in consumer durables where there are a number of well-known brands but the consumer fears a risk against the product category because of the high unit cost. Even in the case of FMCG products, WOM can be effective. Medical, entertainment, financial and beauty-care services can also benefit from WOM as a number of intangibles are involved in these services. The Body Shop, which manufactures eco-friendly cosmetics, has created awareness all over the world through WOM. Marketers have to promote favourable WOM and prevent negative WOM. Viral Marketing is a variant of WOM. Hotmail is probably an interesting example of how viral marketing can work. With millions of users opening their accounts, 'Hotmail' became an important advertising site.

Groups and Brands

An IPL enthusiast may buy more number of IPL merchandise associated with the team he or she will support during the tournament. This is because of the 'deindividuation' which means that we may do 'more' of something when we are in a group.[6]

But strangely this may not be the same behaviour in certain contexts. Social loafing ensures that we do not generally devote more time and effort to something when we are in a group.[7] A consumer may buy a domestic appliance brand when the brand provides a group demonstration (as against a rigorous evaluation of the brand if purchased without the group being around).

Reference Groups and Virtual Reality

Kingfisher used a 'hashtag' to introduce a virtual reality-based campaign to mark one of its events that reached out to a lakh of people.[8] A pulse meter was given to consumers and as soon as the pulse crossed a threshold they would get a Kingfisher drink in the virtual space. Here, we see that consumers could connect with virtual reality images. There was also a provision to post comments on social media channels. Such initiatives not only enable the reference groups to interact among themselves but also promote the word of mouth about the brand (especially, given in the situation that the brand is a hedonic one dealing with fantasies and pleasure).

There are several strategies to deal with the rumours when they carry a negative WOM. One of the first and foremost the key factor is 'not to do anything'. The consumers may actually hear about the rumour when the marketers of a brand attempt to correct it. Cadbury's picked Amitabh Bachchan as its brand ambassador when the credibility of the company took a hit after when worms were found by the consumers in its offering. In 2015, the Volkswagen advertisement got into trouble with its pollution rigging mechanism. WOM and controlling a negative WOM, especially when there are surplus rival brand sites (Walmart and P&G have faced such issues and controversies). The movie, 'The Blair Witch Project' became a runaway success after it constructed an interactive site (www.blairwitch.com). J. K. Rowling (the creator of Harry Potter) sold more than five million copies of her books across the globe because of its WOM rather than portraying any creative advertisement. There are companies in developed markets that attempt to quantify the impact of positive or negative WOM on brands through research studies that track WOM.

Celebrity Usage and Their Impact

Celebrity usage is one of the topical strategies of many brands across categories. Some brands use them for getting attention (Santro when it was launched), some for prolonged association (Lux) and others, perhaps, for the purpose of recall (a brand of bulbs). As in other facets of marketing, it may be worthwhile to analyse the usage of celebrities with certain aspects of the marketing mix, rather than taking a rigid position on the usage or non-usage of celebrities. What is required is a framework that can offer a marketer specific options and follow up the aspects of using celebrities.

Celebrities and Brand Connection

Brands may choose more relatable celebrities if the objective is to establish strong connections with the respective offering. Pepperfry, an e-commerce portal for furniture, roped in Radhika Apte and Shahana Goswami because of their acting prowess and the ability to convey appropriate emotion. Olx, Honda Mobilio and Policybazaar took the humorous route with a stand-up comedian like Kapil Sharma and indiaMART chose Irfan Khan as he would properly fit in with the 'no-nonsense' functional positioning of the brand.

As inputs received from, Amit Bapna (2015), 'Unusual Faces', *The Economic Times*, 19 August.

Mechanism of Celebrity Usage in Advertisements

It is necessary to understand the psychological aspects of celebrity usage in advertisements regardless of whether a celebrity is drawn from films, sports, beauty contests or politics. A celebrity has the glamour and/or charisma to trigger and sustain a following by using the emotional power of 'identification'. Identification, in this context, is the feeling of bonding which the followers (consumers in this context) exhibit towards a celebrity because of the admiration and adoration that may transcend rational motives. This concept is in line with the reference group concept, in which the followers attempt to have a role model whose attitudes and values they like to imitate. This is an important tool that can influence consumer behaviour. The impact of this kind of influence can be illustrated by the example of Vespa scooter. The Italian brand has become fashionable again in some parts of the US because celebrities like Steven Spielberg owns this brand. Though these celebrities may not have been the typical segment the company would have planned to target, the celebrity association may have created consumers, who may not otherwise have been interested in two-wheelers. The 'identification' mechanism is a psychological outlet for consumers and gives a vent to their unfulfilled aspirations and desires. These may deal with materialistic possessions or merely fantasies.

Celebrities and Brands—From Colas to E-commerce

Celebrities have been a part of the Indian culture for several decades.

In the recent times, several film celebrities have been used as a model by e-commerce companies. Likeability, trust worthiness and the appeal of the celebrities to aspirational groups of consumers are some of the reasons why celebrities are gaining popularity in the era of social media (social media drives the word of mouth about celebrities faster than the traditional). A celebrity can either endorse an e-commerce portal or comment on it based on the expert opinion (a celebrity endorsing a personal care and beauty website based on her expertise in this domain).

There are three conceptual aspects that explain the popularity of celebrities in the Indian context.

The Heider theory in terms of its application to consumer behaviour links the equilibrium of a consumer when he responds to a brand and a celebrity associated with it. It operates at the individual level of the consumer links the equilibrium associated with an object (brand), the consumer and the celebrity. In an ideal situation, a consumer would like the website FirstCry (catering to the requirements of new born babies) because Amitabh Bachchan says that he (celebrity) likes the brand (object). The three entities will be strongly tied together with a positive attitude towards one another. According to this theory there is always an equilibrium maintained in the three relationships. In a negative situation, a consumer may change his liking towards a celebrity if the celebrity endorses a brand that the consumer may not like. The reference group concept at the group level is the second conceptual angle that makes the consumer like the celebrity-endorsed brand. According to the reference group theory, any group/influence that is exerted on the consumer's attitude or preferences or values is an associative group that the consumer likes to connect. For instance, there may be a group that likes Fastrack brand and at the group level this may attract like-minded individuals who would like to be a part of the group. Online media has given a fillip to such behavioural formation of groups. At a cultural level, (the third conceptual point) in a collectivistic culture like India (where group belongingness and harmony, group decisions and affiliations overwhelms individual independence), celebrity groups appeal to consumers who are a part of the collectivist culture (this does not mean that there is no individualistic consumer in the culture; it only means that the orientation of the social mainstream is collectivistic). Hence, the classical conceptual perspectives will hold good even when e-commerce websites use celebrities (SRK for Big basket and Yepme, Hrithik Roshan for Myntra's HRX collection, Salman Khan for Yatra and Ranveer Sigh for Quikr). And these celebrity associations may also score on metrics too (Bigbasket reported that its campaign with a celebrity can reduce customer acquisition costs and triple its customer base).[9]

Factors to be Considered in Celebrity Usage

There are a few basic factors to be considered before a brand chooses its celebrity/celebrities (see Figure 8.2). Each of these factors has a major influence on the effectiveness of the celebrity association.

Importance of the Target Segment

The target segment is one of the basic considerations that a brand should take into account. It is a common practice that regional film celebrities are often used for brands that are marketed in a specific region (textiles, fast food, coffee, soft drinks). For a brand that wants to

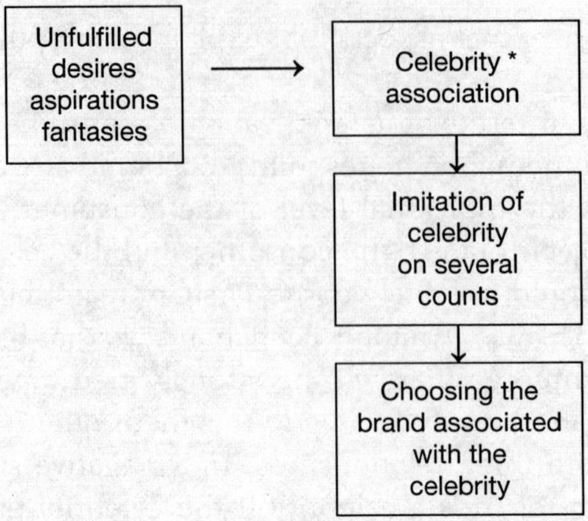

Figure 8.2 Process of Identification

avoid spending money on a high-visibility campaign, a movie star who is very popular in a given geographic region will be effective to influence consumers in that specific region. The advertising execution (visuals, jingle, etc.) should consider the local preferences, culture and language so that 'identification' occurs spontaneously. There is a need to clearly categorize the celebrity based on the appeal. There are film celebrities who have a rather wide appeal. These celebrities may figure across product categories. Amitabh Bachchan, Sachin Tendulkar and Shah Rukh Khan belong to this category. However, a brand has to be careful that excessive exposure does not cause any celebrity wear out. The celebrity may make an impact but not the brand. For example, a brand of jeans, which was targeted at the youth, used a middle-aged Western celebrity who may have appealed to youngsters a few decades back but not anymore.

The Charisma of Celebrities—Beyond the Domains of Rationality

Celebrities may have the power of charisma that even lasts beyond logical thinking. The charisma generates an emotion that overwhelms the cognitive thinking of consumers. One of the disadvantages of using celebrities is that the brand may earn negative publicity if the celebrity gets involved in a scandal or crime. High-end journals on marketing have carried articles on the subject of negative publicity associated with celebrities who get on to the wrong side of law and how.

---

* Choice of the celebrity will depend on the target segment of the brand.

> On March 7, 2015, Filmfare carried an advertisement for a jewellery brand with a celebrity who was prosecuted for a crime months before this ad was published (the celebrity had been associated with the brand even before the conviction with respect to the wrong doing). It is usual for a brand to remove the celebrity association if the celebrity is into bad publicity. It may also happen that the emotional attachment to the celebrity among the consumers could generate sympathy and add to the charismatic appeal of the celebrity.

Kohinoor, the brand of premium *basmati* rice, used Tiger Pataudi and Sharmila Tagore; Pepsi has used several spirited cricketers; Vimal and Digjam, one of the leading brands in premium men's wear, used celebrities from films but not necessarily those who play the hero. These are examples of positive celebrity associations in tune with the identification needs of their respective brands.

Celebrity Clutter in the Category

There is a need for marketers to review the product category for analysing the number and nature of celebrities to be used in the category. In the category of pre-recorded cassettes, no brand has used a celebrity to impress upon the quality of the music, though several brands are attempting to differentiate themselves using variety. As variety becomes a non-differentiator in the present day competition, a classical or playback singer can lend credibility to the brand of pre-recorded cassettes. Cola is a category which was experiencing celebrity clutter. Hence, any brand in this category has to opt for a non-celebrity to build the brand promotion. The 'cola–celebrity' association is very strong, given the consumption of cola in the soft drink market and the advertising exposure created by cola brands. This may have a strong impact on the category itself and any other brand attempting a celebrity route may be eclipsed by the existing clutter.

Is Celebrity a Long–term Brand Association?

Brands may consider celebrities as long-term brand property and hence, may have to carefully choose them. Lux has been using celebrities for several decades. These celebrities, almost always contemporary, have been drawn from films. The usage of celebrity as brand property goes well with the brand proposition of Lux—clear and attractive complexion symbolized by the celebrities for whom this characteristic is a prerequisite. Pepsi can follow the same strategy by associating the brand with popular cricketers over a period of years, especially in a situation where its arch-rival, Coke cannot use celebrities from cricket. This will give the brand a sustainable advantage over the other brands in terms of "identification". This approach can be extremely useful in product categories, which revolves around imagery rather than functional benefits. It is difficult to list out the functional benefits of an aerated soft drink when several other alternatives are available to consumers to quench their thirst. This is also a category where a number of brands are attempting to create an imagery that will appeal to the target segment (youth). In fact, there is a distinct possibility of using an appropriate celebrity who will appeal to at least a small section of the adult population that consumes aerated soft drinks. Niche brands which offer bitter lime, ginger ale other such products attempt such a strategy after researching the profile of the target segment.

Celebrities and Attention-Grabbing Aspects

In an era of brand proliferation, there may be a need to use celebrities, simply to hold the attention of the target segment. There is a need to differentiate between FMCG products and durables before such a strategy is applied. The basic assumption here is that the celebrity may or may not have the credibility to advance the proposition. For example, Crowning Glory, a brand of soap, used Dimple Kapadia, who added credibility to the brand proposition of hair-care with her own lovely, lustrous hair. In contrast, a brand of bulbs used a celebrity simply to get the attention of consumers and move it up the 'recall hierarchy'.

When an FMCG product uses a celebrity just to capture attention (and not as a long-term brand property), there is a need to ensure that the brand is available at retail outlets in the territory of advertising. In order to make the strategy more effective, the point-of-purchase (POP) posters and merchandising displays can be used together with the celebrity-based advertisement. This will enable the recall process to be triggered, apart from creating a top-of- the-mind awareness for the brand. Such integrated approach to celebrity advertising for an FMCG product is likely to have a huge impact on the consumer intention to buy. In fact, wherever it is appropriate, the sales promotion involving the celebrity may additionally impact the consumer's mind-set.

In case of durables, the product offering has to be in tune with the expectations of consumers. It is to be noted that celebrities used in this context may highlight the features or the end benefits but they do not have the expertise (in most cases) to add credibility to the brand proposition. Hence, consumers may be taken in by the appeal of the celebrities and the brands may slip into the 'consideration set' of prospective consumers. This is useful, especially for brands like Santro and Samsung, which did not have much brand equity at the time of entering the market. The strategy has to be followed up with a good customer-interface at the retail outlets. Specific benefits that may motivate the consumer may have to be highlighted by retail personnel or there may have to be a follow-up campaign that highlights the benefits of the brand over those of competition. Santro used this approach (in a comparative advertisement) in a follow-up to its celebrity-based launch campaign. Word of mouth is extremely important in durables. And also excellent service, which may be required to fortify the initial interest triggered by the celebrity appeal.

In certain situations, brands may have to even hold a product-line that may be of interest to consumers to back up a celebrity advertisement. Philips TV (initially launched as PHX in India) and it used a well-known celebrity but the brand PHX did not seem to have picked up in terms of leading the market share associated with a leading brand. It is essential that the interest triggered by the celebrity (in durables) results in purchase of the brand at retail outlets. This is possible only if the brand has a strong marketing mix package. Certain premium brands, known for several decades around the world, can benefit from using several celebrities, even during a short span of time. These brands are so well-known that they have, by themselves, become a global lifestyle statement (see Table 8.1). Hence, the association with celebrities is just a strategy to get attention and project a contemporary image. The brand image, cultivated over time, would be powerful enough to suppress any discrepancy that might have been created by the association of celebrities, who may otherwise project diverging associations. Omega is one such brand that may have had several secondary associations in its advertising (celebrity, features and ad visuals).

Table 8.1 Dimensions of Celebrity Usage

Need	Brand Celebrity	Benefits Usage
Brand awareness	Santro (cars)	Created awareness in a market in which the brand was unknown
Top-of-the-mind recall	Cema (bulbs)	Improved brand recall in a low-involvement category
FMCG—lifestyle	Pepsi (cola)	Attracted youth population orientation
Product-benefit Boost (drink)	Lux (soaps) benefits	Cine stars endorse brand
Relaunch	Colgate Total (toothpastes)	Conveyed the benefit (12-hour protection) through the celebrity
Established brand appealing to lower-priced segments	Sonata watches	Celebrity enhanced the credibility of the brand
Preserving a habit against changing trends	Parker (pens)	Celebrity endorsed a global brand and also retriggered the interest in using the basic pen in a digital era
Reinforcing brand personality	Rajdoot (early '80s)	The rugged celebrity association reinforced the brand personality

These aspects cover only the usage of celebrities and not the other dimensions of reference group concepts that may also be equally useful to the marketer. A celebrity can add to the other elements of the brand, if used in a conceptual manner (see Figure 8.3).

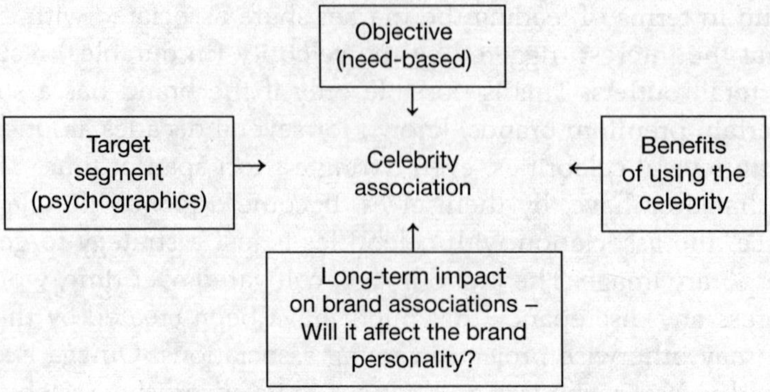

Figure 8.3 Selecting a Celebrity

Box 8.1
The Hyde Effect

Mohammad Azharuddin and Hansie Cronje are celebrities who typify the emergence of the Hyde effect in the Indian context (there have been quite a few in the West). Pepsi and Hamstead (a brand of suiting) used these celebrities to the hilt before they were dropped following match-fixing scandals.

The Hyde effect,as conceptualised by the author,is the trouble a brand brings to the marketer when the celebrity associated with the brand gets into "bad word of mouth". It can be avoided by not banking upon a specific celebrity for obtaining the 'identification'. Pepsi has cleverly avoided the effect by banking on cricket for 'identification' and not on the characteristics of a specific celebrity.

Box 8.2
Can Celebrities Work When Brands are not Created?

One of the interesting aspects of celebrity usage is the question of their impact on the target segment when the latter is not clear about what the brand stands for. A string of popular celebrities like Hrithik Roshan, Shahrukh Khan and Priyanka Chopra appeared for the advertisements of the brand, Home Trade. A brand is built through associations. These may either be benefits or an emotional appeal depending on the product category. Home Trade used celebrity advertising and it is not certain if the target segment was clear about what the brand stood for. It was, in fact, a financial super market retailing options for consumers through the internet. Home Trade implied that the consumer can effectively make financial investments from the comfort of his/her home. A strong focus on the benefits of such an outfit or an unambiguous endorsement of the services (by the celebrity) may have been very effective.

Source: 'Can Celebrities Work When Brands Are Not Created?', *The Hindu Businessline*, 28 Februrary, 2002.

Touch of Reality

WOM and Perceived Risks

WOM and perceived risks open up a few thoughts for marketers. There are four quadrants shown in the diagram (see Figure 8.4). Low risks and high degree of WOM may be associated with fashion and fun products that may range from chewing gums to symbolic mobile phones and iPhones ('Fun and Frolic'). The risks involved are considerably lowered by the branded offerings (well-known ones) and the buzz factor enhances the symbolic appeal of the offerings. Low risks and low WOM is applicable to everyday FMCG that are utility oriented. But even in this context, there may be brands like Colgate Maxfresh that may trigger WOM through celebrity usage or a creative advertisement (a lady police officer seduced by a young man when he is asked to take the breath test to check for alcohol while driving a car). Several FMCG categories may fall under this 'Mundane' category. High degree of perceived risk and low WOM is associated with high-involvement categories that are not amenable to WOM ("State of the Art"). Advancement in specific areas of medical care (artificial saliva recommended by dentists for some patients) is an example. Finally, 'Deep Decisions' are those that are more oriented towards the utility value of categories and brands. For example, a consumer who is interested in buying a washing machine or an electric cooker may rely on WOM to ascertain to what extent a brand provides value. This is different from 'Fun and Frolic' where WOM is more about the symbolic value/acceptance in a specific group.

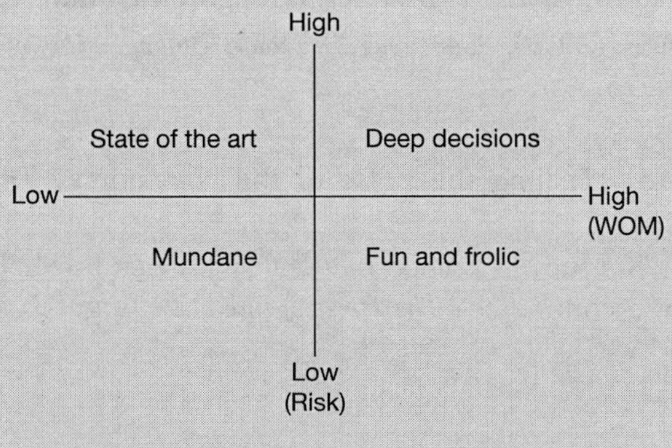

Figure 8.4 Degree of WOM Involved

THE TRIAD ROUTE TO CELEBRITIES AND BRAND ASSOCIATIONS

The triad theory suggests that a consumer will ensure that he/she has an attitude that is in consonance with the brand if he/she likes the celebrity. For example, consumers who may like Amitabh Bachchan may have bought products from Kalyan Jewellers simply because he has endorsed the brand. A non-profit organization like PETA (People for the Ethical Treatment of Animals) may have a celebrity like Paul McCartney (one of the members of Beatles) to advocate vegetarianism. The triad theory works on the principle that consumers who like the celebrity will also associate themselves with the brand/cause advocated by the celebrity. The basic point is that a consumer would want to create equilibrium in himself/herself by adopting the likeability to both the brand and the celebrity. If the consumer does not like the celebrity but likes the brand, he/she is likely to change the attitude towards the celebrity. There may also be a possibility that the consumer might start to like the celebrity to a lesser extent to bring in mental equilibrium within himself. A camera brand, Rebel, used Andre Agassi, the tennis player widely known for his temperamental behaviour on the tennis field—consumers may like the brand but not the celebrity. But in a resultant outcome some of these consumers may start liking both the brand and the celebrity, thus resolving the dissonance into equilibrium.

End Notes

1. Viveat Susan Pinto (2015), 'Philips banks on Bollywood', *Business Standard*, 9 August.
2. Richa Maheshwari (2015), "Users will 'Like' it: Myntra to become Facebook of Fashion", *The Economic Times*, 3 August.
3. Ravi Balakrishnan (2015), 'Such a long journey', *The Economic Times*.
4. Jessu John (2015), 'Fans ask, celebrities answer', *The Hindu Business Line*, 7 August.
5. Hoyer and MacInnis, *Consumer Behavior*, (Houghton Mifflin, 1999), pp. 377–401.
6. Michael Solomon (2015), *Consumer Behavior: Buying, Having and Being*, (Pearson, 2015), pp. 372–373.
7. Ibid.
8. Jessu John (2015), 'Feeling the pulse of the consumers', *The Hindu Business Line*, 7 August.
9. Anand J (2015), 'Startups in Escape Ink deals with Actors: Shah Rukh, Ranveer seek to build trust for e-commerce', *The Times of India*, 29 August.

Exercises

1. Collect celebrity ads from the Indian context. Also collect the celebrity ads of Amitabh Bachchan and Shah Rukh Khan over the years. Compare the brands that had used Amitabh Bachchan and Shah Rukh Khan with the brands that had used other celebrities and comment on the usage of celebrities between these sets of brands.
2. Choose the apparel category. Observe your friends. Note the type of influence that some of them may use in the selection of apparel. Select friends who take the opinion of other friends for the purpose?

CHAPTER 9

Dimensions of Culture and Branding

Consumerist Culture in the Indian Context

The consumerist culture in the Indian context can be traced back to the 1960s and across the stages of acculturation. During the '60s, Western lifestyles were getting reflected in advertisements at the cinema theatres. Forhan's toothpaste, Coke and a few other brands were advertising to create awareness rather than to compete with other brands in the category. 'Ambassador' and 'Fiat' cars had appeared on Indian roads and were a symbol of the rich and successful (though implicitly). There were only a few readymade apparel brands (not widely advertised) and very fewer people wore coats and suits. English news (radio) had a small segment of listeners and broadcasted film songs through radio stations as it was a rich source of entertainment. Radiogram (radio with gramophone that would play songs) was a status symbol while refrigerators at homes were rare. This stage of acculturation can be termed as the emergence of Western symbols (there may have been Western symbols earlier but this was the stage where certain segments of consumers were perhaps being formed from the perspective of consumer culture).

During the '70s and '80s, fashion, music and films (three major indicators of culture) became more Westernized. Cigarette brands were widely advertised. The concept of star-rated hotels was introduced and television, too, got widely diffused throughout the country. This was the stage that initiated consumerism in India. There were some social taboo regarding cigarette smoking, consumption of liquor and permissive movies that stood out from the mainstream culture. Women were still regarded with a 'conservative and home-based' stereotype, even though a cross-section of women were employed. This stage of acculturation can be termed as the acceptance stage with an overtone of resistance (rather than being termed as rejection stage).

After the onset of the 21st Century (i.e., after the year 2000), Indian consumers have reached the integration stage of acculturation (adapting Western lifestyle to a significant extent in their everyday process). YouTube, Facebook, Tablets and Smartphones have transformed the Indian youth in terms of their approach to living. Discretionary income is being used for indulgence in several categories and services. McDonalds, Pizza Hut and Dominos have expanded in the country as eating out has become a part of the culture. Café Coffee day, Barista and the entry of Starbucks indicate how the culture of socializing over coffee is likely to get nurtured over time (Refer to Plate 9.1). Though there is a small number of youngsters who are going abroad for studies, there has been a significant rise in the aspirational efforts on education among youngsters than ever before. There are two-wheeler brands like Pleasure and Scooty Pep that symbolize the new values like self-reliance, independence and a futuristic orientation that are associated with the women of this digital era. Acculturation introduced the concept of personal grooming to women and men in India; the Indian context has extended the direction of acculturation with 'Fair & Handsome', a fairness cream for men.

Culture is one of the major factors affecting consumer behaviour. The attitudes and values of consumers are culture-specific in a broad sense. Culture is a combination of learnt beliefs, values and customs that directs consumer behaviour in a specific society. It is the manner in which the members of the society share certain implicit meanings about values, customs, beliefs, rituals and other aspects that are related to the collective functioning of the society. These are important components of culture. Customs are overt modes of behaviour that are acceptable in a specific cultural context. The different food habits of Indians, for example, are customs that are part of a region-specific culture. From the perspective of marketing, products and brand communication have to take into consideration

Plate 9.1 Entry of Starbucks indicate how the culture of socializing over coffee is likely to get nurtured over time

the customs existing in a specific market situation. A marketer offering an alternative for the morning cup of coffee or tea (to which a large chunk of consumers has been used to for a long time), will find it extremely difficult to change the custom. But with the essential changes in an environment, customs also change and marketers can be successful if they organize their products/brands and position them in an appropriate timely manner. A few decades ago, using nail enamel and lipstick was a taboo among many consumers, especially in villages. While nobody looks twice at someone who uses the products in urban areas, rural consumers are now not averse to using them. A number of health clubs have mushroomed in urban areas because health and fitness are areas of interest to several urban consumers due to their stressed lifestyles. The cultural meanings differ from one context to another. Smartness with regard to personal grooming may be a part of many cultures but adding a tinge of blue to the white apparel (Ujala brand) and adding starch to cotton apparel to impart stiffness (revives the brand) is a unique practice in India

Signs, Meanings and Brands

Semiotics is associated with the process of how we assign meanings between signs and symbols.[1] The object may be soap, which is the focus of the message. Sign is the image that represents the sensory meaning of the object (the image of a dove on Dove soap brand). Interpretant is the meaning that we associate between the sign and the object. Dove brand of soap is mild, soft and pure (dove is of white colour and the colour is associated with purity) (Refer to Plate 9.2).

Plate 9.2 Through its image, Dove symbolises purity

CHARACTERISTICS OF CULTURE

Culture is specific to a context. Different countries have different cultures and hence, consumer behaviour also differs in different countries. This aspect is particularly important to multinational corporations that enter different markets to cater to the diverse cultural needs of consumers. The differences in perception among consumers with regard to products (and, perhaps, even brands) are based on need, usage and importance. In the US, products like cola, burgers, peanuts, popcorn and ketchup are a popular part of the culture while tea, sandwiches, bowler hats, golf and raincoats are an intrinsic part of the English culture. Kimonos, rice, cars and cameras are synonymous with Japan while one identifies beer, music and cars with Germany. Pasta, pizza, espresso coffee, art, wine, opera and shoes are a part of the Italian culture and perfume, wine, cognac, cheese and champagne are intrinsic to the French culture. *Samosa* (spicy eatable), tea, bicycles and incense sticks generally represent the Indian culture, though there may be sub-cultural differences.

Differences across cultures have a number of implications for the marketer. In India, McDonald's does not use beef on its menu as cows are considered to be sacred to a large part of Indian consumers. Money-back guarantees may reassure US consumers but not those in Latin America as they never expect their money back. Pizza Hut offers sea food delicacies in Japan. Procter & Gamble came up with different variations of its TV commercial for its disposable diapers 'Pampers' as it is used widely in different European countries.

Sub-cultures consist of ethnic groups within a culture. These groups have common heritage, religion, beliefs, customs and experiences that differentiate them from other sub-cultures within the culture. There may be certain aspects that stand for the Indian culture, but almost every state in the country reflects a sub-culture. Dressing styles, eating habits, festivals and religious rites and rituals are different in different Indian states. With several professional domains getting into the Indian context, sub-culture may also be found within the professionals belonging to a specific domain. For example, executives in the advertising field or the software field may have certain aspects of a culture that are widely adhered to within the respective group.

Culture and Cultural Norms and Brands

In any culture there are three kinds of cresive norms that are connected with explicit and subtle behaviours.[2] Custom is a basic behaviour.

The role of the wife traditionally was associated with doing the laundry. Ariel Matic with its 'share the load' campaign is trying to suggest that doing laundry is also the man's job.

Conventions are norms consisting of a wider range of customs that govern our everyday behaviour and it is associated with the 'correctness' of behaviour. Wearing clothes, serving food (Indian culture may be different from other cultures) and idol worship are such examples.

Fast foods and fashion offerings may create new conventions that may end up as trends. In the West, food preparations using wheat are vastly different from the preparation of culturally 'correct' food associated with Indian culture. Western apparel for women has created a new sense of style among a cross-section of women.

CONSUMER PERCEPTION AND CULTURE

Figure 9.1 reflects how the perception of consumers is associated with culture of which they are a part of.

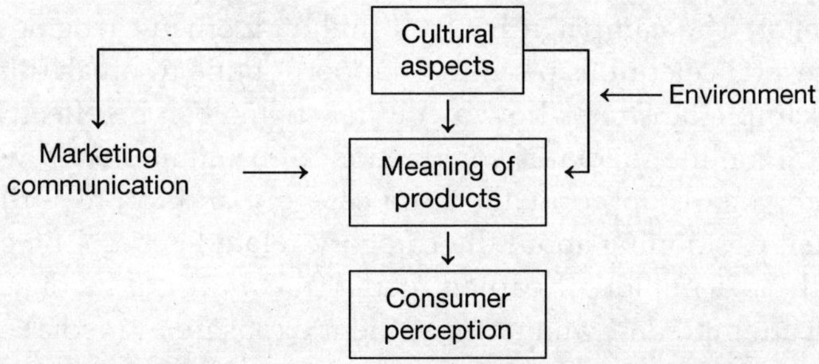

Figure 9.1 Impact of Culture on Consumer Perception.

The cultural aspects include perceptions of consumers about work, leisure, time, festive occasions, ethnicity and gender, which affect the meaning associated with product categories. For example, there may be differing perceptions about clothes to be worn for work and for informal occasions. Meanings can be associated with product categories of liquor and cigarettes. These meanings can vary from one market situation (country/region) to another. Gender can also trigger perceptions. Women have all along, been considered to be delicate, whimsical and expressive. Aggression is more of a male aspect thing, traditionally associated with men. Certain types of clothes are associated with women (transfer of meaning to a product). Marketers have to be sensitive to the 'meanings' associated with the products in a specific market setting. They have to clearly communicate their message in accordance with the perceptions associated with product categories and also ensure that the respective brand gets differentiated through positioning strategies. There is also a possibility that over a period of time, the cultural meaning associated with a product category may change. For example, (cigarette) smoking was considered as a 'sinful' act in conservative South India a few decades ago. It is an accepted practice now, even in villages. Beauty salons that were once considered as taboo are now frequented by a significant number of urbanites. The meaning of 'cosmetic product category' has changed in the Indian cultural context (at least in most of the states). Consumers have moved from the plain talcum powder of the yesteryear to several cosmetic product categories. Bicycles and two-wheelers have given way to four-wheelers as status symbols. In certain categories, marketers have used the term 'tradition' in a correct niche to launch products. Nikhar, a unique beauty soap from Godrej and Santoor from Wipro, make use of the ingredients traditionally associated with skin/complexion care. These brands have also differentiated themselves in the crowded category of soaps using their 'herbal' proposition.

Cultural Taboos and the Indian Context

For decades, a significant number of Indian women had believed in the cultural taboo that pickles get spoilt if touched during the menstruation cycle. This belief has been repudiated by research.[3]

Whisper, the personal care brand, launched a TV campaign in which a young girl is encouraged by an elderly couple to 'touch the pickle' to counter the irrational cultural belief. The campaign had 2.9 million women pledging to 'touch the pickle'[4] with several celebrities providing support online to break the superstitious belief.[5] The example illustrates how a cultural stigma can be effectively broken if a brand uses the online media in conjunction with offline media when the content of the campaign is appropriate to the category and to prove that the beliefs are wrong when positioning about the category-related issues. The campaign was associated with $6.1 million of earned media (the worth of media expenditure if the brand had attempted to gain an equivalent exposure in media).[6]

Using herbal products is very much a part of the Indian culture and brands like Lifebuoy and Hamam from Unilever, which have been a part of the culture for a long time, have launched many herbal variants. Cultural meanings also change because of the environmental changes. Westernization has had an impact on the Indian marketing context with several product categories carrying Western overtones. Anti-wrinkle creams, diet soft drinks, fast foods and status-orientation in the category of automobiles and jeans are a few examples to reflect the impact of Westernization in the Indian context. Even in this scenario, Arvind brand positioned its Ruf & Tuf jean as the aspirational jeans for the Indian youth at an affordable price (when the brand was launched).

Brands and Consumption in a Cultural Setting

There are two kinds of cultural consumption that are important to brands. Sacred consumption which is associated with serious consumption with high involvement and profane consumption associated with mundane or common place consumption.

Brands have the challenge of converting profane consumption into sacred consumption. Personal grooming that largely consisted of talcum powder a few decades back has taken a 'sacred' role with respect to consumption in the present-day context.

Sacred consumption involves the consumer treating the consumption with awe and respect.[7] Fair & Lovely, Dove, L'Oréal, Tresemme, Head & Shoulders are some of the brands that have created significant involvement among consumers who consider personal grooming as a serious ritual.

CULTURE AND EMBLEMS*

A consumer communicates with others in the society (different types of groups he/she is associated with) by conveying a message through the products he/she uses (or is in possession). What the consumer is performing here is the emblematic function in a culture. The music which one listens to may stand for his/her age (ranging from Andy Williams, Beatles, Boney M., Abba to Michael Jackson, Spice Girls and Britney Spears) and the type of reference group he/she belongs to. People observe others and make conscious or unconscious inferences through the products/brands they use.

How can Cultural Symbolism be Used in Sensory Branding?

Dettol, the leading antiseptic brand, has a strong odour; it burns when applied to cuts or wounds and has a specific smell. It has been all along associated with the killing of germs.

The frequency of purchase by consumers (antiseptic liquid) may not be very high. Besides the penetrative capacity of the antiseptic lotion, it cannot be compared to a typical FMCG product. With Savlon (from ITC), which is likely to be a tough competitor, Dettol can run a campaign highlighting its sensory properties and by relating to the 'wellness experience' it can offer. By such an initiative, the brand is likely to transform its sensory properties into a sensory experience that consumers can relate to with greater awareness.

There are different kinds of 'emblems', which convey meanings about the consumer. The different types of emblems are as follows.

1. *Geographic emblems*: Products may vary across regions and hence, have a geographical identification. Traditional and ethnic dresses (for men and women) vary across many Indian states. However, the executives working in the corporate world, especially in urban cities, have a similar dress code to symbolize their business orientation. Jeans/denims worn by youngsters, especially in metros, symbolize their Western orientation. There may be brands that have a global identification. Rolex, Omega and Mercedes are brands that stand for its class and status in virtually all parts of the world. Marketers can use specific aspects of a culture to create brand preferences. There may be new trends in a specific country/culture. For example, Westernization is catching up in a number of developing countries. Certain brands that symbolize Western lifestyles

* Hoyer and MacInnis, *Consumer behavior*, Houghton Miffin, 1999, 445–447

and values (Coke and Nike) are admired by the emerging economies. Jeep Cherokee in Korea costs four times the price of a comparable offering from Hyundai because the brand symbolizes the 'adventure' associated with Americans.

2. *Ethnic emblems*: Food, apparel and rituals are probably some facets through which consumers express their ethnic identification. Kellogg's cereals generated significant trials in India but the ethnic identification of Indians with (traditional) food is so strong that the brand has a long way to go in the Indian market. A number of tea brands attempted different kinds of positioning strategies in different states; Taaza tea is offered in different flavours (tea is taken with diverse tastes across geographical areas.[8] The success of Limca (especially during the '80s) can be attributed to the popularity of lemon juice (cloudy version) across the country. The Western concept of lemonade (clear lime in the aerated soft drink category) has been around in the country for several decades but has not been able to achieve significant success. Though cola is also not of Indian origin, the diffusion of the drink as a symbol of modernism, perhaps, has made it a drink for the masses in many countries that have not been associated with several other aspects of the Western culture.

3. *Social class emblems*: From foods and cosmetics to durable products like automobiles and watches, consumers employ emblems to reflect their social status and to infer the status of others. Fast foods and trendy restaurants (normally located in trendy shopping locations) are associated with the young and the fashionable. A consumer driving a mid-segment car like i10 or Honda City may be accorded a greater status as compared to the one who owns a plain Maruti Alto. Guavas and grapes are associated with the middle class while apples and cashews with the upper social strata. There could be certain pockets in the country where the identity of consumers springs more from caste, religion and background rather than from symbolic consumption (rural markets in certain states). But as liberalization of markets and lifestyle changes impact a specific market, the use of symbolic consumption as an indicator or social emblem will increase.

4. *Gender emblems*: Cigarettes, alcohol, jewellery and clothes are categories that have a strong gender association. These emblems have an impact on strategy formulation. Cigarettes have been associated with men for decades. Even today, a woman smoker is difficult to be found in public places (even in the more modest and liberal Bangalore city). Ms, a cigarette brand, was launched in India during the '80s. The brand targeted the young, modern, professional woman. The brand was careful not to position itself on the 'glamour' platform. Instead, the message was that women achievers are on an even keel with their male counterparts. This appeal was built up in the campaign in a subtle manner. In spite of its low-key launch, the brand was withdrawn (social taboo may have been one of the reasons) and ever since, no cigarette brand targeting women has been launched. Jewellery has been, all along, in the woman's domain. There may be a niche male population interested in the

product category (in urban markets). A brand like Tanishq or Carbon has to be very careful if it were to launch product items for men. A different brand name, perhaps, could be useful. Even in jewellery, Titan has the Tanishq brand more oriented towards the urban culture and a distinct brand Gold Plus to appeal to the traditional culture associated with jewellery, especially in the urban markets. Shaving in India is traditionally associated with men and several cultural aspects have to be taken into consideration when a brand launches shaving systems for women. Gillette launched its Venus shaving kits for women. The target segment has to comprise women who are independent of the family influences on their grooming habits. This is likely to lead the marketer to a niche group of women with a very specific set of values, activities, interests and opinions (AIO). Psychographics can be very useful in identifying the appropriate segment of women. Braun attempted a trial sales promotion during a specific period of time. A brand like Gillette (offering for women) may target niche media vehicles like Femina, Filmfare, and TV channels like MTV to create awareness about the product category and brand. Simultaneous approaches of creating awareness through niche media, a good direct marketing program and demonstration at retail outlets can sell the concept to the target segment. The process of selling a new concept or product to a new class of consumers belonging to a group (niche) with a different set of attitudes and values as compared to the masses in a specific market is given in Figure 9.2.

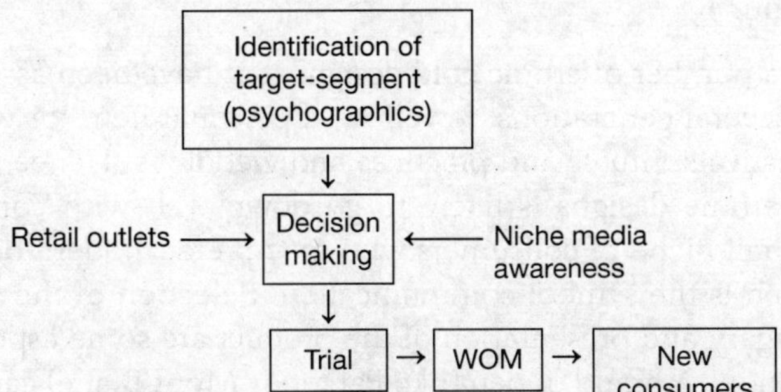

Figure 9.2 Targeting a Sub-culture with Distinctive Psychographics

5. *Reference group emblems*: Membership to a reference group can also be indicated in a culture through reference group emblems. Punks are a group of people who are non-conformists in many ways and identify themselves with groups using products which symbolize 'anti-establishment' (non-conformist) tendencies, dramatic elements and have a shock value (studs, fluorescent hair colours, 'weird' earrings, body piercings, faded jeans, leather outfits and perhaps, some other products that may not

be in common usage in a specific society). Most of these products stand for rebellion, cynicism and tendencies that are not in tune with the surrounding cultural practices and beliefs (rejection of normal practices and unwritten codes). Consumers who are health-conscious reflect their choices with regard to clothes and footwear. These products may have both functional and symbolic value and create a sense of identification. The art of corporate dressing, propagated by several brands in the Indian context, essentially addresses the need for identification among the target segment of corporate executives. There are several younger consumers who use products, brands and styles based on the 'celebrity reference group' from which they may select their role model. These celebrities can be drawn from cricket, films or from other fields depending on the type of target segment and product category. In fact, cola consumption may have significantly increased since celebrities stepped in to endorse the various brands in that category. The identification with celebrities is so compelling that the target segment (youth) tries to toe the line of its role models and hence, uses brands that they endorse. Marketers should consider the implications of emblematic functions on the minds of consumers. One approach could be symbol development that involves identifying cultural principles associated with a category and associating the brand with elements that would reflect the identified cultural aspects. Hero Pleasure, the two-wheeler for women, may have inspired consumers belonging to specific reference groups that had associated themselves with freedom and independence (the brand's proposition was 'Why should boys have all the fun?').

Tanishq showcases a number of ethnic gold designs that have been associated with Indian art and culture for several generations. Jewellery, a personal item for women, has cultural associations with festivals, rituals and practices and weddings. Hence, a brand that incorporates traditional ethnic designs is likely to go down well with consumers in general, though there is a small niche of consumers who may prefer modern designs.

Another approach is the symbol communication. Selection of the setting, formulating the appropriate imagery and presentation of the product are some aspects concerned with symbol communication. A brand of pen (like Parker or Mont Blanc) can be shown in association with a number of up-market products like wine in a vintage glass, a classic model of Mercedes or a Rolex. Such an advertisement needs no words to convey the message of the brand. Its association with other symbolic products/brands conveys the meaning. The elements portrayed in the visuals, reinforces the up-market image of the brand.

The third approach involves organizing and formulating other aspects of the marketing mix to reinforce the symbolic image. An up-market pen brand like Mont Blanc carries a premium price; it is distributed throughout the exclusive outlets or up-market malls and is created through a special raw material. Each element of the marketing mix reinforces the other elements of the mix.

Can a Brand Become a Part of a Script?*

Script is a sequence of actions adopted by a consumer when he/she is familiar with a situation. The consumer carries the schema of these actions and these actions become automatic with regard to the behaviour of the consumer. Eating can have a script; playing or recreation/fitness training can have a script and going to the bank can also be a script. Personal grooming is a ritual and there are several actions on the part of the consumer required in the form of script. Parachute 'aftershower' may be considered as a part of a script associated with the grooming ritual by a cross-section of youngsters. Dove shampoo may become a part of the script associated with the bathing ritual among consumers who are satisfied and loyal to the brand. Knorr soup may become a part of the script associated with the evening snacking ritual of some children.

IMPORTANCE OF ROLE ACQUISITION[9]

All consumers perform different roles at different points in time (role of a child, student, father/mother, executive, sports person, etc.). Marketers should be interested in these kinds of life stage changes or transition of consumers from one role to the other. There are three phases in role transition. The first one is separation from the old role—a business school graduate getting into a corporate job, for example. The next phase is the transition from one role to another. The change to a new identity is revealed by procurement of material objects and possessions that reflect the new identity in a symbolic manner. In the example given, the consumer concerned may like to give up a number of possessions of his/her student life and may want new products/brands (designer wear, a two-wheeler, an up-market watch and a credit card), which is probably positioned for aspirational executives. The final phase is incorporation associated with taking on the new role/identity. This may involve acquisition of more products/associations that reinforce the identity chosen. This happens over a period of time—this consumer can obtain memberships of prestigious clubs, acquire an up-market automobile brand and holiday at a foreign resort. Peter England readymade shorts had positioned its brand to fit in with role transition (the ad was hinting about a beginning of a new role with respect to youngsters, 'beginning of good things').

Ritual–brand Linkage

Ritual is an activity (either symbolic or functional) that is generally repeated over time with multiple fixed and episodic sequences that reflect seriousness, inner intensity and formality.[10] For example, eating and bathing are rituals that serve some kind of functional utility; grooming is another ritual that may reflect some degree of symbolism about your own self. Marketers need to make brands as part

* Hoyer and MacInnis, *Consumer behavior*, Houghton Miffin, 1999, 92–93, Indian edn., 1999.

of a ritual as appropriate to the consumer segment. Sunsilk Natural Recharge is a shampoo brand that has hair strength as its proposition and it makes the brand a part of the 'office going' ritual in its advertisement.

Marie biscuits is a part of the tea-drinking ritual. Parachute Advansed coconut oil advocated that the consumer may apply the oil before washing their hair. Using a hand wash (Lifebuoy, for instance) has become a part of the hand washing ritual.

Role Transition and the Importance of Rituals[11]

Normally, consumers go through certain rituals and get associated with symbols when they assume new roles. They experience discomfort and uncertainty when they begin to take on a new role. This may be because they are not experienced enough to fulfil the expectations of the new role. Hence, they may choose products that are associated with the new role. Consumers may carry in their minds with specific images of 'roles' (doctor, engineer, executive or lawyer) and choose products associated typically with them. As students, young people may take on multiple roles and it may be friend, sportsperson, student representative, etc., and choose brands associated with a particular role. Brands 'shape' the images that consumers carry about roles. 'Just do it' from Nike may appeal to youth who may assume that the role of a friend (in a specific group) or of a sportsperson. Consumers tend to use a mix a constellation of products to identify themselves with a role.

Rituals are important in role transition as they involve others who may enable the consumer to strengthen and reinforce his/her new role. A common example is the transition of a consumer from being single to getting married. Marriage involves a series of rituals and each of these rituals has a number of products associated with it. The consumer uses these products to symbolize his/her role transition with the help from others in the ritual, as also their 'feedback' on both the ritual and the products. This feedback from others is called reflexive evaluation and it helps him/her strengthen his/her identification with the new role. A bride being complimented for procuring good jewellery or a groom drawing praise for the purchases he made for the occasion are examples of reflexive evaluation.

Cultural transition occurs when consumers move from one culture to another. An Indian who settles down in the US is likely to get used to colas and pizzas, thus replacing the food items he/she used in India. The same consumer, however, may also continue to keep or use certain products that reflect his/her parent culture—Indian jewellery, ethnic clothes, Indian music and video cassettes of his/her favourite films.

Consumers in the transition phase represent a significant target market in most situations. Creams and lotions in the beauty market essentially targets unmarried consumers (women) who are likely to go through a role transition (by getting married). Second-hand markets are likely to boom when marketers target products for consumers who are transitioning but are unable to afford new versions of products/brands. Cars and scooters traded in the second-hand markets are examples. Marketers create a perception that certain products are essential for reinforcing the transition when consumers are going through that phase. Titan's proposition as a gift item for the parent symbolizes the growing status of the son/daughter and their gratitude towards the relationship with parents. Wedding gifts are also oriented towards consumers who are in the transition phase. Product constellations can also be emphasized by the marketer. For example, a brand of modern retail outlet can position itself as a retail outlet for groceries/vegetables/commodities for young couples who are in the process of setting up home.

INDIAN CORE VALUES*

The Indian society is driven by a set of core values, though these may vary in the urban context. These values remain basic to the Indian culture and are strongly embedded in most sub-cultures. The variation in the urban milieu may be attributed to changing lifestyles, impact of Westernization and diffusion of technology. Even within the urban context, these values may have further variations or contradictions. Young couples working with high-technology firms may lead a typically Western lifestyle (cars, fast food and weekend holidays) but still hold on to or practice certain religious beliefs and customs, which are totally ethnic in nature. In general, Indian consumers are still culture conscious in the sense that they conform to the cultural expectations of society. Core values are those (i) which are adopted by a significant number of people, (ii) which are enduring and are followed by people for a long period of time and (iii) which enable marketers to understand the behaviour of consumers. The following are some of the core values of Indians.

Family–orientation

Family, for an average Indian, not only includes his own family only but also the extended family—parents, brothers and sisters. That is the reality for a majority of Indians, though the joint family is fast diminishing in the urban context. The commitment of the male consumer (in some cases, the female consumer as well) to the family is such that he, as the chief wage earner, supports the entire joint family. This has several marketing implications. First, the disposable income of such a consumer gets radically reduced and he/she is always looking for value-based brands at a lower price point. This logic works equally for purchases concerning the self and the immediate family members. The brands at the lower end of the market in a number of product categories like tea, soap, toothpaste and shampoo typically cater to these kinds of consumers. This type of consumer also mixes up brands and offerings from the unorganized sector to balance his/her expenditure on such consumption needs. In fact, the low-end brands attempt to upgrade the consumer from the offerings of the unorganized sector (unbranded and local offerings, which may be marketed in an unstructured and haphazard manner). A consumer may buy a branded detergent powder like Surf to wash his/her 'special' clothes and may

---

* For more on Indian core values, refer to www.pearsoned.co.in/cb2rameshkumar

buy lowly priced washing soaps (branded but cheaper) for washing ordinary clothes. He/she may buy shampoo sachets (small packets, which are offered from around ₹ 2 to ₹ 2.50—Chik shampoo was introduced at 50 paise sachets) once in a while. Such implications, in terms of 'value' offerings, (₹ 1 is less than 5 per cent of a US dollar) will not be felt in developed countries. As the consumer feels the need to economize, he/she may also down-trade or buy less expensive brands after using expensive ones. Down-trading occurs as the consumer's response to price increases across product categories or when the cost of essential services like electricity, water or cooking fuel goes up. This behaviour of consumers is important for marketers as there have been constant efforts by the companies to upgrade consumers in several categories. For example, Hindustan Unilever Limited has a number of price points in almost all of its product line-ups. Colgate also has a number of price points and variants like Colgate Herbal, Colgate, Colgate Gel and Colgate Total brands. Consumers may down-trade at any price point in the product-line and not necessarily at the lower end of the market (though brands towards the upper end may experience a degree of price insensitivity). Britannia, the brand of biscuits, (the brand was built over a period of several decades) has a product-line, ranging from the low-end to premium offerings for a niche market. It introduced Tiger brand of glucose biscuits (a major part of the biscuit market is in the unorganized sector and glucose biscuits are extremely popular at the lower end of the market) at the low-end and it was a major success. This shows that consumers at the lower end who are conscious about the 'value' differentiate across product categories even when they are under pressure to bring down their regular consumption expenses.

Mela and Brands: The Unique Aspect of the Indian Culture

Melas associated with religion is an inherent part of the Indian culture. In 2013, the *Maha Kumbh mela* drew about 5 to 8 crores of people over 30 to 40 days. Colgate, Unilever, Dabur and Vodafone are some of the brands that had participated in this *mela*. *Melas* are fairs organized across India during festivals or to mark any special occasion. *Melas* as a marketing platform may be much older than the organized knowledge on marketing. Lifebuoy had fifty hand wash stations across fifty km radius in one of the *melas* while Fair & Lovely was sold by 500 sales men with trays. Colgate had tied up with Airtel to target their audience with promotional messages using a popular radio personality. Yet another interesting aspect is the sensory aspect of a product that can be sampled by a consumer on the spot such as deodorants or a promotional pack of biscuits. *Melas* are likely to remain a part of the Indian culture despite the digitalization that seems to take over several aspects of consumer behaviour.

With inputs from, Ravi Balakrishnan (2015), 'The Mela mindset', *The Economic Times*, 27 August.

Savings

Savings is an inherent value of Indians, given the uncertainty in income generation (there are monthly, weekly and daily earners in the country). Unlike in developed countries, community medical services and assured pension after retirement are not available to most of the consumers. Consumers fall back on their savings to celebrate festivities, specifically weddings in the family and spend as lavishly as possible. In the recent times, consumers have begun spending on durable products after the basic needs have been taken care of. Bicycles, watches and TV's are popular 'entry-level' purchases for the average Indian who is able to take care of the basic necessities. Savings, as a habit, pervades all sections of the society. Consumers belonging to all socio-economic classes are interested in jewellery and for most of them it may mean investing a considerable amount of their savings. Traditionally, jewellery is more associated with women. Families with girl children are more likely to spend their savings on jewellery. Mostly, consumers buy their jewellery from their family jewellers who have been associated with their client-families for several generations. Branded jewellery like Tanishq and Carbon cater to just about 2 per cent of the market and target an up-market niche. The popularity of instalment payments for a number of products ranging from bicycles to computers can be attributed to consumers splitting savings between traditional purchases like jewellery and appliances required for a convenient living.

Festivities

Celebrating festivals is an ethnic practice followed as India's culture in all the states. The sub-culture within a state (territory) determines the type of festival that is to be actively celebrated. For example, Pongal is celebrated primarily in Tamil Nadu. Like most festivals in this country, Pongal has a special association with the farmers of the state. In West Bengal, Durga Puja is celebrated with a great deal of enthusiasm every year. But these festivals are not popular in any other states, even though its variations are celebrated in other parts. Similarly, Onam in Kerala is another example of a regional festival. Such festivals are a huge opportunity for marketers. Given that 76 per cent of the Indians live in rural areas, a number of companies step up their advertising campaigns and logistics during the festive months. Asian Paints, a leading paints brand, associated its brands with festivities in Bengal and found that there was a substantial increase in its sales. Several brands in a number of product categories offer sales promotional programs during festive seasons and lakhs of consumers make use of the 'value-based' deals during these times. A number of consumers postpone their purchases, especially durables, in the hope of getting such deals. Even a niche jewellery brand like Tanishq came out with *'Oraaphis'* (fraternal friendship bonds tied by girls to boys of their choice, usually in the neighbourhood) in gold on Raksha Bandhan. Gold coins with images of gods (a sign of financial prosperity) are given away as gifts by marketers of durable brands, normally through specified outlets in a city.

Shopping as a Ritual

Shopping is a ritual of sorts among both urban and rural Indians. The type of buyers, the shops they buy from and the product they purchase vary across geographical territories and the economic spectrum of consumers. Retail outlets may range from a roadside shop selling vegetables, to Big Bazaar or Croma or Shopper's Stop that promises a considerable degree of ambience, variety and service over other conventional outlets. The fact that insignificant merchandise (in value terms) are retailed through departmental stores is a reflection of the fragmented nature of retailing in India, quite the reverse of what happens in developed countries. Housewives shop almost regularly for buying all the basic commodities and vegetables, even though the trend may be changing in the urban context. Bargaining, especially in the case of commodities and vegetables, is an unwritten rule in the transaction process. The popular departmental store caters to the middle class and has a sales promotion strategy throughout the year across several product categories. In the case of durable products like TV, refrigerators or two-wheelers, the average Indian consumer takes decisions oriented towards 'extended problem-solving'. As part of the great shopping ritual, members of a family go visiting different outlets with the objective of comparing prices and arriving at the best deal in a product category. The shopping of durables by typical Indian consumers can be associated with compensatory style of decision making, with buyers analysing one brand after another (especially when sales promotions are advertised). It is extremely difficult to find retailers (durable categories) who refuse to sell the brand below the marked retail price in order to clinch the deal with the consumer. This has been true in case of FMCG products in the recent times and such shops use the signboard, 'Buy and Save', to achieve big volumes. During October 2016, Flipkart, Amazon, Myntra had organized a dazzling shopping festival with attractive discounts and new products.

The rural Indian scenario presents a unique characteristic, which the marketers have used. In a number of villages and towns (around 6,25,000 villages) *shandies* are held every week and people buy the basic necessities (sometimes even durables like bicycles and watches) from these temporary markets. These are generally held on a specific day in a week and retailers spread their 'product-mix' in make-shift stalls. Most of them stock fast-moving units across product categories that they buy from wholesalers near their place of trade. A number of companies make use of the video-vans that arrange some kind of entertainment (most commonly, a movie) and end with a brand message. Not every village or town, of course, has this make-shift market, which attracts consumers from a number of neighbouring villages. Most consumers in semi-urban and rural areas visit the closest market in the town/city for their purchases. Given the nature of durables (upper-end ones like refrigerators and colour television sets), these brands are not in a position to have a network of outlets reaching out to the most parts of the country (like FMCG companies that reach millions of outlets in rural areas). There are potential markets in villages where higher-end durable categories may be consumed, but the rural households in such categories, unlike their urban counterparts, are spread out while the latter are concentrated in specific pockets. Some of them, however, may be concentrated in a specific state (Punjab, for instance, has a number of such households in rural areas). Marketers of durables can adopt specialized channel strategies. A brand can identify such customers, have a company-owned outlet (depending on its feasibility) and start a direct marketing exercise to reach out to these households. Company-owned outlets are preferred because the company establishes contact with these consumers and can, at a later stage, attempt up-selling and cross-selling of its products. LG, the brand that has a leading share in several categories of durable products opened up sales offices in semi-urban markets in an effort to reach out to consumers in the hinterland.

Mythology

Mythological stories, scriptures and music are an inherent part of the Indian culture that has attracted scores of tourists from different parts of the world. Apart from creating a brand experience in a service like the tourism industry, unique and invaluable, souvenirs and artifacts are also present in the Indian cultural milieu. Such offerings are marketed in places of tourist interest, but the offerings are not branded. Most of these may not even have the right quality in terms of product finishing and durability. Tourism, largely promoted by Government enterprises, has received considerable impetus in the form of infrastructure and service support. But there is a vast potential for creating a brand in this industry—among both foreign and domestic travellers. A value-based branding experience can create a huge market in tourism, which seems to have taken off in a big way only in the upper social crust. Local toy manufacturers cater to specific markets and a large chunk of the industry is in the unorganized sector. Branded toys with Indian cultural themes (with several elements of the marketing mix brought together) can open up attractive avenues for a brand. Even multinational brands like Leo and Mattel can develop ethnic brands and make it affordable for the masses considering the potential that exists in this sector.

Food

As with the most Asian countries, hot, spicy delicacies are widely popular in India. It may be worthwhile to note that food habits have a strong link with culture and are difficult to change. With the exception of Maggi noodles during the '80s, there has not been a 'foreign' food which has become so popular. Bread, which has been used around for several decades, is still not popular barring certain urban and some semi-urban markets. But it is interesting to note that several variants of wheat flour are popular throughout India.

Changing Cultural Trends in Indian Urban Markets

The urban setting is very different from the rural or semi-urban market setting. There are target segments in cities comprising professionally qualified, high-salaried people who are into the routine track of life. The cultural values of this segment reflect the trends in the urban markets (trends with regard to niche consumers that do not cover the majority of the population). This niche is strongly influenced by the lifestyle and aspirations of the West. The following values can be associated with this niche:

Success through Professional Achievement

Success through professional achievement provides an opportunity for brands to take part in the intrinsic and extrinsic motivational levels (of consumers) and are reflected in the consumption of products and brands. Possessing a middle-end car (like Honda City), membership of prestigious clubs and holidaying in a foreign resort are such products and services these consumers are interested in procuring. These products/brands reinforce a feeling of accomplishment in the individuals and are perceived as rewards.

Involvement in Work

As a logical extension of the previous value, contemporary consumers break away from traditional work practices and are involved in high-tension, fast-paced jobs. They experience time pressure, and hence, prefer time-compression or convenient products. A variety of retail outlets across product categories have emerged in the context (ordering of groceries online, direct marketing of brands, one-stop-shop stores, fast-food restaurants like McDonald or Pizza Hut and grocery shops in petrol bunks are some of the examples). There is a growing need for several kinds of services, which may offer high levels of satisfaction. On-call services like plumbing, bill-payment, laundry services and eateries are some of them.

Material Success

Young professionals who are aged in between 25 to 30 years and who are extremely conscious of their materialistic success have emerged in the past decade. This segment is significantly and markedly different from its equivalent counterparts (in terms of education and status) two decades ago. The present-day young adults have tremendous exposure to the environment through education or work experience abroad. They belong to the cutting-edge professions like software or are high-profile entrepreneurs. Higher education, intelligence and aspirations of these consumers have resulted in their acquiring substantial wealth at a relatively young age in the life-cycle stages. The wealth is spent on essential products, which have contributed to the service economy—health, amusement, time management and convenience. Besides, this segment chooses products and brands with a symbolic overtone; probably to tell the society that they have 'arrived'. There is great demand for quality-oriented, branded services like laundry, in-home delivery of food, baby-sitters and pet-care, in a small way, online marketing of essentials.

Middle-of-the-road Approach to Tradition

The niche of consumers, who are urban, highly educated and in the upper end of the socio-economic strata adopt a middle-of-the-road approach towards rituals and other cultural practices. Most of them are neither too permissive nor too traditional in their approach towards tradition. This is similar to the niche of Indian consumers in the West who adopt a similar approach.

Impulse Gratification

While a number of consumers may be using credit cards, the neo-urban young adults exhibit a compulsive need to buy products and services through credit cards. This niche may possess multiple credit cards. Some banks even attempt to get into the consideration set of such consumers by offering discounts to students of premier institutions in the hope that they may be prospective consumers interested in banking with them.

Use of Hi–Tech Products

High-profile consumers use products like mobiles, computers and other hi-tech products in the categories of household appliances and entertainment systems. This lifestyle aspect may be of interest to marketers of high-end products like fuzzy-logic washing machines, plasma television sets and perhaps, products using Bluetooth technology. A company with a rich database of consumers belonging to this segment can have several variations of permission marketing (that essentially deals with getting the consumer involved in the brand's messages that suits his/her interests rather than bombard the consumer with a barrage of direct mailings). This segment is oriented towards information and is independent, involved in its search and has the potential and willingness to spend. A number of brands may address this segment through a media-mix. The penetration of PC's would be high among the members of this segment as would be online information processing even though, eventually, these consumers may transact at a retail outlet. Several brands are positioned to this segment with lifestyle and symbolic appeals. Symbolic positioning can be backed up by a strong cognitive (information-oriented) copy on the Internet. Interactivity can be put to good use if the website can customize the information provided to the consumer. Queries are likely to be diverse in nature and TV commercials can be supplemented by the Internet. There is also a possibility for the brand to develop a brand community on the net. The urban niche is ideal for the marketers interested in one-to-one marketing or relationship marketing.

Symbolic Behaviour and Gifts

As gifting is a part of several cultures, it may be appropriate to consider the process of gifting and its impact on the transfer of symbolic meaning. There are two participants in the act of gifting—the giver and the recipient. There may be a number of occasions when gifts are exchanged. These occasions are determined by a specific cultural setting. Consumers celebrate Mother's Day, Father's Day and Valentine's Day. Offering gifts is a part of the Indian culture. Titan watches were positioned as gifts initially when they were launched.

Stages in Making Gifts

There are three stages in the process of making a gift—gestation, presentation and reformulation.

The gestation stage is concerned with the motive(s) of making a gift. One may have an *agnostic* motive, in which the giver or donor derives emotional pleasure from the act of giving. The motive may be instrumental when the donor expects something in return from the recipient. A consumer may have an obligatory reason to make a gift because the relationship forces him/her to do so.

A consumer may also give a gift because of antagonistic reasons because he/she is forced to give gifts to someone whom he/she does not like and may select something he/she feels is not the best in his/her perception. The nature of the gift is important at this stage. It may be inappropriate to give a close friend a 'token' gift because the relationship demands the gift be of higher value. But token gifts may be appropriate when no gift is expected. Gifts may also convey a specific meaning on certain occasions. De Beers, the global brand in diamonds, has positioned itself for the occasion of engagement/wedding. The value of the gift (in terms of what it costs) may indicate the intensity of the relationship between the donor and the recipient. Making gifts is also specific to a culture. In Japan, it is odd to reciprocate with a gift which is of higher value than the one received. Search time (the time taken by an individual to search for an appropriate gift) also depends on the intensity of the donor-recipient relationship. Another aspect of the gestation stage is taking a decision on when, in a specific relationship, a gift should be made.

Implications in the Indian context

The gestation stage has several implications in the Indian context, which is influenced by changing lifestyles.

1. It may be worthwhile for a brand like Titan or a brand of pens, which is positioned as a gift, to conduct primary research on why the target segment indulges in gift-giving, the kind of monetary value it places on gifts and what kind of gifts are made for obligatory reasons. This can help the brand to understand how the target segment perceives the positioning of the gift. For example, if a brand is being bought for obligatory reasons, the price may be more important than the emotional aspect of the brand. Hence, there may be a need to launch a variant of the brand. If the brand is bought for emotional reasons, positioning can adopt innovative ways of heightening the emotional proposition.
2. Since India does not have too many consumers in the higher income bracket, the role of a token gift can be researched in the process of gifting—the type of token gifts perceived positively, their price and occasions that are used for making such gifts. These aspects can be studied in detail. A brand with a gift proposition can even use the association to launch lesser-priced 'gifts' across product categories.

The Presentation Stage

This is the stage when actual presentation of the gift takes place. The ritual or the ceremonial aspect of giving becomes important in this stage. A gift wrapped nicely with a personal message in it tells the recipient it has been 'selected' for him/her. The timing of the gift and the element of surprise involved in it are also important. This stage also deals with the reaction the donor expects from the recipient and his/her response thereafter. There may be an uncertainty associated with the impact of the gift on the recipient—whether the latter will like the gift or not. The attention elicited in the presentation stage may also be important. Wedding and birthday parties are occasions that focus on the recipient's reaction to guests and what they offer (though in certain cultures it is impolite to unwrap a gift in front of the giver).

In most Hindu weddings (across different states), the process of making a gift assumes significance and is highlighted at the end of the wedding process. In certain sub-cultures (especially in a number of semi-urban areas), money instead of material gifts is perceived to be more important. The intensity of the relationship is associated with the amount of money presented, especially during the gift-giving ceremony. In a number of cultures, gift-giving is built into the process of marriage when it is finalized. It is an accepted convention that the families of the bride and bridegroom exchange gifts. A substantial amount of money, shopping effort and time are spent by both the parties for this ritual. Godrej Storewell is a brand of steel cupboards that has built emotion into the brand by associating it with the wedding occasion, while being presented as a worthy gift. The brand associated itself as a gift item for weddings. The brand has maintained its association with the occasion and the 'bride' in its advertisements and TV commercials.

The reformulation stage is the final stage of the gift-giving process. The donor and the recipient re-evaluate their relationship based on this process. The reciprocity on a subsequent occasion depends on the experience the donor and the recipient had during the process of making and receiving the gift.

Given that the hospitality and reciprocity are an integral part of the Indian culture, the reformulation stage holds the potential for brand positioning. While some brands have positioned themselves on the 'gifting' platform, there is scope for a brand to position itself on the 'reciprocity proposition'. Titan brought in a warm feeling of reciprocity in one of its TV commercials showing a daughter gifting a watch to her parent. Brands can identify the reformulation stage across different occasions and build positioning strategies by using primary research. For example, how do students feel when they receive gifts from parents and friends? How does a member of the family react to a gift from a person who belongs to another family? How does a young executive react when he receives a gift from a colleague?

Cultural aspects with a mix of varied factors can offer valuable insights for a marketer in a specific environment.

Marketing Communication—The Ethnic Way

A number of positioning strategies in the urban context reflect the growing influence of the West. But there have been successful communication campaigns that conveyed the message effectively through the ethnic route.

There are many advantages of using the ethnic appeal (subject to the selection of target segments). Ethnic appeals are normally drawn from the culture of a specific market, which reflects the practices, rituals, taboos and behavioural orientation over generations. These may also be useful in enabling consumers to connect with familiar situations. Ethnic advertising has the ability to dramatize emotions in a specific cultural setting. Ethnic appeals can also be combined with Western appeals. This can be best illustrated when comparing Titan's advertisement with that of Godrej's Storewell. The former has an element of dramatization woven around the 'warmth' expressed through the gift. The aspirational fantasy of gift-giving brought the brand into the consideration set of consumers who shopped for gifts (not just watches). Watch, as a gift, reflected in the visuals of the TV commercials that clearly reflects a Western orientation. The changing lifestyles, especially in urban markets, are conducive to such a positioning strategy. In the case of Godrej's Storewell, the 'emotional' connection (though portrayed as a gift) is achieved against the backdrop of a marriage in which the bride receives the cupboard as a gift.

Ethnic Route

There are different ways in which a brand can be positioned using the ethnic approach. It can

1. Identify specific behaviour(s)/practices that are connected with the brand/product category
2. Identify specific values in a cultural context, which can be inputs to marketing communication
3. Identify certain beliefs that need to be considered before an advertising campaign is formulated
4. Combine elements of a specific culture with changing cultural trends (Westernization) West
5. Capture a sense of nostalgia associated with a specific culture
6. Use cultural stereotypes
7. Identify specific cultural traits, which can be used for product categories/brands

A combination of several kinds of cultural dimensions makes it worthwhile for marketers to consider positioning strategies oriented towards culture.

Cultural Behaviour

There are a number of behaviours that can be associated with a specific culture. Some of these have their origin in certain kinds of beliefs that are associated with product categories. For example, the *bindi* worn by Indian women is considered as an integral part of Indian culture. Hence, it is essential that a brand name for such a *bindi* should have an ethnic sounding name. A Western name is likely to be counter-productive. An interesting example of effective use of cultural behaviour is the Pepsodent TV commercial a few years back. Snacking on the way to school and back has been a cultural habit of Indians for many decades now. It is a behaviour that can be associated with the masses.

The commercial for the toothpaste captures this and the traditional behaviour of the mother scolding her child. This gets the attention of viewers before the brand benefit of 'protection' is conveyed. Regardless of the extent to which this TV commercial contributed to the success of the brand, this example reflects the need for marketers to have insights from the daily life of consumers in a specific cultural backdrop. Even Maggi noodles (noodles is not of Indian origin) was positioned as a 2-minute convenient snack for children. The cultural practice of providing homemade snacks as food to children was the thought behind the Maggi campaign. The portrayal of whiteness in clothes led to the creation of the whitener category for clothes and Robin Blue was almost a household name before Ujala was launched. Whiteness, to masses in India, is the whiteness with a bluish tinge. The practice of using soap for washing clothes is so old that a brand like Ariel, which pioneered compact detergents at the upper end, had to introduce soap at the lower end of the market. It is interesting that Ariel initially advertised that soap was not required if one used a compact detergent for washing. Samsung has introduced a washing machine to ensure that sarees do not get entangled after washing.

Importance of Cultural Values

Cultural values are important for product categories and positioning strategies. Charms, the cigarette for the youth was launched in the '80s and it became a rage among young smokers. Its positioning was in consonance with the changing values. 'The spirit of freedom—Charms is the way you are' was its punchline that stood for adventure, independence and non-conformity. The denim-like packaging added to this appeal. However, cultural values have not changed enough for marketers to launch a cigarette for women (Ms was launched during the '80s). Values are important because they reflect culturally acceptable behaviour. Valentine's Day cards may have been a taboo a decade ago but they have caught on, at least in urban markets. Bacardi, the liquor brand, positioned itself on the 'spirit of enjoyment' (during the days of liquor advertising) and its success among the intended target audience also reflects the changing values. The launch of Close-up toothpaste during the '80s was perhaps ahead of the values of those times. The 'Close-up smile' was advertised in cinema halls and was positioned at teenagers. Later, the permissiveness was marked down by using a different group in the commercial. Charms and Close-up were one of the earliest brands and were symbolic (along with certain changes in the environment) in heralding a new youth culture in the country.

There may also be certain beliefs that have an impact on marketing communication. The Indian obsession with fairness has made Fair & Lovely a strong brand. The recent TV commercial (that was later withdrawn) of the brand is based on the deeply-entrenched cultural belief that a son is better than a daughter. But the daughter proves that she can be as successful as a son and the equality was possible because of Fair & Lovely. Vicco turmeric cream positioned itself as a fairness cream for the 'brides-to-be' to enhance their complexion. Turmeric for skin-care is a part of the Indian tradition in many regions of the country. Vicks Vaporub captured the emotional bond between the mother and son to convey the benefit of the brand. Clinic Plus also captures the care an Indian mother showers on her daughter. The 'family togetherness' is a cultural aspect of India that marketers can use. Lifebuoy had re-launched itself as a family soap. While family soaps like Protex and All-Care have not met with great success in terms of being present in the market for a long time, the 'family' platform (being associated with the family) for Lifebuoy may be appropriate, given the historical presence of the brand.

While Pond's talcum powder was virtually a household name till the '80s, a significant cross-section of talcum powder users may have switched over to creams/lotions because of the belief that 'self-enhancing' powers are better with substitute products. A brand that masses accept because of a cultural belief should launch several variants/better alternatives of the product for the same segment to ensure that the target segment stays with the brand.

Asian Paints is a good example of a company's attempts to associate its brands with several festivals in the country. For example, many families, especially in semi-urban and rural areas of Tamil Nadu, believe in repainting their houses during Pongal. Asian Paints has created specific brands, which can be associated with such occasions.

Mixing Culture with Changing Trends

A type of effective cultural appeal consists of mixing certain cultural beliefs with trendy products or advertising. Promise toothpaste, which had a successful run, highlighted the traditional clove oil used by people to control toothaches. Cadbury's recent television campaign (for moulded chocolate) shows people of different age groups enjoying the chocolate with a well-known celebrity endorsing the brand. Normally, one associates chocolates with children in the Indian context. But decades back the brand 5-Star from Cadbury positioned itself as a 'togetherness bar' for the youth segment. (In fact, this was even before when Charms or Close-up addressed this segment). Snacking is a part of the Indian culture. Positioning a chocolate for adults in India involves a mix of tradition and modernity, which, in this context, is Westernization. Chocolate, in the West, is considered as a favourite with adults as well. Cricket has been so long a part of the Indian culture that Pepsi used it in its campaign 'for the younger generation' and associated the brand with the fun that goes with the game. Raaga collection from Titan is another example of contemporary positioning with ethnic overtones.

Cultural Traits and Their Importance

A few brands have used Indian-ness to make an impact on their target segment. 'Believe in the best' which highlighted the superiority of Indian-made BPL products had featured Amitabh Bachchan in its ad. It is an example of a specific cultural trait being used to reinforce a brand that had already built a strong image over the years. The 'Hamara Bajaj' campaign (the old and the new) blends the modern lifestyle with ethnic beliefs (both these examples are old ones but convey the conceptual point). The message of the positioning is that even though the current crop of young people is Western-oriented, they have a core association with ethnic values. Amway, an Indian beauty and health care company, came up with an ad showing two sisters dressed in traditional and bohemian outfits respectively. While their family members assume that the traditionally-dressed sister would touch their feet, they were sceptical about the other sister. But she smiles and touches their feet. The ad line tried to show that even if somebody dresses in a certain way, it does not necessarily portray anything disrespectful or negative about their character. In India, women have always been told to wear and behave in an 'appropriate' manner. Through their ads and brand messages, companies are trying to portray the changing cultural topography of India where a woman refuses to be judged on what she wears. Also, these brands had encouraged ethnocentrism—buying brands from one's own country.

Other Cultural Appeals

Nostalgia for a specific culture can be a good appeal, especially for a brand which has been in the market for a number of years. Margo soap adopted this approach in its advertisement in which a young woman remembers her childhood days fondly. Subsequently the brand used a well-known female celebrity to endorse the goodness of neem based product on her association with elders who had recommended it. Ayurvedic concepts (now Himalaya) had used the stereotype of a traditional grandmother to promote its products made from the traditional ayurvedic herbs and preparations. Such cultural stereotypes lend credibility to the brand. Bru initially used the stereotype of 'the taste of filter coffee', which is a part of the South Indian culture.

Cultural dimensions can matter to many products and such inputs are valuable to marketers for both Indian and MNC brands.

Touch of Reality

Branding Associations and Cultural Practices

Cultural beliefs and practices can be innovatively used by brands. Meera is an herbal shampoo brand and the brand name, ingredients and packaging have strong associations with the cultural aspects associated with shampoo and beauty. The brand launched an interesting TV commercial that showed a dialog between the mother and daughter (this kind of relationship is very traditional in the Indian culture and the mother giving tips on various aspects of life to her daughter is also a traditional one). The advertisement begins by showing the daughter who says she is weak in maths (also a frequently encountered belief among school-going children and parents). The daughter is shown fidgeting with her hair (also a traditional practice commonly seen) and the mother comments that her hair is also weak upon noticing fallen hair in her daughter's hands. The advertisement ends with snippets of the daughter using the brand and turning out to be strong in maths, with her also acquiring strength from the brand of shampoo.

Hamam, the popular soap brand in the southern markets, introduced herbal variants and it also launched advertisements with clear images of cultural practices. One of the TV commercials begins with a man performing *surya namaskara* (a religious prayer), the lady of the house dressed in traditional apparel and finally ending the commercial with the brand's proposition of 'auspicious beauty'.

End Notes

1. David Milk, "Consumer research and semiotics: Explaining the morphology of Signs, Symbols and Significance, " *Journal of Consumer Research 13* (September 1986): 196–213.
2. George J. McCall and J. L. Simmons, *Social Psychology: A Sociological Approach*, (Free Press, 1982).
3. Shaswati Shankar (2015), "Does the crowd dig crowdsourcing?," *The Economic Times*, September 2.
4. Ibid.
5. http://www.bing.com/videos/search?q=touch+the+pickle&qpvt=touch+the+pickcle&FORM=VDRE, accessed on September 2, 2015.
6. Purva Chitnis (2015), "The hunt for followers," *Business Standard*, September 7, 2015.
7. Michael Solomon, Consumer Behavior: Buying, having and Being, (Pearson, 2015), 109.
8. http://www.hul.co.in/brands-in-action/detail/Brooke-Bond-Taaza/294520/, accessed on October 15,2011.
9. Dennis W Rook, "The Ritual Dimension of consumer behavior," *Journal of Consumer Research 12* (December 1985): 251–264.
10. Ibid.
11. Hoyer and MacInnis, *Consumer behavior,* (Houghton Mifflin, 1999), 439–467.

Exercises

1. Compare Patanjali's toothpaste with Close-up in terms of cultural orientation.
2. Draw a comparison between the urban youngsters in the age group of 20-25 years with the urban population of 50-60 years in terms of their preferences of fast food using cultural aspects.

CHAPTER 10

Retailing and Consumer Behaviour Linkages to Branding

Retailing, in the Indian context, is undergoing a radical change with modern retail outlets spreading across the country. India's retail markets would reach a value of ₹47 lakh crores with the *kirana* (neighbourhood or 'pop and mom' stores) shops contributing to 61% of the grocery consumption by value. There are about 15 million of these shops across the country and a significant proportion of these are managed by family members. Even large multinational brands depend on wholesalers who feed these *kirana* shops in several markets across the country. There are also varying sizes of *kirana* shops depending on their location (in urban or rural areas). A typical *kirana* shop carries merchandise that is absolutely required by consumers residing in the vicinity of the shop. It does not offer extensive selection of merchandise in terms of stock keeping units (sizes of packs and variants) or in terms of the type of product categories.

With several modern retail outlets and malls mushrooming across the country, the historical dominance of *kirana* stores in the country assumes special significance in the Indian retailing context.

Consumer Behaviour at the Cutting Edge of Retailing

With technologies interacting with retailing in a significant manner, consumer behaviour offers exciting applications to marketers. Flipkart and Myntra have apps that consumers can use to discuss with their friends while shopping or even with fellow shoppers in a mall to know their decisions and get an idea about trends.[1] Self-concept and reference group aspects are involved in such initiatives. These groups may comprise people whom a consumer may or may not know personally. For example, people with similar interest may connect online and form a chat group to discuss their choices. Technology and consumer behaviour at the retail point of purchase is likely to open up several avenues to brands that were not available in the previous decades. Another development is the concept of mobile wallets like M-wallet (card-less mobile payment) and Paytm, a company which now boasts of 100 million customers. M-wallet companies can target consumers and offer loyalty-based discounts/other benefits. For instance, consumers may be loyal to M-wallet in a few categories like groceries and mobile charge and these categories may be of interest to M-wallet companies. [2]

The Digital Touch to Kirana Stores

There are several towns and villages where consumers may not be tech-savvy in using computers and gadgets, though they may have mobiles. Small *kirana* stores in towns and villages can supply almost any merchandise to their consumers (Kolar town in Karnataka, for example, has a digital kiosk with a tablet PC).[3] The shop keeper packages the required product ordered by the consumer (it may be any apparel or electronic product, for instance) and within a day or two the customer receives the product. The shop keeper takes the payment from the consumer before he orders the product (12 per cent of the Indian population uses internet). More than 50 per cent of the retail sale takes place in smaller towns (Tier 3 or smaller towns that have a much lesser population as compared to an urban city). The *kirana* shop owner also benefits as he gets the product online without the need for distributors and hence, makes a margin whenever he sells a product.

Decision making on retailing is very similar to CDM on brands where the consumer goes through the entire process beginning with the 'needs' to 'post-purchase decision making'. There are a few interesting and important dimensions associated with consumer behaviour and retail outlet selection:

- Does the retail outlet have psychological implications on the target segment? Titan watches created an exclusive retail network that offered transparent prices and a fine shopping experience for consumers.
- Does the selection of outlets vary in accordance with the types of product categories?
- While buying a TV or washing machine, will consumers visit an exclusive showroom of LG, Samsung or Whirlpool, or will they go to a multi-brand outlet? Will there be differences in the psychographic (and demographic) profile of consumers in terms of choosing the outlets? What is the sequence in which the consumers are likely to go about their decisions? Will they select the brand or the category before choosing the outlet?
- What is the impact of the image developed by a retail outlet? Is Reliance Mart, for example, different from the neighbourhood grocery shop in the perception of consumers? What kind of perception are consumers likely to carry with regard to shopping from an online outlet like Rediff with regard to a brick and mortar outlet like Fountain Head or Landmark?
- Will consumers be interested in store or retail brands? Traditionally, retailers have been stacking manufacturers' brands. In recent times, super markets like Reliance Mart have started carrying retail or store brands.

- What contributes to retail equity (the value a retail outlet holds to a brand), retail image or retail loyalty?
- How do retail outlets handle perceived risks?

Marketers need an in-depth knowledge of the various dimensions that link retailing and consumer behaviour. Research is needed to handle retail decisions in a competitive context. A few companies operate through kiosks at airports, malls and high-traffic areas. Online retailing, too, may perhaps hold tremendous potential in services, where the consumer requires a good deal of interaction with the service provider (financial services, travel services and music downloads).

Importance of Synergy Between Digital and Offline Stores

ShopClues is one of the newer e-commerce portals with a current seller base of two lakhs. It has planned to create hyperlocal stores where it would work with offline stores to deliver products to consumers. Amazon Kirana Now is an initiative where Amazon works with *kirana* shops to deliver products to neighbourhoods. Spencer's Retail has 130 offline stores and it plans to use this base to launch its online stores. This is likely to provide synergies associated with supply chain and logistics.

Inputs from

Writankar Mukherjee (2015), 'Spencer so Retail Plans Ecomm foray with Separate unit', *The Economic Times*, 27 July.

Payal Ganguly (2015), 'ShopClues takes the cloud route to get to the last mile', *The Times of India*, 27 July.

Retail Outlet Selection and Brand Selection[4]

There are three fundamental patterns that a consumer can follow: (i) brand first, retail outlet second; (ii) retail outlet first, brand second; and (iii) brand and retail outlet simultaneously. A consumer wanting to buy a car (information search on brands is followed by retail outlet selection in durables) may collect information on brands and purchase the one he/she wants from a retail outlet based on his/her perception of the price offered and/or post-sales service provided by it. In certain product categories, especially where 'category-killers' (large retail outlets, which deal with several brands and variants) exist, and consumers may first think of the retail outlet and then the brands. Television, refrigerator and audio products retailed through outlets like Croma are such examples. Another dimension may be to compare the brands in the evoked set that are at the retail outlets.

This is possible, especially in the Indian context, where dealers in semi-urban/rural areas develop a bond with consumers. Primary research can be used to find out the specific sequence involved in such a situation. The 'brand first' dimension may need a 'feature-based' advertising and the 'retail outlet first' dimension may require POP material and special training to sales personnel (at the retail outlet) to recognize consumer needs. Further, if it is known that a number of consumers are inclined on visiting their favourite retailer in a geographical area, there has to be more emphasis on regional/local advertising, which highlights the retail shop rather than the brands.

Pop–up Retail Stores

E-retailers have an opportunity to build a positive attitude among consumers through Pop-up stores that come up in malls or high visibility areas for a few days to a few months.[5] Creyate (customized clothing), FabAlley (apparel) and Pepperfry (online furniture store) are examples. It is not the sale associated with these stores that matter; it is the exposure that consumers get to these online stores resulting in the brand enhancing itself in terms of image as well as creating a positive attitudinal impact on consumers.

Retail Outlet First and Brand Second

When a number of consumers follow this sequence of decision making, the point-of-purchase material and building of the image of the outlet become important. The manufacturer of the brand has to ensure that the brand and its variants are available at the key outlets in a locality. Point-of-purchase material to be used at the retail outlet may require primary research on whether visuals or product features are to be used and if the material should be in the regional language. There may also be a need to monitor competition from other outlets to ensure that consumers remain satisfied on counts of service, price, promotional deals and ambience. This is especially applicable to durable retailing in India (in cities). Retailers attempt to increase consumer traffic by providing a number of add-ons.

Brand First and Retail Outlet Second

Consumers think of the brand first if: (a) they have not developed a strong relationship with any retailer to allow the latter to get into the 'evoked retail set' or (b) the brand has got into the evoked set either because of advertising or positive word of mouth. If local or regional advertising (in the shopping guide, which appears every week in the local newspapers) has a list of brand names that have already got into the evoked set of consumers, it will enable consumers to be 'pulled' to the outlet. Primary research may be required to find out the brands in the evoked set. This feedback may have to be provided by the respective manufacturers to the retailers in various geographical areas, especially if the brands have a major chunk of the market and are nationally advertised. Even multinational outlets can use this approach and mention the brands in the evoked sets. This is likely to increase the traffic to the outlet. Besides, the evoked set can also change depending on the strategies of brands. Local advertising can be different from national advertising for the brand. A brand may be advertised on features nationally, but on the plank of effective after-sales service at the retail level because that is the local priority. The combination of 'push–pull' strategy is shown in Figure 10.1.

Figure 10.1 Brand First, Outlet Second: 'Push–Pull' Approach

The interest generated on the brand has to be backed up by good pre-sale services at the outlet.

Discount Stores and E–tailing

Discount stores in the apparel industry were facing a reduced growth due to the increasing discounted sale associated with online e-tailers.[6] Megamart and Brand Factory are some of the retail chains. These chains were attracting consumers who were attracted by the aspirational value of brands but were unable to afford them. How can consumer behaviour be used to analyse the discount chain as brands? Perhaps a new line of brands (that are exclusive to the discount chain) that are offered with regular and well-known brands over the online space may create the appropriate cognition as well as the aspiration (affect in this context) to reposition these discounted brands. Cognition is associated with the features and benefits of the brands and the affect is the aspirational feeling of buying these offerings at 'value' oriented prices.

Brand and Retail Outlet Simultaneously

When consumers think of the brand and retail outlet simultaneously, it means that they have a certain preference for the outlet and will also like to check out the brands in the evoked set at the retail outlet. The marketer has to do primary research to find out specific markets (geographical areas) where consumers have a positive relationship with retailers. This is important because of the retailers' influence on the purchase behaviour of consumers in India. He/she may also check if the retailers have the brands in the evoked set of the target segments. This is to ensure that the retailers who have a bond with the target segment do not disappoint the consumers merely because of the non-availability of the brands and send them to a different retailer.

Retail sales personnel become more important in this situation. Prospective consumers are 'carried over' to the purchase stage by the store personnel and hence, there should be incentive programs for the latter. If a company like LG or Sony is dealing with a number of brands/sub-brands, it has to ensure the availability of specific brands that may interest consumers. If it is a large retail outlet dealing in a number of brands (like Vivek & Co in the southern India), a shop-in-shop arrangement may be preferable. A shop-in-shop arrangement creates a focus on the brand and reinforces the positive opinion a consumer may have had about the brand (in this context). A considerable amount of pre-sales service has to back up the shop-in-shop concept. This concept creates an aura of exclusivity inside the retail outlet and consumers tend to have higher expectations on count of pre-sales service and the attention they receive. A large store is also likely to stock several brands. Hence, all brands in the evoked set have to compete to get into the choice set. Large outlets may also have a provision for lower prices (because of large volumes) and hence, may be in a better position to clinch the deal with consumers who consider the brand and retail outlet together. With malls evolving in cities and towns, brands should consider the possibility of being located in a mall for reasons other than profitability, depending on the target segments involved. Affluent teenagers interested in iPods or digital cameras are more likely to visit the outlets if these are situated in malls/large shopping complexes. Apple had planned to set up 'shop-in-shop' outlets at some locations of Croma.

Durable Brands and Online Channels

With the growth of online retailing channels in India, a number of durable brands are planning online channels. Godrej, Samsung and Whirlpool brands are considering online channels.[7] Godrej Appliances is considering an exclusive range for Flipkart as televisions and home appliances were showing impressive sales growth in their portal.[8] Online sale of durable brands through online channels introduced by the respective brand appears to be imminent in the Indian context. ShopClues.com is another online channel that deals with several categories of durables.

Retail Image—Basics[9]

Megamart, the ₹ 600 crore chain of stores from Arvind Ltd, was strongly associated with the 'discount tag'. The chain was started in 1995. 25 of these stores were converted into the brand 'Unlimited', that would have an added focus on women's and kids wear.[10] This is an example of a retail chain repositioning itself to adapt itself to the environment.

As in the case of brands, retail outlets also form or carry images in consumers' minds. Primary research can point out the perception of consumers on various aspects/dimensions of a retail outlet. A small retailer can also use this approach. A retailer in a given area can develop a perceptual map consisting of the relevant dimensions to get an idea about how consumers perceive a set of competing retailers. Another aspect associated with retail outlets is that consumers tend to use the image of a retail outlet as an indicator of quality in the absence of brand cues. For example, if a packaged unbranded commodity is marketed through a well-known departmental store, the image of the retail outlet stocking the offering will influence the latter's image. Service counters, queue management, billing, merchandise display and the variety of product categories stocked by the retail outlet (apart from SKU's) influence its image. Retail image is also important in Internet marketing. An online retailer has to have an image of 'convenience, trust and quality', much like a brand name, to ensure that loyal consumers continue to transact business with him/her. Besides, as consumers' trust increases with time, the online retailer can get into product categories that consumers may buy more frequently.

Dimensions Associated with Retailing in a Changing Environment

Two leading brands can come together to capitalize on a trend.

Shoppers Stop had planned an alliance with Femina, the well-known women's magazine, to create a shop-in-shop setting within Shoppers Stop called 'Femina Flaunt', a premium fashion outlet for 25 to 35 years-old urban women who live in the top 25 cities with the psychological profile of independence, progressive and being discerning.[11]

The Negative Aspects of Branding Associated with Retail Image

Gripe websites like boycottwalmart, or ihatestarbucksucks.com are examples.[12] Consumers leave a negative opinion on these sites and brands need to be prepared to handle such problems related to brand associations.

Dimensions Associated with Retail Image

In today's competitive era, it would be difficult for retailers to leave a lasting impression if they attempted targeting all types of consumers. The need is to target only specific kinds of consumers and develop relevant associations with them. For example, Shoppers Stop may be associated with a pleasant, easy going shopping experience and a satisfied loyal consumer who can benefit from the deals that the store offers. Food World may be associated with value in FMCG products and groceries. Landmark may be synonymous with the variety it offers in books. Marketers can control the kind of associations that need to be developed to provide the required differentiation. There may be a store that sells well-known brands at a lower price and does not offer much in store help. A network of such stores can develop an image of convenience and value (by planning the locations). Another aspect of store image is the shopping area. Different shopping locations in a city have different kinds of images among consumers. In Bangalore, for example, Commercial Street is more known for textiles than consumer durables. An upmarket consumer durable located there will find it very difficult to attract traffic (unless it is planned on a large scale in terms of merchandise and visibility). Similarly, an upmarket textile store in a predominantly discount-oriented shopping area may not attract the attention of the intended target segment, which may have a symbolic need (of even shopping in an exclusive locality) with regard to the shopping area it visits.

Online Fashion Portal for 'Innovative Consumers'

Aditya Birla group had launched Abof, the fashion portal that would have relatively selective choice but will cater to consumers who are 'discovery-driven', which means that they do not know what they would buy as compared to consumers who are 'intent-driven'.[13] Abof would be different from the company's Trending.com website that offers well-known brands. It is likely to appeal to 'need-for-innovation' type of consumers. The target segment will be between 18 to 25 years. The portal was planned for 55 brands on the range of ₹ 300 to 4000 along with a 3D trial room for a more interactive experience.

There may be several dimensions associated with retail image and extensive primary research has to be done to ensure that a retail store does not select too many dimensions and dilute its store positioning strategy. Product associations can stand for quality, variety, style or price. Service can develop its associations with sales personnel, pre-sales or after-sales service, easy return of faulty goods, shopping ease or delivery. Consumer imagery can be developed by associating a specific type of consumer with a retail outlet. Ambience can be associated with decor, lighting, moving space, layout, cleanliness and comfort. Convenience can be associated with locations and parking. Value can be associated with low prices, bundling of products at a low price, delivery or a combination of these dimensions. Choosing and nurturing the right image is a prerequisite for the long-term profitability of any retail outlet.

Group Buying in the Indian Context

Groupon is an international online retailer service provider that had advocated the concept of partnering with local retailers in several categories and offering significant discounts to consumers if they form a minimum number to obtain a particular offering or brand on a given day (for instance, a brand of TV will be discounted significantly if a minimum number of consumers are prepared to buy it from a retailer on a given day).

In India, the breakaway group of Groupon is Nearbuy.[14] It could soon join the discounting race along with several online portals.

Store brands are the ones that are carried in the name of the store or the name of a private label. As competition intensifies in a category, retailers are likely to develop brands in the name of the store or independent brand names that can be stocked at their retail outlets. National brands, or well-known brands of manufacturers, are likely to face stiff competition from store brands, especially in retail outlets that have high consumer loyalty. Loyal consumers are very likely to try out store brands as their confidence in the store's brand name is likely to be high. Store brands, therefore, should necessarily offer high quality and perhaps, position themselves on value. There is a need to avoid the traditional approach of store brands providing acceptable quality at lower prices. This is essential because many national brands are taking this route in categories like soaps, shampoos, biscuits, commodities, toothpastes and beverages. A retail outlet may research the pattern of consumption of store brands it carries across categories. If the brand has a chain of stores, it may be worthwhile to observe the impact of store brands in different geographical areas.

A retail outlet has certain advantages and it should consider the following before launching store brands:

- *Analysis of product categories*: If there are several national brands across categories with offerings at close price points, a store brand may find it difficult to enter the category. Variety, SKU's and constant sales promotions add on to the appeal of such buying situations (Reliance Mart in a locality that already has a number of departmental stores, but not offering the kind of variety and prices offered by a large format retailer).
- *Distribution of national brands*: If well-known brands are widely available at different price points, a store brand may find it difficult to have a presence in the market in India.
- *Specialised offerings*: There may be specific markets/niches, which may not be served by national brands. Store brands can use these gaps in the market to come out with suitable offerings. Herbal soap is one example and super market chains carry brands like Medimix, Chandrika and Biotique (some of these brands may not be as freely available as national brands in grocery stores). Special Assam tea made by independent brands can be seen in 'More' outlets. There can also be upmarket niches like home-made chocolates and snacks, which can be marketed as store brands.
- *Are there enough brands to develop the market?* There may be categories like floor cleaning and dish-washing powders/liquids that are largely confined to the unorganized sector and these categories may offer scope for the creation of store brands. For example, there are only a few national brands in the category of floor cleaning and a huge market can be developed as the penetration level of the category is low. Store brands have the opportunity of capturing a considerable amount of the neighbourhood markets, if value is provided. Value can even mean the safety of using a floor cleaner associated with the private label.

- *Can demand be met?* A store brand should be available at the outlet to meet the demand for it, if consumers show a marked preference for the brand. This is important because once a consumer finds that the supply of the store brand is not consistent (though of good quality), he/she may go back to one of the national brands, which are usually always available.

Facebook and Indian Retailing

In August 2015, Facebook had 11.2 crore users in India and it had planned to launch a shopping festival named 'Tied Together' on the occasion of Raksha Bandhan, an Indian festival that signifies and strengthens bonding between a brother and sister.[15] Online word of mouth and reference group concepts become important in such online retailing contexts

'Pull–Push' and the Digital Era

Pull is traditionally associated with advertising strategy to 'pull' the customers to the retail outlet and 'push' is associated with the retailer's strategy. Successful brands have to be strong in both 'pull' and 'push' functions. A detergent brand can advertise effectively but if it does not have 'push' strategies, it would lose out on the advantages of using the 'pull' strategy. A new brand entering the market has to be careful in synchronising its 'pull–push' strategies.

With 213 million users on the internet by 2013(Dec) and 254 million users of internet by the end of 2014[16], Indian advertising ('pull') as well as the retailer's ('push') strategies will undergo a radical change. College students using internet under the age of 21 will be counted around 60 million. If an apparel brand like Allen Solly is interested in a cross-section of the younger segment, the brand may connect with the target segment on the digital media (mobile, YouTube or Facebook for example) by showcasing its range and giving lucrative offers; it may even use a virtual mirror that enables a consumer to 'try the apparel', get their feedback (even in the absence of 'touch') and order it online. With technology and online browsing converging, the conventional 'pull–push' strategies are likely to undergo significant changes in the digital era.

Advertising and Retail Outlets

An outlet may deal with several product categories and there may be a need to advertise on two aspects:

1. A continuous form of advertising (taking into account the reach, cost and the choices available for media selection), which would ensure the positioning of the retail outlet on the dimensions of what it 'stands' for (or the type of associations on which it would like to be perceived by the target segment).

2. Specific advertisements on product categories and promotional prices (including sales promotional offers), whenever it is required. For example, a festive occasion may require certain types of advertising, which will 'pull' consumers to the retail outlet (especially in the case of durable products). A retail outlet marketing fast foods and soft drinks may like to target children during their summer holidays. There may also be specific offers targeting housewives.

A planned process helps a retail outlet convey a coherent and focused perception of the image of the store. The following aspects require careful consideration while a policy on retail advertising is formulated:

- The positioning of the product is important and there should be no advertising that dilutes the planned positioning dimensions. An upmarket store dealing with apparel can certainly run sales promotional campaigns. It has to ensure that the upmarket associations are continuously built over a period of time. It also has to ensure that frequent sales promotions do not dilute the credibility associated with the upmarket associations. The firm can have a sales promotion once or twice a year (during a festive occasion depending on its target segment) and emphasize the association with such sales promotion by using phrases like 'Now only' or 'Once in a year' or 'Special sale'. It may also be a good idea for the retail outlet not to deal with seconds (even if prices are reduced). When an upmarket store announces a sales promotion, its objective should be to enlarge its consumer base by offering 'trial value' which really is offering good quality products at prices that are slightly lower than the usual prices so that more consumers are added during the sales promotion period. These consumers may buy frequently from the retail outlet after being convinced about the merchandise of the upmarket store. Apart from creating a new loyal consumer base, the promotional offer will also benefit the existing consumers. An upmarket store should ensure that, apart from layout and ambience, consumers appreciate 'value' at a higher price point.
- Advertising for one product category (with or without an offer) should result in 'spill-over sales'. This means consumers entering the store for a particular item/category should also be motivated to buy some more items apart from their planned purchase.

Gamified Ads and Point of Purchase

In order to enhance the engagement with consumers, brands may introduce interactive ads that can be played on mobile devices. Breaking a brick to know the features of a Samsung phone or collecting *badam* (almonds) on the screen to use them for a drink to be given to a Sultan are examples. Gamified ads are supposed to be much engaging than static ads.[17] These games have a sensory element as they have a peculiar touch or sound.

However, retailers and brands need to work on ways to ensure that this engagement results in brand consumption in terms of consumer loyalty. The basis to such behaviour is the core product offering. Besides, retailers and brands also can introduce extension of such gamified ads at the point of purchase in the form of contests or introduce some digitally-enabled excitement by which consumers can collect points that can be redeemed. Without the point of purchase, digitalization with respect to such ads, the brands may not translate engagement into action (buying).

This can be done by:

1. Having attractive POP material for categories other than the one advertised.
2. Having a good layout, which will attract attention on related products from the viewpoint of either perception or consumption. For example, an offer for soft drinks should ensure that the brand on offer is stocked near snacks. If a lifestyle outlet is advertising for apparel, it has to ensure that shoe brands (which also have a lifestyle appeal) are stocked near the brand of apparel.
3. When a store advertises on just price ('discount' stores), it has to ensure that consumers compare the advertised prices either with their internal reference price (price range normally considered by consumers for the product category), or external reference price (the price of the advertised brand in other outlets).

A synergized approach taking together the image of the store, POP, planned offers and advertising can result in creating an impact on the target segment.

Diversity of Consumer Segments and Consumer–Retailing Factors

Regardless of the format of the retail outlet, several sets of factors play a role in the variety of offerings, SKU's, categories of products to be stocked, atmospherics and layout of the format.

Bannerghatta Road is a busy road in Bangalore. There is Food World, Hypercity, Reliance Mart and several other *kirana* shops of varying sizes within 3 km radius. Consumers belonging to several socio-economic strata live within this geographical area. There are high-end and middle-end apartments and independent houses within the area. Field investigation (interviews) from a few consumers belonging to different segments of consumers yielded the following information:

Segment 1: Young couple with one or two kids; monthly income of ₹ 3 to 5 lakhs

Shopping routine: Visits large shopping formats, stocks up for a week, requires a wide variety, expects a number of fast moving consumer good categories, happy with deals at the outlet, buys imported chocolates. Also buys vegetables and fruits with groceries. May visit the local *kirana* shop if there is unavailability of any product categories. Does not mind impulsive purchases to try out the new offerings in the eatable category. Looks for organic produce.

Segments 2: Family earning ₹ 2 lakhs/month with two kids. Buys fruits and vegetables at the local market/shop.

Shopping routine: Visits large formats but not on a weekly basis. Buys groceries from a local shop closely (ensures it is of a good quality). While visiting large formats, buys groceries. Most FMCG goods bought with the local retailer (soaps, milk additives, toothpastes and other such items). When there is a sales promotion at the retail outlet, this segment uses it. Looks for moderate variety.

Segment 3: Monthly income of the family ₹ 25,000

Shopping routine: Buys vegetables and fruits at the local store. Buys most of the groceries at a large shopping format but also buys groceries at the local *kirana* stores as credit is made available. Variety is not important. SKU's are important as their unit cost is low.

Given the fact that around 60 per cent of an average family's income is spent on groceries/food/drink, it is important for retailers (students studying retailing practices) to note the diversity of consumers, even within a given geographical area (there may also be geographical areas where consumers have similar demographic profiles).

The following sets of factors will be useful to retailers to get an idea about the consumers visiting the store. Some degree of primary research is required.

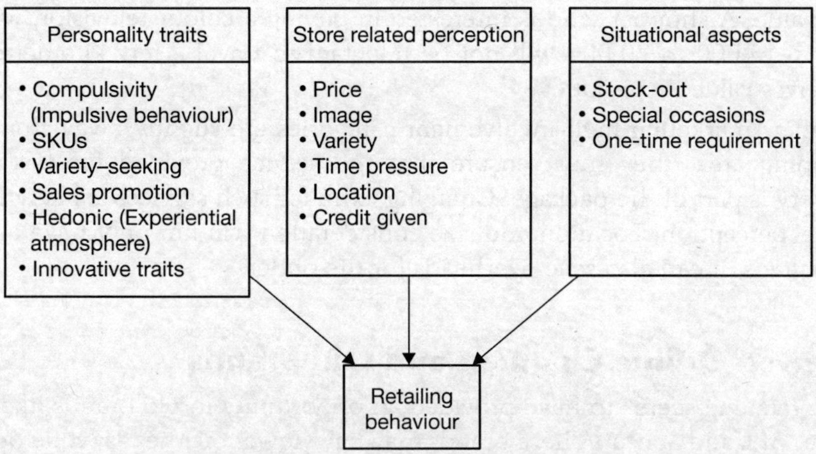

Figure 10.2 Consumer-Store related factors in retailing

Note Discretionary money available with the consumer is an important factor. (The factors in the figure are suggestive in nature)

Location and Size Consideration

Consumers' perception is shaped by an outlet's location and size. Location has to take into account the target segment and the merchandise. Grocery stores should be located in residential areas. But if a large store deals with several categories (and SKU's) of products, it can locate itself in a prime shopping location in the city, as consumers will want to combine their purchases when they visit the location. Consumers, not particular about fast service or convenience, will prefer large outlets. The following aspects should be considered by a retail outlet store when planning its size:

1. The size and retail traffic of competing retailers in a given geographical area.
2. Travelling time taken for the target segment.
3. The importance placed on fast service.
4. The kind of product categories to be marketed by the outlet. Even willingness to travel to an outlet will depend on the product category. Consumers may not mind travelling a distance if they are assured of value in the case of high-involvement categories.
5. Lifestyle brands like Tanishq, Rolex or Reebok may attract better retail traffic if their exclusive outlets are located in a shopping area, which is full of similar outlets.
6. When category killers plan for high-involvement categories, they should consider parking space. Hence, they need not necessarily be located at prime shopping locations (like lifestyle outlets) because consumers will be willing to travel a distance to buy value. A shopper who is interested in buying a colour television which ranges from ₹ 15,000 to 20,000 will not be reluctant to travel a few kilometres if he/she perceives value in an outlet.
7. If outlets marketing high-involvement categories are slightly away from the prime shopping area, they must ensure that the service provided for installation and delivery is part of the package. Charging extra for such services is likely to dilute the 'value' perception. Location and size consideration will not only have an impact on consumers, it can also save overheads for the outlet.

Perceived Online Channels and Old Brands

Online retailing seems to have provided an opportunity to old brands like Onida, Kenstar, BPL and Sansui. These brands may have lower overheads while operating through online channels and hence, will be able to offer lower prices to attract consumers.[18] About 100 million people would be making online purchases in India by 2016.

Risks and Retail Outlet Choice

There are two kinds of risks faced by consumers when they buy a product.[19] One is the social risk (as in the case of acceptance of fashion apparel). The other is the economic risk like repairs, performance, effort and even physical risk, besides the cost of such physical risks (side-effects of using a hair-dye). A retail store has to cater to various kinds of risks associated with the combination of the two.

Different sets of consumers perceive the risks differently across product categories and some primary research is required to identify the appropriate risks associated with a given target segment or product category. Perceived risk is both a consumer and a product characteristic.

Retail outlets also carry a 'risk' perception. New kinds of retail formats like Internet shopping and direct marketing may be associated with a higher degree of perceived risk. The following aspects revolve around perceived risks and specific retail outlet strategies:

1. New kinds of retail outlets (marketing through the internet) should lower the risk by reassuring consumers on the security of their purchase (especially if credit cards are used). Consumers also feel secured when they know that they can return a faulty product without much inconvenience. There may be products, which involve a considerable amount of social risk. Some outlets give consumers the choice of returning the product if they are not satisfied with the purchases. A consumer may buy designer wear or jewellery through the internet, but may not like the design (in spite of sampling it on the site). The option of returning the product encourages him/her to shop at non-traditional outlets. This will also spread a good word of mouth about the outlet.
2. Discount outlets should ensure that well-known brands are available to reduce the perceived risk associated with the purchase.
3. Traditional outlets (large supermarkets) have a clear advantage with high-risk items (it may not be much in durables). Hence, they are in a position to develop store brands in a few categories associated with high economic risks (food categories, kitchen appliances). Store brands (apart from being promoted through POP material) also have the advantage of being associated with the store image.
4. If a retail store dealing in durables provides efficient after-sales service while dealing with well-known brands (especially in an environment where brands score low on after-sales service), it will be able to lower the perceived risk to a significant extent.

Consumer Shopping Types

A retail outlet has to design itself taking into consideration the different types of shoppers and the manner in which they shop. A retail outlet can select specific segments and decide on its target segments. Shopping is viewed as an activity that goes beyond purchasing products. It involves social interaction, learning about new products, trends and sensory stimulation. Shopping orientation refers to specific emphasis on certain characteristics of the shopper. Lifestyles of shoppers determine, to a great degree, the type of shopping they pursue. Inactive shoppers are not much into shopping. Active shoppers are those who enjoy the activity and one of the major criteria in their search may be the price. There are shoppers who are serious about the kind of shopping, which reflects in their lifestyle. Hence, they consider quality, fashion and symbolic aspects of a brand along with the price factor. Service shoppers are those who need and demand high-quality in-store service while shopping. An outlet catering to such shoppers should have friendly, helpful employees. They may have to explain to the consumer, many aspects associated with brand comparison. Dedicated fringe shoppers are those who rely on heavy catalogue shopping. They want to be different and may not socialize a lot. Price shoppers are highly price-sensitive and may be willing to extend their search efforts to identify products/services that are offered at low prices.

There are several implications of shopping orientation/styles on retailing strategies. Inactive shoppers may be more oriented towards online purchasing and may prefer home delivery. Active shoppers may enjoy the buying experience at retail outlets. For example, a supermarket may have a food court to provide the 'experience of socializing' if its target segment consists of active shoppers. A discount outlet, stocked with leading brands, may attract the attention of price shoppers in the appropriate residential area. An outlet would do well to analyse the demographic and psychographic profile of consumers in a specific area and draw inferences about the shopping orientation of consumers in that area. For example, there may be more than two types of orientation with regard to shoppers in a specific area. This may call for different strategies. There may even be a need to use different store brands for different segments. Apart from decor and layout, the merchandise, SKU's and the service provided will vary depending on the shopping orientation involved. A planned approach enables the outlet to take decisions on its viability. Price-sensitive consumers, for example, may expect a high level of in-store service. In this situation, unless assured of huge volumes (which will be possible only by stocking a range of items and brands), it may not be feasible for the outlet to park itself in that geographical area.

Retail Outlets and In-store Purchases

A consumer may visit a retail outlet with an intention of buying a brand or a product, and end up buying additional products as well. Normally impulse purchase is referred to as the lack of rationality in the buying decision. While this may be true in a number of buying situations, there may be exceptions. The decision to buy Bournvita (against Complan, as planned earlier) after entering the store because the brand is on sale is not illogical, even though a certain degree of impulse is involved. An unplanned decision may help the consumer take advantage of a sales promotion. There may be several kinds of 'store' decisions:

- **(a)** *Specifically planned:* The consumer may decide which product or brand to buy even before entering an outlet.
- **(b)** *Generally planned:* The consumer may decide to buy a product category such as cosmetics before entering an outlet.
- **(c)** *Substitute:* The consumer may buy a substitute item after entering an outlet. For example, he/she may buy a brand of fresh juice instead of an aerated soft drink after looking at the promotional material in the store.

(d) *Unplanned:* A consumer may pick up an item he/she didn't think of buying, after entering the store. Research shows that in a number of categories, consumers make item or brand decisions after entering an outlet. Hence, in-store marketing strategies are important for retail outlets. This may be especially applicable to product categories that are not purchased frequently (like mouthwash or antiseptic lotions). Researching the buying decisions of regular consumers will enable a retail outlet to plan an appropriate in-store marketing strategy.

The store atmosphere, which is concerned with layout, lighting, presentation of products, floors, colours, sound, fragrance and behaviour of sales personnel may have an impact on in-store purchases. Atmospherics is concerned with the physical retail environment that can impact the moods of shoppers. Figure 10.3 emphasizes certain important dimensions of retail outlet strategies.

Figure 10.3 Retail Outlet Strategy Formulation

The figure shows that strategy formulation is an ongoing process. There is a need to monitor the expectations of the target segment over a period of time. Food World is present in a number of locations/cities in South India. This may have changed the expectations of consumers with regard to several aspects of retailing like value, service, returning a faulty product etc. Smaller outlets competing with large outlets (at least in specific product categories) have to introduce specific strategies to ensure consumer loyalty.

Importance of Avoiding Stock–outs

Ensuring sufficient stock of several SKU's and reinforcing profitability by turning around the stock is vital in retailing. A company like Unilever probably has around 1000 SKU's across product categories. A retail outlet, today, has to necessarily keep a track of the purchasing pattern—not only with regard to brands and product categories, but also preferred SKU's. There may be four aspects of consumer behaviour associated with a stock-out situation:

1. Purchase behaviour may involve buying a substitute brand or item at the same store.
2. The purchase may be delayed until the preferred brand is available at the same store.
3. The consumer may decide to forego the purchase at least for the time being.
4. The consumer may buy the brand at a second store.

The consumer may also decide to buy all the items he/she had planned to buy at the second store because of the non-availability of the favourite brand in the first retail outlet where he/she had tried to buy it. Generally, in FMCG categories, the consumer either buys a substitute brand at the same store or buys the preferred brand at the second store.

A stock-out situation can also lead to bad publicity for the store. This may, by default, lead to positive publicity for competing stores. There may be a good word for substitute brands as well.

Attitude development may also figure in a stock-out situation. The consumer may develop a negative attitude towards the original store and a favourable attitude towards substitute brands and competing stores.

A retail outlet should constantly monitor the preferences of the target segment with regard to available merchandise and make changes therefore. This approach should also be extended to brands and SKU's/variants. In fact, a large outlet should offer SKU's/variants (in popular product categories) that are not available in a majority of the neighbourhood grocery stores. This provides a strong motivation for consumers to shop at larger outlets. There can also be exclusive packaged deals (FMCG products) that can be made available at large outlets by a special arrangement with the manufacturers of well-known brands. Special services can be introduced to tackle stock-out situations. This may involve home delivering those items for regular consumers. This will strengthen the service orientation of the outlet, apart from providing a way to deal with stock-outs. A stock run-out scenario can result in serious problems, especially if it is a part of the outlet's strategy to eliminate certain products that are not much in demand. The outlet should research, not just the off-take of such items but also the products that are bought with them.

Box 11.1
The Death Spiral—An Important Aspect of Managing Merchandise[20]

Retail outlets can get into what is known as the death spiral. This is a vicious cycle in which the retail outlet keeps eliminating 'non-profitable' items/products. This, in turn, reduces the demand for certain items/products bought with the eliminated items/products. The outlet tends to repeat its 'elimination' round with a new set of items. Over a period of time, the outlet traffic is seriously affected to the extent that the profitability is also threatened. The following example will illustrate the importance of the concept. Shoppers may buy bread regularly from an outlet along with other items. These are regular shoppers, but may form only about 15 per cent of the total shoppers. The outlet may find that cheese, butter and jam are not profitable items and may eliminate them from its merchandise without realizing that those 15 per cent bread buyers also tend to buy cheese, butter and jam (though wholly these may be unprofitable items). By eliminating these items, the store may have, in fact, reduced its consumer traffic. These 15 per cent shoppers may begin going to other stores. So, not only does the traffic reduce but the profits also go down. Once getting caught in this vicious trap, the outlet may lose its consumers eventually and of course the profits (see Figure 10.4).

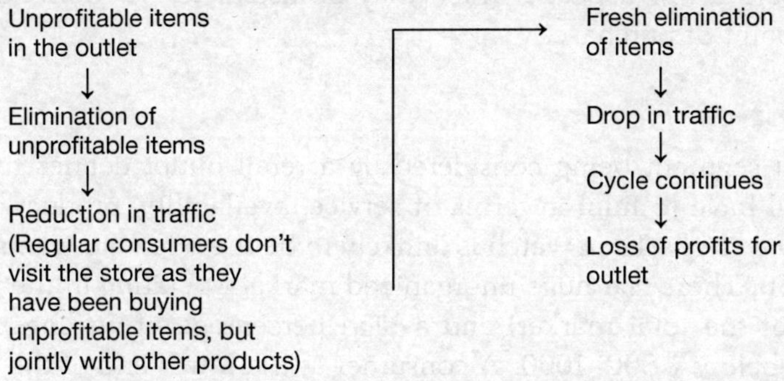

Figure 10.4 The Importance of Complementary Products in Retailing (The Death Spiral)

Dimensions of Retail Equity

Brand equity is the value a brand adds to a product. Retail equity is the value a retail outlet that adds to the brands or products it sells. Purchase happens at the retail outlet and hence, the equity added at this point enhances the image of the outlet. In fact, retail equity draws consumer traffic in product categories like jewellery though names like Carbon and Tanishq have been attempting to build brands in this category. BPL, Titan, Carrier Aircon, Ceat and MRF are some of the brands that have exclusive showrooms. It is this exclusivity that helps brands to build equity. Titan virtually changed the experience of buying watches from the regular bazaar shops to a retail world of comfort and feel-good ambience. This is not to say that multi-branded outlets are not required. The Titan example only reflects the importance of retail equity in building brands.

Importance of Image

As in the case of brand associations, retail outlets also have to nurture and cultivate specific associations in the mind of consumers. In urban cities, the 'retail ladder' is important for marketers and retailers. Like 'brand ladders' in which consumers form a mental hierarchy of brands when they think of a product category, retail equity aims at creating specific associations that create a high degree of recall by placing a retail outlet on top of the 'retail ladder'. For example, when consumers think of value associated with consumables like groceries and commodities, Food World may be on top of the consumer's mind, it may be or Allen Solly for apparel and Health & Glow for health products. Retail equity serves as a differentiator when consumers are confronted with hundreds of retail outlets. Retail equity also helps the outlet have a better buying power with large companies because of the volumes it is capable of achieving.

Developing Retail Equity—Importance of the Target Segment

While the actual process of developing retail equity differs from one product category to another, there are a few aspects, which may be useful to any outlet concerned with retailing and the point of purchase.

Target Segment

The type of target segment being considered by a retail outlet defines the expectations that the outlet will have to fulfil in terms of service, availability, product assortment and layout. A typical buyer of a Titan watch is unlikely to be the one who wants a watch in the range of ₹ 150–250. There is a huge unorganized market operating in the watch category (50–60 per cent of the total market) and a high percentage of watches (around 50–60 per cent) are sold below ₹ 800–1000. A consumer at the lower end of the market may, in

Supply Chain and Consumer Behaviour Contributing to a Brand's Success

450 Million Items per year: 11 Factories, 1770 Stores in 86 Countries

Zara, the fashion brand that has a legendary reputation as a retailer introduced the concept of 'fast fashion' to deliver clothes to retailers twice a week. Its supply chain to support its brand is built around speed and quick responsiveness. It can also accommodate sudden changes in the demand. Besides its factories in Spain, Portugal, Morocco and Turkey, the T-shirts and sweaters are ordered from its Asian factories before six months in advance. The brand generally does not discount or advertise. Zara gets 85 per cent of its prices as compared to the industry average of 60-70 per cent; unsold items account for 10 per cent as against an industry average of 17-20 per cent.

The concepts of 'fast-fashion' aptly backed up by an array of frequent introduction of merchandise and a unique supply chain has not only made Zara, a world-class and trendy brand but it has helped Zara sustain its positioning of 'affordable, fast fashion'[21] (Refer to Plate 10.1). Supply chain provides excellent back up for the behavioural aspects of consumers in the case of Zara.

Plate 10.1 Fast Fashion: Zara

fact, feel uncomfortable in an outlet selling high-end watches. A grocer will only display the products and brands in which the consumers in his neighbourhood are interested. This is the reason why these outlets select product categories and brands with great care. For example, Mother's Recipe, a brand of pickles, may not be available at most retail outlets (including shops) that sell pickles. Awareness of brands and expectations from retail outlets of the target segment is an important criterion for developing retail image.

Dimensions of Expectations

The next aspect to be considered is the various dimensions that a specific consumer segment might be interested in when it comes to a retail outlet. There may be a few situations in which the retail outlet may cater to a broad segment. This happens when an outlet, as a brand, appeals to a big segment. A typical example is of McDonald outlets all over the world. McDonald is known all over the world for its value, cleanliness, consistency and convenience. These expectations have been built over a period of time and hence, it draws consumers from all income, age and lifestyle groups. The brand, even today, offers a variety, which appeals to distinctive segments.

An outlet should research the target segment and identify specific dimensions that can be developed to attract consumers. Convenience for a fast food outlet, fast check-out during peak hours for a departmental store and variety for a music store, are important dimensions. At a time when life is fast, time is scarce and pressures are many, an emerging dimension is the need to enjoy the atmospherics and shop at leisure. Stores like Globus and Shoppers Stop had positioned itself on this dimension (Refer to Plate 10.2). It highlighted the total shopping experience in its visuals, backed by the spread, ambience, decor, product variety and consumer-friendliness. Black and white advertisements made a powerful statement on the feel-good shopping experience. There were advertisements in which customers 'talked' of their experience. Fountain Head, the Chennai-based book store, has also positioned itself on a leisurely shopping experience, which acts as a differentiator for the book store.

Expectations grow and change with changes in the environment. The concept of outlet malls (normally located at the outskirts of the city) is another point of purchase retailing option, which is becoming popular in the West. Manufacturers manage these outlets and offer a good shopping experience apart from discounted, but not damaged, merchandise. Large layouts, open spaces and comfortable car parks apart from low prices, attract a specific segment to these outlets.

Planning the POP Process—A Vital Dimension of Retail Equity

Retailing is about point of purchase and this is the final place at which sale happens. POP strategies have to be planned as part of the overall strategy of the brand/retail store. In the present context of multi-promotional plans, the POP process has to be integrated into the entire promotional plan. This process can be termed as integrated POP plan. Apart from

Plate 10.2 Globus has highlighted the total shopping experience in its visuals, backed by the spread, ambience, decor, product variety and consumer-friendliness

conventional POP material like posters and brochures, a POP plan, today, also considers factors like store layout, parking place, atmospherics (which include mood enhancing elements like music, decor and temperature systems) and systems that enable consumers to transact business with ease and comfort.

Promoting Brands in an Era of Brand Proliferation

A supermarket, in today's context, sells a number of brands within a category. The display or shelf space is limited. Besides, from the consumers' point of view, certain brands may generate greater recall than other brands in the category. In the category of soaps, Liril may generate greater recall than a new brand of herbal soap in the same price range because of the impact of its advertising over the years. While a strongly established brand attempts to retain its existing consumers and also attract new ones from the competitive brands, a new brand has to appeal to consumers to try out the new offering. Added to that is the tendency of even loyal consumers to try out new brands in a category like soaps. This is the backdrop against which a typical FMCG brand attempts to use POP material in the store. A store that deals with 20 brands of soaps or toothpastes may have to promote all the brands most of the time. A special display and POP material have to be organized when the brand is on sale. But as the number of brands increase in most categories, a store may find itself under pressure to promote all of them simultaneously. Furthermore, there are many variants (across FMCG categories) introduced in almost all brands to ensure that the consumer stays with the brand. Colgate has a herbal version, gel version and a Colgate Total, which offers several benefits. All these variants may need to be promoted. Manufacturers need to be convinced that they are getting a fair share of the retailer's attention.

Retail equity establishes a retail association in the mind-set of consumers and also enables the retailer to deal more competitively with manufacturers, depending on how the latter executes that equity.

Retail Service

Service at the point of purchase has been often written about and discussed in great detail. A contemporary dimension is the nature of the service consumers expected in a specific retail setting and the nature of the product category itself. Service, in the retail context, is the overall attention given to consumers that can enhance their (retail) experience. This retail experience can also extend to certain services beyond the point of purchase, as in the case of durables.

Importance of Appropriate Service

A retailer is concerned with the store image and service. The direct result of the service provided can be seen in the way consumers talk about it with their friends/peer-groups. A positive word of mouth (WOM) is the best 'advocate' for the store while a negative one can spell disaster. The importance of WOM is reflected in the fact that large brands in developed markets conduct research studies to quantify its impact in terms of sales gained or lost! Service also helps the store to establish for itself, a specific proposition. This is important as it functions as a differentiator. A consumer will appreciate a service that ensures faster billing with separate counters for less than five items bought in a large store.

Service Varies with Product Categories and Type of Retail Outlets

Service varies with the types of products and retail outlets. But the basic aspect of providing service is concerned with the identification of consumers who need help on entering a large retail outlet. Sales personnel should be trained to provide appropriate and not unwanted service. Unfortunately, service is mixed up with over enthusiasm that is reflected in artificial hospitality at the retail outlet, which certain consumers may not like. The attention given to a consumer should always be perceived as warm, spontaneous and appropriate. It should never be associated with unnecessary intrusion.

FMCG products, commodities and groceries are categories, which require little 'on-store' service. Normally, consumers are discerning enough to sift through the information on brands, prices and sale offers (if this kind of basic information is made available). Hence, the 'off-store' service becomes important. Apart from free home delivery (on certain conditions) offered by super markets, the reassurance provided on the quality of products is extremely important, especially in the case of groceries and commodities and vegetables that are not branded. Consumers visit these large retailers in the hope of finding value on such products (a combination of price and quality). Dissatisfaction on this count can force them to return to their neighbourhood grocer or look for other options. The perception that super markets are shopping places for the middle class is of recent origin and is based on the variety and quality associated with their goods. Consumers should never be let down on this proposition. Complaints about the lack of quality, freshness, and improper packaging and under-weight packages should be immediately attended to and consumers should not get the feeling that the store is doing them a favour by replacing the product. If required, changes in the procurement process or supply chain may have to be made before the store loses its reputation on its core promise. The fact that unbranded products are (relatively) more important from the viewpoint of the store cannot be overemphasized. The store is important for the consumers because it stocks what they really need to buy, as against branded FMCG products, which are picked up more because of the 'pull' effect created by manufacturers.

Speciality Products

High-end products (expensive jewellery, furniture or designer wear) are those that draw consumers because of their lifestyle and symbolic appeals. While brands may also play a role in attracting consumers, a retail store needs to offer a different kind of service. Allen

Solly's exclusive showroom is a good example to illustrate this point. The consumer goes through an 'experiential' service, especially if the product is of personal significance. The product display at Allen Solly's exclusive shop is such that the consumer could go around and feel the fabric before trying it on. Digital kiosks can also be used to give an idea to the consumer about how well the product will match him/her. These kiosks enable the consumer to try out different designs/variations of the brand, enabling him/her to decide on the most suitable one.

In the case of readymade wear, what usually wanted is the 'fit', with which the consumer is concerned even after selecting the design. The retail store personnel can help but in an unobtrusive manner. This aspect of service is also associated with the availability of SKU's and management of inventory that takes consumer needs into consideration.

The experiential service, in which the consumers experience at the point of purchase, can also be extended to categories like perfumes and cosmetics. Lakme introduced a plan at the point of purchase for its Orchids range of cosmetics, in which a consumer could try the product before deciding on the purchase. It should be noted that in such categories, a free trial is possible only in the premium price range.

The Feel of the Product

Experiential service can be extremely effective if applied to audio and video durables. BPL has exclusive galleries in some cities that display its products. Carrier Aircon and Onida are other brands, which maintain such exclusive showrooms displaying a range of products/variants.

If the retail store can help the consumer simulate the experience of listening to an audio system in a 'house-like' setting or the coolness of an air-conditioner in a room similar to the consumer's, it not only helps the consumer but also the store. Such a trend can have a significant impact in detailing the benefits of a brand. A part of the promotional budget can be allocated for such point-of-purchase experience. Retail outlet can be designed to offer the 'in–use' experiences with respect to durable products.

Service for Durables

Leading brands like Videocon, LG or Samsung deal with a number of product categories (audio, TV, refrigerator, microwaves, etc.). Word of mouth has an even greater impact with regard to durables. A consumer of a TV may be a prospective consumer of a refrigerator or an audio system. There are two aspects to be considered with regard to service for durables–service provided by multi-brand outlets like Pantaloons and service provided by an exclusive outlet. A leading brand is likely to be present in about 3000 to 4000 outlets in the country and not all of these are exclusive. Such a differentiation can also help the brand improve its infrastructure and location considerations, apart from enhancing customer satisfaction.

The Credibility Factor

A multi-brand outlet is one where the consumer can compare features/prices and also get a feedback from the store personnel on specific brands. Such a retail store should be very careful in dealing with the consumer when he/she asks for information on specific brands. It is not uncommon to find the sales personnel in the store attempting to promote a specific brand or brands against certain others. This traditional approach of 'pushing' some brands may no longer work in an environment where the consumer is more aware and has sources of information other than from the store personnel. For instance, when the consumer receives a negative feedback about a brand of washing machine (at a retail outlet) and a positive WOM among his friends, he begins to suspect the credibility of the store. The retailer's influence on the consumer is still quite high in India (though the trend is declining in the metros) and the opportunity provided by the situation should be used to build credibility in the transaction.

Analysing the need of the consumer is fundamental to building the credibility of the store. The clutter of brands, benefits and features may confuse the consumer. Confounding the confusion is the advertisements that compare brands on their features, quality and prices and so on. A consumer attempting to upgrade to a feature-ridden colour TV is very different from one who is entering the store to replace a basic colour TV. Pressurizing and selling a feature-ridden colour TV to the uninterested consumer can create post-purchase dissonance. The consumer is likely to feel 'cheated' about being sold a TV that he did not want or one that is too complicated for his needs. Sales personnel may tend to force a brand at a price point higher than the one the consumer wants to buy. The 'need–offer' match that takes place in the initial phase of 'customer–point of purchase' interaction is vital, especially for highly competitive products (low and middle-price range). This is because the major chunk of the market exists in these ranges and the existence of most retail stores depends on these markets.

Product–service interface at the point of purchase enhances the relationship between the retailers and consumers, just as structured 'in-store' and 'off-store' service enhances the customer–retailer interface.

Retail Loyalty

Loyalty being an important strategy for marketers, it is worth analysing how retailers retain consumers and ensure that they come back, after establishing retail equity. With fragmented patterns of retail locations and a high degree of area-wise concentration in urban cities, sustaining consumer loyalty is a major challenge. The research done, both in Indian and Western contexts across categories, shows that loyal consumers significantly enhance profitability. Loyalty, here, is essentially a consumer's commitment towards a retail outlet. This aspect highlights the fact that for some reason, a consumer selects a store for repeat buying in spite of the several alternatives available to him/her.

POINT OF PURCHASE FACTORS

Depending on the nature and size of the retail store, there may be different approaches to enhance the base of loyal consumers. The following aspects may provide a conceptual platform for retailers involved with point of purchase consumers.

Importance of SKU Management

In products like soaps, toothpastes, blades, talcum powders, shampoos and other packaged goods (FMCG), a high degree of branding is taking place. It is not uncommon to find consumers asking for a specific brand in urban markets. But brands like Parachute, Lifebuoy and Chik are strong even in rural markets. The critical aspect to be noted at the point of purchase (even in a super market) is the maintenance of the typical stock-keeping units (SKU) with regard to each product category and brand. Based on the previous purchase data, one can find out what these SKU's are meant for. An SKU is just a unit of the brand. For example, there are sachets, 500 g and 1 kg packages of Surf Excel. Each is an SKU. The normal point-of-purchase strategies that may be often associated with loyalty are service and price. SKU's may play an important role in deciding how a consumer perceives a store. A consumer who is unable to get an SKU of his/her choice at a store after frequenting the store a few times may not want to return to that store again. Availability of appropriate SKU's (according to the location, product category or brand) is important for gaining store traffic—a prerequisite for store loyalty. Does the same size of Ariel or Close-up or Red Label sell uniformly in all areas in the city? How many times does a retailer run out of stock with regard to a specific SKU? Such probing also helps a retailer to manage his/her inventory more profitably.

Price–based Loyalty

Price is one of the several factors that lead to repeat purchase. Any shopper is aware of a couple of retailers in his/her neighbourhood, who may be able to offer packaged goods at a price less than the marked retail price (MRP). This is one of the reasons why consumers stick to their neighbourhood shops in spite of the super markets in their vicinity. Such retailers bank heavily on business volumes. But the catch is that 'price-loyalty' may be a short-term strategy. This is not to say that retailers must not take recourse to discount sales or a reduced MRP. But they must have other plans to back up the 'price-based' strategy. The emergence of a big retailer who offers better prices because of large volume can be a definite threat to a small retailer who uses the 'price-based' strategy. This is the reason why some *kirana* stores offer home delivery during working hours, even for small purchases.

Service and Profitability

While service is certainly an important factor in retaining consumers, its quality and the infrastructure at the point of purchase should be appropriate for the consumer, apart from being profitable for the retailer. Quick and free home delivery may be an attractive service for consumers. But as the retailer builds up a consumer-base over a period of time, this service will become more personal and hence would mean more overheads. This is one of the reasons why large retailers specify a minimum purchase and distance limit for free home delivery. Financial bottom-lines are extremely important when retailers plan for an infrastructure be it a personnel, additional space or technology. Even ambience can be a service, which enhances the shopping experience. The costs of the retailer's AC, the store traffic, repeat purchases and the margin on brands have to be taken into account. The store can have a significant part of low margin–high volume products (like soaps, detergents, coffee, tea or groceries) or high margin–low volume products (like CD's, foreign publications or furniture). Service provided by the store should not be allowed to offset profitability, especially when it is attempting to build loyalty. It is virtually impossible to wean away a loyal consumer from a service that he/she gets used to.

Triggering Retail Loyalty

It is not possible to have a customized strategy for each brand/retail store without specific situation-based inputs. The following guidelines may be considered to come to grips with promoting brands at a retail store:

(a) The identification of the target segment helps in the selection of brands/product categories. Having done that, the store need not stock slow-moving brands or variants. This also minimizes POP efforts. For example, Connexions is a retail store that carries books, CD's, gifts and toys by taking into account the needs of consumers in a specific locality.

(b) The store can identify fast-moving brands and plan promotional activities at the point of purchase. This will ensure that an optimal publicity is worked out for these brands.

(c) Brands on sale can be placed at a specific location in the store. This helps the consumer plan his/her purchase of these brands and also compare and contrast with the variants that are not on sale. Going around the store, a consumer may find on sale a brand of juice and a brand of tea at different locations. If many brands from many categories are on sale, the consumer may miss seeing certain brands or run out of money by the time he comes to the other 'sale' locations in the store.

(d) POP posters have to be displayed at different locations depending on whether a brand is on sale or not. Categorizing 'on-sale' brands also helps the retailer to spread the POP material in the store. This helps attract the attention of customers much better as it breaks the 'adaptation' process by which the latter get used to the POP plethora and end up not looking at any such material at all.

(e) POP brochures are best placed within the vicinity of the respective product category. Placing brochures at the entrance of the store (or distributing them) fails to identify consumers who may be interested in that product category. If awareness is to be created on a new category/brand, it will have to be done in synchronization with media planning.

(f) A brand needs to advertise its promotional sale in local media vehicles that are popular in the area where the store is located. This generates awareness and the selective use of POP material within the store can serve as a recall stimuli. POP planning is an elaborate and structured process, which can improve the image of the retailer in the long run.

Retail loyalty may help retailers deal better with manufacturers, especially when brand differentiation becomes small. Managing the experiences and expectations of the target segment is a prerequisite for retail equity, which can eventually lead to retail loyalty.

Touch of Reality

Consumer Compulsivity in the Indian Modern Retail Setting

Banwari Mittal, Morris Holbrook, Sharon Beatty, Priya Raghubir and Arch Woodside state that the impulse behaviour of consumers consists of several factors being associated with the culture, the personality traits of consumers and the need states of consumers.[22]

They had identified a number of factors associated with these three basic factors. Need for gratification, need for excitement (shopping excitement), impulsiveness (consumer impulsivity), collectivism versus individualism (of the specific culture), materialism and saving mentality are the factors responsible for a consumer's impulsive behaviour.

This approach fits into the Indian retailing context as well. With large modern outlets drawing the masses, consumer impulsivity seems to be triggered on the following lines; consumers get interested in discounts at a large format like Reliance Mart and seem to make purchases that they have not planned for in the respective retail visit.

The excitement of making purchases advertised as the discounted merchandise of the day adds to the compulsivity of consumers. India being a dominant collectivist culture (meaning the need to conform to group norms and practices over individuality), word of mouth spreads fast about 'excitement-oriented deals' in modern retail outlets. The entertainment aspect of spending time in large outlets with good ambience also adds to the shopping excitement. The consumers feel gratified that they have been able to save on the shopping trip, especially when some of these savings are attributed to in-store purchases not planned earlier.

Hedonism as a Retail Experience

Modern retail format is growing at a considerable pace and malls and shopping complexes have recognized the need to extend hedonistic experiences (sensory gratification-based experiences) to consumers. Ambience, layout and spending time in lush surroundings may have enabled the retailers to extend the shopping visits of consumers. The new dimension of the retail strategy is to explore how leisure and entertainment can add value to the retail experience of shoppers. In some of its stores, Shoppers Stop has cafes and reading spaces as well. Apple's retail stores are known for its shopping experiences. Retail experiences can perhaps bring back the shoppers who are lured by online shopping discounts in categories like foot wear and apparel.

End Notes

1. Surabhi Agarwal (2015), "Myntra has an urge to spulrge on social shopping" *The Economic Times*, October 12.
2. Sangeeta Tanwar (2015), 'Growing Share of wallet', *Business Standard*, 12 October.
3. Richa Maheshwari (2015), 'Startup Firms Help Kirana Stores Turn E retailers', *The Economic Times,* 18 July.
4. Hawkins, Best and Coney, *Consumer behavior*, (McGraw Hill 1998), pp.575–599.
5. Prabha Raghavan (2015), 'Makeover: E tailers Pop Up at Retail stores', *The Economic Times*, 3 September.
6. Richa Maheshwari and Sobia Khan (2015), 'Etailers hook shoppers, Factory outlets find going tough', *The Economic Times*, 25 September.
7. Writankar Mukherjee (2015), 'White Goods Makers Fall for Ecomm Charm, Plan Own Sites', *The Economic Times*, 21 July.
8. Ibid.
9. Hawkins, Best and Coney (1998), *Consumer behavior: Building Marketing strategy*, (1998), pp. 575–598.
10. Richa Maheswari, 'Arvind Rebrands Megamart Stores', *The Economic Times*, 10 September.
11. ET Bureau (2015), 'Femina to grow into a consumer brand in Shoppers Stop's Company', *The Economic Times*, 6 August.
12. Michael Solomon, 'Consumer Behavior-Buying, Having and Being', (Pearson, 2015), pp. 137.
13. ET Bureau (2015), 'Aditya Birla group rolls out fashion portal', *The Economic Times*, 17 October.
14. John Sarah (2015), 'Groupon India breaks away, to be called Nearbuy', *The Times of India*, 10 August.
15. Pritha Dasgupta (2015), 'Facebook turns over a new leaf with online shopping fest', *The Economic Times*, 10 August.

16. Harsimran Julka (2013), 'With 254 million users by 2014, India to beat US in internet reach; study', *The Economic Times*, 14 November.
17. Sadhana Chathurvedula and Sharan Poovanna (2015), 'Brands, publishers tap gaming ads to hook users', *Mint*, 22 October.
18. Writankar Mukherjee (2015), 'Old brands get new life, virtually', *The Economic Times*, 21 August.
19. Hawkin, Best and Coney (1998), *Consumer behavior*, (McGraw Hill), pp. 587.
20. Katherine Newell Lemon, Roland T. Rust and Valarie Zeithaml (2007), *Driving Customer Equirty*, (Press: HBS), pp. 100–102.
21. Susan Berfield and Manuel Balgorri (2013), 'Chain Reaction; Zara's Fast Fashion faces Beijing Test', *The Economic Times,* 18 November.
22. Banwari Mittal, Morris Holbrook, Sharon Beatty, Priya Raghubir and Arch Woodside (2008), *Consumer Behavior-How humans think, feel and act in the marketplace*, (Press: Open mentis), pp. 367–380.

Exercises

1. Choose three leading brands from modern retailing in the Indian context and comment on their strategies with respect to discounts and variety offered. You may visit them if possible. Compare them on several retail attributes and benefits
2. Draw a positioning map taking into account the strengths of retail outlets chosen for the previous question. How would you improve on these aspects with respect to one of the brands you had chosen?

Business Cases

CASE 1

Ethnic Consumers Consulting*

It was a humid day in September 2010 in the historic city of Mumbai, where millions of people who barely made ends meet coexisted with a niche segment of consumers who led hedonistic lifestyles oriented towards consumption for pleasure, indulging in the best of brands from across the globe. Nitya Guruvayurappan was busy preparing a presentation for a multinational client on her first probable assignment in her consulting work. With her basic degree in engineering, she had never thought that she would develop so much passion towards consumer behaviour. It was her aspiration to start a consulting company that exclusively dealt with consumer behaviour issues that were unique to the Indian context. With a postgraduate degree from a premier institute and a few years of work experience in the marketing field in a multinational company, she thought it was time to address her aspirations. Guruvayurappan was meeting her first prospective client, a company that

* Dr. S. Ramesh Kumar, Nitya Guruvayurappan and Madhurjya Banerjee wrote this case solely to provide material for class discussion. The authors do not intend to illustrate either effective or ineffective handling of a managerial situation. The authors may have disguised certain names and other identifying information to protect confidentiality.

manufactured hair oil and fairness cream. She remembered a research publication that she had co-authored in 2007, and she wanted to make use of the data to build a case with a practical orientation that would result in interesting insights for the client on consumer values — an area lacking study in this emerging market (see Exhibits 1 and 2). Were emerging markets significantly different from developed markets in terms of their consumer values? Could brand differentiation transcend the usual generic symbolic benefit to accommodate brand symbolism associated with the deeper levels of values? Were existing brands connecting themselves with the diverse value bands associated with Indian consumers? Could values get associated with different socio-economic classes of consumers?

Indian Context — Demographics, Lifestyle and Values

In 2010, India contained a diverse array of product categories, brands, prices, lifestyles and cultures. While marketers were upbeat concerning the consumption of categories and brands stretching from unbranded edible oil to symbolism light-emitting diode (LED) watches, there were unique challenges to marketers: these included the management of marketing mix elements, understanding the diversity of cultures, development of appropriate product lines, localizing global communication and more specifically, understanding the consumer psyche in a changing environment.

As the economy grew between the years 2000 to 2010, so had the spending power of consumers. In 2010, real average household income in India had roughly doubled over the past two decades. Consumption had increased along with rising income, especially with the emergence of India's growing middle class.[1] According to the official definition, urban India consisted of 5,161 towns and cities and included nearly 30 per cent of the population; rural India consisted of more than 600,000 villages and included more than 70 per cent of the population.[2]

Across urban and rural India, the "emerging India" households in 2010 could be classified into five groups based on annual household income. The "deprived" (earning <₹90,000) consisted of 103 million households (HHs) of mostly subsistence farmers and unskilled labourers. The "aspirers" (earning ₹90,000 - ₹200,000) consisted of 91.3 million HHs and included small-scale shopkeepers, farmers — with small areas of owned land — or industrial workers; it was expected that this group would reduce from 41 per cent to around 35 per cent due to their moving into the middle class. The "seekers" (earning ₹200,000 - ₹500,000) consisting of 11 million HHs and the "strivers" (earning ₹500,000 - ₹1,000,000) consisting of 2.5 million HHs were developing into India's huge new middle class. "Seekers" included young college graduates, government employees at intermediate levels and owners of small- to medium-sized businesses. "Strivers," the upper end of the

1. "The Bird of Gold: India's Rising Consumer Market," Chapter 1, www.mckinsey.com/mgi/reports/pdfs/india_consumer_market/MGI_india_consumer_chapter_1.pdf, accessed October 10, 2010.

2. "The Bird of Gold: India's Rising Consumer Market," Chapter 2, www.mckinsey.com/mgi/reports/pdfs/india_consumer_market/MGI_india_consumer_chapter_2.pdf, accessed October 10, 2010.

middle class, were senior government employees, owners or managers of large businesses, professionals and wealthy farmers. In 2010, the middle class numbered some 50 million individuals, but that was expected to grow 10 times and become approximately 41 per cent of the population between the years 2020 to 2025. The "global Indians" (earning > ₹1,000,000) were the other major spending force in India's new consumer market, comprising more than one million HHs: they were senior executives in large corporations, owners of large businesses, politicians and rich farmers with large landholdings.[3]

Changing Values and Lifestyles

In 2010, consumers were characterized by a rising income, aided by the increasing affordability of products. Urban consumers looked more for material success and understood the need to satisfy their desires, rather than practice restraint. They respected their traditions, but did not tie their lives to these traditions. The need for convenience and lack of time resulted in urban consumers becoming increasingly dependent on technology; therefore, technical competence was seen as a must for the urban youth. Urban consumers strove for success and were self-confident about their abilities. Preference for English education was a common factor across all urban consumers and was becoming increasingly important with semi-urban consumers.

As consumerism and media exposure increased, India also saw an evolution in its value systems and beliefs. Indian consumers traditionally saved their money. Contemporary consumers were not looking for cheap goods; rather, they were looking for value and were willing to pay extra for it. The fundamental values of conservatism and risk avoidance were gradually being replaced by an openness to experiment and to spend money on items beyond the essentials: in segments such as the "global Indian," this even translated to conspicuous consumption. This increasing risk appetite also extended to the mindset of Indians in terms of careers and lifestyles: they were willing to try out new career paths and were not bound by the same organization for their entire career lifetimes. Rural Indians saw a lot of migration to the cities and moved beyond their conventional forms of earning livelihood.

The Indian youth was also seeking individuality as opposed to the need for affiliation and social acceptance that was characteristic of older generations. Despite there being close family relationships, families were rapidly growing nuclear and very few parts of urban India still upheld the joint family model. The influence of the West could be seen in the changing lifestyle and trends of the Indian consumer: personal grooming had increased in importance, especially with more women stepping out and making careers for themselves. The work culture had also grown significantly, with more people having jobs in multinational corporations.

---

3 "Next Big Spenders: India's middle class," www.mckinsey.com/mgi/mginews/bigspenders.asp, accessed October 10, 2010.

Category And Brand Summary — Fairness Creams And Hair Oils

Fairness Creams Market in India — Category and Key Brands Summary

In 2010, the personal care industry — which included bath and shower products, hair care, skin care, cosmetics and fragrances — in India was around US$4 billion.[4] Skin care comprised 16 per cent of this segment; the skin care segment consisted of everything from basic creams and moisturizers to specialized products such as anti-wrinkle and dark circle removing creams. The cosmetic industry was expected to grow at a compound annual growth rate (CAGR) of approximately 17 per cent by 2013, and within this industry skin care was one of the most attractive segments, with facial skin care (85 per cent of total skin care sales) outperforming the rest of the skin care segment.[5] Within facial care, facial moisturizers and cleansers accounted for the bulk of sales.

Traditionally, India was a country in which the population had a natural bias towards lighter skin; catering to this bias, skin care in India was flooded with facial moisturizers that either positioned themselves completely as fairness creams and skin-whitening products, or at least offered fairness as an added benefit. Tapping into this huge demand for fairness in India, facial moisturizers were the biggest contributors to skin care in India, comprising almost 50 per cent of the skin care segment.

While Indians were likely to remain partial towards lighter skin, fairness alone was not expected to be the driving force of skin care sales in the near future; rather, exfoliation, nourishment and freshness were expected to become key selling points as almost all skin care products in India already offered fairness benefits. Anti-aging products, comprising just two per cent of the skin care segment, were set to grow as well with multiple brands entering this segment while also offering the whiteness benefit. Furthermore, taking a cue from more developed countries, skin care in India was set to undergo a metamorphosis from a one-product-fits-all mentality to providing separate solutions to suit each different skin type.[6]

Another trend seen in this industry was the introduction of multiple brands in the men's whitening segment. Men accounted for about 25 per cent of the fairness cream

---

4. Pratik Kadakia, Abhishek Nigam and Ashwin Rao, "Outlook for Personal Care Industry: An Indian Perspective," *Chemical Weekly*, www.tsmg.com/download/article/Personal_Care_Chemicals.pdf, accessed October 10, 2010.

5. "Indian Cosmetic Market Ready to Escalate," *PR Log*, www.prlog.org/10931927-indian-cosmetic-market-ready-to-escalate.html, accessed October 10, 2010.

6. Pratik Kadakia, Abhishek Nigam and Ashwin Rao, "Outlook for Personal Care Industry: An Indian Perspective," *Chemical Weekly*, www.tsmg.com/download/article/Personal_Care_Chemicals.pdf, accessed October 10, 2010.

usage in the country and that figure was growing in "absolute terms."[7] This trend was even seen in the comparison of the growth rates of women's and men's fairness creams, which were seven to eight per cent and 25 per cent, respectively.

Penetration and consumption were still challenges in this category. Fairness creams penetrated only 25 per cent of the market, with the South being the largest market (36 per cent). The North and West contributed 23 per cent each and the East contributed approximately 18 per cent.[8] In comparison with China[9], despite India having a higher personal disposable income per household and an increasing population of women in the 25-44 age group (the key consumer segment), it spent only about one-tenth of what China spent on skin care. Pricing in the skin care market ranged from offerings as low as the ₹5 sachets of fairness creams in low income markets to ₹500–600 for the super-premium end of anti-aging creams.

The major players in the fairness cream market were Hindustan Unilever Ltd (HUL), with a market share between 50-70 per cent on its flagship brand Fair & Lovely which also enjoyed a high rural penetration, and CavinKare, which held about one-fifth of HUL's market share with its leading brand Fairever.[10]

HUL's Fair & Lovely fairness cream[11] had been the undisputed leader of skin care products in India for more than a quarter of a century. Fair & Lovely (F&L) was in the popular/economy tier of the market and was targeted at low and middle income Indian consumers across urban and rural India. F&L had a range of product offerings such as Multivitamin, Ayurvedic, AntiMarks and Menz Active. It was available in a range of stock-keeping units (SKUs) from nine gram sachets to 80 gram tubes. In the company's portfolio, it was the flagship skin care brand along with Ponds, and was among their "Super Brands." (An example of F&L's advertising with the case authors' description of its storyboard, as well as the case authors' interpretation of F&L's communication is included in Exhibit 3.)

CavinKare's Fairever[12] managed to retain consumer interest and was the second-best selling brand in facial moisturizers with a 12 per cent value share backed by strong brand equity in South India and constant product innovation. Fairever was available in its base variant and a Fairever Fruit variant perched on the 'naturals' platform. (An example of

---

7. "The Regime of Fairness is Not Limited!" *oneIndia Living*, November 28, 2007, http://living.oneindia.in/men/for-him/men-cosmetics-fairness-creams.html, accessed October 10, 2010.

8. Sravanthi Challapalli, "All's fair in this market," *The Hindu Business Line*, September 5, 2002, www.thehindubusinessline.com/catalyst/2002/09/05/stories/2002090500040300.htm, accessed October 10, 2010.

9. Pratik Kadakia, Abhishek Nigam and Ashwin Rao, "Outlook for Personal Care Industry: An Indian Perspective," *Chemical Weekly*, www.tsmg.com/download/article/Personal_Care_Chemicals.pdf, accessed October 10, 2010.

10. "How fair is Fair & Lovely?," *Rediff India Abroad*, March 9, 2007, www.rediff.com/money/2007/mar/09guest.htm, accessed October 10, 2010.

11. "Fair & Lovely," *Hindustan Unilever Limited*, www.hul.co.in/brands/personalcarebrands/FairAndLovely.aspx, accessed October 10, 2010.

12. "Fairever," *CavinKare*, www.cavinkare.com/fairever.html, accessed October 10, 2010.

Fairever's advertising with the case authors' description of its storyboard, as well as the case authors' interpretation of Fairever's communication is included in Exhibit 4.)

Hair Oil Market in India — Category and Key Brands Summary

Indian consumers were traditionally accustomed to using various natural forms of hair oil as a leave-on conditioning treatment. The most popular hair oil in the Indian context was coconut hair oil, which represented the bulk of sales. Although coconut oil had been the traditional hair oil variety, there were other segments in the market such as perfumed hair oils, light hair oils, cooling oils and tonics or hair gels. Even coconut hair oil was further segmented into plain coconut hair oil and added-value hair oil. In 2010, the $1.28 billion hair oil market in India was categorized into coconut hair oil (50 per cent), *amla* (18 per cent), light (17 per cent), cooling (10 per cent) and tonics and gels (five per cent).[13]

The coconut oil market had been witnessing a change in usage behaviour in both urban and rural markets. The rural consumer, who traditionally purchased unbranded oil, was expected to gradually shift to branded hair oil, given the resistance to adulteration. The penetration of hair oil was high at around 87 per cent and similar across the urban and rural areas.[14]

The use of hair oil had become a deeply ingrained habit in the consumer psyche: it was perceived to encompass multiple benefits such as nourishment, strengthening and revitalizing the hair. Moreover, hair oils also achieved cosmetic benefits as the hair remained soft and shiny after application.

In 2010, the hair oil category in India was slowly reaching saturation as this traditional hair care product was facing tough competition in the urban markets from foreign conditioners. The presence of a huge organized sector and proliferation from the edible oil segment made the hair oils easily accessible to different segments of society, being available at different price points. The market was expected to become such that any brand of hair oil could not charge a price premium based on traditional attributes, as most of them had become hygiene factors and were offered by almost all competing brands. As a result, when newer attributes such as 'cool' oils, herbal products, anti-dandruff and non-greasiness agents were added to traditional coconut hair oils or amla hair oils, this attracted a price premium.

The SKUs in this category ranged from three millilitre (ml) sachets to 300 ml bottles, with the sachet distribution being highly penetrated in the rural markets. The biggest segment was the popular tier with brands such as Parachute and Dabur Amla oil; the economy tier followed with brands such as Nihar, Shanti Amla and other regional brands. The premium tier consisted of brands such as Dabur Vatika and Hair and Care.

---

13. "Marico to move court on coconut oil excise notice," http://epaper.timesofindia.com/Repository/ml.asp?Ref=RVRELzIwMDkvMDcvMTQjQXIwMTgwMg==&Mode=HTML&Locale=english-skin-custom, accessed October 10, 2010.

14. www.equitymaster.com/research-it/sector-info/consprds/consprds-products.html, accessed October 10, 2010.

The leading company in this category was Marico, with its flagship brand Parachute holding almost 50 per cent of the coconut oils segment, which itself was 50 per cent of the total hair oil category[15]. Other big players were Dabur and Bajaj, with their respective brands Dabur Amla and Bajaj Almond leading the segments of the heavy amla and light oil segments.

Parachute[16] was a market leader in its category and positioned on the platform of purity. It was also available in pouch packs such as Parachute Mini, a Re1 SKU, and a 20 ml Parachute sold at ₹5 for the rural consumer. Although historically Parachute had positioned itself on the platform of purity, the communication had evolved over time to appeal to different consumer groups. The brand name extended to a range of variants such as Advansed and Jasmine, and to adjacencies such as shampoo and hair gels. (An example of Parachute's advertising with the case authors' description of its storyboard, as well as the case authors' interpretation of Parachute's communication is included in Exhibit 5.)

Dabur Amla[17] was a heavy amla oil with a composition of natural amla for enriching and strengthening hair; it was available in Re1 sachets as well as bottles. It had non-sticky variants based on flower fragrances. Dabur Amla was targeted at the middle and low income markets with its economy tier pricing, while Vatika from the same company had offerings in the premium end of this segment. (An example of Dabur Amla's advertising with the case authors' description of its storyboard, as well as the case authors' interpretation of Dabur Amla's communication is included in Exhibit 6.)

Preparing the Presentation

Following an analysis of the relevant industries, Guruvayurappan conducted a consumer survey in order to understand the dominant cultural values among consumer groups of these categories across socio-economic classes (see Exhibit 7). Based on this data and an understanding of the communication of leading brands in these categories, Guruvayurappan seemed to have identified an area of differentiation based on cultural values and ritual experiences from which brands in an emerging market could benefit when they were pitched against one another. The challenge was to use some frameworks to understand how brands could differentiate themselves using values unique to the Indian context.

15 "Marico to move court on coconut oil excise notice," http://epaper.timesofindia.com/Repository/ml.asp?Ref=RVRELzIwMDkvMDcvMTQjQXIwMTgwMg==&Mode=HTML&Locale=english-skin-custom, accessed October 10, 2010.

16. "Parachute," *Marico*, www.marico.com/brands_n_business/parachute/index.html, accessed October 10, 2010.

17. "Dabur Amla," *Dabur*, www.dabur.com/Products-Personal%20Care-Amla%20Hair%20Oil, accessed October 10, 2010.

Exhibit 1 Values Questionnaire

Each of the 32 values is defined by five statements which are to be rated on the five-point Likert Scale (strongly agree, agree, neutral, disagree, strongly disagree) by the side. In the final form of the questionnaire, all 160 statements will be mixed up to remove any bias. The defining value will not be shown to the respondents who were asked to mark one (1) against their level of agreement with each statement given below.

Values
Power distance
I often seek opinions from people before making decisions
There are many distinctions between people in my locality
I believe that some people in my locality are clearly more influential than others
I don't think equality is a practical concept
I look up to some people in society as really knowledgeable
Uncertainty avoidance
I don't like being uncertain about things
I search for a lot of information before I do or buy something
I don't like being in unfamiliar situations
It gives me a reassurance if other people are doing/buying the same thing as me
I generally do not experiment while buying things
Forward-looking
I often think about the future when I need to make a decision
I believe in saving money for a rainy day
When I earn some unexpected money, I don't generally spend it on myself
I don't expect immediate results for things I do
I engage in a lot of planning and don't believe in just living for the present
Conservatism
I do not like to stand out in a crowd
I am careful about the money I spend
I don't get too carried away when I am happy or successful at something
I am cautious about my dress and behaviour when I am with people
I don't think I can ever lead a flashy lifestyle

Need for affiliation
It is important for me that others approve of what I do
When in a group, I often behave in a manner that makes me fit in
I often pay attention to others' reactions to my behaviour
In case of uncertainty, I look at others to get cues from them
I often feel bad if my peer group doesn't praise me for something worthy I've done
Family bonding
I have a close relationship with my family
I feel it is very important to bond well with family
Family is the only long-lasting association that people have in life
I could leave an important career if it gave me no time with my family
I feel close to members of family even if there are physical distances
Utilitarianism
I generally buy products only if they are useful
I am not impressed by free offers unless I definitely need the product
I never buy items just because I liked its advertisement
I don't simply follow my heart while selecting products
I make most purchases with a lot of thought
Fatalism
I generally accept things that happen as fate
I don't think we have control over our destiny
If bad things are to happen, they will happen
I feel helpless in losing situations
I can achieve only what is in store for me
Nominalism
I am not sure what many rituals of my religion actually stand for
I sometimes follow practices without thinking much
I don't think I have tried to seek explanations of things that my parents tell me to follow
I am indifferent to most of the cultural practices I indulge in

(*Continued*)

With more time, I would try to learn about cultural aspects like weddings, etc.
Achievement seeking
I am highly ambitious in my career
Being successful is the most important thing to me
I like finding solutions to challenging problems
I need to be acknowledged for my abilities by people around me
I keep seeking milestones even when I have conquered one
Respect for age
I believe my parents know better than me
I always get up from my seat if I see an elderly person standing
It is very annoying to see old people being spoken to rudely
I believe that one can only get better with age as one gains experience
I feel comforted when there is someone older to take care of certain situations
Co-operation
I believe better work can be done by co-operating with peers
I sometimes feel that competing in things may lead to less work getting done
When there is a task to be done, I try to think of how well we can get together and do it
I enjoy donating things to charity
I like taking part in community service at work or in the neighbourhood
Nuclear family
I think small family is a happy family
It's important for both parents to earn money as living costs rise up
I think both parents should share the work in the house
I do not think we have enough space to have both my parents and my children in the house
I have never lived in a joint family.
Group emphasis
I love to hang out with my friends
I'd rather go out for dinner with friends after work than go home alone
I do not like to go alone to have lunch in the office/college canteen

I am not dependent on one or two persons to make my weekend plans
I am in touch with my college/school group through regular meetings
Respect for work
I think success comes through hard work alone
I believe that every field of work is equally appreciable
I always try to give 100 per cent to the task at hand
If my subordinates work hard, I never fail to compliment/reward them
I respect everyone who does his/her work well, even though their social status may not be the same
Seeking prosperity
I want to have all the latest durables in my house
I want my children to have the best education
I think prosperity is related to social status
I would not mind swapping a job just for the salary hike
I want to earn enough for fulfilling all my adulthood desires
Hospitality
I always invite friends and relatives over for dinner
I love to have my relatives from other cities visiting me
It's great to have your colleagues come over for a chat
I am never put off by someone coming over without informing me
I love to have my children's friends dropping by even when my kids are not at home
Social orientation
I am very particular about what I wear and whether it matches my personality
I like to think that what I own is unique to me in some ways
I try to develop an image based on the things I own
I think my lifestyle is an actual reflection of my personality
My friend circle and I have similar views towards life
Self esteem
I seem to have a great deal of self respect

(*Continued*)

In almost every aspect, I am glad to be the person I am
I feel I have a number of good qualities
I take a positive attitude towards myself
I feel I am a person of worth, at least on an equal plane with others
Honour
I believe that the family name should be upheld
I believe in spending lavishly in accordance with my status in family functions
I would be exceedingly averse to borrowing money from people
My family prestige is of utmost importance to me
I'd rather give up durables than part with a family heirloom
Innovativeness
I like to experiment with my ideas
I would like a job that requires frequent changes from one kind of task to another
I like to try new and different things
I often try new brands before my friends and neighbours do
I am not afraid of failing with my creativity
Conspicuous westernized symbols
I like to party regularly
I think social drinking is acceptable and at times necessary
I own several designer clothing items and accessories
I lead a hectic life where take-away food is a significant part of my routine
I feel it is a good thing to inculcate some western practices
Gifting trends
Whenever I go to visit a friend or a relative, I carry a gift along
It's not the cost of the gift that matters to me, it's the thought
The more expensive the gifts are, the better people would think of my social standing
I take a lot of pains to choose the right thing for the right occasion
I feel honoured when people put an effort to buy gifts for me

Personal grooming
I pay a lot of attention to how I look when I go out
I am conscious of my looks even when I am not going out for an occasion
I think first impression is very important and I need to appear well-groomed when meeting someone new
I occasionally indulge in a beauty salon or similar place to shape up my looks
I tend to make opinions about people who are shabbily attired or too casual in appearance
Family hierarchy orientation
It is the men in the family who purchase goods in my household
The main earner has an important say in selecting brands
The women of the house offer suggestions but the men make the decision
Even for toothpastes, soaps, hair oil, creams, etc., one person picks up brands for everyone
The youngsters in my house have become more independent in buying after they started earning
Ethnocentrism
I generally search for brands with Indian names or symbols
I don't think a foreign brand is necessarily better than an Indian brand
I feel an Indian brand is more suited to my needs
I buy regional or national brands due to a strong sense of loyalty
I feel we must buy more local products for helping Indian brands go global
Individualism
I prefer making most of my decisions myself
I generally buy or consume things which reflect my uniqueness
I like to be different from the crowd at times
I am not affected much by what other people do
It is important to me that people respect my individuality
Thriftiness
I am careful about the way I plan my finances
Price promotions in shops often attract me

(*Continued*)

I generally think low-priced goods can serve my needs well
I don't invest or spend money in ventures that I am uncertain about
I would like to save money for a rainy day
Celebrity orientation
I would buy a product that is endorsed by a celebrity I like
I am attracted to advertisements that use celebrities
If a celebrity is endorsing a product, he or she must have tested the qualities
By using the brand of my favourite hero, I feel I am being like him
I change my brands based on my favourite sportsperson/film star's preference
Time orientation (living in the past/present)
I often think about the good old days
I do not believe exciting days are coming ahead in my life
Life was much simpler and carefree during my parents' time
I wish I could have my old favourite brands back — they denoted quality
You cannot be sure about product quality any more these days
Emotional decision making
I often make my decisions from my heart
I feel it is healthy to express emotions
I don't like to always be rational
My opinions about people can be quite subjective
I am open about my feelings with my peers
Neo-mindset orientation
I change habits and behaviour with time
I am often influenced by some of the new happenings around me
I cannot stick to the same old practices all my life
I don't mind breaking off from conventions
I could call myself rebellious to a certain extent

Source: S. Ramesh Kumar, Nitya Guruvayurappan and Madhurjya Banerjee, "Cultural Values and Branding in an Emerging Market—The Indian Context," *The Marketing Review*, 7 (2007), pp. 247–272, reproduced with the permission of the journal's editor.

Exhibit 2 Dominant Values Identification

Category: Fairness Creams

Consumer Class: Middle

VALUES	μ/σ*
Power distance	7.199
Uncertainty avoidance	5.901
Forward-looking	6.734
Conservatism	6.240
Need for affiliation	5.673
Family bonding	6.860
Utilitarianism	7.423
Fatalism	4.397
Nominalism	6.360
Achievement seeking	7.092
Respect for age	7.111
Co-operation	9.186
Nuclear family	7.039
Group emphasis	6.662
Respect for work	8.250
Seeking prosperity	6.073
Hospitality	5.837
Social orientation	5.516
Self esteem	8.288
Honour	4.359
Innovativeness	7.020
Conspicuous westernized symbols	4.236
Gifting trends	7.645
Personal grooming	3.371
Family hierarchy orientation	3.873
Ethnocentrism	5.528

Consumer Class: Upper

VALUES	μ/σ*
Power distance	6.061
Uncertainty avoidance	6.828
Forward-looking	7.017
Conservatism	5.132
Need for affiliation	6.024
Family bonding	6.203
Utilitarianism	6.274
Fatalism	3.410
Nominalism	4.815
Achievement seeking	5.962
Respect for age	5.679
Co-operation	7.217
Nuclear family	6.952
Group emphasis	6.623
Respect for work	8.574
Seeking prosperity	6.638
Hospitality	6.676
Social orientation	6.821
Self esteem	6.776
Honour	6.615
Innovativeness	7.241
Conspicuous westernized symbols	4.774
Gifting trends	7.479
Personal grooming	4.640
Family hierarchy orientation	4.851
Ethnocentrism	5.962

(*Continued*)

Individualism	8.700
Thriftiness	5.569
Celebrity orientation	3.243
Time orientation (living in the past/present)	5.012
Emotional decision making	6.181
Neo-mindset orientation	6.868

Individualism	6.010
Thriftiness	6.676
Celebrity orientation	2.391
Time orientation (living in the past/present)	4.573
Emotional decision making	4.165
Neo-mindset orientation	7.201

Category: Hair Oil

Consumer Class: Middle

VALUES	μ/σ*
Power distance	7.331
Uncertainty avoidance	5.886
Forward-looking	5.568
Conservatism	7.301
Need for affiliation	5.323
Family bonding	6.840
Utilitarianism	8.029
Fatalism	3.692
Nominalism	5.320
Achievement seeking	6.632
Respect for age	5.994
Co-operation	6.384
Nuclear family	5.976
Group emphasis	4.645
Respect for work	6.417
Seeking prosperity	5.675
Hospitality	4.869
Social orientation	4.847
Self esteem	6.608
Honour	5.839

Consumer Class: Upper

VALUES	μ/σ*
Power distance	7.181
Uncertainty avoidance	6.916
Forward-looking	6.930
Conservatism	4.907
Need for affiliation	5.606
Family bonding	7.620
Utilitarianism	6.971
Fatalism	3.755
Nominalism	4.683
Achievement seeking	7.093
Respect for age	6.905
Co-operation	7.968
Nuclear family	6.458
Group emphasis	7.525
Respect for work	9.359
Seeking prosperity	5.982
Hospitality	6.170
Social orientation	6.101
Self esteem	9.148
Honour	4.667

Innovativeness	6.380
Conspicuous westernized symbols	4.088
Gifting trends	6.525
Personal grooming	4.847
Family hierarchy orientation	3.599
Ethnocentrism	4.930
Individualism	6.900
Thriftiness	6.173
Celebrity orientation	2.997
Time orientation (living in the past/present)	5.189
Emotional decision making	6.784
Neo-mindset orientation	6.355

Innovativeness	7.463
Conspicuous westernized symbols	4.371
Gifting trends	7.524
Personal grooming	4.287
Family hierarchy orientation	4.045
Ethnocentrism	4.662
Individualism	8.376
Thriftiness	5.581
Celebrity orientation	3.218
Time orientation (living in the past/present)	5.016
Emotional decision making	5.923
Neo-mindset orientation	6.403

* μ/σ is the inverse of coefficient of variation where μ stands for the mean of the individual ratings and σ is the standard deviation.

Note: The data can be interpreted as the values with the highest μ/σ are the most dominant in terms of having the highest mean while accounting for standard deviation as they are most clustered around the *mean for the individual consumer responses. Higher score reflects higher intensity of the respective factor.*

Source: S. Ramesh Kumar, Nitya Guruvayurappan and Madhurjya Banerjee, "Cultural Values and Branding in an Emerging Market—The Indian Context," *The Marketing Review*, 7 (2007), pp. 247-272, reproduced with the permission of the journal's editor. The authors thank Dr. Ann Foy, editor, Marketing Review for permitting the use of this data in the case study.

Exhibit 3 Communication of Fair & Lovely Brand

Fair & Lovely Sample Storyboard and Ad Interpretation

Storyboard 1

The ad starts in a household with an elderly couple where the husband asks for some more milk in his tea and the wife says there is not enough milk since it is just his pension that runs the household for three people. The husband comments that it would have been good to have a son, which his daughter overhears when walking in. She gets upset on hearing this and decides to do something to prove she can be as good as a son. She finds an advertisement in the newspaper for an airhostess job but is uncertain if she can get it owing to her dark skin. A Fair & Lovely ad plays on the TV and she realizes how it would help her achieve her dream. She walks into the interview confidently and does very well and gets the job. She shares her achievement by taking her parents out to eat, and they are proud of her success.

Storyboard 2:

The ad shows snatches from a young girl's life where on every occasion she is seen acting as a commentator to a cricket game — sometimes to a game in her locality, sometimes to a match on TV — with a make-believe microphone in her hand. One day a friend of hers takes the microphone from her and gives her a tube of F&L instead. Consequently, the girl applies and is hired to perform commentary in a live cricket match, along with a famous Indian cricket commentator. Her co-commentator is awed by her presence and confidence and she is surrounded by a barrage of fans seeking her autograph after the game.

Authors' Interpretation:

F&L has used the running theme of how fairness leads to self-confidence and success in most of their ads. It builds on the Indian mentality (typical to lower and middle classes) that fair skin gets you noticed and hence helps you go a long way in life. The central character is shown as a young woman in her twenties who is ambitious but does not pursue her dreams because she is kept back by her self-consciousness about her looks. She aspires to be in areas that are either dominated by men or which require her to be attractive and confident with a remarkable personality. Sometimes she also bears the brunt of criticism or humiliation from those around her — either family members or people in society who attach a lot of importance to appearance. As a consequence, it impacts her self-esteem and she is motivated into changing her life and proving a point to those people. She is introduced to F&L by a friend or relative or from some other source of information and her life changes — she achieves her dream and is treated with respect and awe by the very same people who earlier would have ignored her. The inferred benefit here is

the confidence to achieve your dreams, because looking good leads to feeling good. F&L uses an approach of creating discomfort and negative emotion in order to magnify the victory and positive emotions as an outcome of using the product even more.

Source: Advertisement reproduced with the permission of Mohit Sud, Brand Manager – Skin Care, Hindustan Unliver Limited, India. The authors analyzed the advertisement for the brand based on their perception of the advertisements as consumers associated with the Indian context.

Storyboard 1: www.youtube.com/watch?v=2a1iXt1yPsk, accessed October 10, 2010.

Storyboard 2: www.youtube.com/watch?v=zRt8E8sfiSw, accessed October 10, 2010.

Exhibit 4 Communication of Fairever brand

Fairever Sample Storyboard and Ad Interpretation

Storyboard 1

The ad shows a group of school girls on a bus going through a village. When the bus halts for a while, one of the girls sees a woman in labour riding on a bullock cart. She runs to help and offer her some water, and asks the man with her why they cannot take her to the nearest hospital soon. The man remarks that the nearest hospital is very far since they do not have one in the village. The girl goes back and sees a bookmark of Fairever packaging which says 'You can change your future.' She decides to study to become a doctor, despite facing opposition from her family who are unable to understand why she is wasting an expensive degree in the U.S. on a small village where she might not even make money; however, she is determined to do what she feels is right and goes to serve the village which was lacking in medical facilities, making her family proud and making herself loved by the villagers. The ad places emphasis on Fairever giving her the confidence to write her own destiny.

Storyboard 2

The ad shows a little girl exclaiming, "They've come," and shows that it is a house with festoons and decorations. A family comes with a beautiful girl (celebrity) and are invited in. It becomes evident that this is a ceremony where the girl meets a boy in an arranged marriage scenario, but the roles are reversed. Not only does the girl come to see the boy, but also the boy serves the families with tea and snacks, and performs music and dance in front of them. The voiceover (VO) says that when Fairever is making women so beautiful, shouldn't it be the men who have to do all this to win their heart. It ends with the girl saying that she likes the boy and the VO says "changing the colors of life."

Authors' Interpretation

Fairever's key benefit was to encourage young women with the thought that they can write their future. It suggested that Fairever gave women the confidence to write their destinies and become successful. In the above ad, Fairever touches on women's confidence and determination to do things without dwelling on the negative elements and stigma associated with being dark complexioned, unlike its competitor. The ad works on an overall positive approach like the first storyboard rather than showing a negative emotion and then overcoming the same. It also uses creative situations to indicate how powerful beauty and confidence can make a woman, as in the second storyboard. Certain campaign ads also took a dig at competition by declaring that the woman was equally powerful and supported the family, and one did not have to be a son to be the breadwinner. This was explicitly targeted at a competitor's campaigns to make women look empowered after they are shown as the weaker sex initially. Gradually, Fairever is using more celebrities and is also placing emphasis on product claims like "four tones lighter in four weeks" and "three times more protection from the sun." It also talks about product features like milk proteins and saffron white essences in the communication to enhance credibility of the claim. Fairever also uses the whiteness meter in its communication in order to establish that it is an equally effective product, given that it competes with a goliath market leader and hence first needs to establish that the functional benefit that leads up to the emotional benefits is actually strong in its product offering.

Source: The authors analyzed the advertisements for the brand based on their perception of the advertisements as consumers associated with the Indian context.

Storyboard 1: www.youtube.com/watch?v=_KljS8_6ofI, accessed October 10, 2010.

Storyboard 2: www.youtube.com/watch?v=vhp3KSOry5c, accessed October 10, 2010.

Exhibit 5 Communication of Parachute Brand

Parachute Sample Storyboard and Ad Interpretation

Storyboard 1

Three young women are out on a picnic and see a waterfall at a distance; one of the women says she is looking forward to taking a shower and shampooing her hair. One of the friends (a popular celebrity) says that first they need to oil their hair and leave it on for an hour, and takes out a Parachute bottle. On being asked why, she explains that hair tends to become dry and rough on shampoo alone and hence it is necessary to moisturize and nourish hair with oil prior to that. The ad closes with the "gorgeous hamesha" tagline and theme music, which is part of the campaign that Parachute women are always gorgeous and do not need to be made up in order to look beautiful.

Storyboard 2

The ad shows a celebrity experimenting with her hairstyle on different occasions. In the first, she has wavy hair, in the second situation it is her birthday and she has straight hair. On the third occasion, she colors her hair in streaks. She visits the hairstylist again and sits in the chair saying, "What shall we try new today?" To this, the hairstylist replies that the first thing they ought to do is an hour's soaking and massage of hot Parachute coconut oil. She explains that when you experiment with your hair and try new things, it tends to lack the nurture and care and becomes dry and lifeless. In order to rejuvenate her hair, she needs the good old coconut oil treatment. The celebrity gets the same done and is ready to try a new hairstyle all over again.

Authors' Interpretation

Parachute has moved out of the many years of mother-daughter related advertising to now appeal more to the youth, especially given that there are so many category substitutes like leave-on conditioners penetrating the youth market. The Parachute campaign is targeted at young women and seeks to assure them that real beauty does not have to dress up and the Parachute women are "gorgeous hamesha" (always gorgeous). The campaign has both functional and emotional elements, with the emotional campaign being the one in which it has captured beautiful women in different moods and settings and generated awareness for this campaign and tagline. It has subsequently leveraged this in its functional ads like the storyboard mentioned above to drive the benefit of nourishment and keeping hair from going dry. For this, it has built on the accepted consumer belief that a lot of its target audience practices the usage experience of a massage and one-hour leave-on of oil prior to shampoo. Parachute has used celebrities in their campaigns to depict the beauty concept while driving the functional need of oiling as their hair is often subjected to a lot of rough handling in their profession. The second ad is an example of the same. It also captures how Parachute as a brand sits on the border of innovation and tradition, as is true of the women it targets: although they want to try out new things and experiment with their hair and styles, coconut oil will still

remain a part of their hair care and hence they are driving the concept of a hot oil massage before a shampoo.

Source: Advertisement reproduced with the permission of Sonal Krishen, HR Manager, Marico India.The authors analyzed the advertisements for the brand based on their perception of the advertisements as consumers associated with the Indian context.

Storyboard 1: www.youtube.com/watch?v=qGPLSvS23KI&feature=related, accessed October 10, 2010.

Storyboard 2: www.youtube.com/watch?v=w7I2cgOWmDs, accessed October 10, 2010.

Exhibit 6 Communication of Dabur Amla Brand

Dabur Amla Sample Storyboard and Ad Interpretation

Storyboard 1

The ad starts with the central character (a celebrity) walking past, waving her silky hair and the VO says "hair is meant to be shown off." The central character is then shown at a celebration where she urges her friend to come and join her on the dance floor. The friend refuses, due to awkwardness about her oily hair. The VO then says "hair is not meant to be hidden." The ad then goes on to say how other oils make hair sticky while Dabur Amla nourishes and makes hair stronger and shinier. The VO concludes with saying that "hair is meant to win hearts."

Storyboard 2

The celebrity (central character) sees a young girl trying to collect money for a charitable cause but no one on the streets seems to be paying her any attention. The celebrity immediately collects a group of young women and they put on a street dance to attract the crowd. They look attractive and happy as they dance uninhibited and letting their hair loose. The VO says that Dabur Amla adds zest to hair and hence fun to your life.

Authors' Interpretation

Dabur Amla has been using celebrities in their campaigns for both hair oil and shampoo. The central character, usually the celebrity, is shown as attractive, confident, willing to take on challenges and comfortable in her personality. The setting is usually one in which a situation requires two women, the protagonist and another character, to let their hair loose and enjoy, wherein the non-user is reluctant because her hair isn't attractive enough. The benefit communication explains the merits of amla in the hair oil and how it nourishes and strengthens hair, leaving it shiny and soft. It focuses on how women's crowning glory is their hair and hence insists that they shouldn't settle for anything less when it comes to taking care of their hair. Dabur has taken on competition explicitly with their other line extensions like Vatika, wherein they do comparative advertising in which they show packaging that looks identical to the immediate competition without naming them explicitly — like Parachute or Bajaj (almond category) — and compare superiority of their own brand versus those competitors. Amla on the other hand finds them as the market leaders by a significant margin and hence their communication is limited and targeted mainly at the middle-tier market.

Source: The authors analyzed the advertisements for the brand based on their perception of the advertisements as consumers associated with the Indian context.

Storyboard 1: www.youtube.com/watch?v=qyO6A4weVTk&feature=related, accessed on October 10, 2010.

Storyboard 2: www.youtube.com/watch?v=9apExNucf2M&feature=related, accessed on October 10, 2010.

Exhibit 7 Methodology Used for Data Collection

1. Two categories close to the Indian consumer and the prevalent cultural context — hair oil and facial creams — were selected in order to understand the effects/implications of cultural values on branding.
2. An industry analysis was performed and a perceptual map of available brands was developed in order to understand the parameters for brand differences and subsequent classification of those for the categories identified. This helped in understanding how different social class segments perceive the various brands and hence which are more likely to be consumed in specific segments.
3. A list of 32 core Indian values were generated based on literature, consumer reports and the authors' subjective judgment based on their experience in the Indian context as consumers. A measurement scale was composed for each of these values such that each value has five points of measurement in its scale and five levels from "strongly agree" to "strongly disagree." Respondents were expected to express their agreement or disagreement with the items in the scale for each value. Stratified sampling of the target population was performed — with appropriate representation obtained from each social class — and the above questionnaire (after randomization of the statements) was sent to them. Upper and middle socio-economic classes were covered for the categories chosen. Sixty-four respondents from each of the strata were selected for each of the categories. This would equal a total of 384 respondents (in two strata for each of three categories).
4. Coefficient of variation was used as the metric for dominant value identification to minimize variation and find the values in which the ratings congregate closer to the mean value.
5. Analysis of advertisements and communication of prominent brands in each category and for each social class was performed. Gaps in the values between those dominant in Step 4 and the ones reflected in the perception of advertisements (as perceived by the authors of this case) for each social class and the respective category were identified. The final recommendation was based on bridging this gap with the dominant cultural value in each class.

CASE 2

HDFC Life Insurance: Building a Service Brand*

Akshat Kumar, senior manager of digital marketing at HDFC Life, had a complex problem to solve. He had started off as a software engineer in a world class firm and after his management program, had decided to let his passion for consumer behaviour dictate his carrier track. Kumar's new assignment demanded all his knowledge and experience to crack the complexities of branding within the insurance market in India. HDFC Life had come out with several advertising campaigns to differentiate HDFC Life from other competitive brands. There was huge potential for an insurance brand if it was positioned well in the minds of consumers. A survey, commissioned with conceptual inputs, created further complexity in terms of consumer response. Were consumers in the industry immune to positioning

* S. Ramesh Kumar and Akshat Kumar wrote this case solely to provide material for class discussion. The authors do not intend to illustrate either effective or ineffective handling of a managerial situation. The authors may have disguised certain names and other identifying information to protect confidentiality.

strategies? Did they see value in several brands? Were concepts of brand equity valid in such services? How could the survey's insights be used to develop a positioning for the brand HDFC Life?

Introduction

Changing lifestyles and higher literacy among consumers along withthe entry of several well-known banks into the field of insurance had increased the awareness of insurance brands among consumers over the last decade. According to the Confederation of Indian Industry, the value of the Indian insurance industry was INR41 billion.[1] Up to 2012, only about 1/5 of India's population was covered under various life insurance products. The penetration of health insurance products was even lower. There was a larger market for insurance products in India in 2012 than ever before. Given this fact, a lot of international players had also entered the Indian market in joint-ventures with Indian companies.

Innovative products, aggressive marketing and multiple distribution channels enabled insurance companies to sell their various products. Where people traditionally bought insurance to pay for expenses such as education and retirement, increased aspirations led them to buy policies to pay for houses and wedding ceremonies.

One of the biggest trends in the Indian insurance industry was the emergence of online products known as online term plans. With more than 120 million Indian people on the internet, the product had shown tremendous growth. Since the average transaction price for such a product was low (one could purchase life insurance coverage of US$200,000 for as low as US$ 110 per annum as a premium[2]), more people were purchasing this insurance off the internet without the help of either an insurance agent or traditional banks to guide them.

HDFC Life

HDFC Life, one of India's leading private life insurance companies, offered a range of individual and group insurance solutions. It was a joint venture between HDFC, India's leading housing finance institution, and Standard Life plc, the leading provider of financial services in the United Kingdom.

HDFC Life had multiple products online. As of 2012 ten products were available online. Since the products could be bought online, there was a significant focus by the brand on the digital medium used to reach out to consumers.

---

1. http://business.mapsofindia.com/insurance/, accessed October 3, 2012. As of Oct 3, 2012 US$1 was approximately equal to INR52.
2. Conversations with employees in the insurance industry.

Since insurance products are more or less the same, differentiation could only be created through imagery and service. Most of the insurance brands were creating brand associations through positioning strategies.

Marketing Campaigns of HDFC Life

1. Rajasthan Royals IPL 2012, Sar Utha Ke Jiyo[3]

   Indian Premier League (IPL) is a popular cricket tournament sponsored by film and business celebrities. Among the many teams that participate in this cricket tournament are the Rajesthan Royals. The campaign highlighted the characteristics of self-belief, pride and confidence associated with the players of and how they had achieved success despite the odds they had faced in their lives.

   Through this campaign, the brand showcased the significance of brand value. When a team gets onto the field, full of zeal to perform their best, it doesn't really matter what the result is in the end; the point is to play the game for pride and self-respect.

2. Neighbour, Click2Protect, Sar Utha Ke Jiyo[4]

   The campaign suggested that term insurance is very important to secure one's family adequately, and sought to make consumers feel concerned about the well being of their family.

3. Rajasthan Royals IPL 2011, Sar Utha Ke Jiyo[5]

4. Parents' Teachers Meeting, Child Plan, Sar Utha Ke Jiyo[6]

   The campaign was intended to make parents aware of financial planning for their children due to the competitive realities in today's world.

5. Rakhi, HDFC Life Re-branding, Sar Utha Ke Jiyo[7]

   In this campaign, a brother gives a blank cheque to his sister, and tells her that she can fill it out once he gets a job. The gift is given in on a festive occasion that celebrates the bond between a brother and a sister. The campaign was meant to suggest that youth should buy insurance and become financially independent early on in their careers.

---

3. www.afaqs.com/advertising/creative_showcase/index.html?id=34763&media=TV&type=Indian, accessed April 8, 2012.

4. www.afaqs.com/advertising/creative_showcase/index.html?id=32918&media=TV&type=Indian, accessed April 8, 2012.

5. www.afaqs.com/advertising/creative_showcase/index.html?id=27812&media=TV&type=Indian, accessed April 8, 2012.

6. www.afaqs.com/advertising/creative_showcase/index.html?id=26785&media=TV&type=Indian, accessed April 8, 2012.

7. www.afaqs.com/advertising/creative_showcase/index.html?id=25219&media=TV&type=Indian, accessed April 8, 2012.

Customer Segmentation

Most of the HDFC Life products were available online, so geography was not a limitation. The primary audience was males looking life insurance coverage to provide for their families in case of their demise. The target segment included executives and businessmen.

HDFC Life communication focused on needs relevant to different life cycles. The five different life cycle stages emphasized were:

- Unmarried.
- Just married.
- Purchasing a home.
- Children and education.
- Support for old parents.

The typical consumer was a 25 to 40 years old, male professional with disposable income who lived in a large city with a population of between 2 and 7 million people. He wanted to make a variety of future short-term and long-term investments like buying a car or house, while saving for a marriage and providing for his parents. These consumers primarily purchased insurance for tax savings.

The ads were addressed to informed urban consumers who wanted to take charge of their family and protect them with insurance. The target segment had access to the internet and was comfortable doing ecommerce transactions on the internet.

For lifestyle habits of customers, see Exhibit 1.

ICICI Prudential Life

ICICI Prudential Life was a life insurance company that had launched a low-cost online term plan in the Indian market and within a year of launch, it became one of the top-selling online life plans in the country.

With the successful acceptance of its existing online products and the in-depth customer insight it had gathered, ICICI Prudential Life had helped the company improve its online product offerings and create a new online term plan with better features and more benefits. The online application process on ICICI Prudential Life's website made it an easy and hassle-free experience for customers. Innovative products, aggressive marketing and the online channel had enabled ICICI Prudential Life to sell their various products easily.

The brand had leveraged its celebrity association with Amitabh Bachchan (a film celebrity in India) who was shown in marketing materials using a tablet and asking consumers to visit the website and complete the entire process of buying insurance in less than 10 minutes.

Marketing Campaigns OF ICICI Prudential

1. Security Check, iCare[8]

   Through this campaign, the brand highlighted the ease of buying insurance online — quick and easy. With tablets and smartphones, the insurance policy could be bought anywhere.

2. Train, Jeene Ka License[9]

   Through this marketing message, the brand attempted to illustrate the need for insurance before taking risks, even if this risk was just starting a new business.

3. Future Calculator, Jeetey Raho[10]

   Through this campaign, the brand tried to provide the means to consumers to measure their future needs against some financial planning which they could achieve through insurance.

4. Smart Kid Child Plan, Suraksha Zindagi Ke Har Kadam Par[11]

   The brand used the importance of saving for children's education to create awareness of its offerings associated with children.

5. Retirement – World's Best Job, Jeetey Raho[12]

   Through this campaign the idea was to relate to the younger working man, who could then wisely save for his future. The brand had to make retirement aspirational for the hesitant Indian consumer.

SBI Life

Formed in 2001, SBI life Insurance was a joint venture between SBI — India's largest bank — and BNP Paribas Assurance — France's banking and financial services provider. SBI Life extensively leveraged on the network of its branches to sell its insurance products. Customers were perhaps attracted to the association of SBI with the insurance brand. SBI Life had yet to launch specific online insurance products.

---

8 www.afaqs.com/advertising/creative_showcase/index.html?id=31962&media=TV&type=Indian, accessed April 8, 2012.

9 www.afaqs.com/advertising/creative_showcase/index.html?id=26243&media=TV&type=Indian, *accessed April 8, 2012.*

10 www.afaqs.com/advertising/creative_showcase/index.html?id=21529&media=TV&type=Indian, accessed April 8, 2012.

11 www.afaqs.com/advertising/creative_showcase/index.html?id=21501&media=TV&type=Indian, accessed April 8, 2012.

12 www.afaqs.com/advertising/creative_showcase/index.html?id=14825&media=TV&type=Indian, accessed April 8, 2012.

Marketing Campaigns of SBI Life

1. Scooter, Zindagi Hai Jine Ke Liye[13]

   Through this campaign, the brand SBI Life meets wealth creation needs one gets all the time in the world to relish the small joys of life. The idea was also to bring out the trust factor associated with SBI, the larger umbrella brand, in a subtle manner.

2. Celebrate Life, Zindagi Hai Jine Ke Liye[14]

   The idea behind this campaign was to get young people to think about old age and how to secure their retirement. The brand highlighted the serious importance of thinking about one's old age while celebrating and enjoying youth.

3. Heera, Celebrate Life[15]

   The campaign message to the consumers was to start investing early to avoid problems later in life. This message was coupled with the emotion of love. The underlying thought for the campaign became: "Never let money get in the way of expressing your love."

HDFC Life – Digital Marketing Initiatives

The idea behind digital marketing was to increase the distribution mix through the website and establish an online channel to generate business. The marketing objective was to strengthen HDFC Life brand's equity through increased visibility of online products on the website.

HDFC Life was interested in exploring the brand perception associated with itself and its competitors. It desired an exploratory study that would provide reveal the brand perception of insurance buyers of insurance. HDFC Life was also interested in the perceptions of prospective online insurance buyers.

Methodology

With the initiatives taken by HDFC Life, the brand wanted to delve into the brand perceptions of buyers of HDFC Life and its competitors, namely ICICI Prudential Life and SBI Life Insurance. The company believed the perceptions of prospective online insurance buyers should be analyzed to provide a comparison between several aspects associated with the three brands. This study was an exploratory one and the company was interested in commissioning more studies based on its outcome.

[13] www.afaqs.com/advertising/creative_showcase/index.html?id=26608&media=TV&type=Indian, accessed April 8, 2012.

[14] www.afaqs.com/advertising/creative_showcase/index.html?id=18022&media=TV&type=Indian, accessed April 8, 2012.

[15] www.afaqs.com/advertising/creative_showcase/index.html?id=14949&media=TV&type=Indian, accessed April 8, 2012.

A research agency based in Bangalore was engaged in May 2012 for the data collection. The survey was conducted with more than 120 respondents in the cities of Mumbai, Bangalore and New Delhi.

Exhibit 2 is an advertisement for HDFC Life. Exhibit 3 provides information on the responses of consumers who had bought the HDFC Life brand of insurance. Exhibit 4 provides the responses of prospective buyers of the insurance policy through the online channel. Strangely, responses from the buyers of SBI Life and ICICI Prudential insurance policies on all the factors covered in Exhibit 3 were very similar in nature.

Kumar had to decide on the future course of action for HFDC Life's brand, taking into consideration the results of the consumer survey that did not seem to get him anywhere.

Exhibit 1 Lifestyle Habits of the Buyers of HDFC Life Insurance

S. No.	Lifestyle Habit
1.	The consumer cares for his family
2.	The consumer is concerned about long term security of his family
3.	The consumer wants to be financially independent
4.	The consumer is aware of his financial needs
5.	The consumer invests money either during festivals or at the end of the financial year on insurance
6.	The consumer likes to consult people before a purchase making decision
7.	The consumer likes to research to find out the best available investment options
8.	The consumer searches on the internet to read review about various insurance products
9.	The consumer is deeply concerned about the investment if it concerns his children
10.	The consumer who makes the purchase decision is concerned about health issues and likes to protect himself by buying insurance
11.	The consumer spends time reading newspapers, watching TV or browsing internet to help him make decision and evaluate options
12.	The consumer is always looking for help to resolve investment issues
13.	The consumer wants to be associated with brands that service him well.
14.	The consumer is looking for financial options which are not too complex and can be purchased easily
15.	The consumer's financial demands are triggered by personal life cycles like new job, birth of a new baby

Source: Field survey commissioned by the authors. The survey was commissioned by Research Services Bureau, Bangalore, May 2012, Mumbai, Bangalore and New Delhi, India.

Exhibit 2 HDFC Advertisement

Source: Company files.

Exhibit 3 Responses of the Buyers of HDFC Life Insurance Policy

S. No		Average
1	I came to know about HDFC Life insurance through print/tv/radio/internet ads.	4
2	I have tried to get more information about the HDFC Life insurance products.	4
3	I felt the need for buying HDFC Life insurance was triggered by a personal need.	4
4	I bought the HDFC Life insurance after I had gathered all the relevant information about the products.	4
5	I was convinced by the agent or salesperson to buy the HDFC Life Insurance.	4
6	After buying HDFC Life insurance, I tried to gather more information about their other products	3
7	I buy HDFC Life insurance, as the entire process is less complex.	4
8	I find HDFC Life insurance buying process to be time effective.	4
9	I find HDFC Life insurance buying process as high on ease of buying.	4
10	I trust HDFC Life insurance hence I buy their products.	4
11	I buy HDFC Life insurance for long term security.	4
12	I find the insurance buying service to be approachable for HDFC Life.	4
13	I feel my needs are taken care of when I am buying HDFC Life insurance online.	4
14	I feel secure when buying HDFC Life insurance.	4
15	I feel financially independent when buying HDFC Life insurance.	4
16	I feel a sense of social approval when buying HDFC Life insurance.	4
17	I know HDFC Life insurance online is committed to serving customers and I am ready to let go of small errors on the part of the brand.	4
18	I find the quality of service with HDFC Life insurance to be consistent.	4
19	I find the process of buying HDFC Life insurance as beneficial for me.	4
20	My need to buy HDFC Life insurance is synonymous with life events like marriage, new job, home loan, new-born baby, security for old parents, etc.	4

S. No		Average
21	I am going to buy HDFC Life insurance products again.	4
22	I am going to recommend HDFC Life insurance product to friends and family.	4
23	I considered the opinion of my friends and family while buying the HDFC Life insurance product.	4
24	I have considered a few things suggested by my friends and family about the HDFC Life insurance product, which I was myself, not aware of.	4
25	I have derived benefits in terms of savings by buying HDFC Life insurance.	4

Note: A 5 point Likert scale was used to capture the responses. Higher response indicates a stronger agreement with the respective statement.

Source: Field survey commissioned by the authors. The survey was commissioned by Research Services Bureau, Bangalore, May 2012, Mumbai, Bangalore and New Delhi, India.

Exhibit 4 Responses of Prospective Online Buyers of Insurance

S. No		Average
1	I find it extremely convenient to buy insurance online.	4
2	I can choose from multiple products when buying insurance online.	4
3	I can make an informed buying decision when buying insurance online.	4
4	I buy insurance online because I save money.	4
5	I trust online buying and I am feel secure sharing my details online for buying insurance online	4
6	I considered the opinion of my friends and family on social media when buying insurance online.	4
7	I may buy SBI Life online insurance as the entire process is less complex.	4
8	I may find find SBI Life online insurance buying process to be time effective.	4
9	I may find SBI Life online insurance buying process as high on ease of buying.	4
10	I would like to trust SBI Life online insurance.	4
11	I may buy SBI Life online insurance for long term security.	4
12	I may find the online insurance buying service to be approachable for SBI Life.	4
13	I would think my needs are taken care of when I am buying SBI Life insurance online.	4
14	I would think SBI Life insurance online is committed to serving customers and I am ready to let go of small errors on the part of the brand	4
15	I may buy HDFC Life online insurance as the entire process is less complex.	4
16	I find HDFC Life online insurance buying process to be time effective.	4
17	I find HDFC Life online insurance buying process as high on ease of buying.	4

S. No		Average
18	I trust HDFC Life online insurance.	4
19	I may buy HDFC Life online insurance for long term security.	4
20	I find the online insurance buying service to be approachable for HDFC Life.	4
21	I feel my needs are taken care of when I am buying HDFC Life insurance online	4
22	I know HDFC Life insurance online is committed to serving customers and I am ready to let go of small errors on the part of the brand.	3
23	I may buy ICICI Prudential Life online insurance as the entire process is less complex.	4
24	I find ICICI Prudential online insurance buying process to be time effective.	4
25	I find ICICI Prudential online insurance buying process as high on ease of buying.	4
26	I trust ICICI Prudential Life online insurance.	4
27	I may buy ICICI Life online insurance for long term security	4
28	I find the online insurance buying service to be approachable for ICICI Prudential Life.	4
29	I feel my needs are taken care of when I am buying ICICI Prudential Life insurance online	4
30	I know ICICI Prudential Life insurance online is committed to serving customers and I am ready to let go of small errors on the part of the brand.	4

Note: A 5 point Likert scale was used to capture the responses. Higher response indicates a stronger agreement with the respective statement. Though SBI does not have any online offerings, the exhibit attempted to capture the perception of respondents about probable SBI online offerings. Source: Field survey commissioned by the authors. The survey was commissioned by Research Services Bureau, Bangalore, May 2012, Mumbai, Bangalore and New Delhi, India.

CASE

3

Himalaya Face Wash: Brand Associations and Lifestyles*

India was one of the emerging markets that had witnessed a radical change in the lifestyles of consumers in the last decade. About 60 per cent of the country's population was below the age of 35, and youth comprised a significant proportion of the population. Professional personal grooming and the use of branded personal care products had become almost an everyday requirement for the urban population. The face wash category was one that had attracted several brands, which consumers were trying out both for their benefits as well as for the experience. The Himalaya Drug Company (Himalaya), which had the Himalaya brand of face wash, was interested in obtaining insights into how the lifestyle of consumers was associated with the use of this category. Several brands had positioned themselves according to various attributes and benefits. Himalaya wanted to understand the impact of values and lifestyles both on the category and on the brands in this category. They made use of a

* Dr. S. Ramesh Kumar and Eric Minj wrote this case solely to provide material for class discussion. The authors do not intend to illustrate either effective or ineffective handling of a managerial situation. The authors may have disguised certain names and other identifying information to protect confidentiality.

consumer survey — which was conducted in July and August 2011 — that investigated the lifestyle of consumers and connected it to various brands through the concept of laddering. Were the attributes and benefits of the brands associated with the lifestyles of the consumers? How were values related to brand association? Himalaya hoped to obtain insights through these questions that were part of a case study by Professor Ramesh Kumar, who was interested in connecting concepts with practice and who looked forward to exploring various aspects of consumer behaviour and brand associations.

Introduction

The Indian population had experienced a radical shift with regard to lifestyle changes and consumer preferences over the last two decades. Significantly, brand associations and marketing communication had played an important role in shaping the culture of consumers as they were offered more choices for consumption[1]. One of the important motivational factors for consumers was to let their values guide them in several facets of life[2]. Consumer behaviour and preferences made up one of the important facets through which consumers bought, consumed and developed attachments to brands[3]. Thus, brand associations were linked to the values of consumers[4].

The face wash category had recently drawn in several brands. The target segment was youth in the age group of 18 to 25 years. Given the newness of the category and its potential in a market such as India where about 60 per cent of the population was below the age of 35,[5] Himalaya was interested in understanding the psyche of consumers by analyzing their values. A value in this context referred to a preferred mode of existence as compared to other modes from which a consumer could choose. Aspiration through professional success, orientation towards the future, choosing symbols as a mode of expression and having a fun-filled life were some of the values that could be associated with the face wash category as well as with several other personal care categories that had been advertised in India for the last five decades or so.

Methodology

The purpose of the case study was to help Himalaya expand the existing user base for its face wash brand by using insights from the examination of brand associations and life-

---

1. Solomon R .Michael, *Consumer Behavior: Buying, Having and Being,* Prentice Hall of India, New Delhi, 2002, p. 461.
2. W.D. Hoyer and D.J. MacInnis, *Consumer Behavior*, Houghton Mifflin, 1999, p. 409.
3. *Consumer Behaviour*, p. 461
4. S. Ramesh Kumar, N. Guruvayurappan and M. Bannerjee, "Cultural Values and Branding in an Emerging Market," *The Marketing Review*, 7.3, 2007, pp. 243–272.
5. "Census of India," February 13, 2011, http://philatelynews.com/2011/india/census-of-india/, accessed August 20, 2011.

styles. An extensive literature review was carried out to understand how to narrow down the values relevant to the category from the study of psychographics (that is, looking at activities, interests and opinions).

For the purpose of the study, a sample of 53 female respondents (within the age group of 22 to 30 years) was chosen. The data was collected in July and August 2011 in the city of Bangalore through questionnaires that were personally administered. The sample of female respondents in this particular age group was chosen because of the similarities in the target segments for the three face wash brands (EverYuth, Clean & Clear and Himalaya) that were considered for this study. Their profile was inferred by studying the relevant advertisements of these brands. A description of the brands' advertisements is provided in Exhibit 1.

The authors wanted to use a research methodology that involved the study of the lifestyles of consumers to assess their values, instead of using the concept of laddering[6] (which does not involve the lifestyles of consumers extensively). The authors felt that a detailed understanding of lifestyles could be obtained, and that such details would be useful in the analysis.

The objective of the methodology was to convert the lifestyle statements into values. After the ads of the three brands were analyzed for the values they reflected,[7] 72 lifestyle statements were constructed. The association of these lifestyle statements with values was also tested, initially with five respondents. The lifestyle statements were constructed around 24 values that were identified as being relevant to the target profile of face wash users.

The responses from the 53 respondents who used a face wash (Clean & Clear, Himalaya or EverYuth; (see Exhibit 2) were used to establish the relevance of a set of values for face wash users, taking into consideration the lifestyle indicators reflected in the survey. The challenge for Himalaya was to convert these lifestyle statements into values.

The authors arrived at the attributes and important aspects associated with the face wash category based on their analysis of the three brands and their own perception of the benefits that a face wash should offer. The category-level attributes and benefits were important as the brands needed to take them into consideration regardless of the theme they might have for their marketing communication.

Popular Face Wash Brands

Clean & Clear

The Clean & Clear face wash brand from Johnson & Johnson was positioned as a teenage girl's "skin's best friend" and as ideal for all skin types[8]. The product was available in three variants: the Daily Care range for regular facial cleansing and for removing oil, dirt, and

6. T. J. Reynolds and D.B. Whitlark," Applying Laddering Data to Communications and Strategy and Advertising Practice," *The Journal of Advertising Research*, July/August 1995, pp. 9–17.

7. Ramesh Kumar, et al., "Cultural Values and Branding in an Emerging Market."

8. "About Clean & Clear," www.cleanandclear.in/about-us, accessed August 20, 2011; "Clean & Clear: Foaming Face Wash," www.cleanandclear.in/product/foaming-face-wash/cleansers, accessed August 20, 2011.

other pollutants; the Oil Control range for maintaining oil balance and for refreshing the skin; and the Acne Clearing range for pimple control. Clean & Clear's proposition was to derive confidence by means of a clean and clear skin[9]. The face wash also contained antibacterial ingredients. The advertisements for the brand focused on teenage girls as well as middle-aged women and highlighted the need to look trendy and cool. The advertisements showed several activities associated with the lifestyle of teenagers[10]. The product's proposition was a solution for maintaining the oil balance of the skin and for controlling pimples[11].

EverYuth

EverYuth's Naturals brand of face wash was positioned as an anytime solution for refreshing face cleansing[12]. This face wash was advertised as providing purity, freshness and beauty[13]. It was available in four variants, which were advertised as being made from natural fruit extracts. The Lemon face wash, the Neem variant, the Cream variant and the Fruit face wash covered a wide range of skin care benefits. The advertisements for the brand communicated its proposition as a time-saving solution that offered instant beauty[14]. The commercials created the favourable associations of satisfaction, appreciation and confidence that were enjoyed by the user because of the instant beauty offered and highlighted the ingredients of the product[15].

Himalaya Herbal

Himalaya's face wash ranges were positioned as natural and herbal products that were soap free[16]. Its ads made use of the idea of a friend as a "problem solver" to convey positive emotions about the brand and to provide assurances about the effectiveness of

9. "Clean & Clear Deep Action Cleanser Ad," www.youtube.com/watch?v=1xIucrG4lu8, accessed August 20, 2011.

10. "Clean & Clear's Foaming Face Wash Ad," www.youtube.com/watch?v=GZ4YWDg7Qxo&feature=related, accessed August 20, 2011.

11. "Clean & Clear Deep Action Cleanser Ad," www.youtube.com/watch?v=1xIucrG4lu8, accessed August 20, 2011.

12. "EverYuth's Light and Clear Face Wash Ad," www.youtube.com/watch?v=s0acI4xAWg8, accessed August 20, 2011.

13. "EverYuth Face Washes: Feel Fresh!" www.everyuth.com/face-wash.html, accessed August 20, 2011.

14. "EverYuth's Light and Clear Face Wash Ad," www.youtube.com/watch?v=s0acI4xAWg8, accessed August 28, 2011.

15. "EverYuth's Fruit Face Wash Ad," www.youtube.com/watch?v=_Qjk4TWEkIk&feature=related, accessed August 28, 2011.

16. "Himalaya Herbal Healthcare: Hydrating Face Wash Cream," www.himalayahealthcare.com/products/hydrating_facewash_cream.htm, accessed August 28, 2011.

using it[17]. The Neem face wash was positioned as the solution for common skin problems and offered hassle-free and convenient skin care[18]. The advertisements also depicted men appreciating and admiring the user's beauty (implicitly suggesting that the user would appear attractive to the opposite sex)[19].

Exhibit 2 provides data on the lifestyle of the target segment, and Exhibit 3 the benefits of the face wash category. Exhibit 4 shows an advertisement for the Himalaya face wash brand that reflects its herbal proposition of oil-free skin.

The Challenge For Himalaya

Himalaya's challenge was to link the various aspects of the advertisements, the consumer values derived from the lifestyle data and the category attributes and benefits in order to enhance its brand associations, taking into consideration its competitors (EverYuth and Clean & Clear).

The authors would like to thank Antaash Sheikh, manager, marketing communication, Himalaya Drug Company, and Professor Dinesh Kumar, chairperson, research and publications, Indian Institute of Management, Bangalore, for all the support provided

17. "Himalaya Herbal Healthcare's Oil Balancing Face Wash Gel Ad," www.youtube.com/watch?v=EAiDlu-8exC8&feature=related, accessed August 28, 2011.

18. "Himalaya Herbal Healthcare's Neem Face Wash Ad," www.youtube.com/watch?v=vdnzfpq1mu0&feature=related, accessed August 28, 2011.

19. "Himalaya Herbal Healthcare's Neem Face Wash Ad," www.youtube.com/watch?v=vdnzfpq1mu0&feature=related, accessed August 28, 2011.

Exhibit 1 Description of the Advertisements of the Three Face Wash Brands

Himalaya Face Wash

Central Character	A teenage girl or a middle-aged woman who is attractive, fashionable, and socially active; is focused on her career or education; and is concerned about the way she looks.
Setting	Problem-solving approach.
Influencer	Friend, narrator.
Analysis of Ads (Television)	The ad centers on urban girls who are particular about their looks. The ad for Himalaya Oil Balancing Face Wash associates excessive facial oil with stickiness and depicts this as an issue causing inconvenience and social rejection. The product is recommended by a friend who describes the benefits of its herbal ingredients, which guarantee an oil-free face leading to soft facial skin. The association of social acceptance of the user's looks after using the brand is also conveyed.
Inferred Consumer Segment	Targeted at women between the ages of 16 to 25 who have oily skin or skin-related problems and are concerned about their looks.
Inferred Benefit Segment	Himalaya's Oil Balancing Face Wash claims to reduce excess facial oil and to keep the skin soft, providing confidence; the Neem Face Wash claims to help in removing acne and in keeping the skin clear.
Tri Components	Affective components such as the feel-good factor, self-acceptance, embarrassment, panic and confusion can be observed in the ad. The cognitive components in the ad relate to the description of the ingredients and beliefs about their benefits.
Motivation Function	The ad focuses on the importance of self-image and the benefits of the products. (Ego: Defensive and Utilitarian)

Clean & Clear Face Wash

Central Character	A teenage girl who is attractive, fashionable and socially active; is concerned about the way she looks; is open to trying out the latest products and trends in fashion; and is independent in nature.
Setting	Problem-solving approach.
Influencer	Friend, narrator.
Analysis of Ad (Television)	The ad focuses on urban girls who face the problem of oily facial skin. The product promises to keep the skin oil free for eight hours. The characters are young, attractive and trendy females who are keen on keeping themselves abreast with changes in fashion. They seek social praise by being well groomed.

(*Continued*)

	The ads also portray the concern, nervousness and lack of confidence among women due to skin problems. They show that care should be given so that the hectic lifestyle of the consumers does not cause oily skin and pimple problems. The helpful nature associated with the friend who recommends the brand to the main character creates an emotional appeal.
Inferred Consumer Segment	Targeted at women between the ages of 16 to 25 who have oily skin or face skin-related problems and who want to maintain a good appearance despite their busy schedules.
Inferred Benefit Segment	Clean & Clear Deep Action Cleanser claims to reduce excess facial oil, keeping the skin oil free for the next eight hours and providing confidence. Clean & Clear Foaming Face Wash claims to help in removing acne and in keeping facial skin oil free.
Tri Components	Affective components such as the feel-good factor, self-image, concern, nervousness, individualism and confusion can be observed in the advertisement. Cognitive components consist of the price, the ingredients and the benefits related to the product's usage.
Motivation Function	The ad focuses on the importance for the target segment to boost their self-image through the benefits of the brand. (Ego: Defensive and Utilitarian, Value Expressive)

Everyuth Face Wash

Central Character	Young women who are conscious about their looks and concerned about their health, who are involved in a lot of social activities and who want to have an identity of their own.
Setting	Problem-solving approach.
Influencer	Narrator.
Analysis of Ad (Television)	The advertisement shows urban women who have a busy lifestyle. The ad depicts the anxiety women face when they need to get prepared for a social interaction. The brand is positioned as the quickest solution for refreshed, clean, fair and soft skin. The ad also shows the opposite sex appreciating the user's beauty, thus highlighting the enhanced self-image resulting from the use of the brand. The ad also highlights the natural ingredients of the product and their benefits.
Inferred Consumer Segment	Targeted at women between the ages of 19 to 30 who have a busy lifestyle.
Inferred Benefit Segment	Refreshed and soft skin after using the brand and its quick application.

Tri Components	Affective components such as the feel-good factor, individualistic feeling and confidence are observed in the advertisement. Cognitive components include the natural ingredients and the benefits related to the product's use.
Motivation Function	The ad focuses on the importance of boosting the user's self-image and the benefits of the product. (Ego: Defensive and Utilitarian, Value Expressive)

Source: Authors' analysis of the advertisements of the three brands.

Exhibit 2 Lifestyle statements — Activities (A), Interests (I) and Opinions (O) of the targeted consumers for the face wash category

AIO	Statements	Mean
A	I get upset when I don't see the products that I want in a store.	2.87
I	I like to read the stories of people who I aspire to be like.	3.38
O	People like to travel to a lot of places for sightseeing and for memorable experiences.	4.04
A	I feel confident after I choose and use my brand of personal care products.	3.75
I	I like to watch movies that are intelligent and have female protagonists.	3.75
O	I take pride in performing even the smallest activities.	3.7
A	I only eat at certain restaurants.	2.77
I	I like to have maids do the cooking all the time.	2.26
O	Certain kinds of brands show that you are not elegant and classy.	3.15
A	I particularly enjoy shopping or visiting malls/retail stores.	3.81
I	I spend more time shopping for goods I fancy than for goods that I need.	3.36
O	Shopping is more a source of entertainment for me than a necessity.	3.09
A	I go out in the evening for drinks and entertainment.	3.64
I	I like to party on weekends or whenever I get time.	3.57
O	Malls/pubs/discotheques are the places to hang out for enjoyment and fun.	3.34
A	I often take advice from my parents about what I should buy.	2.68
I	I respect all traditions and often try to conform to them.	3.74
O	Traditions are contemporary and relevant in the present day.	3.68
A	I do purchase products out of emotional attachment.	3.49
I	Purchasing my favourite brand makes me happy.	3.89
O	I have a sort of emotional bonding with the product I use.	3.55
A	I find clothes made of khadi (homespun cloth) comfortable to wear.	3.32
I	Ayurvedic products appeal to me.	3.13
O	I love my country.	4.28
A	I purchase a lot of personal grooming products.	3.38

I	I prefer going to a beauty salon than shopping for beauty and grooming products.	3.28
O	I tend to form opinions about people who are poorly or too casually dressed.	2.72
A	I generally buy brands that reflect my uniqueness.	3.47
I	I like to be stand out from the crowd at times.	3.72
O	It's important that people respect one's individuality.	4.09
A	I often buy personal care product with friends.	2.94
I	I prefer to watch TV alone rather than to watch a movie with a group of friends.	2.34
O	Talking over the telephone is better than meeting people for communication.	2.38
A	I love to cook for my friends and family.	3.34
I	I feel upset when my friends don't call me to go shopping with them.	2.79
O	Shops should have seating arrangements to accommodate family and friends while one is shopping.	3.57
A	I usually eat out for fun after shopping.	3.96
I	I find searching for remedies for beauty-related problems satisfying.	3.36
O	Finding the right product for me and/or for others gives me a sense of achievement.	3.55
A	I often advise my friends/colleagues/relatives about the products they should buy.	3.23
I	I like to tell my friends/colleagues/ relatives what would be right for them.	3.28
O	I take initiatives at work/college that showcase my talents.	3.58
A	I often try new brands before my friends/colleagues do.	2.85
I	I like to try a new product to see what it has to offer.	2.89
O	There are always better products available.	3.58
A	Sometimes, I buy cosmetics/beauty care products that were not on my shopping list.	3.62
I	I buy products simply because I liked the advertisements.	2.51
O	Free offers and promotions cannot sell products that are very rarely useful.	3.38

(*Continued*)

A	I only buy products that are popular/common with my friends/colleagues.	2.64
I	I like to be in touch with all the people I know through social networking.	3.28
O	Using similar brands strengthens my bonds with others.	2.7
A	I purchase brands/products that suit my personality and not what others are buying.	3.64
I	I think my lifestyle is an actual reflection of my personality.	3.53
O	My image is based on the things that I own.	2.91
A	I enjoy bargaining while shopping.	3.13
I	Price promotions in shops often attract me.	3.51
O	Low cost personal care products may be of good quality.	2.41
A	I use only tried and tested products.	3.49
I	I like to use my credit/debit card for purchase through the Internet.	3.47
O	I feel that only a few products are genuinely useful.	3.49
A	I enjoy joy rides and roller coaster rides.	3.47
I	I do not visit the cinema without finalizing what movie I should watch.	3.13
O	I do not like surprises.	2.17
A	I only shop for brands that have celebrity endorsements.	1.96
I	I like to read fashion magazines and other articles that inform me about the latest trends.	3
O	I trust the products that celebrities use.	2.32
A	I don't mind smoking at social gatherings.	2.02
I	I like to be up-to-date with the latest trends.	3.32
O	I am often influenced by some of the latest trends.	3.11
A	I often buy foreign brands.	3.25
I	I like to party regularly.	2.85
O	I think social drinking is acceptable and, at times, necessary.	2.98

Source: The data was obtained from the consumer survey conducted by the authors at Bangalore in July—August 2011. The data was collected using a Likert scale. 1 denotes "Strongly Disagree" and 5 denotes "Strongly Agree."

Exhibit 3 List of Attributes and Benefits of the Brands in the Face Wash Category

Attributes/Important Aspects	Category Benefits
Many variants	Groomed looks
Moisturizer/pH neutral	Refreshed looks
Natural/herbal ingredients	Beauty maintenance
Antibacterial/germ protection	Complexion enhancement
Value for money	Feeling of being benefited
Unique/special component	Spotless beauty
Certification	Security of the offering

Source: The attributes/important aspects at the category level were obtained from the authors' analysis of the brands in the category.

Exhibit 4 An advertisement for the Himalaya brand of face wash

Source: The Himalaya Drug Company (reproduced with permission from the Himalaya Drug Company).

CASE 4

Himalaya Drug Company: Repositioning a Herbal Bath Soap*

Sushil Goswami, brand manager of soaps at India's Himalaya Drug Company, was facing a challenge. The company was well known for its herbal offerings, which were made according to the Indian Ayurvedic practice that used herbs as medicine. It had recently launched Himalaya Soap, a product that had to compete intensely with several well-known brands in a market that also included other herbal brands, and Goswami believed that in order to meet the competition, the Himalaya brand of soap had to convey a proposition that ran deeper than just a herbal identity. Further, Goswami thought the brand needed to be repositioned so it could build a long-term brand identity that would contribute to its equity. Goswami decided to conduct customer perception survey that would provide valuable insights into repositioning Himalaya soap.

* Dr. S. Ramesh Kumar, Venkata Seshagiri Rao and Narayana Trinadh Kotturu wrote this case solely to provide material for class discussion. The authors do not intend to illustrate either effective or ineffective handling of a managerial situation. The authors may have disguised certain names and other identifying information to protect confidentiality.

Indian Soap Industry

The Indian beauty and personal care segment grew by almost 100 per cent over five years, with the majority of sales taking place in urban areas.[1] Many fast-moving consumer goods companies were expanding their distribution networks to target rural consumers because of saturation and increased competition in the urban segment. In particular, the soaps category saw sales growth despite an increase in the prices of raw materials. The soap market penetrated 98 per cent of households in India.

Based on the price band or spread, the major brands of the Indian soap industry were divided into three segments: premium, semi-premium and mass (see Exhibit 1). Hindustan Unilever Limited (HUL) was the market leader in the soap category, boasting an overall market share of 49.8 per cent.[2] With its portfolio of soap brands, which were spread across various consumer segments, HUL competed with other brands such as Lux, Dove, Pears, Breeze, Rexona, Liril and Lifebuoy.

In terms of other competitors, Cinthol represented the major brand of Godrej Consumer Products. Wipro made its presence known by making Santoor and Chandrika. The Indian Tobacco Company launched its products on a positioning of "Nature and Science" in 2006, and it introduced the soap brands Fiama Di Wills, Vivel and Superia. The baby soap market was dominated by Johnson & Johnson. Reckitt Benckiser's flagship brand, Dettol, positioned itself as a "healthy soap for everyone" or, in the Indian language of Hindi, "Suraksha Parivar." Other major players included Park Avenue, which offered a deodorant soap, and Karnataka Soaps and Detergents Limited, with its Mysore Sandal Soap.

Company Profile: Himalaya Drug Company

M. Manal incorporated the Himalaya Drug Company (Himalaya) in the year 1930. By 2012, Himalaya operated in 82 countries. The company's vision was to introduce Ayurveda to society in a contemporary form and to unravel the mystery behind this 5,000-year-old system of medicine. The corporate mission demanded that Himalaya would establish itself as science-based, problem-solving, head-to-toe brand, harnessing nature's wealth and promoting healthy living. In line with this mission, the company focused on developing products that would help customers lead healthy lives. To achieve this goal, Himalaya used cutting-edge technologies to produce safe, natural and innovative remedies, operating in the pharmaceutical, personal care and animal health categories.

When the beauty and personal care market started to acknowledge the benefits of non-synthetic chemical ingredients based on natural extracts, the company diversified its beauty and personal care offerings, drawing inspiration for its brand identity from the

1. "Beauty and Personal care in India," *Euromonitor International*, 2012, www.euromonitor.com/beauty-and-personal-care-in-india/report, accessed December 21,2013.

2. "Bath and Shower in India," *Euromonitor International*, 2012, www.euromonitor.com/bath-and-shower-in-india/report, accessed December 21, 2013.

Himalayas, the mountain range from which its name was derived and which represented purity and elevated ideals. This mountain range was also home to a source of natural herbs.

Himalaya followed a unique business model that developed Ayurvedic and herbal drugs in an allopathic manufacturing setup and distributed these pharmaceutical products through a network of medical representatives. The company enjoyed a strong presence across India, with products sold mainly through store-based retailing, including chemists/pharmacies, supermarkets and hypermarkets. Himalaya also opened up its own retail outlets to highlight its range of products, which included a wide portfolio in beauty and personal care products (e.g., baby, hair, skin and oral care). The largest-value sales contributors were Himalaya's skin- and hair-care products, with other categories contributing much less.[3]

Himalaya Soaps

Himalaya Soap, a herbal healthcare product, was introduced in March 2011, as a category extension of its existing beauty and personal care offerings — face wash and toothpastes. At the outset, Himalaya launched four variants of its new range of herbal soaps: Refreshing Cucumber Soap, Protecting Neem & Turmeric Soap, Nourishing Cream & Honey Soap, and Moisturizing Almond Soap. Himalaya Soaps could be differentiated from those of its competitors based on the soaps' range of natural ingredients. Traditionally, Ayurvedic pharmaceuticals commanded relatively high prices because Ayurveda was perceived as offering a skilled, customized approach as compared to the more homogenized approach of traditional allopathic medicine. Himalaya's products were priced to reflect the company's belief that consumers do not mind paying a higher price for products that are made from natural ingredients and that offer the same benefits as standard cosmetics.

The print advertisement of Himalaya's Protecting Neem & Turmeric Soap, with the interpretation of its storyboard, is presented in Exhibits 2, 3 and 4. The key value proposition of the brand came from its offering of Neem and Tulasi, which had long been a part of skin-care regimens in the Indian culture.

Within the same price range, the primary competitors for Himalaya Soaps included Medimix, a herbal offering that focused on Ayurvedic functional benefits; and Lux, a non-herbal offering that focused strongly on emotional benefits. Lux had established itself on the functional benefit of complexion care over decades, and reigning celebrities made up a part of its imagery throughout its advertising history.

Consumer Insights

Goswami planned the consumer survey with the objective to understand the dimensions of brand image associated with the soap used by three sets of users:

3. "Himalaya Drug Co., Beauty and Personal Care (India)," *Euromonitor International*, 2011, www.euromonitor.com/beauty-and-personal-care-in-india/report, accessed December 21,2013.

- Users of Lux, a popular brand of non-herbal bathing soap; it was felt that the perception of the users of a leading brand would be useful to the repositioning of Himalaya soap brand.
- Herbal users of Himalaya bathing soaps.
- Herbal users who did not use Himalaya bath soap. (Users of Medimix herbal bath soap were identified because the brand competed directly with Himalaya.)

The questionnaire had three parts: dimensions related to the functional benefits of soaps, brand image dimensions, and advertising dimensions. Responses from 35 respondents from each of the three user categories (i.e., 105 respondents in total) were collected through a simple random sampling process. The survey responses were analyzed using suitable analytical methods from which to derive inferences.

The results of the study indicated that the brand image developed throughout the chosen dimensions remained the same among the three categories of consumers considered (see Exhibits 5, 6 and 7). The results also showcased the similarity in purchasing decisions of Indian consumers across categories for various benefits, such as fragrance and moisturization. These survey responses indicated that advertising played a dominant role in building brand image. The positioning maps are presented in Exhibit 8.

Preparing To Reposition The Himalaya Brand

The soap market was highly competitive, and Himalaya faced some strong competition from other herbal soap brands. (Although only the Medimix brand has been discussed in the case, there were other national brands, such as Santoor, Chandrika and Hamam, and regional brands, such as Krishna Tulasi, all of which made the herbal soap market highly competitive.) The advertising campaigns and brand positioning seemed to be cluttered with functional, emotional and celebrity appeals. With the proliferation of brands in the soap category, Goswami felt a clear message that provided Himalaya soap's differentiating proposition needed to be conveyed to consumers.

Himalaya was a strong herbal brand, and Goswami knew that it had to quickly cultivate a strong consumer base. To do so, the company would have to develop a stronger positioning strategy, one that it would be able to sustain in the long term. Using the herbal aspect of Himalaya's soaps as a value proposition was likely to become generic, especially when other brands had entered the herbal soap market. In terms of Himalaya Soap's positioning within the market, something more was needed — but what?

Goswami recognized that he had to make a few important decisions, and time was of the essence. He turned to the data that had been captured by the survey, expecting that it would help him with his decision-making process.

Exhibit 1 Classification of major soap brands in India

Premium Segment (>₹ 25 per 100 grams)	Semi-Premium Segment (₹ 15–25 per 100 grams)	Mass Segment (<₹ 15 per 100 grams)
Dove	Santoor	Breeze
Fiama Di Wills	Cinthol	Rexona
Mysore Sandal	Liril	Lifebuoy
Pears	Lux	Superia
J&J Baby Soap	Dettol	Chandrika
	Vivel	Medimix

Source: Authors' analysis of price bands of various soap brands in India ($1 = ₹70 approximately in 2013).

Exhibit 2 Communication of Himalaya Brand

Source: The advertisement has been reproduced with the permission of Himalaya Drug Company.

TV Commercial — Himalaya Soaps

The ad starts with a fresh, happy, young working woman setting off to her office early in the morning. After working all day long, when her husband comes to pick her up in the evening, she has no option but to use powder to make up for the lost freshness in her skin. After realizing that health or beauty soap will not help her, she remembers the Himalaya Neem & Turmeric soap that keeps the skin beautiful and protected at the same time. In the voice-over, the benefits of the soap, in terms of its natural ingredients, are elaborated: turmeric, which is known to add glow to the skin; and neem, which is known to offer great protective benefits for beautiful skin.

The commercial ends with the woman leaving her office the next evening, after experiencing the day-long freshness provided by using Himalaya soap. Her husband, who comes to pick her up again, is also delighted to meet her.

Note: The description of the TV commercial is based on the authors' interpretation of the cited source.

Source: www.youtube.com/watch?v=yy_ceCiNyXI, accessed August 10, 2012.

Exhibit 3 Communication of Lux Brand

TV Commercial — Lux Soap

This ad depicts the functional advantage of the soap by using the jingle, in the regional language, "sone se bhi sunehri twacha" ("skin brighter than gold"). This ad starts with displaying the main ingredients of the soap, such as sandalwood and moisturizing cream, which provide the functional benefit of glowing and smooth skin to young women. It also shows how everyone is attracted to the young woman, and the style of walking reflects the confidence the woman has after using the soap. In summary, the soap conveys the functional benefits and psychographics of young, and confident women.

Source: www.youtube.com/watch?v=ZUzeR4I0EBM, accessed on August 10, 2012.

Note: The description of the TV commercial is based on the authors' interpretation of the cited source.

Exhibit 4 Communication of Medimix Brand

TV Commercial — Medimix Soap

This ad conveys the functional benefit of soap users having young and healthy skin. The ad starts with a daughter telling her mother that if her mother joins her college, everyone will mistake them for sisters because of her mother's healthy skin. The daughter asks whether her skin is healthy because of genes. The mother clarifies that everyone will have good skin in the absence of skin problems. The daughter asks how one could get rid of skin problems and doubts that it is possible. The mother tells her that the magic lies in her hands, and that magic is Medimix soap. The voice-over mentions that this soap is made up of 18 herbs. The ad ends with the mother saying that because of Medimix, there will be no skin problems, and the daughter saying that her mother's words do not need confirmation from anyone else.

Thus, this ad intelligently mixes the functional benefits of Medimix and couples them with an emotional touch of a mother with healthy, young-looking skin who inspires her daughter. By focusing on the confidence that a daughter has in her mother, this ad tries to reinforce the confidence of the users of Medimix soap in healthy skin.

Note: The description of the TV commercial is based on the authors' interpretation of the cited source.

Source: www.youtube.com/watch?v=w3a1GfRq7Rs, accessed August 10, 2012.

Exhibit 5 Response to Importance of Functional Benefits by Three Sets of Users

Functional Benefit	Responses Himalaya Soap users	Responses Medimix Soap users	Responses Lux Soap users
	μ	μ	μ
Moisturization	3.83	3.86	3.91
Youthful skin	3.71	2.74	3.66
Glowing skin	3.45	3.71	3.46
Fragrance	3.80	3.80	3.8
Natural ingredients	4.23	4.49	4.03
Freshness	3.91	3.31	3.51
Price	3.69	3.43	3.66
Hygiene (germ-free)	4.17	4.26	4.03

These values indicate the mean intensity of the attribute on a scale of 1 to 5; the higher the value, the greater the agreement of the respondent.

Source: Consumer survey undertaken by the authors at Bangalore in August 2012.

Exhibit 6 Response to brand image dimensions by three sets of users

Mean Values by Segment	Responses Himalaya Soap users	Responses Medimix Soap users	Responses Lux Soap users
My soap gives me confidence when I use it	3.49	3.03	2.94
When I use the soap that my friends use, it improves my sense of belonging	2.31	2.29	2.26
My soap gives me a sense of individuality when I use it	2.91	2.94	2.74
I heard about my soap from my friends/ family or online communities	2.69	2.86	2.94
I heard about my soap from ads in the media	3.54	3.69	3.31
Packaging of a soap is a criterion in selection of a soap	3.49	3.43	3.26
I prefer soaps that convey pride of ownership in addition to mentioning skin benefits they provide	3.17	3.17	2.80
I want my soap to have a distinguished colour from other soaps	2.49	2.63	2.37
If I don't find the soap I am looking for, I am ready to switch to another soap	3.63	3.31	3.26
Slogan of a soap brand influences my selection of the soap	2.43	2.29	2.49
I will even try soaps that I have not heard of 'til now	3.20	2.57	2.49
I will buy that soap that comes to my mind when I think of a soap	3.46	3.00	3.03
I will buy only those soaps that I know	3.00	3.89	3.80
Celebrity endorsement is a key factor when I purchase a soap	2.31	2.14	2.09

These values indicate the intensity of the attribute on a scale of 1 to 5; the higher the value, the greater the agreement of the respondent.

Source: Consumer survey undertaken by the authors at Bangalore in August 2012.

Exhibit 7 Response to brand communication dimensions by three sets of users

Mean Values by Segment	Responses Himalaya Soap users	Responses Medimix Soap users	Responses Lux Soap users
I prefer soaps whose ads are creatively different from other soap ads	3.23	3.09	3.03
I prefer soaps whose ads communicate their features and usefulness	4.06	4.03	3.66
I prefer soaps whose ads showcase Indian culture and values	2.86	2.83	2.69
I prefer soaps that show how I can transform my life by using them	2.57	2.49	2.69
I don't mind if the brand-image celebrity used for the soap ad does not represent the soap's brand image	3.06	2.86	3.17

These values indicate the intensity of the attribute on a scale of 1 to 5; the higher the value, the greater the agreement of the respondent.

Source: Consumer survey undertaken by the authors at Bangalore in August 2012.

Exhibit 8 Positioning Maps of Brands

(a) Natural Ingredients Versus Price

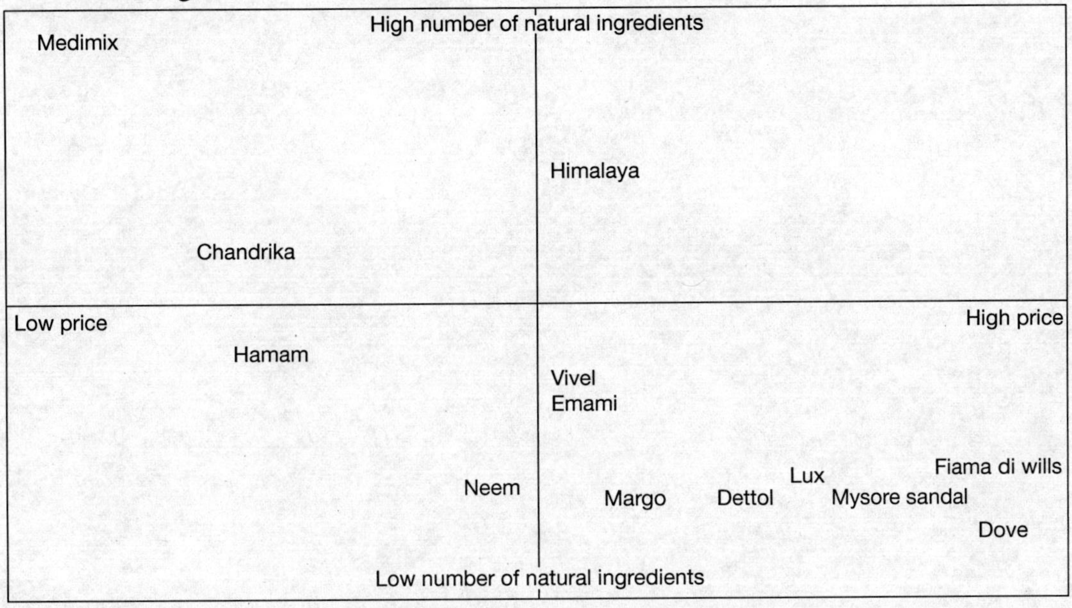

(b) Moisturization Versus Fragrance

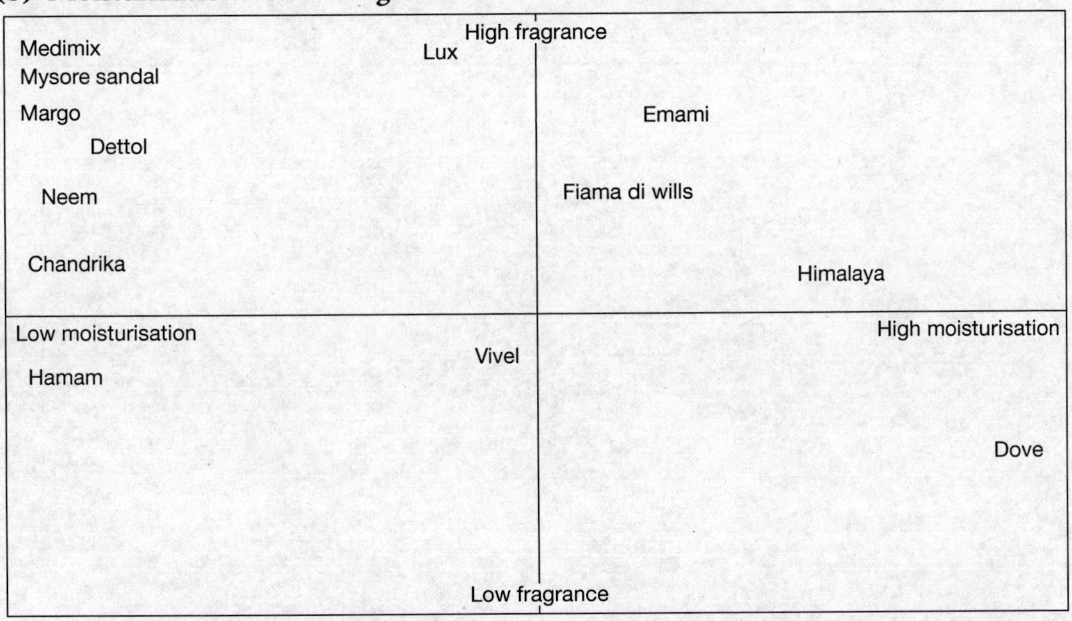

Source: The authors' perception of TV commercials of soap brands/benefits offered with prices for 75 gram pack.

Bibliography

Al Ries and Jack Trout (1982), *Positioning: The Battle for Your Mind*, Warner Books, New York.

Al Ries and Jack Trout (1986), *Marketing Warfare*, McGraw-Hill Inc., New York.

Al Ries and Laura Ries (1998), The 22 Immutable Laws of Branding, *Harper Business*.

Anat Keinan and Ran Kivetz (2008), "When Virtue is Vice," *Harvard Business Review*, July–Aug.

Anderson and Narus (1991), "Partnering as a Focused Market Strategy", *California Management Review, 3*.

Amit Sharma and Purva Bhatia "Retail Biggies bet on leisure, entertainment to up footwalls" *The Economic Times*, July 23, 2008.

Arun Kumar Jain, *Competitive Excellence—Critical Success Factors (200)*, Vikas, New Delhi.

Asia Business News, *BBC*, July 8, 2008

Banwari Mittal, Morris Holbrook, Sharon Beatty, Priya Raghubir, and Arch Woodside (2008), *Consumer behavior–How humans think, feel, and act in Marketplace*, Open mentis.

Bernd Schmitt (1999), *Experiential Marketing*, The Free Press, New York.

Blattberg R., Gary Getz and Jacquelyn S. Thomas (2001), *Customer Equity—Building and Managing Relationship as Valuable Assets*, HBS, Boston.

Blattberg, R., and Deighton, J. (1996), Managing Marketing by Customer Equity Criterion, *Harvard Business Review, 12*, 161–173.

Boulding, William, Ajay Kalra, Richard Staelin and Valerie Zeithaml A (1993), "A Dynamic Process Model of Service Quality: From Expectations to Behavioral Intentions," *Journal of Marketing Research, February, Vol. 30, Iss 1*, 7–27.

"Branding is 20 Century Concept", Amit Ranjan Rai's interview with Paco Underhill, *Business Standard*, May 27, 2008.

Byravee Iyer, "Confidence Code", *Business Standard*, April 15, 2008.

Chuck Pettis (1996), Technobrands, *American Marketing Association*, Chicago.

Collins, J. C., and Porras, J. I. (1996), Built to Last: Successful Habits of Visionary Companies, Century, UK.

"Cool Hunters and Mavens", (book extract), *Business Standard*, July 18, 2000.

Cotte, J., Ratneshwar, S., and Mick, D. G. (2004), "The Times of Their Lives: Phenomenological and Metaphorical Characteristics of Consumer Timestyles", *Journal of Consumer Research* Vol. 31(2) Sep 2004, 333-345.

"Customer Retention is not Enough," (2001), *McKinsey Quarterly*, April.

David A. Aaker and James M. Carman (1982), Are you Overadvertising?, *Journal of Advertising Research*, Aug–Sep, 57–70.

David A. Aaker (1991), *Managing Brand Equity*, The Free Press, New York, 116.

David A. Aaker (1996), *Building Strong Brands*, The Free Press, New York.

David Aaker and Kevin Lane Keller (1990), "Consumer Evaluations of Brand Extensions", *Journal of Marketing*, Vol. 54, Jan, 27–41.

David A. Aaker (2000), *Brand Leadership*, The Free Press New York.

David Aaker (1997), "Building Brands without Mass Media", *Harvard Business Review*, Jan–Feb.

David Aaker (1997), "Take Your Brand to Where Action is", *Harvard Business Review*, Sep–Oct.

David L. Loudon and Albert Della Bitta (1988), *Consumer Behaviour—Concepts and Applications*, McGraw Hill Inc, New York.

Deal, T. E. and Kennedy, A. A. (1982), *Corporate Cultures*, MA: Addison–Wesley.

Del I. Hawkins, Roger J. Best and Coney Kenneth (1998), *Consumer Behaviour Building Marketing Strategy*, The McGraw Hill Co. Inc., New York.

DeLozier, M.W. (1976), *The Marketing Communication Process*, McGraw-Hill, New York.

Del Hawkins, Roger Best and Kenneth Coney (1998), *Consumer Behaviour–Building Marketing Strategy*, McGraw Hill.

Dennis Rook, Brands W. (1999), *Consumer, Symbols and Research—Sidney Levy on Marketing*, Sage, London.

"Digital Challenge", Knowledge @Wharton 2008, *The Economic Times*, Jun 4, 2008.

Donald E. Schultz, Dennis Martin and William P. Brown (1984), *Strategic Advertising Campaigns*, Crain Books, Chicago.

Douglas B. Holt (1994), "Consumers' Cultural Differences as Local Systems of Tastes: A Critique of the Personality/Values Approach and an Alternative Framework", *Asia Pacific Advances in Consumer Research*, Vol 1, 178–184.

Dwyer, F. R., P. H. Schurr, and S. Oh (1987), "Developing Buyer Seller Relationships", *Journal of Marketing*, 51(2), 11–27.

Edward M. Tauber (1975), "Discovering New Product Opportunities with Problem Inventory Analysis", *Journal of Marketing*, Jan, 67–70.

Everett M. Rogers (1963) *Diffusion of Innovations*, The Free Press, New York, 3rd edition (1983).

Evert Gummesson (1991), "Marketing Orientation Revisited, the Crucial Role of the Part-time Marketer", *European Journal of Marketing*, Vol. 25(2) 60–75.

Fornell, C. (1976), *Consumer Input for Marketing Decisions: A Study of Corporate Departments for Consumer Affairs, Praeger, New York*.

Fred Wiersema (1996), *Customer Intimacy*, Knowledge Exchange, California.

Frederick F. Reichheld and Phil Schefter (2000), "E-Loyalty", *Harvard Business Review*, July–Aug, 105–113.

Garth Hallberg (1995), *All Consumers are not Created Equal*, John Wiley and Sons, New York.

George E. Belch (1993), "Towards Development of a Model and Scale for Assessing Consumer Receptivity to Foreign Products and Global Advertising", *European Advances in Consumer Research, Vol 1*, p. 125.

Gopalan S. and Rivera J. B. (1997), "Gaining a Perspective on Indian Value Orientations: Implications for Expatriate Managers", *International Journal of Organizational Analysis*, 5(2): 156–179.

Govindakrishnan Seshan (2008), "Beyond Breakfast", *Business Standard*, Feb 5.

Great McCracken (1989), "Who Is the Celebrity Endorser? Cultural Foundation of the Endorsement Process", *Journal of Consumer Research*, 16(3), 310-321.

Griffith, D. A. and Ryans Jr. J. K. (1995), "Strategically Employing Natural Channels in an Era of Global Marketing", *Journal of Marketing Practice,* 1(4): 52–72.

Gupta, V. (1998), "A Dynamic Model of Technological Growth: Diffusion of Japanese Investment Networks Overseas", *Unpublished Ph.D. Dissertation.*, The Wharton School of the University of Pennsylvania, Philadelphia, PA, USA.

Harper W. Boyd, Jr., Michael L. Ray and Edward C. Strong (1972), "An Attitudinal Framework for Advertising Strategy", *Journal of Marketing,* Apr. 27–33.

Harper W. Boyd, Ralph Westfall and Stanley F. Stasch (1990), "Marketing Research—Text and Cases", *All India Traveller*, New Delhi (authorised by Richard DIrwin Inc, U.S.A.).

Hawkins I., Roger J. Best and Kenneth A. Coney (1998), *Consumer Behaviour*, McGrill Hill Inc., USA

Henning T. and Ursula Hanseh (2000), *Relationship Marketing,* Springer, Hannover.

Henry Assael (1987), *Consumer Behaviour and Marketing, Chapter 4,* Kent, Action Boston.

Henry Assael (2001), *Consumer Behaviour and Marketing Action, (6th Ed.)*, Thompson Learning.

Hoyer and MacInnis (1999), *Consumer Behaviour*, Hongton Miffin, Chennai.

Husain, A. S. (1961), *The National Culture of India, Bombay*: Asia Publishing.

Inng Tan, Jim McCullough, and Jeannie Teoh (1987), "An Individual Analysis to Cross-cultural Research", *Advances in Consumer Research, Volume 14*, 394–397.

Jagdish N. Sheth, D. M. Gardner and D. E. Garrett (1988), *Marketing Theory and Evaluation*, John Wiley, New York, 24–33.

Jack Trout and Steve Rivkin (1995), *The New Positioning*, McGraw-Hill Book Co., Singapore, 63–65.

Jack Trout and Steve Rivkin (1999), *The Power of Simplicity*, McGraw-Hill, Singapore, 153–154.

Jack Trout and Steve Rivkin (2000), *Differentiate or Die*, East-West Books, Chennai.

Jack Trout (2001), *Big Brands, Big Trouble*, East-West Books, Chennai.

Jagadish N. Sheth and S. Ram (1987), *Bringing Innovation to Market*, John Wiley and Sons Inc., New York.

Jagadish Sheth and Atul Parvatiyar (2000), *Handbook of Relationship Marketing*, Sage, London.

James F. Engel, Roger D. Blackwell and Paul W. Miniard (1995), *Consumer Behaviour*, The Dryden Press, New York.

James H. Gilmore and B. Joseph Pine II (2000), *Markets of One*, HBS Press, Boston.

Jerry Wind and Vijay Mahajan (2001), *Digital Marketing*, John Wiley, New York.

Joe Marconi (1997), *Image Marketing*, NTC Business Books., Chicago.

John A. Quelch and David Kenny (1994), "Extent Profits, Not Productlines", *Harvard Business Review*. Sep–Oct.

John Philip Jones (1998), *What's in a Brand? Building Brand Equity through Advertising*, Tata McGraw-Hill.

Joseph Alba, John Lynch, Barton Waitz, Chris Janiszewski, Pickard Lutz, Alan Sawyer and Stacy Wood (1997), "Interactive Home Shopping, Consumer Retailer and Manufacturer, Incentives to participate in Electronic Market Place", *Journal of Marketing*.

Joseph Pine B. (1997), *Mass Customisation: The New Frontier in Business Competition*, Irwin.

Joseph Pine B., Don Peppers and Martha Rogers (1995), "Do You Want to Keep Your Customers Forever", *Harvard Business Review,* Mar.–Apr., Vol. 2, 103–114.

Joseph Sirgy M. (1982), "Self concept in Consumer Behaviour: A Critical Review", *Journal of Consumer Research*. Dec., pp 287–300.

Joseph T. Plummer (1984), "How Personality Makes a Difference". *Journal of Advertising Research*, 25 Dec–Jan

Kanagal, Nagasimha Balakrishna and Ramesh S. Kutmar (1998), "Customer Product Interfacing: A Strategy for Consumer Durables", *The Hindu*, 15 July.

Kathleen Brewer Doran, Babson College (1997), "Symbolic Consumption in China: The Color Television as a Life Statement", *Advances in Consumer Research,* Vol. 24, 128–131.

Kevin Lane Keller (1993) "Conceptualizing, Measuring and Managing Customer based Brand Equity", *Journal of Marketing*, Jan 1–13.

Kevin Lane Keller, Brian Sterntherl and Alice Tybout (2002), "Three Questions You Need to Ask About your Brand", *Harvard Business Review,* Sep.

Knautz, R (1997), Corporate Social Responsibility, *Policy Spotlight,* V. I(7), *Free-market.net.*

Kohli, A. K., and B. J. Jaworski (1990), "Market Orientation: The Construct, Research Propositions, and Managerial Implications", *Journal of Marketing,* 54(2): 1–18.

Kotler Philip (2000), *Marketing Management—Planning. Analysis, Implementation and Control,* Prentice Hall, New Delhi.

Krugman P. (1997), "In Praise of Cheap Labor", Slate, March 20, www.slate.com/Dismal/97–03–20/Dismal.asp.

L. L. Berry and A. Parasuraman (1991), *Marketing Services: Competing Through Quality,* Free Press, New York, 45–70.

Laufer, R. and Paradeise, C. (1990), *Marketing Democracy. Public Opinion and Media Formation in Democratic Societies*, Transaction, New Brunswick.

Leon Schiffman G. and Lazer Kanuk Leslie (1997), *Consumer Behaviour,* 6th ed., Prentice Hall of India, New Delhi.

Leslie Demonte, "Talking in One Voice" *Business Standard* 13 Nov 2007.

Madhukar Angur, University of Michigan Flint, Rajan Nataraajan, Auburn (1996), "An Assessment of International Cultural Content Difference (ICCD)—An Exploratory Study", *Asia Pacific Advances in Consumer Research,* Vol. 2, 128–132.

Marshall, C. E. (1985), "Can we be Consumer-oriented in a Changing Financial Services World?", *The Journal of Consumer Marketing,* 2(4): 37–43.

Martin Lindstorm, Don Peppers and Martha Rogers (2001), *Clicks, Bricks and Brands*, Kogan Page, UK.

Mckenna, R. (1991), *Relationship Marketing: Successful Strategies for the Age of the Customer,* MA, Addison-Wesley, 74–91.

Michael Haywood K. (1989), "Managing Word of Mouth Communications", *The Journal of Services Marketing,* Vol. 3, Spring.

Michael Munson J., University of Santa Clara; Shelby H. McIntyre, University of Santa Clara (1978), "Personal Values: A Cross-cultural Assessment of Self-Values and Values Attributed to a Distant Cultural Stereotype, *Advances in Consumer Research,"* Vol. 5, 160–166.

Milind M. Lele and Jagdish N. Sheth (1987), *The Customer is Key,* John Wiley and Sons, 200–207.

Min Ha.C., (1994), "Assessing the Roles of Cognitions, Country of Origin, Consumer Patriotism and Familiarity in Consumer Attitudes toward Foreign Brands", *Asia Pacific Advances in Consumer Research,* Vol. 1, 103–108.

"Motorola to sing youth tunes", *Times of India*, May 15, 2008

Naresh Malhotra (1981), "A Scale to measure Self-concepts, Person-concepts and Product-concepts", *Journal of Marketing Research* Vol 18, Nov., 456–464.

"No Open and Shut Case", *knowledge@Wharton*, 2008.

Nylen, D. W. (1990), *Marketing Decision Making Handbook,* N.J.: Prentice-Hall.

P. W. Turnbull and D.T. Wilson (1989), "Developing and Protecting Profitable Customer Relationships", *Industrial Marketing Management,* 18, 233–238.

Palmer and Bejou (1994), "Buyer Seller Relationships: A Conceptual Model and Empirical Investigation", *Journal of Marketing,* 10, 495–512.

Parasuraman, A, Valerie Zeithaml and Leonard L. Berry (1985), "A Conceptual Model of Service Quality and its Implications for Future Marketing", *Journal of Marketing,* Fall, p. 44.

Patrica B. Seybold (2001), "Get Inside the Lives of Your Customers", *Harvard Business Review,* May.

Peter R. Peacock (1998), "Knowledge Discovery in Databases", *Marketing Management,* AMA, Chicago.

Peters, T. J. and Waterman, R. H. (1982), *In Search of Excellence,* Harper and Row, New York.

Philip Kotler (1973–1974), "Atmospherics as a Marketing Tool", *Journal of Retailing,* Winter, 48–64.

Philip Kotler (1999), *Marketing Management–The Millennium edition,* Prentice Hall of India.

Philip Kotler, Dipak Jain and Suvit Maesincee (2002), *Marketing Moves,* HBS Press.

Piercy, N., and Morgan, N. (1991), "Internal Marketing the Missing Half of the Marketing Programme", *Long Range Planning,* 24(2): 82–93.

Prasad Sangameswaran, "Front-end Game", *Business Standard,* May 27, 2008.

Priyanka Joshi, "Screenage" *Business Standard,* Nov 27, 2007.

Preethi Chamikutty, "Dyed in the wool Desi" *The Economic Times,* May 14, 2008

Preethi Chamikutty and Pallavi Rao, "Marketers and Brands Eye Airports", *The Economic Times,* May 21, 2008.

Preethi Chamikutty and Sangeetha Rao, "Terminal Velocity" *The Economic Times,* May 21, 2008.

Preethi Chamikutty, "Pure for Sure", *The Economic Times,* Jun 24, 2008.

Rajiv Banerjee, "Hitching a hike back", *The Economic Times,* May 28, 2008.

Rajiv Banerjee, "Full of Beans", *The Economic Times,* July 16, 2008.

Ramesh Kumar S., and Swaminathan S. (1998), "Paradigms on Brand Loyalty", *The Hindu-Businessline,* 28 Aug.

Ramesh Kumar S., and Swaminathan S. (1998), "Synergising Marketing Communication", *The Hindu Businessline,* 5 Nov.

Ramesh Kumar, S. (2000), "What Ticks E-tailing", *The Hindu-Businessline,* 9 Aug.

Ramesh Kumar, S. (2000), "Respecting the Boundaries of Brand Positioning, *The Hindu-Businessline*, 20 Jan., Madras.

Ramesh Kumar, S. (2000), *Applications Exercises in Marketing,* Vikas, New Delhi.

Ramesh Kumar, S. (2001), *Managing Indian Brands—Marketing Concepts and Strategies,* Vikas, New Delhi.

Ramesh Kumar, S. (2002), "Concept of Customer Mapping, A Practice-Orientated Tool", *International Management,* U.K., Sep.–Oct.

Ramesh Kumar, S. (2007), *Marketing and Branding—The Indian Scenario*, Pearson Education, New Delhi.

Ramesh Kumar, S. (2008), *Conceptual Issues in Consumer Behaviour—The Indian Context*, Pearson Education, New Delhi.

Ramesh Kumar, S. (1998), *Marketing Nuggets—Conceptual Dimensions in Marketing,* Vikas, New Delhi.

Ramesh Kumar S. and Karan Bajaj (2002), "Cultural Dimensions and MNC Brands—A Study in the Indian Context", *South Asian Journal of Management,* July–Sep.

Ramesh Kumar, S. (2001), "Synergising Online and Offline Strategies", *Ivey Business Journal,* Nov–Dec., *Ivey Business School*, Western Ontario, Canada.

Regis McKenna (1995), "Real Time Marketing", *Harvard Business Review,* July–Aug., 87–95.

Reichheld F. F. and Phil Schefter (2000), "E loyalty: Your Secret Weapon on the Web", *Harvard Business Review,* July–Aug.

Reichheld, F. F. and W. E. Sasser Jr. (1990), "Zero Defections: Quality Comes to Services", Harvard Business Review, 69(1) 105–111.

Reichheld F. F. (1996), "Learning from Customer Defections", *Harvard Business Review,* 74, Mar.–Apr.

Reichheld, F. F. (1996), "Learning from Customer Defections", *Harvard Business Review, 74 (No. 2),* Mar–Apr, 56–69.

Renee Dye (2000), "The Buzz on Buzz", *Harvard Business Review,* Nov.–Dec.

Reynolds. J. (2002), *A Practical Guide to CRM,* CMP Books, New York.

Richard Cross and Janet Smith (1996), *Customer Bonding—Pathway to Lasting Customer Loyalty,* NTC Business Books, Illinois.

Ranganath Nayak and John M. Kelteringham (1993), *Breakthroughs!,* Mercury, Oxfordshire.

Robert A. Westbrook (1980), "Interpersonal Affective Influences on Consumer Satisfaction with Products", *Journal of Consumer Research,* 7, 49–54, Jan.

Rogers Everett (1995), *Diffusion of Innovation,* The Free Press.

Roland T. Rust, Valarie A. Zeithmal, and Katherine Lemon (2000), *Driving Customer Equity,* HBS, Boston, 100–102.

Roland T. Rust, Valarie A. Zeithmal, and Katherine, N. Lemon (2000), *Customer Equity,* Free Press.

Russel Winer (2001), "A Framework for Customer Relationship Management", *California Management Review,* Summer, 89–105.

Russell W. Belk, and Wendy J. Bryce, (1986), "Materialism and Individual Determinism in US and Japanese Print and Television Advertising", *Advances in Consumer Research,* Vol 113, 569–572.

Russell Winer, S. (2001), A Framework for Customer Relationship Management, *California Management Review*, Summer.

Saha, A. (1992), "Basic Human Nature in India Tradition and its Economic Consequences", *International Journal of Sociology and Social Policy,* 12(1-2):1 SO.

Sahlini Singh, "iPhone mania grips the world", *The Times of India,* July 10, 2008.

Shay Sayre (2001), *Qualitative Methods of Marketplace Research,* Sage, London.

Shunu Sen, "On Branding", *The Hindu-Businessline,* 6 Apr., 2000.

Shushi Vyas and Shatrujeet N., "Holding Fort", *The Economic Times,* Dec 19, 2007.

Shobana Subramanian, "Fine Blend", *Business Standard,* Aug 7, 2007.

Sinha, P. and H. S. R. Kao (Eds.) (1997), *Social Values and Development,* 31–55, Sage, New Delhi.

Sinha, J. B. P. (1978), "Power in Superior-subordinate Relationships: The Indian Case", *Journal of Social and Economic Studies,* 6: 205–218.

Sinha, J. B. P. (1990), *Work Culture in an Indian Context,* Sage, New Delhi.

Smith, A. (1776), *An Inquiry into the Nature and Causes of the Wealth of Nations,* Strahan and Cadell, London.

Srinivas, M. N. (1972), *Social Change in Modern India,* University of California Press, Berkeley.

Storbacka, K. T. Storandvik and C. Gronroos (1994), "Managing Relationships for Profit: The Dynamic of Relationship Quality", *International Journal of Service Industry Management,* 5(5), 21–38.

Subroto Sengupta (1980), *Brand Positioning—Strategies for Competitive Advantage,* Tata McGraw Hill, New Delhi.

Sugirtharajah, S. (2001), "Traditions of Giving in Hinduism", Alliance 6(3), www.allavida.org/alliance/articles/2001/-pr20011009%5F10.cfm.

Susan Fourmier, Susan Dobscha and David Glen Mick (1998), "Preventing the Premature Death of Relationship Marketing", *Harvard Business Review,* Jan.–Feb.

The 100 Top Brands, *Business Week,* 6 Aug 2001.

Theodore Levitt (1981), "Marketing Intangible Products and Product Intangibles", *Harvard Business Review,* May–June, 94–102.

Theodore Levitt (1980), "Marketing Success Through Differentiation—of Anything", *Harvard Business Review,* Jan.–Feb.

The Marketing White Book 2007–2008, *Businessworld.*

Timothy B. Heath, David L. Mothersbaugh, Michael S. McCarthy, (1993); "Spokesperson Effects in High-Involvement Markets", *Advances in Consumer Research,* Vol. 20, 704–708.

Turner, G. B., and Spencer, B. (1997), "Understanding the Marketing Concept as Corporate Culture", *European Journal of Marketing,* 31(2): 10–21.

Valarie A., Zeithaml and Mary Jo Bitner (1996), *Services Marketing,* McGraw Hill.

Vijay Vishwanath and Jonathan Mcark (1997), "Your Brand's Best Strategy", *Harvard Business Review*, May–June.

Webster, F. E. Jr. (1992), "Changing Role of Marketing in the Corporation", *Journal of Marketing*, 56(4), 1–17.

Werner Reinartz and V. Kumar (2002), "The Mismanagement of Customer Loyalty", *Harvard Business Review*, July.

Whan Park C., Bernard Jaworski J., and Deborah Maclnnis J. (1996), "Strategic Brand Concept—Image Management", *Journal of Marketing*, Vol. 50 Oct., 135–145.

World Business report, *BBC News*, Jun 26, 2008.

www.fragland.net accessed on Jun 26, 2008.

www.cafecoffeeday.com/contact.htm (accessed on July 18, 2008)

Zaltman, G. (2003), "How consumers think: Insights into the mind of the market", *HBS*, 80–90.

Index

P

Q

R

S

Credits

Plate No.	Page No.	Credit Line
Plate 1.1	7	Eye-Stock / Alamy Stock Photo
Plate 1.2	9	ZUMA Press Inc / Alamy Stock Photo
Plate 1.3	16	Helen Sessions / Alamy Stock Photo
Plate 2.1	33	Kristoffer Tripplaar / Alamy Stock Photo
Plate 2.2	44	Courtesy: Titan Edge (Creative), (c) TITAN COMPANY, used with permission
Plate 4.1	87	Courtesy: Zomato Community Blog, used with permission
Plate 4.2	99	david pearson / Alamy Stock Photo
Plate 4.3	99	Dinodia Photos / Alamy Stock Photo
Plate 5.1	112	Anil Ghawana / Alamy Stock Photo
Plate 5.2	115	Matthew Horwood / Alamy Stock Photo
Plate 6.1	118	Anil Ghawana / Alamy Stock Photo
Plate 6.2	120	https://www.soulflower.biz/
Plate 6.3	122	Courtesy: Paper Boat Drinks, used with the permission of Hector Beverages
Plate 7.1	152	ACORN 1 / Alamy Stock Photo
Plate 7.2	155	Idealink Photography / Alamy Stock Photo
Plate 9.1	194	Realimage / Alamy Stock Photo
Plate 9.2	195	PSL Images / Alamy Stock Photo
Plate 10.1	239	Mira / Alamy Stock Photo
Plate 10.2	240	Courtesy: Globus Stores Pvt. Ltd., Pacific Mall Kaushambi, Sahibabad Industrial Area, Ghaziabad, UP, used with permission